Andrew Palmer is CEO of Idarat Ltd. and of Idarat Resilience JLT. He has spent much of his life dealing with international business, in the Middle East, Russia, Asia, Africa, Australia and North America as well as Europe. He is a member of Chatham House and holds an MBA from the Lord Ashcroft International Business School, Anglia Ruskin University. His website is: http://www.newpirates.info

'This is a masterful tome, intellectually robust and commendably pragmatic. It should be on the required reading list of politicians, senior naval and military officers, legal advisors and shipping owners. If only they were better informed, we would strike a blow at this dreadful phenomenon.'

– Commodore Pat Tyrrell, OBE Royal Navy

'Andrew Palmer has written the first, and so far only, book that gives an in-depth analysis of the modern scourge of piracy on the high seas.'

– Major General Julian Thompson, from the foreword to this book

'*The New Pirates* will become the definitive work on the subject and be an invaluable intellectual asset for scholars, students and practitioners in government and the armed services. The author has worked on anti-piracy programmes and is an acknowledged expert in encountering this threat to maritime security.'

– Professor Jack Spence OBE, King's College London

THE NEW PIRATES

MODERN GLOBAL PIRACY FROM SOMALIA TO THE SOUTH CHINA SEA

ANDREW PALMER

Foreword by Major General Julian Thompson

I.B. TAURIS

LONDON · NEW YORK

Published in 2014 by I.B.Tauris & Co Ltd
6 Salem Road, London W2 4BU
175 Fifth Avenue, New York NY 10010
www.ibtauris.com

Distributed in the United States and Canada Exclusively by Palgrave Macmillan
175 Fifth Avenue, New York NY 10010

ISBN: 978 1 84885 633 2
eISBN: 978 0 85773 493 8

A full CIP record for this book is available from the British Library
A full CIP record is available from the Library of Congress

Library of Congress Catalog Card Number: available

Printed and bound in Sweden by ScandBook AB

TABLE OF CONTENTS

LIST OF ILLUSTRATIONS

ACRONYMS

AIS	automatic identification system
AMISOM	African Union Mission in Somalia
APMSS	Anti Piracy Maritime Security Solutions Ltd., now MMWC Ltd.
ARPCT	Alliance for the Restoration of Peace and Counter-Terrorism
ARS	Alliance for Re-liberation of Somalia
ASWJ	Ahlu Sunna Wal Jama'a
BDI	Baltic Dry Index
dwt	dead weight tonnage
EDG	emergency diesel generator
EPLF	Eritrean People's Liberation Front
ERA	explosive reactive armour
ESU	Exploration Security Unit (Puntland)
EU NAVFOR	European Union Naval Force
FARC	Fuerzas Armadas Revolucionarias de Colombia (Revolutionary Armed Forces of Colombia – People's Army)
FOB	forward-operating base
GT	gross tonnage
HEAT	high explosive anti-tank (ammunition)
HHN	Hobyo-Haradheere Network (Haradheere = Harardheere, Harardhere or Xarardheere)
HRA	high risk area, i.e. the area at high risk of piracy which is bounded by Suez and the Strait of Hormuz to the north, 10°S and 78°E
ICG	International Crisis Group
IED	improvised explosive device
IGAD	Inter-Governmental Authority on Development (East Africa)
ILO	International Labour Organization
IMB	International Maritime Bureau

IMO	International Maritime Organization
IOCC	International Code of Conduct for Private Security Companies
IRIN	News service of the UN Office for the Coordination of Humanitarian Affairs
IRTC	Internationally Recommended Transit Corridor
ISI	Inter-Services Intelligence
ISMC	International Safety Management Code
ISPS Code	International Ship and Port Facility Security Code
K&R	kidnap and ransom
KLA	Kosovo Liberation Army
KPC	Kuwait Petroleum Corporation
LNG	liquefied natural gas
LPSV	large pirate support vessel
LRAD	long-range acoustic device
LRIT	long-range identification and tracking
MEND	Movement for the Emancipation of the Niger Delta
MILF	Moro Islamic Liberation Front
MS	Motor ship
MSCHOA	Maritime Security Centre – Horn of Africa
MV	Merchant vessel or Motor vessel
NSA	National Security Agency (US)
NSS	National Security Service (Somalia)
NVCG	National Volunteer Coast Guard (Somalia)
OCHA or UNOCHA	United Nations Office for the Coordination of Humanitarian Affairs
OCIMF	Oil Companies International Marine Forum
OFAC	Office of Foreign Assets Control (US)
OLF	Oromo Liberation Front
ONLF	Ogaden National Liberation Front
OSJI	Open Society Justice Initiative (US)
P&I	protection and indemnity (insurance)
PAG	pirate action group
PFDJ	People's Front for Democracy and Justice, formerly the Eritrean People's Liberation Front
PLF	Palestine Liberation Front
PMPF	Puntland Maritime Police Force
PMSC	private maritime security company
PPN	Puntland Piracy Network

PSC	private security company
RIB	rigid inflatable boat
RPG	rocket-propelled grenade
RUF	rules for the use of force
SAMI	Security Association for the Maritime Industry
SSC	Sool Sanaag Cayn (Somalia)
SIMAD	Somali Institute for Management and Administrative Development
SNM	Somali National Movement
SOLAS	International Convention for the Safety of Life at Sea
SRC	Supreme Revolutionary Council
SSDF	Somali Salvation Democratic Front
SSP	ship security plan
TCO	transnational criminal organization
teu	20-foot equivalent units (containers)
TFG	Transitional Federal Government (Somalia)
TFI	Transitional Federal Institution (Somalia)
TNG	Transitional National Government (Somalia)
UAE	United Arab Emirates
UIC	Union of Islamic Courts
UKMTO	UK Maritime Trade Organisation
ULCC	ultra large crude carrier
Unicef	United Nations International Children's Emergency Fund
UNCLOS	United Nations Convention on the Law of the Sea
UNCTAD	United Nations Conference on Trade and Development
UNHCR	United Nations High Commissioner for Refugees
UNODC	United Nations Office on Drugs and Crime
VLCC	very large crude carrier
WFP	World Food Programme

ACKNOWLEDGEMENTS

I owe an immense debt to those who have helped me, commented on the draft and generously given their advice and time, notably Christopher Ledger and Major General Julian Thompson, David Lentaigne, John Knott and Professor Jack Spence.

I also wish to thank the staff of the British Library for their support: may this unique institution long support the independent researcher. In addition, I have benefitted greatly from events organized by the UK Defence Academy and Chatham House. I also thank Dryad Maritime Ltd. for permission to use charts prepared by them.

Friends and family have also supported me over the lengthy period that I have been researching and writing, particularly my wife, Sahar, who has put up with the mess of papers and books for far too long, and Emma Pegler who has provided a quiet bolt-hole for writing in the country, away from phones.

I dedicate this work to Caroline and Olivia.

FOREWORD

Andrew Palmer has written the first, and so far only, book that gives an in-depth analysis of the modern scourge of piracy on the high seas. At present there is probably more nonsense spoken and written on the subject than on any other topic. There is very little coverage on piracy in the British media, as well as almost total ignorance of the potentially disastrous impact that piracy might have on the British economy and indeed every household in the land; especially if piracy becomes linked to terrorism.

It is impossible to understand piracy today, especially Somali piracy off the east coast of Africa and the Indian Ocean, unless one has a good grounding in its underlying causes and how it has developed. Piracy has flourished in Southeast Asia, principally in the South China Sea and East Indies for centuries, as it has in the Caribbean and off the coast of South America ever since the days of Drake and Hawkins. Southeast Asian piracy waned and waxed over the centuries, but never completely died out. Piracy in the Caribbean and South America disappeared completely during the nineteenth century and only started making a comeback in the last third of the twentieth, kick-started by the drugs trade. Whereas the more recent growth of piracy off the coast of West Africa is perhaps the least reported of all. There is also the involvement of local elites, Nigeria being what the author calls 'an archetype of the predatory state'; Somalia being another. He quotes Cameron Thiers:

> The state as predator does not consume the population-as-prey, but rather consumes the resources of the population. The aim of the governing elite in such a state is their own enrichment, and the resultant impoverishment and destitution of large sections of the population is a matter of no concern to them. The predatory elites operate like the mafia, the state becomes a racketeering enterprise in which the rules are written for the benefit of the corrupt, undermining normal markets in order to create clients dependent on the predatory elite.

Andrew Palmer goes on to point out that Somalia and Nigeria are not the only 'predatory states' in Africa and suggests that:

> The error that international organizations have consistently made in Somalia, and in countries like it, is to attempt to build a state and its supporting institutions, by supporting men who in fact are only the leaders of armed factions, and whose agenda is to exploit the resources of the country for their own ends. So by working to limit conflict and to create stability, international organizations, and outside powers, have too frequently achieved the precise opposite of what they have publicly stated as being their objectives.

Although piracy in other parts of the world is given due coverage, the bulk of the book is devoted to Somali piracy – its causes and how it might develop. The last two parts of the book ask if there are answers and includes geopolitical conclusions. Politicians, journalists, and those involved in business and commerce, and in defence should read this book, and especially the last two parts. Navies by themselves cannot extinguish piracy. Piracy in the early nineteenth century almost vanished partly because of the efforts of the Royal Navy in particular, but also because owners started arming merchant ships, so attacking them became too difficult for anything other than a warship with a disciplined crew. Andrew Palmer is not suggesting that merchant vessels should be armed. He makes an exception for slow, low-freeboard ships or tugs that might need to carry armed guards. The knee-jerk reaction by some shipping companies to use armed guards in all ships is both expensive and fraught with legal pitfalls. Furthermore some of the folk employed in this role have no maritime knowledge, being more familiar with driving armoured 4 × 4s in Iraqi and Afghan urban areas, and providing close protection to VIPs.

It is up to shipping companies to put their houses in order by making their ships 'resilient'. Andrew Palmer explains what this involves. For far too long the shipping industry has either been complacent, or put in place inadequate or just plain inappropriate, measures to counter piracy: and sad to relate the UK owners are among the most sluggish in this respect.

This is an important book, the result of deep and extensive research, by a man who knows his business.

Major General Julian Thompson, CB, OBE

MAIN SHIPPING ROUTES IN THE NORTH-WESTERN INDIAN OCEAN

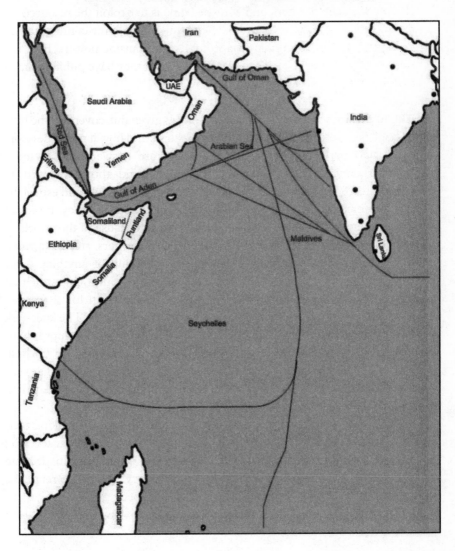

INTRODUCTION

Tacitus wrote, in the introduction to *The Histories*, 'The story I now commence is rich in vicissitudes, grim with warfare, torn by civil strife, a tale of horror even during times of peace.' I can only echo his words.

In looking at modern piracy it is inescapable that this book concentrates on Somalia, although other places are now emulating Somalia's experiences. When I started writing this book I thought that I was writing an account of modern piracy, but, like a traveller entering a new land, I found that the environment was far more complex than I had at first imagined. The book therefore includes an account of the political and economic undercurrents in the Horn of Africa, the criminal tendencies of African elites and the follies of the 'War on Terror'. If this was not sufficient, I also found myself considering the depression that has hit the global shipping industry, the best methods to protect a ship from pirate attacks, the mechanism of ransoming ships and their crews, and the operation of the insurance market and maritime law as it applies to piracy.

In a way, looking at modern Somalia in detail is rather like looking under a rock: you see many things that are normally hidden and observe a vision of the world in which deep-rooted, and normally hidden, forces are exposed to view. This is not a pleasant story: virtually every form of human depravity can be found in Somalia, but in the main it is the Somalis who are the real victims, and the causes of most of their suffering lie in the greed and folly of a few.

Piracy has a long history, as old as seafaring itself. In 75 BC, Julius Caesar was captured by Cilician pirates, who plagued the Mediterranean at the time, and after he was ransomed, he returned and captured them. Plutarch, in his *Life of Julius Caesar,* describes how Caesar then crucified them all, just as he had often told them that he would do when he was held captive on the island – though they had thought that he was just joking. Some people today imagine that summary 'justice', along Roman lines, would quickly sort out our current problems with piracy in the Indian Ocean and the South China Sea, although few would go as far as crucifying them; only Saudi Arabia today retains this ancient punishment.

In the *City of God*, St Augustine tells the story of a pirate captured by Alexander the Great. The Emperor angrily demanded of him, 'How dare you molest the seas?' To which the pirate replied, 'How dare you molest the whole world? Because I do it with a small boat, I am called a pirate and a thief. You, with a great navy, molest the world and are called an emperor.' St Augustine thought the pirate's answer was 'elegant and excellent'.

The theme of this book is that maritime piracy is a symptom of deep and underlying problems. Piracy arises where governance breaks down and where people are desperate enough to risk their lives in perilous attacks on the high seas, where they are as likely to be the victims of storms and the other dangers of the seas, as they are to be captured, injured or killed by those they are attacking. Thedor Mommsen described pirates in his day as, 'the ruined men of all nations', and the truth remains that piracy is the resort of those wretched men who can see no other avenue of advancement. The life of the modern Somali pirate is often extremely short: skiffs are sent off to sea without adequate fuel and drinkable water for a return trip; only by hijacking a vessel can pirates in such a situation hope to return to their homes. On 8 October 2009 Reuters quoted the remarks of a Somali pirate, who said, 'We are missing more than 30 of our friends who went out to sea over the last two weeks to carry out hijackings.' Most succumb to the perils of the ocean, though it is reported that some die as a result of 'turf wars' between Somali groups.

Piracy, in case there is any confusion in the mind of the reader, is committed by private individuals and includes acts of hijacking, kidnapping, robbery and criminal violence on the high seas; but such acts within the territorial waters of a state are not technically regarded as piracy. Similar actions by a state, and its agents, are not acts of piracy. As *Jane's Defence Weekly* noted in May 2005, 'Piracy covers a wide spectrum of seaborne crime.'

We also consider the possible links between 'terrorism' and piracy, which again are highly complex, secretive by nature, and complicated by the fact that modern terrorism is largely funded and manipulated, if not directly controlled, by the agents of states. Terrorist groups, or 'independent militias', are too often the 'deniable' agents of the secret services of a state, or of their own irregular, or intelligence, agencies, such as the Iranian Revolutionary Guards, or Pakistan's Directorate for Inter-Services Intelligence (ISI). The list of such engagements is long; Israel's Mossad has established Hamas, the Russian FSA is deeply involved in the Chechen Republic, and is alleged to have initially provoked the recent conflict in that unhappy place, and the United States has a long history of similar involvement in Central America.

We need an effective and long-term solution to piracy, and one of the most important aspects of the answer to this puzzle is the reduction of the present vulnerability of merchant ships to attacks. There are methods and non-lethal defensive equipment available today that make virtually any merchant ship resilient and protected against attacks by pirates. The deployment of naval forces and aerial surveillance can help, and good intelligence is vital.

Just as the conditions that give rise to piracy are complex, so are the answers. Action to deal with piracy needs to be, as this book will show, multi-layered and systemic. There are no 'one-shot' solutions.

We do have to be careful in our responses to modern piracy. In dealing with any complex problem of this type, with myriad threats of causation, we always need to be aware of the socio-political dynamics of the situation, the values of the culture from which piracy has sprung, and the perceptions of the local people.

As a society we also need to take actions that do not compromise our own values and social principles. By international agreement in 1948 we accepted the Universal Declaration of Human Rights, which recognized and acknowledged that 'the inherent dignity and the equal and inalienable rights of all members of the human family is the foundation of freedom, justice and peace in the world'. Shooting anyone in a small boat off the coast of Somali and Indonesia, who may be a pirate, as suggested by some in the United States, is hardly the way to resolve the problem. In any case any master responsible for such actions is likely to face the prospect of a trial. In fact, the International Maritime Organization's Maritime Safety Committee (MSC) at its 86th session (27 May–5 June 2009),

> agreed that flag States should strongly discourage the carrying and use of firearms by seafarers for personal protection or for the protection of a ship. Seafarers, it was agreed, are civilians and the use of firearms requires special training and aptitudes and the risk of accidents with firearms carried on board ship is great.

Since then the deployment of armed teams on merchant ships has become a commonplace, although there are a number of issues that we will look at in more depth later in this book. One problem is the confusion between pirates and fishermen. In the waters of the Red Sea, Gulf of Aden and Indian Ocean fishing boats look exactly like pirate vessels, are equipped with firearms for self-defence, and often follow large vessels, because their propellers bring fish to the surface. Too many fishermen have died at the hands of guards who could not tell the difference.

Governments that overreact to threats can ultimately do more damage to their own societies than any damage from piracy. Western countries need to retain their hard-won respect for human rights, which benefits all citizens, even when this leads to great frustration in dealing with pirates, who follow no such codes. We understand that policemen have to follow the law, even though the criminals they are dealing with are free to lie and steal.

Caesar lived in different times, as did the Royal Navy officers of the eighteenth and nineteenth centuries who were free to exercise summary justice and execute pirates. The 1809 campaign of the Royal Navy in the Persian Gulf, under Captain John Wainwright, which saw the destruction of pirate ships and stores at Ras Al Khaimah (now part of the United Arab Emirates) and attacks on Linga and Laft in Persia (now Iran), would be difficult to repeat in modern circumstances.

The dangers of overreaction by a state, when it acts to suppress piracy, is illustrated by another incident from ancient history. In 68 BC pirates attacked Ostia, which was then the main port of Rome; they set it on fire, destroyed the consular war fleet, and kidnapped two prominent senators, together with their bodyguards and staff. As a result the Roman Senate passed the *Lex Gabinia* (in 67 BC), which gave Pompey the Great extraordinary proconsular powers, which he used to raise a great fleet of 500 vessels that swept the pirates from the seas in less than three months. Historians argue that the powers granted to Pompey the Great under the *Lex Gabinia* undermined the resilience of the Roman Republic, and were a critical step in its subsequent downfall.

In addition to identifying the causes of modern piracy, and outlining its operations around the world, this book addresses the necessary responses to piracy and highlights the fact that we can expect to see piracy becoming endemic and global. The fundamental reason for this change in the importance of piracy is the decline of the global economic and political system that has been in place for nearly 200 years (which it is convenient to date from the conclusion of the Congress of Vienna in 1815). In many ways we are returning to the political and economic situation prior to 1815; a world of multi-polar powers, threatened by famine, conflict and without the financial certainties that have underpinned the world during our lifetimes.

It is important to understand that everything in our world is interconnected; the fact that giant oil tankers can be regularly attacked while carrying the crude oil on which our economies are so clearly dependent is not something that we can view in isolation, and that the failed economies of Africa and Asia often sit astride key lines of communication and control raw materials that are in increasingly short supply. Piracy is one of the threads out of which the emergent world of the twenty-first century is being woven; we need to understand it, because it can tell us much about the fabric of our new economy.

CHAPTER 1

PIRACY: THE BACKGROUND

OUR PERCEPTIONS OF PIRACY

For most of us, children's stories and films made us believe that pirates are mythical and romantic figures from a more dangerous age, exciting to look at from the safety of our world, an escape from the boredom of a predictable and secure environment. One can question whether humans naturally seek adventure, but our historical experience has been of danger and threat, and we are in many ways adapted to cope with such stresses; thrills and danger have an attraction for most of us; if this were not the case, then roller-coasters would close and horror filmmakers would go out of business. As a species we like to imagine how we can deal with hazards, a trait that has obviously had beneficial survival value.

Piracy is no longer about a romantic vision of the past, or of rare events in far-flung parts of the world, but is now a reality of life in the twenty-first century, and something that no amount of high-tech armament can effectively banish. In my opinion it is one of the symptoms of our changing world. In fact it is not only a symptom of change, but it also serves to illuminate emergent economic and political realities.

It is important to make comparisons with piracy in the past, which highlight the connections between past events and current developments. It is likely that places like Madagascar, and the islands of the South China Sea, which have been pirate centres in the past, will see piracy re-established in the twenty-first century.

THE RE-EMERGENCE OF PIRACY IN THE TWENTY-FIRST CENTURY

In the great sweep of history piracy is best understood if it is seen as a normal state of affairs at sea, and the relative peace of the past 150 years as an intermission. Relative is perhaps the operative word; the world has never been entirely free of piracy. A friend recalled to me a story told to him by his father, a Royal Navy officer in the 1930s, who saw the pirates he had just captured beheaded, on the beach, by the Chinese authorities. Such attacks continued to be a problem in the South China Sea, and in the coastal waters of the Philippines and Indonesia, throughout the twentieth century.

It is important to remember that the oceans, away from territorial waters, are essentially lawless; the sea is the territory of no country. The strict definition of piracy refers to hijacking and kidnapping on the high seas, outside the jurisdiction of any state. While it is true that some international treaties and conventions govern the high seas, and some states claim extra-territorial powers, in the main piracy takes place in a lawless environment. For those used to the idea that laws govern every aspect of their lives this represents a strange and unsettling concept. There is also an interesting juxtaposition of the ideas of human rights and international law, and the reality of dealing with the inhabitants of territories like southern Somalia, whose judicial system is now very basic, where it operates at all. This is a dilemma that lacks any obvious solution, given that summary execution has gone out of fashion. Logically the nations of the world should agree to extend the jurisdiction of the International Court to deal with piracy, but this would give greater power to that body and many governments, including the US administration, which would undoubtedly resist such a development.

CAUSES AND FACTORS

The reasons for the growth of piracy are fivefold.

(1) In territories (that may be parts of otherwise effective states) that lack effective governance, or where the governing state and its apparatus (the military, judiciary, police, bureaucracy and political structure) is itself controlled by the corrupt, or criminal, i.e. the state is predatory, then there is no effective restraint on the activities of those wishing to engage in crime, whether that crime is drug smuggling, arms running, slavery,

human trafficking, or piracy. However, it is rarely the case that there is a state of total anarchy; even criminals need some structure. Many states exercise only partial, or spasmodic, control of areas of their territory. This is obvious in the case of Colombia and Peru, but it is also the case in most of Africa, and in countries like Yemen and Pakistan.

(2) Such territories have access to the sea, and to major shipping lanes.

(3) The inhabitants of such territories are desperate enough, and have the necessary sea-going and military skills to undertake such a hazardous venture. Poverty alone is not a sufficient cause.

(4) Piracy on the grand scale requires management and the existence of effective criminal organizations. Piracy is a crime, and needs to be considered on the same level as the drug trade and human trafficking.

(5) Finally, in order to be truly effective, piracy requires strong backers, links to international criminal organizations and to members of a national diaspora. These factors have been especially important in the case of Somali piracy.

David Anderson makes the important point, when writing about Somalia, that:

Piracy is *not* a function of the failure of the Somali state – and this assumption has perhaps been the most pervasive yet the most misleading of all. The reinvigoration of Somali piracy is connected to the reconstruction of the state in what was Somalia, not its collapse, and its consequences are therefore very serious for the future. Strengthening the state will *not* necessarily lessen piracy, though changing the character of the transactions conducted by state actors probably will.[1]

Piracy in Somalia is not the result of state failure: that simple conclusion is far too readily reached by people who examine the chaotic mess that is Somalia, without adequate consideration of the situation. The reality is that the failure of the original Somali administration has caused a phase transition to another state of being, a period of virtually continual internal conflict and chaos. Marten Scheffer, writing about complex systems, refers to 'critical transitions' in dynamic systems, including societies that can transit between alternative stable states.[2] Stable government is therefore not inevitable, but is merely an alternative state. Scheffer argues that the loss of resilience increases the fragility of a system (including a state) and that 'it can be easily tipped into a contrasting state by stochastic events'.[3] He adds that when such a change occurs the cause is often sought, incorrectly, in the stochastic, or chance, events, rather than in the fundamental issues that have given rise to a loss of resilience within the system.[4]

Piracy is enabled by a lack of effective governance, and weakly, or ineffectively, governed areas are ideal for its operation, whereas total chaos would not permit the criminal 'business' of piracy. As Anderson says, it was the attempts by local strongmen and clan forces to recreate new forms of governance, particularly in Puntland, that have enabled piracy to develop, because piracy needs basic structures and communications. The proto-state of Puntland in the past provided an ideal support system for piracy.

In the language of complexity theory, Somali society moved from one attractor to another and has stabilized in its current state; therefore, a move back to a 'national state' with a central government is not inevitable. Much of the failure of international policy towards Somalia in recent years has been due to the failure to understand the nature of control exercised by 'proto-states' within Somalia and the resultant inability to acknowledge the relative stability of the present system. There has been an overwhelming desire to 'restore' the Somali state, which frequently leads individuals and organizations to ignore the facts on the ground; particularly the importance of developments in Puntland and Somaliland.

Piracy, on the scale now practised in Somalia, requires a number of structural support systems. First, the captives have to be housed and fed in protected areas, where there is little risk that they will be captured, killed or injured by violent gangs. Local people are employed to feed and guard captives and their ships. The equipment and supplies needed by the pirates have to be provided, though securing arms is not a huge problem. The government of the United States has generously donated large quantities of weapons from time to time to groups it supports, and these have then been freely sold in Mogadishu's arms souk. Saudi Arabia, Eritrea and other countries in the region have also supplied weapons from time to time; all in contravention of the long-standing UN arms embargo. Money has to be transferred, not only to the men who man the skiffs and motherships, but also to the backers, local and foreign, and to those supplying intelligence from around the world on the movement of shipping and the cargoes carried.

There was even a basic form of stock market in Somalia where people could buy shares in pirate operations. Reuters reported in December 2009 that in Haradheere pirates set up a cooperative in August 2009 to fund their hijackings offshore, and this operated like a type of stock exchange. A local pirate, called Mohammed, told Reuters:

> Four months ago, during the monsoon rains, we decided to set up this stock exchange. We started with 15 'maritime companies' and now we are hosting 72. Ten of them have so far been successful at hijacking.[5]

Piracy actually paid for the social infrastructure of Haradheere, until the Islamists moved in 2010. According to a local official, 'the district gets a percentage of every ransom from ships that have been released, and that goes on public infrastructure, including our hospital and our public schools'.[6]

Like any successful business, piracy in the region has meant increased imports of goods, including 4 × 4 cars and the employment of many in selling and supporting local customers.

Euromonitor said in 2010: 'Surprisingly, air travel is actually enjoying positive performance in Somalia: Damal Airways, Daallo Airlines and Jubba Airways are all performing well.'[7] Damal Airlines operate to Sharjah and Dubai in the United Arab Emirates from a number of airports in Somalia, including Bender Qassim International Airport, Bosaso and the reopened Mogadishu Airport, and there are regular flights from Jomo Kenyatta International Airport, Nairobi and also 'khat' flights out of Nairobi's Wilson Airport, delivering khat from Kenya to a number of destinations in Somalia. The available evidence is that piracy, far from being a threat to Somalia, is transforming the economy of central Somalia. Kenya is also enjoying a property boom, as Somalis have invested their ransom money, and their profits from other enterprises, criminal and legitimate. In the period 2005–10 property prices in Nairobi increased between two- and three-fold.[8] Far from being isolated from the rest of the world, successful Somali businessmen (including those making money from piracy) are able to travel freely and invest their money abroad. The same air routes also deliver the navigation and communications equipment needed by the growing pirate 'companies'.

This may sound counter-intuitive, but in fact we have been fed so much non-reflective analysis by the media that we all too frequently accept such conclusions. Typical of this is a comment by David Randall in *The Independent*:

> Western security agencies say that Somalia has become a safe haven for militants, including foreign jihadists, who are using it to plot attacks across the impoverished region and beyond. As many have pointed out,

the only lasting solution to the problem of piracy on the high seas is a political solution to anarchy on dry land. Until then, the capture of ships and crews will continue.[9]

A more balanced view is that Somalia is a territory in which a number of groups are violently competing for control of the resources of the country, and that the conflict at a local level is still fundamentally tribal, whereas foreign elements, and those Somalis allied to them, including the agents of states, often express their desire for influence and control by the use of ideological language, including support for and opposition to Islamic extremist philosophies. A political solution to the many problems of Somalia will not be possible until the inhabitants of the former Italian colony of Somalia decide that they wish to renounce violent conflict, something that Somaliland (the former British colony) did in the period up to 2010. Given the strength of the competing parties, which are variously supported by agents from the United States, Ethiopia, Egypt, France, Eritrea, Saudi Arabia, Iran and Kenya, in addition to criminal elements from Italy and elsewhere, and individuals espousing 'terrorism', and the current commitment of the UN, and other international bodies, to an imposed political solution, it is extremely unlikely that any lasting political solution for Somalia will be forthcoming in the near future; that is, one that is acceptable to the Somali people and the various international powers. However, one can only hope that the process initiated by the Garowe Principles can bring greater stability to Somalia.

It is difficult not to agree with David Anderson when he says that 'Fundamentalism and terrorism are explicitly *not* the causes of piracy.'[10] Somalia is a tribal society, in which conflict for scarce resources has deep historical roots. This is not in itself unusual; the history of the Scottish Highlands, of the Scottish Borders, and of Afghanistan, all give examples of such cultural predispositions. Modern Yemen and the southern provinces of Saudi Arabia also exhibit such behaviour.

A COALITION OF INTEREST GROUPS

Piracy in the twenty-first century is, in the main, the work of organized criminal gangs. The gangs may be small and opportunistic – groups of fishermen, off-duty policemen, or customs officers – but increasingly the threat has been from sophisticated professional pirate groups, well organized and with adequate funding. Somalia is currently the epicentre of these developments, but the lessons learnt there are being applied by criminals elsewhere in the world. That is not to say that piracy in Southeast Asia and the west coast of Africa will precisely mirror the Somali experience – there are different influences and traditions in each area – but the size of the multi-million dollar rewards realized by the Somalis will inevitably result in copycat behaviour.

Piracy, as it has developed in Somalia, involves a complex network of interest groups. The hierarchy of control involves local politicians and businessmen, tribal leaders and warlords, foreign investors, including members of elites living in the Arabian Peninsula, foreign criminals, expatriate Somalis, corrupt lawyers, bankers and officials. Like other forms of transnational criminal organizations (TCOs), modern piracy has seized the opportunities presented by globalism and new technology to become more effective. Furthermore, it has exploited the lack of restrictions placed on its activities in Somalia and Yemen. Like any other form of criminal activity, it is normally impossible to prove the involvement of individual players in piracy – piracy is like an iceberg; most of the information is hidden below the water-line. Only the operatives at sea, the actual pirates, are likely to be identified.

The driver of all such criminal activity is predation. Predation, in the human context, means the act of preying on others, taking material wealth from them and threatening them with the loss of life or injury. Such criminals can be compared to natural parasites, or species, like lions, that kill other animals in order to survive. The term has become popular as a description of the behaviour of political elites in African and Middle Eastern countries, in taking large shares of national wealth by the use of corruption and bribery, as well as the straightforward seizure of the wealth of others; as when politicians, generals and princes take the land of ordinary people without adequate (or any) compensation. In all societies that are not governed by the rule of law, and where despotic power is exercised, the individual lives a Hobbesian existence, 'the life of man, solitary, poore, nasty, brutish, and short'.

It is important to understand the concept of predation, because it underpins not only the behaviour of criminal gangs, including Somali pirates, but also the behaviour of elites in regions like the Horn of Africa and Arabia. Jane Novak refers to 'Yemen's pervasively corrupt environment', and says that 'officials are determined to retain the cash flows derived from corrupt practices and criminal enterprises'.[11] She could have been writing about any number of countries.

THE GROWTH OF PIRACY

For a long time the growth of piracy off Somalia was inexorable, doubling year on year. In 2009 the International Maritime Bureau (IMB) recorded 217 attacks on vessels by Somali pirates, nearly twice the 2008 figure, which in turn was over twice the 2007 figure of 44, and was over twice the 2006 figure of 20 attacks. In 2010, to early April, the IMB reported 36 attacks by Somali pirates, of which seven were successful, including the hijacking of the South Korean VLCC (very large crude carrier) *Samho Dream* on Easter Sunday 2010. What does need to be remembered is that the IMB's figures are not reliable. The main reason for this is that shipowners are reluctant to advise their insurers of problems where no claim arises, and because of the perception that pirate attacks are bad publicity. The Kuwait Petroleum Corporation (KPC) denied that the MV *Album*, a 105,000-ton tanker, was attacked on 30 December 2009, even though the attack had been notified to the IMB. In this case it was clear that their publicity department thought that the attack could discourage clients from buying oil from KPC. During discussions, shipowners have freely admitted that they do not report all attacks; this is a particular problem off West Africa, where the authorities are distrusted, as they are thought by many to be in league with the attackers.

There is evidence that on occasions up to 80 per cent of West African attacks are unreported, although the incidence of unreported attacks off Somalia is much lower, because the presence of international warships that are able to come to the aid of merchant ships, is an incentive to radio for help. It is important to bear in mind the unreliable nature of the data whenever you look at piracy. However, two things are beyond dispute. Somali pirates (and their Yemeni associates) accounted for over half the recorded attacks in 2008–9 and in the period from 2006 to 2010 Somali piracy grew exponentially, from 20 in 2006 to the IMB's figure of 217 in 2009. On the basis of the reports to the IMB in 2009 there were 406 attacks globally, of which 53.5 per cent were by Somalis.

The precise number of attacks is less important than the tremendous growth in the Somali piracy 'industry'. There is good reason to believe that the Somali contribution to global pirate attacks may actually be below 50 per cent of the total; however, it is clear that the Somali form of piracy is far more lucrative than the robberies on the high seas so common in the South China Seas, or the murderous assaults off the Niger Delta. Somali piracy has been far and away the most profitable form of piracy seen in modern times, and there is no doubt that the bulk of money raised from piracy today is paid to Somalis and their business allies.

Numerous estimates of the amounts paid in ransom are printed, but my understanding is that shipowners and their underwriters are very careful to keep such information secret. It is also likely that the sacks of US dollars parachuted down onto the decks of hijacked vessels do not represent the whole picture and that at least a percentage of ransom payments is transferred via more conventional channels. In Somalia piracy is a business, operating with the support of politicians, local businessmen and other key constituencies, whereas in the Philippines and Indonesia piracy is predominantly a cottage industry of robbery at sea by local gangs. It must, however, be remembered that the triads were behind the series of hijackings and ship reflaggings, which occurred in the South China Sea in the 1990s, and that they, and their business associates, are still involved in the hijacking of barges laden with cargoes like palm oil, which can easily be resold.

What happened in Somalia has been a game-changing situation, which in the space of a few years moved piracy from a minor inconvenience, which was extremely unlikely to affect any particular merchant vessel in transit to and from the Red Sea, to a major problem. It is often said that the shipping industry and insurers were slow to react to the increase in the threat, but until the beginning of the 2009–10 pirate season off Somalia (which normally begins in September–October with the ending of the summer monsoon, and lasts until the following summer, with a slight interruption caused by the weaker winter monsoon) it was possible to say that the then current level of attacks was extraordinary and would not be repeated, particularly given that the introduction of international warship patrols off the coast of Somalia and in the Gulf of Aden was seen by many as an effective deterrent. At each stage industry analysts tended to look back at the historic data, and that approach failed to predict the dynamic nature of Somali piracy and its innate ability to improvise and respond to changing circumstances.

However, the expediential growth of pirate attacks has been reversed, and in 2012 there were only 75 attacks by Somali pirates and 14 hijackings, according to the International Maritime Bureau, out of a global total of 297 attacks and 28 hijackings.[12] Somali piracy had not been eradicated, but the days of ever-increasing hijackings are over, at least for the time being. The announcement in January 2013 that 'Afweyne', a major pirate leader, was retiring, was one indication of the sea change in the Somali piracy industry.[13]

THE NEW PIRATES

Any understanding of the nature of modern piracy must be grounded in an understanding of the nature of Somali piracy and the socio-political structures and background that nurtured its development. At the date of writing Somalia is still the heart of the piracy industry and the model for aspirant pirates around the world. It is therefore essential to look at Somalia in some detail.

CHAPTER 2

THE POLITICAL DEVELOPMENT OF SOMALIA

SOMALIA: SOCIETY AND CLANS

In order to understand fully why Somalia has evolved into an ideal base for piracy it is necessary first to look at Somalia's history since independence, and the origins of the modern country. The Somali people occupy a large region in the Horn of Africa, which includes Somalia, the so far independent state of Somaliland, the Republic of Djibouti, the Ogaden (or Somali) territory of Ethiopia and parts of northern Kenya. There is also a large, and growing, diaspora, with Somali communities in Nairobi, Kenya, Yemen, Saudi Arabia, the United Arab Emirates, the United States, the United Kingdom, the Netherlands, Sweden, Italy, Australia, and a number of other countries. The current Somali elite has strong ties to the diaspora, because this group is better educated and wealthier than the Somalis living in Africa and have become an important source of investment funding for the country.

Historically Somalis have had a reputation as traders and merchants, and Somali seamen settled in European ports from the nineteenth century. The homeland of the Somalis is mainly semi-desert on the plains, and apart from the settled farmers of the south, the majority of Somalis have been pastoral nomads, with small populations of traders and artisans living in long-established towns, such as Mogadishu. The Somali territories are backed by the Golis and Ogo mountain ranges, which rise to a height of over 2,000 metres, and are linked in the west to the Ethiopian highlands[1]; rainfall from this area ensures that Somaliland is normally well-supplied with water.

17

Central Somalia, known as the Haud, has no permanent water; this area includes the provinces of Nugaal, Mudug and Galguduud.

In the south the land is well-watered by Jubba and Shebelle rivers, which rise in the Ethiopian highlands; in a small way they are to Somalia what the Nile is to Egypt. The Italians selected the Shebelle valley for plantations and started building irrigation systems in 1919.[2] Initially cotton was grown, and in 1926 banana cultivation was introduced by Italian settlers. The Shebelle flows east to Balad, then south where it normally evaporates in a series of marshes near Jilib, although when in flood its water reaches the Jubba River. The Jubba River, which is navigable from the sea to Bardera, enters the Indian Ocean near Kismaayo, a port that has seen fierce fighting between militia groups over the last few years.[3] This area is by far the richest arable zone in Somalia, and late President Siyad Barre rewarded his supporters with farmland in this area.

Ioan Lewis, the historian of modern Somalia, says that Somalis belong to the Hamitic ethnic group; they have connections with the Oromo and Bantu tribes and also with Arabia. He also notes that the largest element of the Somali population (*Samale*) consists of four principal groups of clans or 'clan families': these comprise the Dir, Isaq, Hawiye and Darod, which Lewis says are all 'primarily pastoral nomads'. There are also a number of sub-clans. The Dir clans, the Ise (or 'Esa') and Gadabursi, live mainly in Somaliland and Djibouti, but can also be found in the Harar province of Ethiopia. Lewis states that the Isaq, who were originally a sub-clan of the Dir, live mainly in the centre and north of Somali, but also move into the Ogaden. He says that the largest of the Somali clan families are the Darod who occupy the eastern part of Somaliland, and what is now known as Puntland, the provinces of Bari, Nugal and Mudug, together with most of the Haud and the Ogaden (the Ethiopian Somali province) with a presence in the south of Somalia and north-eastern Kenya. The other Samale clan family are the Hawiye, whose territories traditionally stretch north into Mudug, and include Hiraan, Galguduud and the area around Mogadishu (*Muqdisho*).

Lewis adds that the Sab tribes, the Digil and Rahanweyan (or Digil Mirifle), are separate from the Samale, and tend to be cultivators, having settled mainly in the well-watered river valleys of the Jubba and Shebelle.[4] The Sab tribes have developed a distinctive variant of the Somali: Af-Maymay. In addition some Somalis are the descendants of Bantu slaves, who live mainly in the southern river valleys. Other minority groups, who have a caste-like position within Somali society, are those who engage in occupational activities: these groups include the Midgans, Tumals and Yibirs and are collectively known as *sab*. The Digil Mirifle also include many whose ancestors were non-Somalis – foreign craftsmen and traders who were adopted into, or joined, the clan.

Among pastoralists there is a fierce sense of independence. The traditions of Somalia are overwhelmingly those of a nomadic society, one in which camels have been of critical importance. In fact, Lewis says, 'on a social as well as economic transactions the pastoralists operate on a camel standard'. Wedding gifts are therefore calculated in terms of camels and the blood price for a man's death is 100 camels, 50 for the life of a woman. The price for injuries is calculated in the same manner.[5]

Somali pastoralists learn their genealogies by heart and, in this way, understand which groups to identify with; but the most important single linkage is to their '*diya*-paying group', the group of men who pay and receive blood money, which varies in size from a few hundred to a few thousand. Lewis says: 'It must be appreciated that the nomadic Somali are a warlike people, driven by the poverty of their resources to intense competition for access to water and grazing.'[6]

Apart from the farming areas of the southern rivers and the north-west, where millet is cultivated, Somali pastoralists have dominated the country and their concept of territory is determined by the migration of the livestock, which is moved constantly to graze on new pastures. The Somalis have in the main not owned their country, but have occupied such parts of it as they need for the moment. The normal Somali pastoralist is known as a *warenleh*, or spear-bearer, a warrior.[7] Those who are learned in religion are known as *sheikhs*, but normally these men have no political power; Sheik Sharif Sheik Ahmed, formerly president of the Transitional Federal Government (TFG), is an exception.

In summarizing the impact of Islam on the Somali character Lewis says:

[W]hile the Somali draw many of their distinctive characteristics, especially their strong egalitarianism, their political acumen and opportunism, and their fierce traditional pride and contempt for other nations from their own traditional culture, they also owe much to Islam. And it is typical of their mutual dependence upon these two founts of their culture that the highly pragmatic view of life and, as it must seem to some, fatalistic trust in the power of God and His Prophet. Above all, Islam adds depth and coherence to those common elements of traditional culture which, over and above their many sectional divisions, unite Somalis and provide a basis for their strong national consciousness.[8]

The Somalis are Sunni Muslims, of the Sha'afi School of Law, and traditionally Sufism has been an important element of their faith. It is often claimed that Somalis are not attracted to religious extremists and that Al-Shabaab (or 'Harakaat al-Shabaab al-Mujaahidiin' to give it its full title) accordingly has little appeal to the Somali Muslims. While this may be true, it is also important to remember the history of Somalia's national hero, Sayyid Muhammed Abdille Hassan, and his *jihad* against the British in the early twentieth century. Like modern Islamists he was strongly influenced by *Wahhabi* ideas from Saudi Arabia. The idea of a *jihad* against foreign forces is therefore not a new concept in Somalia. However, Lewis says that, fundamentally, 'Somalis are staunch pragmatists, valuing what can be shown to produce results.'[9]

Somalia, for most of its history, has therefore been dominated by a pastoral majority, who looked down on the inhabitants of the small towns that grew up on the coast for the purposes of trade, and on those who chose to practise settled farming. The concept of territory has consequently been fluid; the Somalis follow their grazing animals in search of water and fodder. Somali society has never been dependent on urbanization and has retained its pliable view of territory. Leimsidor refers to 'the transnational nature of Somali society', which he says is, 'a factor informing almost every aspect of Somali migration and central to Somali society in general [...] For Somali society, however, the term implies a society in which ethnic and clan identities supersede legally determined national identities and borders to the point in which legal status, physical barriers, and conventional categories of self-identification are rendered almost irrelevant'[10] (Figure 2.1).

A BRIEF HISTORY OF SOMALIA TO 2008

Living on the edge

The fundamental and historic issues in Somalia are that the territory is arid and agriculture is marginal. Any change in the weather, particularly a period of drought, can rapidly have dire consequences; faced by drought people can either die, or migrate. Somalia has therefore lacked resilience, and individuals of necessity have a dependency on the clan or sub-clan for survival; it is not a land where an individual can survive for long without the support of the larger group. Conflict is also a part of inter-tribal relationships, as raiding is an effective survival technique for the strong, when times are tough.

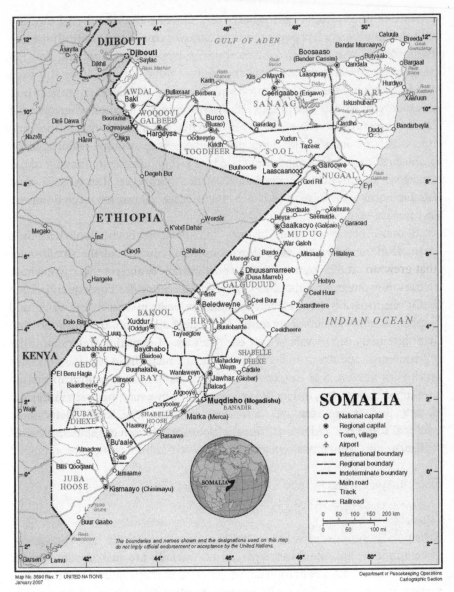

Figure 2.1 UN map of Somalia

Somalia is, and has been in the past, a territory where humans live at the edge of existence, a place where life is normally hard. Because Somalia has historically been resource poor and dependent on livestock herding (notably goats and camels) it never had sufficient capital of its own to build up the

21

infrastructure of a state, or a rigidly hierarchical society. In the nineteenth century there were a few ports along the Somali coast, which were essentially trading bases; the tribesmen of the interior ran their own affairs, and no government's writ ran throughout the land.

The Somali people came to occupy much of the Horn of Africa, but never developed the institutions of a state, as understood by Europeans. For a nomadic race the territory of Somalia was like the sea, something over which no man could claim possession, except for the small area of established arable farming. By the end of the nineteenth century their territory was caught up in the scramble for Africa. The British Navy also had problems with Somali piracy in the nineteenth century. According to F.L. James:

> In 1825 the British brig *Mary Ann* was treacherously seized and plundered, and broken up by the coast Somalis near Berbera, and most of the crew murdered. A sloop of war was at once dispatched by the Government of Bombay, to blockade the coast and open fire upon the people, who fled in all directions. Through the intervention of El Haji Sharmarkay, the governor of Zeila, the survivors of the *Mary Ann* were recovered, and the Somalis bound over to abstain from future attacks on English vessels, and to pay the full value of the plundered property by annual instalments; but in 1855 the practice of plundering and murdering strangers on the coast was renewed, and the tribes were again fined £3000, and the harbour of Berbera blockaded by two of the Honourable East India Company's cruisers.[11]

There may be a lesson here for modern navies.

Colonialism

Britain took the port of Aden in 1839 to use as a resupply base for vessels travelling to India. Aden was dependent on supplies from Somalia, but the British resisted the temptation to occupy the Somali coast. Other powers moved into the region. In 1859 France obtained the cession of the port of Obock and in 1869 the Italians obtained an interest in the port of Assab, in what is now Eritrea. In the 1860s Egypt also sought to re-establish old Turkish claims to the Red Sea and the Somali coast; in 1869 the Egyptians raised their flag at Bulhar and Berbera in Somalia, a fact that initially caused Britain concern, but that it accepted as not being a threat to imperial interests. However, the Egyptians abandoned their claims to their

Somali possessions in 1884, in order to deal with the Mahdi's revolt in the Sudan.[12] In 1887, in order to forestall other powers, Britain established a protectorate over Somaliland, the northern portion of Somalia, after Egypt abandoned its claims to the territory. As there was no overall authority in the Somali territories the activities of foreign governments encountered no serious local resistance. As Lewis explains: 'Foreign aggression thus encountered not a nation-state, but a congeries of disunited and often hostile clans which themselves were regularly divided by bitter internecine feuds.'[13]

Once the Egyptians withdrew, Britain was not the only state to seek control of portions of the Somali and the Red Sea coast. In 1885 Italy proclaimed a protectorate over Eritrea from Assab to Massawa, and in 1889 it signed the Treaty of Ucciali with Ethiopia, which the Italians regarded as bringing that country into their sphere of influence. In 1884 a British officer obtained the consent of the northern Somali clans for a British protectorate, allowing the appointment of British agents on the Somali coast. The British provided security in the ports of Berbera and Bulhar, thus protecting the export of animals to Aden and keeping other powers out of northern Somalia. In 1885 France obtained the cession of Jibuti (Djibouti). In 1889 Italy claimed the Somali coast to the east of the British Protectorate, signing treaties with the Sultans of Obbia and Alula. Then in 1892 the Sultan of Zanzibar ceded four ports, including Mogadishu, to Italy for 25 years in return for an annual rent.[14]

In this way the division of Somali territory between Britain, France and Italy (and the subsequent Ethiopian acquisition of the Ogaden) determined the future of the country. As we will see, the area that was formerly British Somaliland declared independence as the Somaliland Republic in May 1991 and it has remained an oasis of relative calm and good government, in contrast to the chaos that has marked the former Italian colony of Somalia in the same period.

The pre-independence history of the Somali territories in the twentieth century included the consolidation of Italian power, the start of the Italo–Ethiopian war in 1934, by which the Italian Fascists sought to avenge the Italian defeat at Adowa in 1896, and which led to the Italian invasion of Ethiopia. By 1941 the British had defeated the Italians in Somalia and Ethiopia and established a military administration over the whole of Somalia, except for Djibouti. In 1950 the UN granted Italy a ten-year mandate over its former colony of Somalia, and transferred the Ogaden to Ethiopia.

Independence

On 26 June 1960 British Somaliland became independent followed a week later by Italian Somalia. The two countries then merged on 1 July 1960 to form the Somali Republic, which in reality lasted until January 1991, when President Siyad Barre was overthrown. No effective government has controlled Somalia since that date.[15]

Adan Abdulle Osman was the first provisional president of the new republic. Lewis says that the new state had the framework of a European-style centralized state and administration, but that 'no serious thought had been given to considering how appropriate these would prove in the local setting, or above all in conjunction with the highly decentralized nature of traditional Somali political institutions'.[16] This problem has been ignored in most of the 'solutions' subsequently proposed by international bodies. The new state also faced serious problems in the integration of the two ex-colonies, which used different methods of administration, accounting and law. In addition, the former British colony used written English for all documents, while the former Italian portion of the country wrote in Italian, there being at the time no written form of Somali. The political and economic focus of the new state was inevitably Mogadishu and from the beginning there was a sense in former British Somaliland that they were being excluded. The referendum held on 20 June 1961 to approve the constitution was not popular in the north – about 50 per cent voted against – whereas in the former Italian territory it was strongly supported.[17] This was an ominous sign, and foreshadowed later developments. Somalia attempted, without success, to include land from northern Kenya in its territory, but Kenyan nationalists resisted such moves.

There was also conflict within Ethiopian-run Ogaden, which started in 1963 with the formation of the Ogaden Liberation Front. In 1954, as part of the UN-approved settlement, Britain had formally recognized the Ogaden as Ethiopian territory, an event that the local tribes considered contrary to their 1896 protection treaty with Britain. It was foreseeable that the wish of the Somalis in the Ogaden to secede from Ethiopia would cause trouble and equally certain that any Ethiopian government would resist these pressures. With the advantage of hindsight it is easy to criticize the decisions made 60 years ago by those who sought to resolve the problems of the Horn of Africa, but self-determination was not seen as a matter of major importance at the time and the geopolitical considerations favoured the support of a strong Ethiopian state. The Somalis see Ethiopia as a colonial power, occupying the Ogaden. Conflict between Ethiopia and Somalis is something that has deep roots; Somalis, whose sense of history is as acute as that of the Irish, remember the campaigns of Ahmed Guray against the Ethiopians in the early sixteenth century. In recent times this conflict led to the Somali–Ethiopian war of 1977–8, which was disastrous for the Somalis and resulted in a massive refugee crisis; Siyad Barre only agreed to a peace accord with Ethiopia in 1988.

Somalia's history since independence has been dominated by the figure of Siyad Barre, who became president in October 1969 and ruled for over 21 years, until 1991. After Barre came the deluge, violence, conflict and corruption that originated from the failures of his regime, and still beset Somalia to this day.

The rise of Siyad Barre

Following the start of the original Ogaden conflict in 1963 a new civilian government was formed in June 1967, after elections that saw the first peaceful transfer of power in Africa, following the defeat of President Adan Abdulle Osman. Abdirashid Ali Shermarke became president and Mohamed Haji Ibrahim Egal prime minister. President Shermarke was the father of Omar Abdirashid Ali Sharmarke, the TGF prime minister in 2009–10.

After the elections of 26 March 1969, when almost all the elected candidates joined the government party, the stage was set for effective dictatorship, or one-party rule, as the various political groups rapidly consolidated around the Somali Youth League (SYL). By the end of May 1969 the SYL parliamentary cohort had swelled from 73 to 109. In addition, the 11 Somali National Congress members formed a coalition with the SYL; this coalition held 120 of the 123 seats in the National Assembly. Basil Davidson said that massive corruption followed the political chaos and vote rigging.[18] Fifty candidates challenged the election results, but the Supreme Court refused to intervene; Somalia had started its transformation into a predatory state. At that point, over 40 years ago, Somalia began its descent into chaos, *tempest-tost*. The stage was thus set for the tragedy of Siyad Barre, a Macbeth-like figure who, after trying to do his best for Somalia, set his seal on its ruination, and from whose rule so many 'fled the snares of watchful tyranny'.[19]

Ruth Gordon says, 'After a decade of parliamentary democracy, the seething tensions of antagonistic clans provided the setting for the military coup of October 1969.'[20] There is another view, that clan tensions were not the cause, and that what ultimately drove Shermarke and his colleagues was greed, unrestrained by law, or custom. For him it was the chance to gain all, with no care of the future of his country; he was corrupted by power. He was the forerunner of the Somali leaders who followed.

On 15 October 1969, on a visit to the north-western town of Las Anod, the administrative capital of the Sool region, President Shermarke was shot dead by one of his bodyguards. Less than a week later, on 21 October, the day after the late president's funeral, the Somali army carried out a bloodless *coup d'état*, banning political parties, suspending the constitution, promising to end corruption and closing the National Assembly. General Siyad Barre was appointed Head of State and President of the Supreme Revolutionary Council.[21]

The Somali revolution

The new military government, having seized power in October 1969, established a Supreme Revolutionary Council (SRC), which initiated a policy of reform. Lewis says that the SRC's intention, '... which was popular initially, was to clean the Augean stable and restore Somali virtues with a concerted onslaught, under energetic leadership, on the real enemies of progress: poverty, disease and ignorance.'[22] On the first anniversary of the coup the regime officially adopted 'Scientific Socialism' as its ideology; Barre was back then in charge of a revolution. Somalia also became a client state of the Soviet Union. The regime ran campaigns against corruption and tribalism. Revolutionary Youth Centres were established and a leadership cult was developed using Chinese, North Korean and Soviet models. General Siyad Barre was referred to as the 'Father' of the nation and the 'Victorious Leader' in a manner similar to the idolization of North Korea's leaders, and quite alien to Somalia's traditional nomadic culture. Marxism–Leninism was blended with Islamic concepts. Soviet-style controls were introduced for much of the economy and imports were controlled by a state agency.

As initial public enthusiasm for the new regime weakened, the government reacted by crushing any opposition. The apparatus of a police state was created; a force of people's vigilantes was formed. Allegiance to the new order was enforced by the National Security Service (NSS) and National Security Courts, which had arbitrary powers. The right to assembly was limited and any expression of opinion that did not conform to government policy was suppressed. However, the Somali government, at this time, did function effectively.

One undoubted success of Barre's regime was the adoption of a written form of the Somali language in 1973, and there were ambitious plans to teach all to read and write. In 1974 Somalia joined the Arab League, creating stronger links with conservative Islamic governments, a move that may have been intended to provide support against potentially hostile neighbouring states. Then, during 1974–5, Somalia was affected by severe drought. This drove many pastoralists to seek help from the government, and in 1975 many were settled in the southern river areas, or in fishing communities. The government therefore dealt effectively with the drought, in contrast with its neighbours. This drought was a periodic event, the like of which affects Somalia from time to time.

The Somali–Ethiopian war

The breach with the Soviet Union in November 1977, which followed when a new pro-Soviet government in Ethiopia sought Soviet support, dropping Ethiopia's previous pro-US stance and the Soviet Union in a complete *volte-face*, changed its regional allies in the Horn. The breach was initially very popular in Somalia. Somalia failed to balance this unforeseen realignment by coming to terms with the West and its membership of the Arab League. Although it secured some money from Saudi Arabia, this could not compensate for the loss of superpower support. When, after several years of conflict between the Ethiopian government and local Somali groups in the Ogaden (backed by the Somali government), Somalia announced a general mobilization and committed itself to war with Ethiopia in February 1978, the stage was set for military disaster. In March the Somali military was hammered by Cuban-manned fighter-bombers and tanks; the Ethiopian advance in the Ogaden was irresistible, and on 9 March it was announced that Somali forces were being withdrawn from the Ogaden.

Authoritarian control

The disastrous defeat in the Ogaden in 1978 and a failed military coup in April of that year put enormous pressure on the regime. The regime reorganized itself in 1979 with a new constitution and 'people's parliament'. However, despite the previous attacks on tribalism, Barre became increasingly dependent on his tribal connections in order to retain power. His clan, the Marehan, was a sub-clan of the Darod, and the Darod came to dominate government organizations, such as the SRC.[23]

Barre's 21 years in power are really divided into two halves: 1978 marks the watershed. Although he was initially successful in achieving his objective of changing Somali society, he was soon swept off course by events that were largely not of his making. No Somali government could have stood by while the Somali inhabitants of the Ogaden revolted after the fall of the Ethiopian empire. Somalia would inevitably have been sucked into this conflict to support its kith and kin. The withdrawal of Soviet support, likewise, was not due to the actions of the Somali government, but was caused by the greater attractiveness, to the Soviet Union, of influence over Ethiopia. After 1978 the regime was therefore severely weakened, a situation that was greatly exacerbated by the resultant refugee crisis. President Barre, thereafter, only retained his hold on power during the next 12 years by intensifying his authoritarian control over Somalia, and increasing his dependence on a group of men, largely from the same clan background as him, who sought to exploit the power of the regime for their personal gain – while all the time he publicly denounced the curse of tribalism in Somalia. In the second half of his rule the government turned progressively personal, rather than directed by a revolutionary organization. It is also the case that Barre and his family became increasingly greedy, exploiting his position, particularly in collaboration with Italian interests.

Barre can therefore be seen, at one level, as essentially a victim of consequences, who almost unwittingly created the type of predatory regime he was fighting when he came to power. However, the reality was far from this romantic vision; his regime became cruel and profoundly corrupt. The Barre family, which included his five wives and at least 30 children, acquired property and bank accounts in Switzerland. Barre's eldest son, Colonel Hassan Mohammed Siad, who had an apartment in the Raphael hotel in Rome, dealt with the bribes paid by Italian construction, engineering and communications companies for their share of business in Somalia. Italian politicians quickly identified the opportunities to profit personally from the substantial aid budget for Somalia. Italy therefore did not react forcefully when in July 1989 Salvatore Colombo, the bishop of Mogadishu, was murdered, neither did Italy impose sanctions when an Italian biologist was beaten to death by the Somali secret services in June 1990.[24]

Barre's tragedy lay in the fact that, by the end of his period of rule, he became the complete opposite of what he had claimed to be when he seized power. His life mirrored that of the pigs in Orwell's *Animal Farm*.

Internal strife

The refugee crisis of 1978–80, which resulted from the defeat in the Ogaden, was another unexpected event. By 1979 there were officially 1.3 million refugees in Somalia and more than half were settled in the north.[25] Lewis notes that 'the economy of the country simply did not possess the resources to absorb so many uprooted people, even when the majority were ethnically Somali and indeed kinsmen'.[26] The regime also exploited the presence of the refugees, particularly those located in the north (present day Somaliland Republic). It oppressed clans that it considered to be hostile, notably the Issaq, in addition to using the refugee problem as a justification for seeking foreign aid. Human Rights Watch noted that:

Northerners were dismissed from and not allowed to work in government offices dealing with refugee affairs, so that they would not discover the truth about the government's policies. Instead, refugees, registered with UNHCR were given jobs in the offices dealing with refugee matters.[27]

After the war with Ethiopia, Africa Watch reported that:

[M]any Ogadeni refugees were recruited into the WSLF [Western Somali Liberation Front]. The WSLF was ostensibly being trained to fight Ethiopia to regain the Ogaden, but, in fact, terrorized the Isaak [Issaq] civilian population living in the border region, which came to fear them more than the Ethiopian army. Killings, rape and looting became common.[28]

Barre's regime had begun the process of fighting its own population and, in the end, like a serpent eating its tail, devoured itself.

The oppression of the Issaq developed into a full-blown civil war, which finally led to Somaliland declaring its independence, and the aftermath, to this day, makes any confederation of Somalia and Somaliland extremely unlikely. It marked the beginning of the end of Barre's regime, although the process took ten years. The Somali National Movement (SNM), based in Ethiopian territory, was the vehicle used by the Issaq to resist Barre's regime. Africa Watch noted that:

The government's practices consisted of a variety of brutal tactics to subdue the local population that bred outrage in those who stood by helpless. Apparently despairing of peaceful political change, an increasing number of Isaaks [Issaq] began to look to armed conflict as the only hope of defeating the government. Many supported the armed opposition, politically or logistically, and a growing number of Isaak [Issaq] men joined the ranks of the SNM as fighters. In turn, the government justified the growing terror by the emergence of the SNM, making a vicious cycle of violence inevitable.[29]

The SNM was not the only armed opposition group: the Somali Salvation Democratic Front (SSDF) was created by those members of the Mijerteyn sub-clan of the Darod involved in the attempted coup of April 1978. The SSDF obtained support from the Ethiopians, a sign of things to come. In 1991 the SSDF, under the command of Colonel Abdillahi Yusuf and General Mohamed Abshir, established what was to become the proto-state of Puntland, dominated by the Mijerteyn.

In April 1988 Barre and Mengistu Haile Mariam concluded a peace agreement, mainly to stop each other supporting the other's opponents, but this came too late for the north, where the conflict developed into all-out war from 1988 to 1991. At least half a million people fled abroad from the area and thousands of civilians died. Ogadeni refugees, in many cases, took over the homes and businesses of the Issaq. Other sub-clans were armed and encouraged to fight the Issaq. Lewis makes the point that 'in its desperate fight for survival, Siyad's family and clansmen sought to exploit to the full segmentary lineage[30] rivalry within the Somali nation'.[31] The man who had come to power promising to end corruption became dependent on it, and the man who had tried to abolish clans finally armed the clans against each other in a murderous circle of violence, setting Darod on Hawiye and everyone else on the Issaq.

Siyad Barre and state predation

Siyad Barre reportedly said: 'When I leave Somalia, I will leave behind buildings but not people.'[32] By the end of his regime Somalia was marked by oppression, corruption on a grand scale and clan patronage. He left office a deeply corrupt tyrant, hated and feared by virtually all Somalis; a monster. His regime became so brutal as to almost defy description. The Africa Watch Committee said in 1990: 'Both the urban population and nomads living in the countryside [were] subjected to summary killings, arbitrary arrest, detention in squalid conditions, torture, rape, crippling constraints on freedom of movement and expression and a pattern of psychological intimidation.'[33] In fact, the systems developed under Barre represented the most extreme form of state predation seen in Africa at that time. But Somalia is not North Korea; ultimately, controlling a pastoral society is like trying to control the wind, and the traditional institutions of clan and faith remained, although in the old Italian territories Barre's regime had tried hard to undermine the authority of the clan system.

A man who had, at the start of his period in office, promised much and had performed some valuable services for his country, ended his days as a dictator, whose government even took money from the Italian mafia in return for dumping chemical waste on the Somali coast. Apologists for Somali piracy have claimed that piracy was in part a response to the dumping of chemical waste by European companies on their shores, but have neglected to point out that this problem originated in an agreement by the then Somali government.[34]

Bayart et al. referred to Italian press reports that revealed 'the influence wielded by the P2 masonic lodge in Mogadishu [during President Siyad Barre's time], together with that of the Italian chemical industry, anxious to find a dumping ground for its toxic waste through the intermediation of members of the Honourable Society.'[35] The complete criminalization of the Somali state is no better illustrated than by this deal with the Italian mafia. In fact, Bayart et al. said of Siyad Barre's government, and similar regimes in Africa: 'It was not at all inaccurate to describe their governments as mafias.'[36]

William Reno response was that Siyad Barre:

Built a political network from the late 1970s and after on the basis of distributing parts of the formal and clandestine economy to strongmen who he thought he could trust. In practical terms, this meant he relied upon the social bonds of shared kinship and clan identity to authoritatively exercise power. Increasingly suspicious of his own state's institutions, he financed this alliance through skimming foreign aid and manipulating creditor-mandated land tenure reforms to distribute land to his political allies. External pressure to privatize state assets gave him political cover to hand these resources out to his associates. The president had a distinct geographical advantage in handing out these resources too. His close political allies generally did not come from the places that were being exploited. This, along with their tendency to bring along private militias made up of otherwise unemployed youth, insulated them from the social consequences of their predatory behavior since they owed their power to the president's favor and could provide their own immunity from customary sanctions for anti-social behavior. Thus their dependence on the obligation to heed local community interests signified organizational shifts toward something more like a predatory private commercial syndicate than a government.[37]

The UN Development Programme simply claimed: 'The 21-year regime of Siyad Barre had one of the worst human rights records in Africa.'[38]

Barre stained his hands with blood, killing politicians, businessmen, religious leaders and young students, in fact anyone who could even remotely be seen as threats. George Ayittey reported on one incident:

> [O]n July 16, 1989, in the early hours of Eid al-Adh, a Moslem holy day, government forces swooped down and arrested six prominent imams after morning prayers. Whole sections of the crowd of worshippers were gunned down. Innocent people were rounded up by the hundreds, and many were murdered and buried on the Jasira beach. Over 1,000 died that day.[39]

In the later period of Barre's tenure, in the 1980s, the elites connected with his government, in particular the Marehan and the Dhulbahante of the Darod clan family, took part in land-grabbing in the irrigated Jubba and Shebelle valleys, taking *aziendas* formerly run by Italian settlers and deposing local farmers.[40] Dustin Dehérez says that 'Conflicts over land – the heart of the conflict in Southern Somalia – turned violent because the traditional conflict mediation system was corrupted by Barre's power politics.'[41]

On 26 January 1991 Barre fled Mogadishu pursued by General Aideed of the USC militia, an organization whose members were mainly Hawiye. This is the last date that the Republic of Somalia could be said to have had an effective administration and, for over 20 years, Somalia has remained the archetypical failed state.

Conflict continued, except in Somaliland, which declared its independence on 18 May 1991, and has since remained an island of relative calm. Somaliland thus removed itself from the endemic chaos and violence, which continues to shape life in the former Italian colony of Somalia to this day, and Somaliland ceased to be part of the Somali problem. The failure of the international community, particularly the African Union, to recognize Somaliland in 1991 was short-sighted, and contrasts with the universal recognition accorded to South Sudan in July 2011. In public discussions in 2009 the then TFG prime minister, Omar Abdirashid Ali Sharmarke, made clear that he still regarded Somaliland as part of 'his' state, when he said, 'stabilisation plan that will begin the process of restoring peace to Somalia including Puntland and Somaliland',[42] a view that too many foreign governments have encouraged.

The legacy of Barre's regime

The 21 years of Barre's regime split Somalia deeply along clan lines in a way that had not been true in the past. By arming the clans and encouraging internecine conflict, Barre separated the country into fragments. What emerged were not militias based on the major clans, but groups that were divided into sub-clans and then divided again; each man was like Ishmael: 'His hand shall be against every man, and every man's hand against him.'

Towards the end of Barre's rule, chaos and conflicts were particularly bad in the south. There militias battled for control of the banana exports, which generated large revenues, and for control of the agricultural lands of the Shebelle and Jubba valleys. Catherine Besteman noted that the unarmed residents of this area were easily targeted by mobile militias and were killed so that other Somalis could claim their land and their harvests:

> Valley residents were defenceless. Genocidal acts in the valley took the form of mass killings, abduction and involuntary marriage of local women by militia members, and the deliberate starvation of entire communities by the seizure of food supplies.... Militias massacred groups of villagers who defied their efforts to exert control in the valley. Several villages, for example, lost all their men in such acts. Militias forcibly divorced young Somali Bantu women from their husbands in order to abduct them into involuntary marriages.[43]

Upon the declaration of independence by Somaliland in May 1991, the territory of which is similar to that of the old colony of British Somaliland, the territory of Somalia basically reverted to its colonial division. However, although warlords and armed groups fought for control of the area that had been Italian-run before independence, one quasi-independent area developed – Puntland, in north-east Somalia, dominated by the Mijerteyn clan. Since 1991 it has maintained control over its own affairs, although without a declaration of independence, and has been a quasi-state throughout that period. It will be necessary to look at it in greater detail, as Puntland developed into a pirate state, the trade promoted and supported by its elites.

The failure of government in Somalia has been profound. After the collapse of Barre's administration, which started with such lofty ambitions, there was no belief that a governing body was the solution to the country's problems. Instead the Somalis returned to an earlier era, before the changes introduced by Europeans had come into effect. Power in Somalia ultimately moved into the hands of local businessmen, their militias and the groups of aspirate politicians. Their objectives were limited to their own enrichment and the consolidation of local power bases. In order to gain access to foreign funding they were (and are) more than happy to say whatever makes the foreigners happy, whether it is about the importance of representative institutions, support for the general population, suppression of terrorism, or peace with Somalia's neighbours (and recently the suppression of piracy). Do not believe a word. It is true that foreign influences in the form of revolutionary Islamic groups have been introduced into the equation, but the essence remains the pursuit of power. Somalia remains the most obvious example of a predatory state; in fact it is possible to argue that it is the most advanced development of this style of exploitation of a territory, although the Congo is not far beyond.

The economic reality of Somalia is that it has had an economy based on scarcity, not on growth, and that the competition is for the control of limited resources; foreign aid, payments from international organizations and governments, the trade in goats and camels to the Middle East, and payments for fishing. Until the advent of the era of large pirate ransoms, there were no alternative sources of income in the country; although the trade in goats, and other livestock, still brought in more money than piracy even at the height of the piracy boom. Although the prospect of oil production would be a game-changer for the whole Somali economy, enriching any government authority that can control the revenues; whether Puntland, Somaliland, or a central government based in Mogadishu.

Because wealth is so closely linked to disbursements by foreigners, Somalis have developed a proficiency in outwitting, or confusing, those who control such payments. The CIA is therefore told that rival militias are harbouring terrorists, the aid agencies are assured that food aid is being delivered to those truly in need (and not being supplied to local militiamen and their families, or sold off in the markets), and those governments who believe that the root cause of all Somalia's ails is the lack of a controlling state receive fulsome, and deceitful, undertakings that the TFG will stop piracy and crime throughout the whole country. In short there is too often a conspiracy between donor and recipient, whereby falsehoods are accepted because they suit the agendas of both sides. The CIA is paid to chase terrorists, action in Somalia ensures the flow of funding from Congress, likewise the European Union and the UN have a budget for 'good governance', and for good accounting reasons they like to spend it. And so often the intrigues and stratagems of those involved on both sides contrive to mislead the public. The UN Monitoring Group made the observation:

> The principal impediments to security and stabilization in southern Somalia are the Transitional Federal Government's lack of vision or cohesion, its endemic corruption and its failure to advance the political process. [They added] Arguably even more damaging is the Government's active resistance to engagement elsewhere in the country. Instead, attempts by the Government's leadership to monopolize power and resources have aggravated frictions with the transitional federal institutions, obstructed the transitional process and crippled the war against Al-Shabaab, while diverting attention and assistance away from positive developments in the country.[44]

It would difficult for an official body to produce a more damming assessment. In other words, the TFG becomes part of the problem, not part of the solution.

It can therefore be argued that since the Somalis experienced 'government' in the Western sense, they are less inclined to try it again, and that if foreigners attempt to impose a national government on Somalia, as it happened in Ethiopia in 2006–8 with US support, the independent forces within Somalia will ensure the failure of any such enterprise. There is of course little prospect that the United States and its allies will attempt to take on another 'Afghanistan' in the foreseeable future, not only because it would be extremely difficult to see what advantages would accrue to the Western powers from such actions, but also because the United States is less able to afford such adventures.[45] However, a 'proxy war', using Ethiopian forces, remains an attractive option, one that was used again in 2011 when Kenyan and then Ethiopian troops entered southern Somalia.

The history of Somalia since 1991 is of chaos punctuated by disaster. For over 20 years, there has been constant manoeuvring by groups seeking international support and recognition as the national government. The first conference at which various competing groups, mainly clan-based, were able to pursue this objective was held in Djibouti in July 1991. But the reality was that Somali clans lost the ability to cooperate; as Lewis noted, 'clans became effectively self-governing entities throughout the Somali region as they carved out spheres of influence'.[46] The chaos and continuing drought created a catastrophic famine, which is estimated to have killed half a million people. As a result of this, the UN Security Council authorized a peace-keeping mission in April 1992.

When this proved to be ineffective in December 1992, a US-led military operation known as UNITAF, or 'Operation Restore Hope', was launched. Unfortunately, the name chosen proved to be wholly inappropriate. The Americans decided that, as the new sheriffs in town, they would enforce law and order, and attacked militias, including those led by Aideed. On 5 June 1993 Aideed's militia killed 24 Pakistan peace-keepers. As a result, the UN declared war on Aideed. The United States then took the fight to downtown Mogadishu in October 1993, in a disastrous confrontation known in the book[47] and film of the same name as *Black Hawk Down*. The loss of US soldiers and helicopters represented a huge embarrassment for the Americans, who had acted as though they had nothing to fear from Aideed's ragged Somali fighters; in the chaos hundreds of Somalis were killed and the bodies of US servicemen were dragged through the streets of Mogadishu. In reality, the US officers in charge of the operation had completely misjudged the situation and displayed an arrogance that made such a confrontation unavoidable. The Australians, who also deployed to Somalia as part of the same mission, were far more successful in gaining the trust of Somalis and reducing tension.

Following these events, former President Clinton announced that all US troops would leave Somalia by 31 March 1994. By March 1995, the expensive UN operation had ended and, as Lewis says:

> The final exodus was marked in Mogadishu by extensive looting as the UN base, built with Somalia's aid budget, was besieged by Somali scavengers. A few months later, as the country again began to descend into chaos, the very foundations of the $160 million UN headquarters had disappeared.[48]

If ever there was an apt metaphor for the failure of that international intervention in Somalia, it was that, at the end, it was reduced to an expensive hole in the ground.

The next stage of international involvement included a peace plan promoted by the regional group, the Intergovermental Authority on Development (IGAD), and launched by the president of Djibouti in 2000. This initiative was also supported by the European Union, the UN, the United States, Egypt, Italy and Libya. A conference was held at Arta in Djibouti and was attended by a collection of Somalis, some self-appointed. However, Somaliland took no part in the proceedings. This assembly, which contrived to create the illusion that it was representative of the Somali people, chose Abdiqasim Salad Hassan as president of the Transitional National Government (TNG). However, the TNG, faced with the realities of life in Somalia, was never able to ascertain real authority within the country and controlled only a small area in Mogadishu (like the TFG in 2010–12). By 2002 the experiment of the TNG had collapsed, though the UN tried to revive it unsuccessfully.

In October 2002 the IGAD and international organizations reran the Arta Conference, this time at Mbagathi in Kenya. The conference included all the main warlords, but was even less representative than the Arta Conference. The meetings in Mbagathi were confrontational and even violent; each group sought its own advantage and there was little real concern for the welfare of the country. The whole affair was chaotic and confused, and finally in 2004 Colonel Abdillahi Yusuf, who had been the autocratic president of Puntland, was appointed president of the TFG. Samatar and Samatar (the 2009 UNCTAD Secretariat) said:

> Unfortunately, incompetence, malfeasance, and the conflicting self-interest of some IGAD countries as well as officials of the Conference itself practically ensured that warlords (the main culprits responsible for the suffering of the Somali people) and corrupt politicians and their mainly illiterate clients dominated the process and appointed members of the Transitional Parliament and cabinet ministers.[49]

Ethiopia was keen to ensure Abdillahi Yusuf's selection and bribery played a large part in his success, in the same way Ali Geedi was nominated prime minister. Finally, in 2005 the TFG moved back to Somalia, first to Jowhar and then to Baidoa, far from Mogadishu. Although the UN and the European Union attempted to treat the TFG as the legal government of Somalia, and funded it, it had no following, nor credibility, within Somalia. Some of its members also became involved in the US-funded Alliance for the Restoration of Peace and Counter-Terrorism (ARPCT), the name of which described its attraction to the United States. Bronwyn Bruton says of the ARPCT: 'The Central Intelligence Agency's involvement was hard to hide, and ARPCT's creation caused a popular revolt.'[50] The objective of the CIA was to use local militias to capture any Al-Qaeda members hiding in Somalia.

While the international community was attempting to support the morbid TFG, a local development, the Union of Islamic Courts (UIC), supported by Somali business leaders, enjoyed real success in imposing law and order and reducing the power of warlords in Mogadishu. Although some of the UIC's measures, such as the attempts to ban the use of *qat* and football matches, went against the grain of Somali opinion, there was widespread relief at the improvement in conditions. The UIC also regarded piracy as being un-Islamic and took effective action to stop it in central Somalia in 2006–7. However, the United States (with its anti-terrorist focus), and its ally Ethiopia, saw this movement as a threat to their own interests, and alleged that it included elements that the United States regarded as terrorist. The United States appears too often to exhibit an unreflective reaction, whenever presented with allegations of terrorism. Its triggered response served the interests of the Ethiopian government well, which had no wish to see the re-emergence of a Somali state, although not those of the United States.

The Ethiopian invasion of Somalia: 2006

The Ethiopians invaded Somalia at the end of 2006, removing the UIC from Mogadishu and installing the puppet government of the TFG in Mogadishu. US backing for Ethiopia was open, and US aircraft bombed targets within Somalia. The Ethiopians were eventually forced out of Somalia after two years, by the increasingly effective tactics of their opponents, and by the predictable reaction to their brutality. From the ruins of the UIC was spawned a much tougher Islamic movement, Al-Shabaab, which benefitted greatly by being seen as a national resistance movement, opposing foreign invaders.

Writing in 2008 Lewis summarized the failure of international policies:

Reflecting on this tragic mess, it is easy to see how once again the process that led to the formation of the TFG had repeated all the major mistakes of previous steps in the circular and unproductive Somalia 'peace process'. The most crucial was to fail to insist on the parties actually making peace before trying to make a government.[51]

As the Crisis Group noted, when Ethiopia invaded Somalia in December 2006, 'It quickly defeated the UIC but was forced to prop up Abdillahi Yusuf's weak and, for many Somalis, illegitimate TFG, Abdillahi Yusuf's TFG was thereafter perceived to be an Ethiopian puppet.'[52] Ethiopia described Somalia as a terrorist centre, and it seems that US agencies were strongly influenced by such views. It has been said that the 2006 invasion, 'carried an imprint' of the United States. Bamfo noted that, 'Less than a month after Ethiopian troops went into Somalia, the United States quietly poured weapons and military advisers into Ethiopia. By January 2007, there were about 100 of these advisers.'[53] In addition, the United States provided intelligence and airpower. On 7 January 2007, a USAF AC-130H Spectre gunship,[54] probably operated by the 16th Special Operations Squadron, flying from the US base at Djibouti, attacked suspected Al-Qaeda members in southern Somalia. The targeting of the attack was based on joint military–CIA intelligence and on information provided by Ethiopian and Kenyan military forces operating in the border area. US sources would not confirm that US forces were operating on the ground in Somalia, along the border between Somalia and Kenya, although one official emphasized that 'we are working very, very closely' with Kenyan forces. A carrier task force, with the aircraft carrier *USS Eisenhower*, was deployed in the Indian Ocean to provide air cover.[55] There were reports on US blogs that the US involvement in the Ethiopian invasion was actually much greater; a senior military intelligence officer is quoted as saying, 'US ground forces have been active in Somalia from the start. In fact they were part of the first group in.' These ground forces were said to include CIA paramilitary officers based in Galkayo, Puntland; Special Operations forces, and US Marine units operating from Camp Lemonier in Djibouti. US planes and helicopters with their markings obscured were also said to have struck UIC targets in Somalia from 25 December 2006.[56]

These reports were not repeated in the mainstream media in the United States, but *The Washington Post* did announce that US military personnel entered southern Somalia to try to determine exactly who was killed in the AC-130H attack. As a result, accounts of wider US special forces engagements are credible. It also seems that the AC-130H attack failed to kill the intended victims, but that eight to ten other people died. Furthermore, it was alleged that the United States undertook a series of attacks aimed at Aden Hashi Ayrow (Ayro), the head of the military arm of the UIC. This was not confirmed by US spokesmen, but the United States did confirm that one of the objectives of the 2007 attacks was to kill Fazul Abdellah Mohammed, Abu Taha al-Sudani and Saleh Ali Saleh Nabhan. The United States believed that they were members of the Al-Qaeda cell in East Africa who were responsible for the bombings at the US embassies in Nairobi and Dar es Salaam in August 1998, which killed hundreds of people.[57] Ayro, who was blamed for the 2005 killing of the BBC news producer Kate Peyton, and who, as reported by *The Times*, 'had almost certainly been behind the earlier murders of a number of foreign aid workers',[58] was eventually killed by the United States in Somalia on 1 May 2008. His death was reportedly caused by four Tomahawk cruise missiles fired from a US Navy ship off the Somali coast, when he was in the central Somali town of Dhussa Marreeb. The attack killed him, his brother and a number of other top Al-Shabaab leaders.[59]

The United States was therefore fully engaged in the Somali conflict. It did not just use precision weapons aimed at particular individuals. The AC-130H Spectre is not designed for the assassination of individuals; it is an area-denial weapon, which can kill large numbers of people in a designated area, using its 40 mm howitzer and cannons: it is best deployed against bodies of troops. If targeted at an individual, it will almost inevitably kill other people, as 'collateral' damage. Given that the United States had other, more precise, weapons available for such missions, such as the Predator, it would seem that there were two possibilities. The first is that the AC-130H was never targeted at 'terrorists', and that the stories released to the media were cover stories – the aircraft may have been assisting Ethiopian forces in their invasion of Somalia, attacking troops or militia on the ground. The second possibility is that the United States lacked accurate information on the position of the men it wanted murdered, and was prepared to set up a wide 'killing zone' in which anyone present – civilian, militia or terrorist – would be killed.

Reports that other AC-130H Spectre attacks and US military engagements took place during the same period are plausible;[60] you do not deploy a carrier task force offshore just to support a relatively minor anti-terrorist operation. A report from the UAE-based Al-Khaleef news agency also claimed that 11 US Marines were captured by the Somalis in the south of the country in January 2007, while the Americans were operating with Ethiopian forces.[61] What is certain is that the United States fully supported the Ethiopian invasion of 2006 and that it committed US forces to the conflict, but in a way that was 'deniable', or could be portrayed as a part of an anti-terrorist campaign. There was also a report in *The New York Times* in June 2007 that US special forces had been operating in Puntland against members of the UIC. Hassan Dahir, the vice president of Puntland, was reported as saying, 'Three Americans came into the mountains with us. They are counter-terrorism experts and they are investigating the computers that the militants were carrying.' Eight men from the ousted UIC administration were killed in Puntland, out of a party of 15 travelling through the territory. They had come by boat to north-east Somalia in an attempt to cross the Gulf of Aden and leave Somalia.[62] In fact, it is clear that the United States conducted a 'secret war' within Somalia in 2006–7, similar to its earlier involvement in Laos during the Vietnam War.

It is important to understand the extent of the commitment of the United States to the December 2006 Ethiopian invasion, because in my opinion this strategic entanglement still strongly colours American policy towards Somalia. My own impression, based in part on feedback from a US 'Special Forces' officer, is that US policy in the Horn of Africa does not 'do complexity' and that a rather simplistic, 'black and white', approach too easily finds favour with US decision-makers. There remains a 'War on Terror' focus within the US establishment that does not always fit with the facts on the ground, and there is too often a naive belief in the power of technical solutions and in force as a solution to all problems. In 2010 there was obviously planning for a rerun for the 2006 invasion on the part of the United States, but no action seems to have taken place, and the reasons for that probably lie in the extreme weakness of the TFG and the reluctance of the Ethiopian army to commit to another bitter and expensive fight in Somalia at that time. It is possible that small groups of US special forces, and CIA operatives, continue to operate within Somalia, probably from bases in Puntland, and from across the Somali border in Ethiopia and Kenya, as well as from Camp Lemonier in Djibouti, but this is conjecture.

Given the huge size of the US intelligence community and the US military resources committed to the 'War on Terror', a cynic could claim that the perception of a terrorist threat in Somalia fits the agenda of many in the US security system. In 2010 I spoke to a US army officer who suggested that a rerun of the disastrous US-backed Ethiopian invasion of Somali of 2006 was desirable from a military point of view.

Ethiopia and the United States also cooperated in intelligence matters: 'A US government official confirmed to Human Rights Watch that agents of both the Central Intelligence Agency and the Federal Bureau of Investigation questioned detainees in Addis Ababa in early 2007.'[63] Human Rights Watch also recorded that the United States had maintained a presence within Somalia: 'One detainee described being taken to a US outpost near the Kenyan border, but still inside Somalia, where two plainclothes US officials interrogated him for several hours before he was flown to Kismaayo and Addis Ababa.'[64]

The behaviour of the Ethiopian army within Somalia was harsh and only served to increase the hatred felt for them. Amnesty International said in 2008: 'Violations of human rights and international humanitarian law, including rape and unlawful killings of civilians, have been committed by all parties to the conflict in Somalia, most notably TFG and Ethiopian forces.' Amnesty International also reported that one person claimed that they had received individual reports of 12 extrajudicial executions allegedly committed by TFG and Ethiopian forces between the start of November and early December 2007, including one case where a young child's throat was slit by Ethiopian soldiers in front of the child's mother.[65]

Ethiopia withdrew its forces in 2008, but at the end of December 2011 it re-entered Somalia in force, taking the town of Beledweyne in central Somalia from Al-Shabaab.[66] Then in February 2012, Ethiopian troops, together with Somalis, took the key town of Baidoa from Al-Shabaab.[67] They were still controlling the town at the end of 2012.[68]

MODERN SOMALIA

The problems of Somalia are systemic

It is important when looking at Somalia to remember that a short-term timescale is meaningless, and that there are no simple solutions. The problems of Somalia are systemic and deeply rooted in the territory's geography, history and society.

The situation in Somalia today is the result of the intersection of a number of complex issues, to which there is no single, or simple, solution. The long-term constraints on life in Somalia have conditioned the territory's development. The socio-economic environment of Somalia is very much the product of its geography, the semi-acrid nature of much of its landscape and the periodic droughts that affect the territory. Somalia has always been a marginal territory, as far as human settlement is concerned; whereas in more favoured climes geography, although of great importance, has not acted as such a continual restraint on human development. In Somalia Malthusian constraints created a society that was all too frequently operating on the edge of survival.

Somalis are a people who have always lived on the edge; they have developed the ability to respond to changes in the environment. This has made them adaptable, and able to exploit changes in their circumstances quickly. Somalis have always been excellent traders and the way in which they have developed piracy shows how effectively they can exploit emergent opportunities. The poor environment and the marginal nature of agriculture have also discouraged the development of hierarchical forms of government. Historically the Somali territory has not generated the wealth to support a large government bureaucracy. As a result, a clan-based society relying on the loyalty to their *diya*-paying groups emerged.

Dragon's teeth: The failure of US counter-terrorism policy

US policy in Somalia appears to be driven largely by fears over the existence of terrorist organizations and concerns over the potential for Al-Qaeda to use Somalia as a base. Jeffrey Gettleman reported in March 2010 that the US authorities regard Al-Shabaab as essentially a proxy for Al-Qaeda and that 'several high-ranking Qaeda agents were still active in Somalia'. The Americans have trained the TFG's militias and provided them with equipment and intelligence.[69]

Although the international media has frequently portrayed the current chaotic situation in Somalia as being caused by Al-Qaeda-linked terrorists and internecine conflict, there is a tendency to overlook the pernicious influence of US policy. The United States has tended to describe the 2006 assault on the UIC as an attack on terrorists. US officials frequently describe all Somali Islamists as terrorists; for example, on 14 December 2006 Jendayi Fraser, the US assistant secretary for African affairs, announced that the UIC was controlled by Al-Qaeda.

The Ethiopian invasion of 2006 provided an ideal environment for Al-Shabaab to develop. Radicalized by the horrors of the Ethiopian occupation, and with a perception that 'Crusader' America was one of Somalia's enemies, nationalist Somali Islamists with no interest in a jihadist agenda were sidelined.

There seems to be little understanding by US strategists of the depth of its failure in 2006–7, and there are many indications that US policy remained too focused on an anti-terrorism agenda. Ted Dagne, an African affairs specialist at the US Congressional Research Service, when giving evidence to a US House of Representatives subcommittee in June 2010, said, 'the Ethiopian invasion, with the support of the United States, is seen by some as having contributed to the emergence of Al-Shabaab and the proliferation of other extremist groups in Somalia.'[70]

Hoehne summarized the situation in Somalia elegantly, when he wrote:

> The Manichean perspective of the (perennial) struggle of 'good' against 'evil', which is variously assigned to 'Islam' against 'the West' or the other way round, has manifested in Somalia. Much like in other settings where the US-led War on Terror reigns and *Al-Qaeda* got involved, propaganda and violence are used to forge binaries that 'distort rather than illuminate the political landscape'.[71]

It is difficult not to agree with this judgement.

The irony is that past US policies have damaged US interests in the region, and created an environment in which Islamist fundamentalism may look like an attractive option. The United States has been careful to disguise the true extent of its involvement in Somalia, but Ethiopia has in many instances only been a proxy for the United States. As we will see, the United States has not appeared to be primarily interested in dealing with piracy and its implications, a fact that led to a divergence of opinion with the British at the UN in April 2010. US policy is to oppose Al-Shabaab and other Somali Islamists at every turn. As Hoehne said, 'Somalia since 2006 is possibly the clearest example of the failure of US (and Ethiopian) counter-terrorism policy, which actually has produced what it was supposed to counter.[72]' Hoehne added:

In the aftermath of the 9/11 attacks, local and regional actors, including Somali warlords and Ethiopia quickly appropriated the newly introduced 'anti-terrorism' rhetoric in order to attract resources and support. Still, at the local level the civil war in Somalia continued to be primarily over the question of who controls which parts of the country (and the related resources, such as ports, junctions, and road-blocks) or even 'the state'. Only since 2006 ... has the warfare in Somalia gained an 'ideological' quality pitting radical Islamists and their global networks against forces of an increasingly militant West and its allies.[73]

The Transitional Federal Government (TFG)

The TFG was formed as a result of the Arta Conference in 2004, with Abdillahi Yusuf as the first president; it finally ended its unhappy existence in August 2012 with the country's Transitional Federal Institutions (TFIs) implementing the Roadmap for the End of Transition, otherwise known as the 'Garowe Principles' after the two Somali National Consultative Constitutional Conferences held in Garowe, Puntland, in December 2011 and February 2012. The changes included the drafting of a new provisional constitution, and the selection of the members of parliament by a group of 135 traditional Somali elders, with the advice of a technical selection committee.[74]

Only time will tell whether the Roadmap offers any improvement of governance for the average Somali, but the country has been ill-served by politicians, who in the main appear to see personal enrichment as their main goal. The UN Monitoring Group summarized the problem in their June 2012 draft report saying:

> The final year of the Transitional Federal Institutions' term of office is due to expire in August 2012. But the transfer of power to a more effective, legitimate and broad-based national authority is threatened by the efforts of diverse Somali political leaders and their supporters to hijack or derail the transitional process – outcomes that would fuel continued instability and conflict, potentially reviving the fortunes of an embattled Al-Shabaab.

The concerns of observers are largely based on their understanding of recent history. As Jason Mosley wrote in June 2012, '... lessons from earlier phases of Somalia's post-1991 trajectory appear to have been overlooked or ignored. Most obviously and recently, missteps from Ethiopia's 2006–9 invasion and occupation are being repeated: a political crisis is being approached primarily through a security lens.'[75]

Since the collapse of the Somali government in 1991, successive generations of Somali leaders have engaged in corrosive political and economic practices that have aggravated the conflict and helped thwart the restoration of peace and security in the country. Under the TFIs, the systematic misappropriation, embezzlement and outright theft of public resources have essentially become a system of governance, embodied in the popular Somali phrase 'Maxaa igu jiraa?' ('What's in it for me?').[76]

The TFG never had popular support within Somalia and suffered from its association with Ethiopia and international bodies. The TFG was a powerless entity, grossly inflated in importance by the international community, and its status as the 'government' of Somalia was nothing less than grotesque. Human Rights Watch, in its World Report for 2011, wrote:

> The TFG lost further ground to al-Shabaab during the year [2010] and at this writing controls just a few square blocks around the presidential palace at Villa Somalia in Mogadishu, with the AU [African Union] forces defending the capital's port, the airport, and a few other strategic sites.[77]

While it is true that the African Union forces cleared Mogadishu by 2012, and that Kenyan and Ethiopian forces drove Al-Shabaab from territory that it had controlled, these changes were not the result of a strengthening of the TFG's capabilities, but were due to outside intervention and the weakening of Al-Shabaab.

Rashid Abdi and Ernest Jan Hogendoorn also claimed that 'the weak and increasingly fractious Transitional Federal Government seems incapable of extending its authority or becoming even modestly functional'.[78]

The UN Monitoring Group, in their February 2010 Report, summed up the situation in southern Somalia in similar terms:

> Somalia's frail Transitional Federal Government has struggled ineffectually to contain a complex insurgency that conflates religious extremism, political and financial opportunism, and clan interests. Beneath a superficial ideological overlay, armed opposition groups have essentially degenerated into clan militias, manifesting the same kind of fluid alliances and fissile tendencies. As a result, southern Somalia remains a patchwork of fiefdoms controlled by rival armed groups – a political and security vacuum in which no side is strong enough to impose its will on the others.[79]

There were also disputes between the TFG administration and members of the Somali Parliament, also known as the Transitional Federal Parliament, or Transitional Federal Assembly. It was reported that, 'Fistfights are common in Somalia's unruly parliament, where lawmakers have even pulled guns on each other.'[80] In January 2012 some members were injured in a dispute over the election of a new speaker. This unelected body, whose members were appointed in 2004, as noted above, unsuccessfully attempted to extend its life until 2014.[81]

In February 2011 the International Crisis Group (ICG) concluded that:

> Somalia's Transitional Federal Government (TFG) has squandered the goodwill and support it received and achieved little of significance in the two years it has been in office. It is inept, increasingly corrupt and hobbled by President Sharif's weak leadership. So far, every effort to make the administration modestly functional has come unstuck.[82]

The ICG continued:

> The level of corruption within the TFG has increased significantly, and many local and foreign observers regard the current government as the

most corrupt since the cycles of ineffectual transitions began in 2000. A cabal within the regime presides over a corruption syndicate that is massive, sophisticated and extends well beyond Somalia's borders. The impunity with which its members operate and manipulate the system to serve their greed is remarkable. They are not fit to hold public office and should be forced to resign, isolated and sanctioned.[83]

On 5 March 2012 the UN Security Council stated that 'The Security Council further welcomes the consensus in London that the mandate of the Transitional Federal Institutions will end in August 2012 and that there will be no further extension of the transitional period.'[84] The record of the past few years gives little hope that a new Somali government will be able to resolve the country's problems and internal conflicts.

There were signs of hope for ordinary Somalis in 2012. Jeffrey Gettleman reported in April that more than 300,000 residents had come back to Mogadishu in the previous six months and that the local economy was showing real signs of life. However, Gettleman added:

But the folks on the hill – meaning Villa Somalia [the TFG], the hilltop presidential palace – still seem as dysfunctional as ever. Two men are claiming to be speaker of Parliament, paralyzing all lawmaking, and millions of dollars are missing, a former government official recently revealed.[85]

In June 2012 the UN Monitoring Group did give a positive report on the decline of Al-Shabaab:

Al-Shabaab has suffered a series of reversals over the past year and has been significantly weakened by internal divisions. In August 2011, the group withdrew its forces from most of Mogadishu, and in October 2011, Kenyan forces, accompanied by a loose coalition of anti-Shabaab Somali militias, entered south western Somalia, securing long stretches of the common border. Ethiopian troops followed suit in November 2011, occupying parts of northern Gedo, and launching cross-border offensives in Bay, Bakool, Hiiraan and Gaalgaduud regions in March 2012. Under sustained military and economic pressure, Al-Shabaab has since ceded even more territory, and its leadership seems increasingly divided.[86]

Arms sales and military incompetence

In its 2010 report, the UN Monitoring Group added a damning assessment of the TFG's military competence:

> The military stalemate is less a reflection of opposition strength than of the weakness of the Transitional Federal Government. Despite infusions of foreign training and assistance, government security forces remain ineffective, disorganized and corrupt – a composite of independent militias loyal to senior government officials and military officers who profit from the business of war and resist their integration under a single command. During the course of the mandate, government forces mounted only one notable offensive and immediately fell back from all the positions they managed to seize. The government owes its survival to the small African Union peace support operation, AMISOM, rather than to its own troops.[87]

The UN Monitoring Group also pointed out that the TFG

> is handicapped by entrenched corruption at all levels: commanders and troops alike sell their arms and ammunition – sometimes even to their enemies. Revenues from Mogadishu port and airport are siphoned off. Some government ministers and members of parliament abuse their official privileges to engage in large-scale visa fraud, smuggling illegal migrants to Europe and other destinations, in exchange for hefty payments.[88]

The sale of arms by the TFG was open and apparently unrestrained.[89] The bulk of the first shipment of arms from Ugandan stocks, which was supplied to the TFG in the summer of 2009 by the United States,[90] in breach of the UN arms embargo, quickly ended up in the Mogadishu arms bazaar. The price of an AK-47 type rifle in Mogadishu reportedly dropped from $600 to $300 within a week.[91]

It is worth looking at the past behaviour of the TFG (and its predecessors), if one is to understand the true objectives of this entity. In 2002 Andre Le Sage undertook what he called a detailed analysis of the ways in which the TNG (the predecessor of the TFG) functioned in practice. Le Sage could have been writing about the TFG when he said that the TNG 'has established the trappings of a national government. . . . Although they are robust in appearance they are weak in practice given the government's lack of territorial control and inability to raise revenue through taxes.'[92] Le Sage added that, although the TNG was dysfunctional and ineffective, it did have the support of the Mogadishu business community, and that support could only be explained by looking at the links between the TNG and local businessmen. He said that the Arta Conference, which established the TNG, was partly financed by Abdurahman Boreh, a Somali with strong links to Ismael Omar Guelleh, the then president of Djibouti. Boreh was a major investor in the SomTel telephone company (as was the TNG's first prime minister, Ali Khalif), and he was also connected to a group of Mogadishu businessmen who paid for some of the TNG's operating costs. This group included Mohamed Deilaf. Deilaf developed his business on the back of international aid contracts for the transportation of food (in 2010 the UN Monitoring Group pointed out that such contracts continue to offer rich rewards for local entrepreneurs) and also smuggled goods into Kenya, transhipped via Somalia to avoid Kenyan customs duties. Deilaf was then one of the richest businessmen in Mogadishu and had also supported the *shari'a* courts in south Mogadishu. Le Sage argued: 'The failure of Somalia's militia-factions to provide a stable investment and trade environment motivated Mogadishu businessmen to identify an alternative to the inefficient and costly protection racket established by the feuding warlords.'[93] Le Sage pointed out that the strength of the TNG was based on 'the symbiotic relationship with this group of businessmen that … [dominated] the regional currency supply import markets and other UN/NGO contracts.'[94]

The currency import business was the system whereby some Somali businessmen had Somali currency printed abroad, imported it and used it as the local medium of exchange. The printing and issue of currency was therefore a private venture and no Somali 'government' was involved in the process. Banknotes are not always produced by government banks; in Hong Kong three banks issue banknotes, as do eight banks in the United Kingdom.[95] This group of businessmen in fact provided the main financial support to the TNG because it was more cost-effective to pay the TNG to provide protection from the militias than to pay the militias. Another reason for supporting the TNG was that it regarded at least part of their payments as loans, rather than as revenue. The businessmen could therefore expect to be repaid from foreign aid; when the TNG received $15 million from Saudi Arabia, this gift was used to repay local business supporters.

The protection afforded by the TNG also allowed this group of businessmen to issue new Somali Shilling banknotes, printed for them abroad. However, so many new notes were put into circulation that it caused local inflation. The businessmen of course profited handsomely from issuing money that had only cost them the expense of printing, i.e. from *seigniorage*, a right that the TNG should strictly have claimed. Le Sage therefore concluded that the TNG was little more than a business cartel, with its officers and officials sharing the profits of trade and aid with local businessmen. Nearly all the individuals concerned also came from the Hawiye clan.[96] Having noted the tendencies to corruption within the earlier incarnation of the TFG/TNG and its historic connections with Somali business interests, it is important to understand that the same drivers to predatory exploitation still exist today.

It was always difficult to regard the TFG as an embryonic Somali government. In essence it consisted of a group of predatory political entrepreneurs who would exploit any economic opportunities to profit from the resources of Somalia. In May 2006 the Chinese International Oil and Gas Company signed a production-sharing agreement with the TFG for exploration in north Mudug, which was controlled by Puntland. It is estimated that there may be 5–10 billion barrels of oil in the area.[97] The Chinese are also exploring for oil in the Ethiopian-controlled Ogaden, where a Malaysian company has already discovered large quantities of gas.

The possibility that there are large amounts of oil has been a hidden factor in Somali politics for many years. In the 1990s the World Bank undertook a geological survey of Somalia's oil prospects, and Thomas E. O'Connor, the principal petroleum engineer for the World Bank survey, said, 'It's there. There's no doubt there's oil there.' From 1986, the Barre regime allocated the exploration rights in nearly two-thirds of Somalia to the US oil companies Conoco, Amoco, Chevron and Phillips. It has even been suggested that the likely existence of oil was a factor in the United States' willingness to deploy military forces to Mogadishu in 1992. Certainly it was common knowledge in the US administration that Yemeni oil reserves (estimated at 1 billion barrels) were part of a great underground rift, or valley, that extended across northern Somalia.[98] The government of Somaliland is nowadays actively seeking oil industry partners to exploit its likely reserves. Recent discoveries in the Rift Valley and in the Mozambique Channel, the levels of exploration in Ethiopia and the importance of the reserves in South Sudan have underlined the fact that East and Central Africa are two of the more important and undeveloped oil regions in the world. At a time when China's increasing demand is putting pressure on traditional suppliers and the threat of 'peak oil' grows as old fields see production decline, any new oil supplies, no matter where they are, are of huge importance. The new Federal Government of Somalia is also showing its interest in oil. In August 2013, Soma Oil and Gas Exploration, whose one of the directors was former UK Conservative leader Lord Howard of Lympne was awarded rights in up to 12 oil blocks in Somalia. According to the *Financial Times*, 'The company, which has not undertaken a seismic survey before, was incorporated in the UK [in July 2013] with capital of £0.001'.[99] In September 2013, a press release from Kilimanjaro Capital announced that Soma acquired rights in the Amsas-Coriole-Afgoye (ACA) oil search block, just south of Mogadishu.[100]

It has also been reported that Somalia's new government is talking to major international oil companies like Exxon Mobil, Royal Dutch Shell and BP about resuming exploration programmes abandoned when the East African state collapsed into anarchy in 1991.[101] The concern here is that the Somalia Federal Government will attempt to claim oil resources in Somaliland and in the territory of Puntland, which has itself granted oil exploration rights. This will result in further instability and possibly give rise to conflict. In fact the UN Monitoring Group said in July 2013 that:

> In the absence of clear constitutional agreements between federal and regional governments and the introduction of best-practice transparency mechanisms for the management of signature fees and royalties and taxes on future oil production, oil companies should cease and desist negotiations with Somali authorities or risk fuelling non-transparent practices and political disagreements that could exacerbate clan conflict and constitute threats to peace and security.[102]

From experience in other parts of Africa, such as Nigeria and Angola, the rent-seeking focus of local elites probably ensures that the population sees no benefit from oil wealth, and that it can actually fuel further conflict. It is not clear what the US response would have been if their support to the TFG resulted in China obtaining ownership of enormous new oil reserves. It is likely that in the future China will take a more active role in Somalia in order to gain access to its hydrocarbon and other mineral resources. However, interestingly, China has pursued a quiet, commercially-focused policy in Somalia, not taking a leading role in international efforts to improve the situation in the territory.

The involvement of China in Somalia has been a matter of interest to the US government in recent years, a concern that the WikiLeaks cables have shone a light on. In February 2010 the US embassy in Nairobi reported to Washington that:

China is especially interested in potential opportunities for petroleum exploration [in Somalia]. China is reported to have secured the rights to oil blocks in the Puntland region. Media reports indicate that in January, the acting TFG Minister of Petroleum met with the Chinese Minister of Petroleum in Khartoum to discuss an upcoming mission to Somalia. While no formal engagements have been reported, we understand that Chinese officials and businessmen are laying the groundwork for trade and investment in the oil and gas sectors, primarily through informal relationships with local and regional authorities. [In the same cable the embassy added that] Somalia's rapidly growing telecommunications sector is powered predominantly by Chinese equipment. Chinese companies provide 'soft loans' to the telecom operators to purchase equipment. Our contacts shared some details of a deal that was signed in 2008 for approximately USD 25 million. They told us that this scale of business deals is common. Chinese companies are some of the few that are willing to send technicians into Somalia to set up and maintain the equipment. Anecdotal reports indicate that there are often Chinese businesspersons within the country and most are associated with large telecommunications projects.[103]

The US embassy cable also warned that 'TFG and Puntland officials tell us that China's priority area of engagement remain its quest for natural resources, especially oil.'[104]

Somali business successes

The power of local businessmen, identified by Le Sage in 2002, remains an important factor in the Somali political ecosystem. The UN Monitoring Group said in 2010 that 'A handful of Somali contractors for aid agencies have formed a cartel and become important powerbrokers – some of whom channel their profits – or the aid itself – directly to armed opposition groups.' These businessmen included the Adaani family, who are one of the largest contractors for the WFP in Somalia, and which the UN Monitoring Group claimed have long been financiers of armed groups.[105]

It is a mistake to think that, because Somalia does not have a functioning government, businessmen cannot make money there. The most successful modern Somali businessman is Abdirashid Duale, CEO of the money-transfer company Dahabshiil. Dahabshiil transfers about $1 billion a year from the Somali diaspora into Somalia, from its head office in Dubai, and its operations centre in Hargeisa, Somaliland. The company employs more than 2,000 people across the world.[106] Somali businessmen have also made large profits from telecommunications, particularly from mobile phone networks. *The Economist* pointed out the unexpected advantages of operating in a failed state:

> No government means no state telecoms company to worry about, no corrupt ministry officials to pay off (there is no ministry), and the freedom to choose the best-value equipment. Taxes, payable to a tentative local authority or strongman, are seldom more than 5 per cent, security is another 5 per cent (more in Mogadishu), and customs duties are next to nothing. There is no need to pay for licences, or to pay to put up masts.[107]

Businessmen therefore control the economy and negotiate their way around the militias in the same way that European businessmen negotiate around government regulations. Businessmen are a vital factor in the Somali environment and are too often overlooked.

Rent-seeking politicians

The UN Monitoring Group has reported on the TFG rent-seeking predisposition and given the example of what it calls 'brazen incidents of visa fraud', involving TFG officials and members of parliament. According to the Monitoring Group, Somali politicians claimed that they had to travel abroad on official business, to attend a conference for example, and that they needed to be accompanied by a bogus delegation of government officials. Requests for visas to visit foreign countries were, as the UN Monitoring Group noted, typically accompanied by a *note verbale* or other introductory document from the Somali embassy, often with a supporting letter from a minister, the speaker of parliament or one of his deputies. If the requests met with approval, the other members of the delegation would pay each as much as $15,000 for the opportunity to travel. Many did not return.[108]

One informant told the UN that senior government officials, including the prime minister and the speaker of parliament, were responsible for such requests. The UN Monitoring Group reported that its investigations,

> have linked a number of senior officials of the Transitional Federal Government to the practice of visa fraud, including the Deputy Prime Minister and Minister of Fisheries, Abdirahman Ibrahim Adan Ibbi, the Minister for Women's Affairs and Gender, Fowsiya Mohamed Sheikh, and the Minister of Constitutional Affairs, Madoobe Nunow Mohamed.[109]

These scams had serious security implications. Some of those who have obtained visas in this way were criminals; several members of a Puntland-based pirate militia obtained asylum and travel documents in Europe in 2009. The Monitoring Group noted that: 'One obtained asylum in Sweden, one travelled via Italy to the Netherlands and one reportedly obtained entry into the United Kingdom. All three subsequently returned to the region to resume their involvement with pirate militias.'[110] It would be interesting to know what type of business was transacted during these visits.

Large numbers of refugees continued to flee Mogadishu in 2010. According to UNHCR, a total of 21,500 people were displaced in the two months from 1 October 2010. Of these, 12,500 people left the city, and the remaining 9,000 moved to areas within Mogadishu.[111]

The TFG was careful to restrict reporting in Somalia, no matter what its spokesmen said during their visits to Western capitals. Amnesty International, in a July 2010 report, claimed that there were 'threats against journalists and media outlets by the Transitional Federal Government authorities and armed groups associated with the government.'[112]

The European Union attempted to assist the TFG in 2010 by training some of its recruits at a Ugandan army base in Bihanga. However, Rashid Abdi of the International Crisis Group said:

> If you deploy these troops who have been well trained, they will look at the political environment and feel this not the kind of politics I was trained to serve and they will desert. That is the danger and the reality in Somalia.[113]

This is not the first time that Western-trained Somalis troops would desert for better pay and conditions. In April 2010, it was reported that hundreds of Somali soldiers trained by the French at US expense in Djibouti in 2009 deserted the TFG, because they were not paid their monthly wages of $100, and that others even joined Al-Shabaab. Colonel Ahmed Aden Dhayow of the Somali army said that about half of them deserted. He added: 'Some gave up the army and returned to their ordinary life and others joined the rebels.'[114]

The failure of the TFG

As shown above, the TFG achieved nothing for Somalia, and actually made the situation worse. The support of international organizations did not have the effect that was desired. It must be hoped (at the time of writing) that its successor will be more effective. As Olivier Cromwell said, when dismissing England's Rump Parliament in April 1653, 'You have been sat too long here for any good you have been doing. Depart, I say, and let us have done with you. In the name of God, go!'

In the opinion of the International Crisis Group, 'Nothing highlights the general ineptitude of the TFG in forging political alliances and achieving wider reconciliation better than the botched power-sharing agreement with the ASWJ.'[115] The ASWJ (Ahlu Sunna Wal Jama'a) was an effective enemy of Al-Shabaab in south and central Somalia. But the TFG, although forced into a power-sharing agreement by external pressures, did nothing to support the ASWJ, and an important opportunity was lost.

Foreign governments, notably the African Union countries, Turkey and other Muslim countries, did much in recent years to try and support the TFG and improve the situation in Mogadishu. The international will is there, as was shown at the London Conference in February 2012, but unless Somalis can show real leadership and act in the interests of their community the hopes for the TFG's successor organization cannot be high. As William Hague, the British foreign secretary, said in February 2012, 'the fact that we have not succeeded in turning Somalia round is not for a lack of effort by the international community ... but because the problems are so vast and complex'.[116]

The Road Map: The provisional constitution and the new federal parliament

In August 2012 the TFG finally left the stage and the Somali National Constituent Assembly adopted the provisional constitution. This was followed by the inaugural meeting of the new federal parliament, with Professor Mohamed Osman Jawari as its new speaker.

On 10 September 2012 Hassan Sheik Mohammud, a 56-year-old university lecturer, was elected as Somali's next president. Sheik Mohammud, who is Chairman of the Peace and Development Party, defeated the TFG's president, Sheik Sharif Sheik Ahmed, 190 votes to 79 in the second round run-off. Sheik Mohammud has worked as a community activist for various non-governmental organizations, including the Center of Research and Dialogue, the International Peace Building Alliance and Unicef.[117] He is also co-founder of the Somali Institute for Management and Administrative Development (SIMAD). He, like the outgoing president, is from the Hawiye clan.[118]

The difficulties faced by the new president were illustrated by the fact that within two days of his election three suicide bombers dressed in

Somali army uniform attempted to enter the Jazeera hotel, in Mogadishu, which was President Mohammud's temporary residence – all were intercepted by security forces and killed before they were able to enter the hotel.[119]

At the time of writing, the history of Somalia is still being written. It is to be hoped that Al-Shabaab will continue to lose out in the struggle for control of central and southern Somalia, but it is important not to engage in wishful thinking. Although Al-Shabaab retreated from Mogadishu, Baidoa, Hudur, Beledweyne and other towns, it probably controls about 60 per cent of southern Somalia and still has important sources of income. Al-Shabaab also has strong links to extremist Somali groups in Kenya, so it is not totally dependent on its Somali operations and can continue to be a threat even if totally removed from the Somali territory.[120]

This UN-backed Road Map is not complete. In August 2012 the UN secretary-general said:

> Since the end of the transition period is expected to usher in a new phase of peacebuilding, the United Nations has begun to develop plans for an inter-agency review of the United Nations presence in Somalia. The review, to be led by the Department of Political Affairs through an interdepartmental process, will be undertaken in the second half of 2012, in close consultation with the Somali authorities, the African Union, IGAD and other relevant regional and international stakeholders.[121]

An optimist hopes for the best, despite the past; a pessimist says that nothing will change. You can take your choice. My own feeling is that things can get somewhat better and that new developments may well deliver some improvements for the ordinary Somali. The discussions with Somaliland show that a long-term future plan for the whole of Somalia may be on the cards, although Somaliland will almost certainly retain its independence.

Somalia is not going to be a 'normal' country anytime soon, but with the hoped for oil production in Puntland, which will mean that piracy is no longer attractive, and continued international action against Al-Shabaab, in the words of D:Ream's song, 'Things Can Only Get Better'. Let's hope it is true for Somalia; even if it did not work out for the British Labour Party, which used the song in its 1997 election campaign.

SOMALIA'S NEIGHBOURS: REGIONAL CONFLICTS AND ALLIANCES IN THE HORN

Background

Somalia does not exist in a vacuum, but sits in the centre of a complex network of regional conflicts and alliances. In the same way, piracy has become a regional issue, not merely a Somali one. It is therefore necessary to look at the regional players in order to understand the context of Somali piracy.

Somalia, which has the longest coastline of any African country, controls the southern part of the Gulf of Aden, provides key lines of communications to Ethiopia and has significant unexploited mineral reserves, including oil. It is of immense strategic importance.

While 'terrorism' attracts the attention of the international media, the greatest source of conflict within the region is intra-state rivalry; 'terrorists' may too often turn out to be the deniable assets of state security organizations. The greatest threat to Western interests in the Horn of Africa is that the Gulf of Aden and the Red Sea could be controlled by hostile powers, because this is a vital maritime line of communication. Somali piracy has shown the vulnerability of this route and its importance to the Western economies. The Bab el Mandeb strait, between the Red Sea and the Gulf of Aden, is only 12 miles across, the shipping channel is narrow and mines, which Iran has in numbers, could easily close the waterway; any claims that Al-Qaeda is involved would be a useful distraction for the real perpetrators.

Ethiopia

Ethiopia's relationship with Somalia has been dominated by conflict for hundreds of years, and has its roots in fifteenth- and sixteenth-century struggles between Ethiopia (Abyssinia) and Muslim leaders like the Sultan of Ifat, Haq ad-Din and Ahmad Gran. Raiding parties clashed and low-level conflict was a fact of life for generations; but by the end of the nineteenth century Ethiopia expanded into the Ogaden. In the early twentieth century the Dervish campaign for Somali independence attacked Ethiopian outposts as well as the British colonial power. However, it was only in September 1948, with the post-war settlement of regional borders under the UN, that Ethiopia finally established control of the Ogaden. Independent Somalia aspired to recover the Ogaden, to control the part of northern Kenya into which Somalis had moved in the nineteenth century, and to integrate French Somaliland; in no case were these ambitions achieved. The disastrous Somali–Ethiopian war of 1977–8, which had been preceded by the 1964 clashes, was a reaction to chaos within Ethiopia on the one hand, and on the other hand, a long-held wish to 'recover' lost territory. The 2006 invasion of Somalia by Ethiopia, and the continuing involvement of Ethiopia in Somali affairs, therefore followed an ancient pattern. The enmity between the two societies is deep and abiding.

Ethiopia, which faces a potential conflict with Egypt over the use of Nile water, sits at the heart of the Horn of Africa and is Somalia's main neighbour. Over the past few years the United States has treated it as a key ally in the region. However, Helen Epstein, writing in the *New York Review of Books* in 2010, described the Ethiopian government as, 'a regime that is rapidly becoming one of the most repressive and dictatorial on the continent'. She said: 'The government uses Chinese spy technology to bug phone lines and Internet communications, and countless journalists, editors, judges, academics, and human rights defenders have fled the country or languish behind bars, at risk of torture.'[122]

There is a strong dislike among Somalis for the Ethiopians, a historic and deep-rooted antagonism. This prejudice was only reinforced by the behaviour of Ethiopian troops during the 2006 invasion and subsequent occupation. The Ethiopian army subjected civilians to executions, torture and rape. In 2008 Human Rights Watch noted:

Ethiopian forces have been implicated in numerous violations of the laws of war, including acts by individuals that amount to war crimes. They have indiscriminately bombarded populated areas with mortar shells, artillery, and rockets. They have increasingly responded to insurgent ambushes and other attacks by firing indiscriminately at anyone and everyone in the general vicinity. And incidents of killing, rape, and looting involving ENDF personnel have greatly increased.[123]

Human Rights Watch reported a number of horrific incidents. In one case an interviewee described how Ethiopian soldiers shot one girl and gang-raped another; 'They shot her in the chest... The other girl did not want to talk about it but she said three of them were raping her at the same time.'[124]

Conflict between ethnic Somalis and the Ethiopian government continues in the Ogaden to this day. The Ogaden National Liberation Front (ONLF) remains active, and this is one of the main reasons for Ethiopia's continued involvement in Somalia and Somaliland. About 4 million ethnic Somalis live in Ethiopian territory, and the Ogaden is now being explored for hydrocarbons, not a resource that the Ethiopians can afford to concede. On 24 April 2007, ONLF fighters overcame the Ethiopian troops who were protecting Chinese oil-exploration workers in Obole, in the Degehabur zone. Seventy-four people were killed, including nine Chinese workers. As a result, the Chinese Zhoungyan Petroleum Exploration Bureau suspended its seismic tests in the Ogaden.[125] The Oromo Liberation Front (OLF) is also active, and has been involved in unsuccessful negotiations with the Ethiopian government. A clandestine OLF network in Ethiopia also infiltrated state organs.[126]

It is almost certainly the case that the Ethiopians wish to keep Somalia in its weakened and fragmented state, as a strong Somali state would inevitably renew the challenge to Ethiopian control of the Ogaden. Somali distrust and dislike of Ethiopia is historic, and virtually any involvement of Ethiopia in Somali affairs inevitably causes tension. The use of Ethiopia as an ally and advisor by the United States has been one of the major errors of US policy in Somalia, and the fact that Ethiopia was a member of the Inter-Governmental Authority on Development (IGAD), which also included Uganda, Kenya, Sudan, Eritrea and Djibouti, which set up Somalia's TFG in 2004, served to weaken the authority of the TFG from its inception. Ethiopia has also failed to recognize the independence of Somaliland, or to promote its interests in the Organization of African Union, while giving it low-level support. In short, Ethiopia has made it a matter of national policy to control what happens in Somalia and to ensure that a strong Somali state is not allowed to re-emerge.

One of Ethiopia's main strategic problems is its need to secure reliable access to the sea. Since Eritrean independence in 1993, Ethiopia has lacked a coast and access to the Red Sea. It has had to rely on the ports of Massawa and Assab under Eritrean control, and then, when relations worsened, on the port of Djibouti. In recent years, Ethiopia has also been using the port of Berbera in Somaliland in order to reduce its dependence on Djibouti. However, a new issue has emerged in the Ethiopian equation: the country is on the verge of becoming a major energy producer.

Gregory Copley, writing in August 2010, said that the Malaysian oil company, Petronas, proved as much as 4 trillion cubic feet of gas reserves in the Ogaden basin region of Ethiopia, and plans were announced for a pipeline linking the Ogaden to Djibouti to be constructed and operational within five years.[127] As additional funds flow into the Ethiopian treasury, Ethiopia will be able to upgrade its armoury and increase the effectiveness of its army. Copley argues that Ethiopia's new wealth will allow the country to compete more effectively against Egypt and Eritrea, and that it is likely to make a real effort to reacquire access to the Red Sea, probably through the port of Assab. He also makes the case that: 'The radical Islamist forces operating in Somalia have long been supported by Eritrea, along with their support from Iran, Egypt, and Libya, as a means of tying down Ethiopian forces and promoting secessionist moves by ethnic Somalis and Oromos in Ethiopia.'[128]

Somalia is a cockpit, in which other states have fought out their conflicts. Ethiopia's enemies, including Eritrea and Egypt, have intervened in Somalia in order to discomfort Ethiopia, not because of any real interest in the affairs of the Somalis. Ethiopia has sought to prevent the emergence of a strong Somali state and to remove potential support for its own ethnic Somali population.

Yemen

Yemen is a failed state, and, as noted, its former president, Ali Abdullah Saleh, who transferred power to his vice-president, Abed Abdu Mansour Hadi on 23 November 2011, had a close relationship with the late Colonel Abdillahi Yusuf, the former president of Puntland and of the TFG.[129] It is profoundly corrupt – its ruling elite is as predatory as any in the region and there is no obvious solution to the series of internal conflicts that could see the country split into two separate states. The independence of South Yemen, a former British colony, could well occur in the next few years, and the northern rebellion could restart at any time. The presence of Al-Qaeda has been an additional source of confusion and, despite Yemeni government stating the contrary, it seems that a working relationship was established between Al-Qaeda and President Saleh in 2009 in return for assistance against groups that opposed President Saleh's government. Yemen has continued its current programme of disinformation by claiming that the conflict in the south is against Al-Qaeda, whereas it is actually against southerners who wish to reassert South Yemen's independence.

In April 2012 it became clear that President Hadi was not going to act as a puppet for Saleh, when the head of the Yemeni Air Force, General Mohammed Saleh al-Ahmar, Saleh's half-brother, accepted orders from the new president to leave his post.[130]

Saleh attempted to convince the United States to give him arms and money to fight Al-Qaeda, while actually putting most of Yemen's efforts into conflicts with the two rebellions, and it seems that the conflict in South

Yemen was actually his greatest concern. Saleh also threatened the United States, referring to the high poverty rate and illicit arms flows into both Yemen and Somalia, saying, 'If you don't help, this country will become worse than Somalia.'[131]

Since Saleh left office, it appears that the United States has increased its support for Yemen, primarily because of the perceived threat from Al-Qaeda. US tactics include the use of missiles launched from drones, of the type used to kill a US citizen, Anwar a-Aulaki, in Yemen during 2010,[132] together with training and logistical support for the Yemeni military. Much of the fighting in May 2012 was in the south, in the area of the former British Protectorate of South Yemen. On 14 and 15 May airstrikes and ground assaults left dozens of people dead, including civilians.[133] The response was a suicide attack a few days later on a rehearsal for a military parade in Sana'a; nearly a hundred soldiers died.[134]

The complexities of the Yemeni situation are as knotted and deeply woven as those of Somalia. The various conflicts and rivalries include those between Saleh loyalists (still deeply embedded in the army and security agencies) and the Ahmar clan, the determination of the southern provinces to break away from Yemen, the bitterness felt by the northern tribes, and then, to add to the explosive mixture, elements of Al-Qaeda. The new government is deeply unpopular in the remote provinces; the tribes have no fixed loyalties, creating a natural sanctity for terrorists. Nothing is quite as it seems, nothing is black and white.

Eritrea

After gaining independence Eritrea was dominated by its former president, Isaias Afwerki. Afwerki was the leader of the Eritrean People's Liberation Front (EPLF) during the struggle for independence, which was achieved in April 1993. The EPLF renamed itself the People's Front for Democracy and Justice (PFDJ) in February 1994. Isaias Afwerki ruled on the basis of decree, the country's constitution having been suspended, and the PFDJ being the only political party permitted in the country.

The US ambassador to Eritrea, Ronald K. McMullen, was advantageously positioned to observe the situation on the ground between 2008 and 2009 and, thanks to WikiLeaks, we can now read his dispatches to Washington, which were insightful and well written. In a country that discourages independent reporting, diplomats are one of the few groups well placed to observe the political and economic situation in Eritrea. In 2008 Ambassador McMullen described President Isaias Afwerki as:

An austere and narcissistic dictator whose political ballast derives from Maoist ideology fine-tuned during Eritrea's 30-year war for independence. He is paranoid and believes that Ethiopian PM [Prime Minister] Meles tried to kill him and that the United States will attempt to assassinate him.[135]

The fact is that Isaias Afwerki ran a thoroughly unpleasant regime with no regard for human rights and a record of arbitrary arrest, torture and imprisonment. In another cable, in March 2009, Ambassador McMullen said that:

The accelerating decline into dictatorship began in 1996 with an alleged assassination attempt against Isaias by Ethiopian PM Meles Zenawi, followed by the bloody 1998–2000 Border War, and the 'treason' of the inner-circle critics called the G-15. Severe persecution of any potential opposition increased.

By December 2009 Ambassador McMullen's views about Eritrea were even more negative. He wrote:

Things are getting worse and worse in Eritrea. The regime is facing mounting international pressure for years of malign behavior in the neighborhood. Human rights abuses are commonplace and most young Eritreans, along with the professional class, dream of fleeing the country, even to squalid refugee camps in Ethiopia or Sudan. The economy continues to sink; exports for 2008 totaled only $14m and vital hard-currency remittances have fallen to 43 per cent of the 2005 level. 'He is sick,' said one leading Eritrean businessman, referring to President Isaias' mental health. 'The worse things get, the more he tries to take direct control – it doesn't work.'[136]

Human Rights Watch confirmed the negative opinion of the regime:

Death in custody is common from ill-treatment, torture, starvation, and denial of medical care. In April 2010 a woman held for over two years in a shipping container because she would not renounce her unregistered religious faith died at the Sawa military training center from maltreatment.

Their summary report in January 2011 added:

> Torture and other forms of cruel, inhuman, and degrading treatment in detention are routine. Former detainees report that detention almost always includes severe beatings, often leading to permanent bodily harm. Punishments also entail mock drowning, being hung by the arms from trees, and being tied up in the sun in contorted positions for hours or days.

On 23 December 2009 the UN Security Council put an arms embargo on Eritrea because it had 'provided support to armed groups undermining peace and reconciliation in Somalia'. The resolution 'demanded that all States, in particular Eritrea, cease arming, training and equipping armed groups and their members, including Al-Shabaab'.[137] Eritrea's support was for the Somali groups opposed to Ethiopia. As the UN Monitoring Group reported in 2010: 'Since 2006, and possibly earlier, Eritrea has supported opposition to the Transitional Federal Government, which it perceives as a proxy for the Government of Ethiopia.'[138] The Monitoring Group added, 'In addition to military support, the Government of Eritrea has consistently provided financial support to Somali armed opposition groups, including ARSAsmara, Hizbul Islam and Al-Shabaab.'[139]

SOMALIA – A FAILED STATE?

It is a common fallacy to claim that the problems of Somalia are mainly due to the fact that it is a 'failed state', and that once Somalia has a proper national government, all will be well with the country. As noted previously, with reference to Marten Scheffer's ideas, it is possible for Somalia to experience a phase transition after Barre's regime fell, and for the current situation of warlordism to be actually an alternative and stable condition. If this is the case, the return to a national state will not be inevitable. It will require significant and fundamental changes.

Unfortunately, it appears that the idea of a return to a national state being accomplished with relative ease, and given sufficient international support, is held with conviction by virtually all governments and international institutions, including the UN and the European Union. The experience of the last 20 years or more belies this belief, but faith in this solution to Somalia's problems is deep-rooted. In February 2012, at the London Conference on Somalia, British Prime Minister David Cameron was reported to have said that the world reached a turning point in helping Somalis reclaim their country, and added, 'Unless we can help the people of Somalia to build a stable future, the problems will keep reoccurring.'[140]

Some Somali commentators even claim that the current situation in Somalia is actually the result of foreign intervention. Mohamed Sharif Mohamud, a former Somali diplomat, said, 'Yes, displacement, refugees and a lack of state authority are problematic. But these issues result directly from sustained foreign intervention and the deliberate fragmentation of the country into fiefdoms, enclaves and tribal territories.'[141] While such claims play well with some Western decision-makers, and it is true that foreign intervention has frequently compounded a bad situation, Somalis are primarily the authors of their own disorder.

Another common error is to claim that the problems of Somalia are due to tribalism, or the role of clans; if tribalism was the direct cause of Somalia's problems, a number of other nations that have strong tribal elements would have similar problems. On the face of it, Somalia is one of the exceptions to the African norm, whereby groups of unrelated peoples were corralled within boundaries originally imposed by colonial regimes. Somalis are a single people, who speak a common language and have one religion, Islam. There are Somalis in Kenya, Ethiopia and Djibouti, who never came under the direct control of a unitary Somali state, but Somalia should have in theory avoided many of the problems of African 'nation-building'. But, as Christopher Clapham forcefully pointed out, 'the idea that viable states can be constructed throughout Africa on the basis of the territorial units established by colonial control has now reached the end of the road'.[142] Clapham added that in the case of Somalia the structures and values associated with ethnicity help undermine statehood, and that Somalis' shared attitudes towards political authority and control do not support the maintenance of an effective state.[143] He concluded:

Eventually, the African diplomatic system and the world as a whole will have to come to terms with the fact that the demarcation of the continent between crisply delineated sovereign states based on the old colonial frontiers....is now is many areas no more than a fiction.[144]

What Clapham saw in 2001 has still to be grasped by the international community over ten years later, as the weak, incompetent and corrupt TFG lost all credibility and retained its position in Mogadishu only because of the presence of the African Union Mission to Somalia (AMISOM). AMISOM is a force originally of just over 5,000 African soldiers from Burundi and Uganda, whose primary mission is to support the TFG. The numbers of AMISOM troops are steadily increasing, and in February 2012 the UN Security Council agreed to increase its numbers to 18,000. The secondary aims of AMISOM are 'to facilitate the delivery of humanitarian aid and to create the necessary conditions for reconstruction, reconciliation and the sustainable development of Somalia'.[145] To add to its difficulties, it is also empowered to use 'all necessary means' to reduce the threat from Al-Shabaab.[146]

It is possible to propose a number of contradictory interpretations of events in Somalia, all of which may be credible. Somali society is complex and highly fragmented and, like a well-cut diamond, it shows a large number of different facets to the observer. In order to produce a workable theory of Somali society, it is necessary to look at its fundamentals.

The underlying cause of the present condition of Somalia was the abuse of the state by the politicians who led the post-colonial governments of that country. With few exceptions, the post-independence governments of Somalia were predatory, and political elites used and abused state power to increase their personal power and wealth. Somalia is a country, in which the nation state, when it existed, failed to address the problems of the people. Since January 1991, Somalia has experimented with a combination of local forms of governance in places like Puntland and Somaliland, and with the exercise elsewhere of power by business elites in alliance with militias, often fronted by 'political' leaders (or 'warlords').

Writing about Sierra Leone, and the possibility of state collapse there, William Reno referred to the 'fragments of elite networks, strongmen striking out on their own' and to the likelihood that 'entrepreneurs and their supporters will exploit anarchy and anger as an opportunity to rob the countryside on their own behalf';[147] this is precisely what happened in Somalia.

Power in Somalia tends to coalesce around specific groups, which may appear to be political or religious in nature; but these are always coalitions of interested parties, based on local elites. The local elites include businessmen, members of political families, tribal leaders, militia groups and others. These groups, or nodes, tend to have a relatively short life and, after their break-up, the individuals and elements that formed them then coalesce around new groups; the attractors that bind these groups together are weak, and can easily be overcome. The same individuals appear time and again in new guises. The evidence is that Somalis are essentially pragmatists and that the only long-term goals of their aspirant elites are power and money; they are rent-seeking.

Modern Somalia is a territory controlled by networks. Imagine that Somalia is linked by communications pathways that branch from autonomous centres, and that the encoding of the system is a function of Somali culture. The system not only lacks a dominant hierarchy, but there are strong factors within the protocols of the system that resist the emergence of such a hierarchy (that is a strong centralized government). A function of the centres is that they can break up and reform quickly and that the appearance of these centres may be different, but they perform essentially the same functions. Their essential function is to acquire money for their participants, whether they are politicians, businessmen or militiamen. There is little sign that the elite groups show any real concern for the welfare of the mass of their compatriots. For such individuals it is more important to make money on transport, security and sale of international food aid than to ensure that those who are really in need benefit from foreign aid. In the same way attendance at conferences organized by the international community to discuss the problems of Somalia and to promote a unified government appear to be primarily, as far as the Somali elites are concerned, opportunities to gain foreign currency and other forms of material benefit. The TFG's representatives travelled to Western capitals in early 2010 in order to gain funds for their administration but, at the same time, were careful to negotiate an oil development contract with China, which they hoped would be their source of future enrichment.

The chaotic condition of Somalia has enabled its elites to exploit a number of criminal opportunities; piracy is the best known, but there are also large-scale smuggling of goods and drugs into Kenya, kidnapping for ransom, toll-collecting at road-blocks, slavery, prostitution, people trafficking and stealing food aid. Hardly any form of criminal exploitation of humans is practised in some way or another in Somalia. Even the threat of killing hostages for their organs exists. The weak, particularly women and children, are preyed on ruthlessly, and it is understandable that any form of government, Islamic or not, that gives better protection to the vulnerable will be popular. The elites, who in the main behave no better than criminal gangs, have adapted and found that the current state of anarchy offers them a steady flow of revenue, without the need to pay taxes, or comply with laws and regulations.

It is also necessary to understand that Somalia's last effective government ruled over a predatory state, the collapse of which, in 1990, was a relief to all.

From a Somali perspective, the worse outcome today is not necessarily the lack of a formal state, but the return of an effective predatory administration that seeks to control and exploit the resources of the territory for the benefit of a small elite. The 'failed state', as defined by Western governments and international organizations, is a state that lacks an effective government, with a monopoly of control over its designated territory. But the problem with this term is the word 'failed': it automatically suggests, without examining the condition of the state being discussed, that it can be restarted and given the benefit of international advice. In the case of Somalia, it may be truer to say that the state, in the European sense of the Westphalian concept of the state, is an illusion.

The international political community abhors a vacuum and, in terms of the world system, Somalia is a vacuum. Foreign governments feel that they cannot write off the territory of Somalia as an area of the Earth's surface without governance in the European style; they want to have an authority with whom they can negotiate treaties, exchange diplomats, agree on the exploitation of Somalia's mineral wealth, including its oil and its extensive fishing grounds. There is also the feeling that a national government can stop piracy. So keen were foreign governments to have such an authority that they enabled the TFG, which did not even control the city of Mogadishu at the beginning of 2010 – the frontline then starting approximately 500 metres from the 'presidential' residence – to take Somalia's seat at the UN, and to enter into agreements with the governments that purport to deal with territory that the TFG has never controlled, nor has any likelihood of controlling. It could be said of the international community, as Tacitus said of a disastrous Roman campaign against the Parthians, that 'Unmistakeable facts were ignored in favour of appearances.'[148]

We are also continually told that if such ungoverned territory is not controlled (that is by a government friendly to the Western powers), Al-Qaeda will inevitably use Somalia as a base. Such assertions normally start with the assumption that Somalia will be the 'next Afghanistan'. In 2010, both the UK and US governments warned in no uncertain terms of the dangers to their countries of terrorism originating from Somalia. Somalia is, however, far from being an ideal terrorist base. In 2007, the Combating Terrorism Center at West Point released a report called *Al-Qa'ida's (Mis)Adventures in the Horn of Africa,* in which their team of area experts and terrorism scholars analysed Al-Qaeda's attempts to establish bases of operations and recruit followers in the Horn of Africa. The report's conclusions were:

Conventional wisdom suggests that Somalia, a failed state, would be an ideal safe haven for al-Qa'ida. Our analysis, however, indicates that weakly governed regions such as coastal Kenya, not failed states like Somalia, provide an environment more conducive to al-Qa'ida's activities. In Somalia, al-Qa'ida's members fell victim to many of the same challenges that plague Western interventions in the Horn. They were prone to extortion and betrayal, found themselves trapped in the middle of incomprehensible (to them) clan conflicts, faced suspicion from the indigenous population, had to overcome significant logistical constraints and were subject to the constant risk of Western military interdiction.[149]

The report also found:

al-Qa'ida failed to gain traction in Somalia in the early 1990s because: (1) its members were perceived as foreigners; (2) it significantly underestimated the costs of operating in a failed state environment; and (3) its African vanguard did not understand the salience of either local power structures or local Islamic traditions. In a region dominated by clan-based authority structures and moderate Sufi Islam, the benefits of joining a foreign Salafi terrorist organization paled next to the costs of leaving one's clan.[150]

Al-Qaeda appears to have made headway in its relationship with Al-Shabaab, but at present its importance in Somalia is low, although the threat of an increased Al-Qaeda presence has refocused the attention of the US security and intelligence establishment on Somalia.

Since the fall of President Siyad Barre, there has been no wish on the part of the Somali population, or their elites, to return to the state of governance that they overthrew in 1990. This may be inconvenient for the rest of the world, but at present it is a state of affairs with which we should learn to live. In the nineteenth century much of the world was in this state, where control was exercised over territories by traditional leaders and where boundaries remained unclear and mutable, lacking any precision. Until the Congress of Berlin in 1885, when European states divided up the map of Africa, Africa had largely been in such a state. The boundaries of some of the states of the Arabian Peninsula remained undefined until recently. Even today maps have left 'undefined border' between Saudi Arabia and the United Arab Emirates. It may be that in the future parts of the world will return to the pre-imperial state of territorial uncertainty. Somalia may be showing us that the concept of the state is more fluid than we had imagined; and that the only legitimate state should be one that is accountable to all its inhabitants, rather than an institution that controls the inhabitants of a given territory, which is no better than colonialism.

FAILED STATES AND PIRACY

Chabal and Daloz say: 'At one extreme of the spectrum there are countries, like Somalia, where the very shell of the state has shattered utterly and where politics has become a naked power struggle between warlords.'[151] They also observe that:

> The logic of warlord violence in Somalia is, again unsurprisingly, both political and criminal. ... What distinguishes warlordism in Somalia from that found in other parts of Africa, therefore, is its structured social and political clan foundations, rather than its criminal tendencies.[152]

Piracy did not emerge, in its modern form, by accident, rather it was consciously developed and supported by clan and political leaders in Puntland and became a way in which a predatory economy was extended outside the territory actually controlled by the local predatory elite. It was not inevitable that piracy would arise in Somalia, because it was a failed state; but because it was a failed state, local leaders were able to develop modern piracy without constraint. In other words, the failure of the Somali state created an environment where anything was possible, and there was no restraint on predatory and criminal activity. The form of piracy developed in Puntland is dynamic, adaptive and effective. There is a clear hierarchy of control and the bulk of the profits are retained by clan leaders and major investors.

CHAPTER 3

STATELESS TERRITORIES AND CLANDESTINE NETWORKS

THE AFRICAN REALITY: DEALING WITH UNGOVERNED SPACES

It is important to stress that Somali piracy has emerged from a specific set of circumstances. It is not, as the pirates would have us believe, merely a response to foreign fishing boats in Somali waters, or the dumping of dangerous waste on their shores. In the main, the foreigners who did this have made some type of bargain with the Somali elite. Somali piracy as practised today is the result of developments within Somalia, and came about because of deliberate decisions by Somali leaders. It was not a reaction to the deeds of foreigners. In Somalia a political tendency, which is seen throughout Africa, has developed into its most extreme form: the exploitation of a territory by predatory elites.

In the rest of modern Africa, legal and illicit businesses intersect in a grey zone, full of ambiguity; Carolyn Nordstrom refers to 'il/legal' transactions. Our understanding of the nature of the pirates themselves needs to be based on this reality. The men in pirate skiffs are just hired hands, taking whatever work is available. They are not, in their own eyes, criminals, nor do they take responsibility for the effects that their work has on those they hijack. However, those who hire them and run pirate companies are well aware that what they are doing is regarded as criminal in the wider world, and they have links to criminals living in other parts of the world, including India, the

Middle East and Europe. Pirate leaders have used the traditional clan-based structures, which developed to support the maintenance of warrior groups, and have applied them to the business of piracy, where they have proved extremely effective.

It is important to understand the impact of what we can call the 'post-state socio-political system', which is now a commonplace within Africa, not merely in Somalia. It is not sufficient today to refer to 'failed states', because this leads to the idea that the state in Africa can be 'saved', or restored. It is important to understand that in parts of Africa, like the Congo and Guinea-Bissau, the state is, in the words of Lorenzo Bordonaro, 'essentially vacuous, an empty shell',[1] and in Somalia it has ceased to exist. We need to consider a future in which, in some territories, the state ceases to have any relevance and may not be 'restored' in the Westphalian sense; Somalia is showing us a possible future for other parts of Africa. Chabal and Daloz, writing in 1999, said:

> We are thus led to conclude that, in most African countries, the state is no more than a décor, a pseudo-Western façade masking the realities of deeply personalized political relations. There may well appear to be a relative institutionalization of the main state structures but such bodies are largely devoid of authority.[2]

International organizations, including the UN and Western governments, are ill-equipped to operate in this environment, because they are so committed to the Westphalian view of the state. They attempt to recreate the state and state institutions in their dealings in Africa. They are unable to envisage an alternative to this model. You can observe this at international conferences where diplomats make formal statements of policy and agree draft communiqués; this process is done within a set of well-established rules. In this system Somali politicians are treated as if they represent a normal state, like Germany or Turkey, because diplomatic convention requires that states deal with other states. The reality is that Somali politicians are at best optimists, and they may represent no one, except themselves. The way in which the TFG in Somalia was supported by Western agencies and governments demonstrated the failure of these organizations to develop a genuine understanding of the dynamics of the Somali socio-political system at the beginning of the twenty-first century. It is easy to be extremely critical of the TFG and the rent-seeking behaviour of its leaders, but in reality they acted logically and in accordance with a realistic appreciation of the situation; it is just that their actions and their words did not match.

Bordonaro refers to the 'contemporary *irrelevance*' of the state in Guinea-Bissau;[3] if the state is irrelevant in Guinea-Bissau today, it has been irrelevant in Somalia for decades. In the European sense, the state has ceased to exist in large areas of Africa and what has replaced it is a series of networks of elites: businessmen, politicians and traditional leaders, whose power and influence may be local or transnational, and who connect to internal and external agents. Bordonaro describes them as 'the cluster of informal, commercially oriented patrimonial networks growing out of the interplay between political authority and the clandestine economy'.[4] Taylor describes these networks as, 'a combination of political, economic and socio-cultural forces linked to the international sphere and transactional in nature'.[5]

As Christopher Clapham forcibly points out, 'States are not unchanging features of the global political order', and he reminds us that:

The idea that the whole world ought to be divided among states exercising full authority over their territories and populations dates only from the era of European colonialism and, in turn, from the creation of a global economy in which statehood was regarded as necessary to secure and regulate access to resources in hitherto inaccessible or uncontrolled areas.

Clapham, with his typical pragmatism, concludes that we have to be able to coexist with such ungoverned spaces, because 'The alternative project of attempting to restore universal statehood is chimerical.'[6]

However, if ungoverned spaces are not states, what are they? On Victorian maps of Africa and Arabia, there were large white spaces, labelled '*terra incognita*', unknown lands. These spaces were not part of the Westphalian system; they did not produce diplomats and did not participate in the structure of rules that states used to govern their relationships. Perhaps we should now write '*terra ex lex*' across the maps of Somalia and other failed states; a land without law. These territories lack a 'state' in the Westphalian sense, which makes it possible for them to participate in international diplomacy and to deal with other states in accordance with international law. It is arguable that the key attribute of a state under the European system is the ability to conduct relationships with other states, according to a common set of rules. The sovereignty of pre-colonial African kingdoms and the like was generally ignored, largely because they did not participate in diplomatic relations.

However, political structures do exist in virtually all human societies, although they may lack sophistication. Political structures, at their most basic, are ways by which power is exercised by members of communities. In Somalia local groups control resources and territory (although such control may be temporary) and these structures can be pre-state, or proto-state (the case of Puntland being an interesting one), and in rudimentary forms may merely equate to the control of territory exercised by criminal gangs in inner cities. As the study of Somalia shows, customary law can be effective, even in ungoverned spaces.

SOMALI CUSTOMARY LAW: *XEER*

What is remarkable about Somalia today is that it has no functioning system of laws, and therefore the consequences of actions do not need to be considered, providing clan obligations are observed. It was for this reason that the early promise of the UIC – which was an attempt to reintroduce the rule of law into that country – was so important, and why its destruction was such a disaster for Somalia. Peter Eichstaedt quotes a Kenyan human rights worker, Frederick Okado, who said of Somalis being kept in Kenyan jails: 'They're not used to the fact that if you hit someone, there will be consequences. In Somalia, you can hit someone or even kill them, and no more steps will be taken.'[7] We use the term 'lawless' without thinking, but that is the effective state of Somalia today. In such a situation the distinction between illicit and licit business is effectively non-existent, and so a businessman can just as easily invest in a mobile phone company, or in piracy: it is just an investment decision.

Strictly speaking, Somalia is not lawless, but it does lack a consistent system of criminal and civil legal redress in the sense understood in most of the world. Somali society, that is the clan-based system, relies on a combination of Islamic *shari'a* law and customary law, known as *xeer*. *Xeer* law is not the same as *shari'a* law; it is an oral system that has not been formally codified and is exercised by male clan elders, known as the *xeer begti* or *isimadda*. *Xeer* law is pre-Islamic in origin. According to Andre Le Sage, the general principles of *xeer* law include:

- collective payment of *diya* (blood money, usually paid with livestock, including camels) for death, physical harm, theft, rape and defamation, as well as the provision of assistance to relatives;

74

- maintenance of inter-clan harmony dealing with 'socially respected groups', including the elderly, the religious, women, children, poets and guests;
- family obligations including the payment of dowry, the inheritance of a widow by a dead husband's brother (*dumal*), a widower's rights to marry a deceased wife's sister (*higsian*) and the penalties for eloping;
- resource-utilization rules, regarding the use of water, pasture and other natural resources and the provision of support to relatives and the poor.[8]

Xeer can be divided into two broad categories: *xeer guud* and *xeer gaar*. *Xeer guud* includes the general aspects of traditional clan law that regulate common, day-to-day social interactions, civil affairs, and means of dispute settlement within a clan and between different clans. *Xeer gaar* regulates economic issues between clans and sub-clans in such areas as pastoralism, fishing and frankincense harvesting.[9]

What distinguishes *xeer* from most other systems of law is that it is based on the relationship between groups (of men) rather than between individuals. The whole *diya* (blood money) paying group is collectively responsible for a crime committed by one or more of its members. Ioan Lewis says that a Somali's 'most binding and most frequently mobilized loyalty is to his "*diya*-paying group"'.[10] As Lewis notes, a *diya*-paying group consists of 'a few hundred to a few thousand fighting men' and he adds that:

An injury done by or to any member of the group implicates all those who are party to its treaty. Thus if a man of one group is killed by a man of another [group], the first group will collectively claim the damages due from the second. At the same time, within any group a high degree of co-operation and mutual collaboration traditionally prevails.[11]

In dealing with pirate groups it is important to understand that the principles of the *diya*-paying group will be applied in their dealings with others. Thus, if a pirate is killed by the marines of a particular country, say France or the United States, the Somali *diya*-paying group to which the pirate belonged will see it as their duty to seek the payment of *diya* from the country concerned, and, if this is not forthcoming, they will see it as their entitlement to revenge the dead pirate by killing a Frenchman or an American, even if the Somali pirate died while trying to kill innocent seafarers. Somalis are not used to the idea that the individual may be responsible for his actions; their system is collective. An example of this approach was the action of Somali pirates in refusing to allow seven Indian seamen to leave Somalia in April 2011, even though their ship the *MT Asphalt Venture* was released after a ransom of $3.6 million had been paid. Reuters quoted a pirate called Ahmed, who said:

> The ship has just sailed away but we have taken some of its Indian crew back because the Indian government is currently holding our men. We need the Indian government to free our men so that we can release their citizens.[12]

Xeer is essentially a warriors' code. In practice women do not have direct access to the system unless a man brings a matter to the elders; so the rape of single women will not normally be dealt with (and women have to be careful not to be found guilty of immoral behaviour, even when they are the victims). Another important aspect of *xeer* is that because an act, such as the murder of another man, is dealt with by the payment of *diya* by the group, the individual perpetrator will not normally be punished. As Gundel says: 'In general, the collective responsibility imposed on *mag*-groups by the *xeer* is seen as removing responsibility from individual perpetrators of crimes.'[13] Thus, a Somali rapist or murderer does not take direct responsibility for his crimes. This is a fundamental difference from the English common law system, and virtually all the other legal systems, which are based on each individual taking moral responsibility for his or her actions. This is not merely a 'cultural' difference, but a gulf that distinguishes *xeer* from Western legal systems and also from *shari'a* law, because Islam holds that each Muslim is accountable to Allah for his or her actions in this world. In our dealings with Somali pirates we always need to keep an understanding of *xeer* in mind, because the Somalis will not behave in the way that we would expect otherwise. We are dealing with a group, a gang, not individuals who feel responsible for their own actions. It is possible to compare the outlook of *diya* group members to that of people in traditional societies, from Sicily to Pakistan, who value 'honour', or respect, and are even prepared to kill their own family members who fail to comply with the local codes. But *diya* group members go much further than that.

If we are truly to learn from the problems of Somalia, we need first to examine our own preconceptions, to stand back from our own certainties. A need for certainty is one of the reasons why Westerners find it so difficult to deal with the chaotic and disordered situation in Somalia. Western patterns of thought reflect ingrained habits, unexamined assumptions; the disorder of modern Africa is a profound and existential shock to visitors, and Somalia sits at the extremity of chaos.

HIDDEN TRADE NETWORKS IN AFRICA

We can only understand the situation in Somalia if we throw out our conviction of the inevitability of the state, and see Somalia, and many other African territories, as existing nodes or intersections of complex networks of power, focused on enriching those who control the key connections within these networks. These networks are in essence trading networks, not mafias in the way that they are commonly understood, though the products traded along the networks may be illicit or licit. The World Food Programme uses local businessmen to deliver critical supplies of food to refugees. Medicines and life-saving supplies pass along such networks, but the same networks can distribute weapons, ammunition, traffic people, illegal drugs and navigation equipment for pirates. These networks are as fluid as quick silver and can rapidly reconfigure themselves. New players can enter and old ones depart, and *ad hoc* arrangements can be put in place overnight (Figure 3.1).

Figure 3.1 Ilyushin Il-76 loading

Somalis, who are traders by tradition and have always existed in a harsh and forbidding environment, have adapted easily to this new milieu. Dhows, Antonovs and Ilyushins are the workhorses of these trade routes. In his heyday, Russian arm smuggler Viktor Bout operated Russian- and Ukrainian-crewed Antonov An-12s and Ilyushin Il-18s out of Sharjah into Africa carrying all sorts of cargo, and he hauled aid, peacekeepers, militias, gems and guns indiscriminately. Some aircrafts came to grief in the Congo, crashing on the volcanic runway at Goma. As one commentator put it after yet another crash in the Congo, the 'Ruskies drilled the lava at Goma today and bought the farm'; all five Russian crew members of an Antonov An-12 died in that incident in September 2007. Recent events have also cast suspicion on small and battered cargo ships, running cargoes into Somalia from the Persian Gulf.

The key issue in Somalia today is neither terrorism, nor piracy, but the way in which to deal with a society that exists without a 'state'. Somalia is not the only territory with this problem; the Congo and Guinea-Bissau are obvious examples. It is only in this environment that piracy has flourished, because piracy is supported and enabled by 'clandestine networks'. In a normal state, there are a number of legitimate entities that provide the socio-political environment in which the nation operates. In the United Kingdom, for example, the structures of law, parliamentary democracy, Church, Crown, the Army, Royal Navy, RAF, police, the Bank of England, press and multiple local and national organizations provide a complex framework within which government and organizations within the state must operate. Illicit organizations, like criminal gangs and terrorists, exist within the territory of the British state, but they are subject to confrontation and sanction; they do not form part of the core framework of the country, notwithstanding corrupt policemen and politicians.

This is not the case in Somalia, where the difference between licit and illicit actors and networks is actually irrelevant. Some institutions and organizations within Somalia operate with great integrity – the money transfer system is one example – but illicit networks are interposed within the system, like layers of a cake, and colour the behaviour of the society. Carolyn Nordstrom points out that a single transaction, for example the sale of arms, may be legal at some stage in the process and illegal at another stage.[14] Nordstrom's thesis, set out in convincing detail in *Global Outlaws*,[15] is that hidden trade networks facilitate the transfer of assets from third world countries into industrialized economies, and that these networks are interwoven with licit trade systems. Illicit networks are not just a shadow economy; they form part of the real economy. As Nordstrom says:

'The unregulated – the illicit and the smuggled – is fundamental to the world of business, economics, and politics as we know them in the modern world.'[16] She adds:

> Legality is a fluid concept . . . . The vast majority of those who participate in the extra-legal do not think of themselves as criminals, as smugglers, as 'really' breaking the law. In their perspective, states, being only 'somewhat' important, are only somewhat noticed, somewhat respected. Vast extra-state economic networks are equally, and sometimes more, important. Multiple nodes of power. Multiple constructs of privilege. Each balancing the hegemony of the other in global realities.[17]

In other words, the size and complexity of interwoven trade flows and the layered intricacy of corporate structures and financial planning have made it virtually impossible for governments to control the flow of goods across their borders and impossible to tax it effectively. Globalization is far more than the assembly of consumer goods in low wage countries; it is the movement of power from states to those organizations controlling trade flows, and the loss of the ability of the state to level taxes effectively on international corporations. Nordstrom says: 'Reputable multi-national corporations most commonly violate the laws controlling trade.'[18] Neither is this just an African, or a developing economy problem. Nordstrom quotes a US customs official who declared:

> You want to know who we most commonly catch breaking the law? The big-name corporations whose products we all buy every day. We bust them and they just call their 'friends' in DC. We then get a call telling us to drop the case. We have no choice, the call comes from people too powerful for us to fight.[19]

The illicit section of the world economy is closely interwoven with the legitimate section in much of Africa and other developing areas. As Nordstrom comments:

> The links between the shadows and the formal sector should be evident by now: profiteers assist the transfer of military goods and payments in precious resources; these profits fuel formal businesses as well, and the profits – both material and political – that can be gained in business can be converted into political power when successful businesspeople run for

office or back other of their choice. Military, business, and politics intersect in these transactions that blur il/legal distinctions, and public policies are often in actuality crafted in the shadows.[20]

Piracy can be seen as just such an intersection: legitimate traders provide key equipment and supplies; at some point these supplies are diverted to pirate gangs. In the same way, ransom money can pass into legitimate channels and buy properties in the Persian Gulf and Kenya, whereas some of the ransom money can pass to groups like Al-Shabaab, designated as terrorists by the UN; all the while ebbing and flowing from illegitimate to legitimate to illegitimate.

Nordstrom also argues that the shadow economies of the world may be the shape of things to come:

[T]he shadow sovereigns of today may foreshadow new power formulations barely emergent on the horizons of political and economic possibility. It may be convenient to think that globalism most powerfully affects the cosmopolitan centres the world. But perhaps.... Mozambique and Angola, Africa and Asia, are the sites where new configurations of power shaping the world are most visible. For it is here that ... the breakdown of entrenched institutionalization, the politics of survival, and the creativity of development meet in the most direct of ways.[21]

CRIMINAL NETWORKS

Woven into the shadow economy are the real criminal networks – the distributors of illegal drugs, the traffickers in women and children, the organized fraudsters. But they frequently work with amoral politicians, corporations who bend the law and use legitimate businesses as fronts or partners. It is worth turning to books like Gregory David Roberts' semi-autobiographical novel *Shantaram*, an epic account of life in Mumbai's criminal underworld, which rivals Dostoevsky's work.[22] For many of the world's population, criminals – or powerful elites operating in the shadow economy – have a much greater impact on their daily life than politicians, priests, mullahs or doctors. These people control the slums, decide where it is safe to go, determine if your company gets business, provide work, kill your friends and can sell your sister into a brothel – and there is nothing you can do about it. The police and politicians pay these people and control the sources of revenue in your world. The impact of crime on ordinary people is staggering; the International Labour Organization (ILO) estimated that at least 2.45 million people were victims of human trafficking in 2009.[23] However, gangs and criminal foot soldiers are only the public face of crime; the real money is made by 'respectable' men in suits with professional qualifications who operate from offices and banks. Many legitimate businesses also knowingly deal with criminal enterprises in order to obtain resources, including finance, so there are too often no clear boundaries between the criminal and non-criminal world.

Antonio Maria Costa, then Head of the UN office on Drugs and Crime (UNODC), said drug money often became the only available capital when the financial crisis spiralled out of control in 2008, and that the UNODC had found evidence that 'interbank loans were funded by money that originated from drug trade and other illegal activities'.[24] Large and respected businesses may also have had their roots in criminal activities, smuggling and the like. Governments, via their intelligence agencies, use criminal enterprises when it suits their purposes. Our world is not clearly divided between right and wrong; there are many shades of grey.

Western policies towards the illicit economy often fail to understand the way in which it is so deeply embedded in most societies. Billions of people exist in an environment in which those operating in the shadow economy exert a foul and miasmic influence over their lives. You cannot live in Naples, Moscow, Sao Paulo, Johannesburg or Lagos without negotiating with representatives of the illicit economy at some level or another. And if you are poor and live in the slums, gangs control your district and dictate the rules under which you exist. If you live in Mogadishu, Galkayo or Eyl, the gangs may be clan-based, but they are controlled and focus on making a living in an environment where there is no 'rule of law'.

Somali piracy is run on business lines; all expenditure is accounted for and the investors are offered a return proportionate to their 'investment' – in the same way that Queen Elizabeth I of England profited handsomely from Francis Drake's adventures and plunder of Spanish vessels. It is also well connected to Somali political and business elites, to the widespread and effective Somali diaspora networks, and to other international criminal networks. Until recently Puntland was the key political base for Somali piracy; local politicians were funded by competing pirate groups. But recent policies have shown that Puntland intends to move away from piracy.

Piracy has been strongly connected with Yemen and its political elites. There are also ancient connections between East Africa, including the Horn, the Indian sub-continent and the Persian Gulf – connections cemented by marriage and ancient obligations. The trade routes across the Indian Ocean are thousands of years old, and this has developed deep-rooted inter-dependencies, which remain relevant today.

The existence of these support networks provided piracy with a secure base and facilitated the trade of piracy in the past. In short, Somali piracy is a node on the transnational criminal network.

In addition to the supply chains that provide for the pirates' needs for weapons, ammunition, radios, GPS and other navigation equipment and, if rumours are to be believed, bulker fuel, there are also intelligence-gathering operations that give pirate bosses information on ship movements and assist with hijacking negotiations. A recent development has involved pirate associates putting pressure on the families of hijacked seamen, particularly in India. Families in India are asked for money to feed their loved ones kidnapped by Somalis, and receive heart-rending telephone calls from the hostages, informing them that the hostages will be tortured unless the ship is ransomed quickly. It is also said that, once Indian seamen return from captivity, some remain afraid that pirate associates will keep threatening them, unless they refrain from talking to the media about their experiences.[25] All this provides at least circumstantial evidence that Indian criminal enterprises are partners in Somali piracy.

Somali pirates monitor the media and attempt to influence it by convincing people that piracy is a 'people's enterprise', which has emerged as a response to the behaviour of greedy foreigners – a Robin Hood venture – rather than the brutal criminal enterprise that it is in reality. Do not believe everything that you read on the internet: there is no romance in Somali piracy. It preys on seafarers, mainly men from Asian countries who are paid little for a hard life at sea, and pirates have tortured, mutilated and killed seamen in order to make money from their trade.

CRIME AS A GLOBALIZED BUSINESS

Piracy is a transnational crime. As noted earlier, Somali piracy has benefitted from venerable cross-Indian Ocean connections, but these connections mirror the behaviour of other major criminal organizations. Madsen says that 'International crime represents both a cultural and a political exemplification of the internal logic of globalization.'[26] Global criminal businesses need partners, and as James Richards says:

> Colombian drug cartels are operating in Western Europe; Russian gangsters are operating in Eastern Europe, the United States, and Asia; the Chinese Triads dominate Asia and the west coast of the United States; and the Mexican criminal organizations dominate the world methamphetamine trade. Not only are these organizations operating globally, they are forming strategic alliances with each other, with rogue governments, and with terrorist organizations. These international criminal organizations ... and their strategic alliances are the dominant problem facing local, national, and international law enforcement today.[27]

In a sense, criminals are the real beneficiaries of globalization and of the virtual world we now inhabit. Their legal and financial advisors have ensured that all the benefits of offshore banking, shell companies, corporate secrecy and tax avoidance, that the very rich and large corporations have been exploiting for years, are also available to transnational criminal organizations.

Criminal organizations therefore network effectively and form relationships with groups that can offer new skills and give access to new criminal markets. One bizarre example is the working relationship between the Italian mafia and the Chinese gangs in Italy, as mentioned by Madsen:

> Chinese organized crime chose Italy because of the presence of very well-established endogenous crime organizations, which they correctly saw not as competitors, but as potential associates ... the profits accruing to Chinese organized crime in Italy is estimated at 1 billion euros a year.[28]

Because they are businesses, criminal organizations are as market-driven and profit-seeking as any corporation – the essential difference being that some (but not all) of the business they do is defined as illegal by the states in which they operate, except of course in lawless territories. Criminal organizations can also cooperate with terrorist groups and can form close alliances. Makarenko highlights the relationship between the Albanian mafia and the Kosovo Liberation Army during the Kosovo conflict, which involved heroin trafficking and the supply of weapons.[29] The Provisional IRA in Ireland also funded its operations by smuggling weapons, robbing banks and selling counterfeit goods. In recent years the Real IRA, Continuity IRA and INLA have all moved into this territory, becoming involved in drugs, protection rackets and prostitution.[30]

In Somalia, groups like Al-Shabaab are likely to continue to seek income from criminal activity, including piracy and smuggling goods into Kenya.

Modern criminal organizations form adaptive networks with self-organizing nodes. Global organized crime is uniquely flexible and adaptable, as well as violent, ruthless and unscrupulous. As Juan Carlos Garzón comments:

> Criminal structures are increasingly adopting a network form. They have been moving away from cumbersome – almost bureaucratic organizations that tried to monopolize illegal economies, toward the configuration of cells that specialize in certain parts of the production chain or in a specific market (like the protection market). ... The real leader is the person who has the contacts and the connections, the person who has developed a significant concentration of relationships....[31]

It is becoming increasingly difficult to halt the operations of criminal groups; if one limb is cut off, a new one rapidly grows.

One of the most effective transnational criminal gangs of recent times is D-Company of Dawood Ibrahim, which Rollins et al. described as, 'a 5,000-member criminal syndicate operating mostly in Pakistan, India, and the United Arab Emirates'. They added that it 'provides an example of the criminal-terrorism "fusion" model'.[32] They concluded that Dawood Ibrahim 'is capable of smuggling terrorists across national borders, trafficking in weapons and drugs, controlling extortion and protection rackets, and laundering ill-gotten proceeds, including through the abuse of traditional value transfer methods, like hawala'.[33] There has been no indication that D-Company is involved with Somali piracy, but gangs like this might give Somali pirates a major boost in capability and it is certain that similar organizations are deeply involved in piracy.

In Somalia, individual gangs have developed specialization skills, and the job of guarding hijacked ships and feeding their crews is normally sub-contracted to specialists. Others are involved in moving ransom money and investing it. There are financial links to 'investors' among the wealthy and criminally inclined in Europe, the Indian sub-continent and the Middle East. In other words, Somali piracy is a widespread criminal network with international connections.

The public face of piracy is, of course, men like Abshir Boyah (as we will see in detail later on). But in order to succeed, Somali piracy has connected itself to the deep transnational criminal networks that move money and intelligence around the world. It is important to grasp this connectivity to a wider network because, as in so many other things, Somalia shows us the world in a sharper light. Piracy is deep-rooted, adaptable and resilient, and more people are involved than we think.

MONEY TRAIL

Somali pirate groups are nodes within an international criminal network. They have clear structures within Somalia and cooperate with each other where necessary, even though individual gangs do sometimes fight over ransoms. The responsibility for money laundering may be outsourced to Somalis based in other countries or to non-Somali specialists. There are stories, which cannot be substantiated for obvious reasons, that a strong Indian connection exists and that the ancient links across the Indian Ocean to East Africa, via Arabia, are as important as they ever were, encompassing all types of 'trade', illegal as well as legal. Stories that circulate about the role of Indian criminals in communicating with the families of hijacked crew members, lend credence to such claims.

Too much can be made of the importance of *hawalas* as a 'secret' money-transfer method; but let's remember that other criminal organizations successfully launder and transfer much larger sums of money using normal banking systems. In March 2010, Wachovia paid US federal authorities $110 million in forfeiture for allowing transactions connected to drug smuggling.[34] As Misha Glenny says: 'The Caymans, British Virgin Islands and all the other offshore banking centres are the back door through which criminal money can enter the legitimate, if increasingly opaque, money markets.'[35] Jeffrey Robinson concludes:

> Like all multinational enterprises, transnational organized crime and global terrorism need the legitimate financial world. In this respect, criminals operate exactly like multinational corporations. They use the same global financial infrastructure to handle their corporate affairs. [He adds that criminals rely on professionals, and] Lawyers, bankers, accountants, company formation agents and brokers may or may not know the origins of the money they're handling, but most know they don't want to know.[36]

In the case of the wealthy, similar techniques are used to avoid the payment of tax, an imperative that also drives corporations to use complex offshore structures, not easily understood, or uncovered, by revenue authorities.

Somali crime needs to be understood in the context of other criminal activities in Africa and the Middle East. First, the revenue from Somali crime, including piracy, is not enormous by the standards of international organized crime. Somalia has other scams and criminal enterprises, but the gross revenue from ships hijacked in 2009 was probably no more than $74 million, and could have been as low as $50 million. Once costs were deducted, it might be assumed that around 50 per cent was profit and that, say, $20–30 million passed to investors. Compared to the revenue flow made by investors in drug smuggling, or the profits made from illegal arms dealing, this is a relatively small sum, even if the profits from smuggling refugees to Yemen and smuggling goods to Kenya are added in. In contrast, the annual value of opium grown in Afghanistan is about $64 billion, and the Taliban's tithe on opium cultivation alone brings in $90–160 million a year.[37] However, within the Somali economy this is still a considerable amount of revenue, and Somali businesses and political elites have thrived on this income. There are other sources of revenue within the Somali economy, including illicit sales of food aid, smuggling goods into Kenya, transporting migrants to Yemen, arms dealing, legitimate profits from livestock exports, providing transportation and security for the World Food Programme (WFP), telecommunications and money transfers (*xawilaad*). Money, food, medicine, weapons and materials also flow into Somalia in the form of foreign aid and from remittances by Somalis living abroad.

It is clear that a large amount of the profits made by Somalia's businesses have been invested in the relatively safe economy of Kenya;[38] money may also have been invested in the Gulf States, Europe and other centres. The payment of $9.5 million for the ransoming of the South Korean VLCC *Samho Dream* in November 2010[39] – a record at the time – was game-changing, although it was eclipsed in April 2011, when it was reported that $13.5 million was paid for the ransom of the tanker MV *Irene*[40]; those negotiating future ransoms will undoubtedly use these sums as benchmarks.

Not all of the ransom money ends up on the decks of hijacked ships; a proportion is sometimes paid via more conventional channels. Mick Palmer, Australia's inspector of transport security, acknowledges that following the money trail is crucial to fighting the problem, since 'no criminals are in business to lose money, they only get involved to get money'.[41] However, as Christopher Ledger says:

There's been a lot of inventive reporting on very slim evidence. What happens to the money is exceedingly opaque, partly because of the way

Somalis communicate with each other, and also because of the impenetrable way their finance system works.[42]

The fact that most ransoms are paid in cash means they simply disappear into the Somali community, rather than ending up in banks or other financial institutions, but it is worth trying to follow the money trail in order to identify the investors and the politicians involved in the trade. The money trail may as well end up in Mayfair, Boston, Hong Kong or Dubai. In the words of Jeffrey Robinson, organized crime is a business.

MONEY TRANSFERS IN SOMALIA: *XAWILAAD*

Although some of the proceeds of ransoms may be transferred using Somalia's *xawilaad* services, this does not mean that these services are themselves part of the criminal economy. What is fascinating is that, while Somalia (with the exception of Somaliland) is a territory without formal legal institutions, its economy is reliant on a sophisticated financial system that enables expatriate Somalis to remit large amounts of money to their families in Somalia. Without this money, Somalia would not be able to survive. It is the flow of money from the Somali diaspora – money from Somalis in North America, Europe and the Gulf States – that keeps the territory going. *Xawilaad* services are also a vital support to the international aid programme and Somali traders who can export goods. The Somali word *xawilaad* is equivalent to the Arabic word *hawala*, which means a method of transferring and setting off debts that relies on trust between the participants.

Economic life in Somalia became dependent on *xawilaad* in the absence of conventional banks after the fall of President Barre. It then grew rapidly in the late 1980s and early 1990s as the civil war spread across the country, and in the late 1990s growth continued because of demand from refugees and aid agencies.[43] Then, on 7 November 2001, President George W. Bush announced that the United States was blocking the assets of a number of individuals and organizations, including Al-Barakaat, which was then the largest *xawilaad* business in Somalia. This came like a bombshell and had a profound impact on the Somali financial system. President Bush even claimed that Al-Barakaat and another transfer company, Al-Taqwa, were

tied to al-Qaida and Usama [Osama] bin Laden, raise money for terror, invest it for profit, launder the proceeds of crime, and distribute terrorist money around the world to purchase the tools of global terrorism. ... Al-Barakaat's founder, Shaykh Ahme Nur Jimale, is closely linked to Usama bin Laden. He has used Al-Barakaat's 60 offices in Somalia and 127 offices abroad to transmit funds, intelligence and instructions to terrorist cells.[44]

As Anna Lindley points out, the US 9/11 Commission 'found that the designation of Al-Barakaat and others had been driven by the perceived need to show the world that the US was serious about its financial "War on Terror", and that the evidence against Al-Barakaat was actually quite weak'.[45] In other words, Bush undermined Al-Barakaat on the basis of an imagined connection. Ibrahim Warde said:

In reality, after the initial euphoria, the Al-Barakaat case became an embarrassment for the financial warriors. It came to illustrate many of the dysfunctions of the financial war – the power of rumour and innuendo, the flimsy nature of what passed for evidence, and the unaccountability of bureaucrats. It highlighted the asymmetry of the financial war [on terror], showing how self-aggrandizing mid-level bureaucrats could inflict further misery on one of the world's poorest countries.[46]

George Bush's actions had a serious impact on the Somali economy, keeping between $400 million and $1 billion of foreign remittances out of Somalia. An examination of the money-transfer business shows that remittances from Somalis working in other countries is the territory's largest source of income and that livestock exports ($300–400 million) is second; piracy and other criminal enterprises are well down the list. The UN estimates that in 2001 about $500 million was remitted to Somalia from abroad by expatriate Somalis and a significant percentage of the population was dependent on such transfers – up to 40 per cent of households in some cases.[47]

Since 2001 other businesses have replaced Al-Barakaat, notably Dahabshiil and Amal. Dahabshiil has over 1,000 branches and agents in 40 countries; Amal has about 300 foreign agents and over 350 outlets in Somalia.[48] Lindley says that remittance services, 'are able to count on significant local solidarity because they provide a service on which many depend, but must be careful to work with respected local people and preserve good relations with local elders'. She also adds that 'Their business is caught up in complex ways in Somali politics.'[49]

The remittance business provides an interesting example of a successful and thriving commercial enterprise in Somalia that is not dependent on criminal connections, that exists in a stateless environment (except in Somaliland, although Puntland is a quasi-state) and that provides a valued and critical service to the whole community. The primary function of such institutions is to transfer funds into Somalia. There is no direct evidence that Somali *xawilaad* enterprises transmit the proceeds of ransom payments out of the country, although it would be difficult for their agents to know what the sources of funds were (and Somalia is a very long way from supporting such a regulatory infrastructure). It is also the case that, because a financial transmission system may be used by criminals, there is no argument for closing it down, owing to the fact that such a large percentage of the Somali population is dependent on the money that it transmits from abroad. There is no alternative to these enterprises in Somalia and they are one of the few success stories in modern Somalia. It is important to understand their role in the Somali economy, rather than just focus on their possible misuse.

THE CRIMINALIZED OR PREDATORY STATE

Although it can be argued that Somalia has ceased to be a state in any meaningful sense, it does retain quasi-state institutions in Puntland and the vestige of a government in the shape of the transitional institutions in Mogadishu. It is therefore relevant to consider how such a state or quasi-state functions and how the history of the last government of Somalia is an indication of how a new Somali government may function.

Under Siyad Barre Somalia was reduced to a predatory, or criminalized, state; crime flourished with the support of sympathetic state institutions. In the cases of weak and failing states, the relationship of the ruling elites to quasi-legal and illicit enterprises can serve to maintain those elites in power. Reno refers to 'fusion regimes', which he says 'combine the facade of formal state bureaucratic institutions and the trappings of international sovereignty with the control of resources in illicit markets'.[50] Jean-François Bayart wrote of the 'Somali road to development' under Siyad Barre, which he said,

appears to be based on the occupation of the most dubious niches of international economic activity (various forms of trafficking, including of drugs; and the dumping of toxic waste, for example) and on the unregulated exploitation of the mineral, oil and wildlife resources of the sub-continent. Politically, it seems to take the form of the radical privatization of the state, the criminalization of the behaviour of power-holders, and even the transformation of factional struggle ... into armed conflict, as has happened in Chad, Uganda, Angola and Liberia.[51]

Reno argues that the associates of Barre, like the associates of Mobutu in Zaire and Samuel Doe in Liberia, 'used their connections [for] illicit commerce', hoping to 'claim state power and use international recognition of sovereignty to construct their own fusion regimes that they could exploit as the real basis of their power'.[52] There can be little doubt that were the successors to the TFG, or any other Somali group, to control Somalia, then a 'fusion regime' of the type described by Reno could be put in place.

The representative of the TFG told the UN Security Council in November 2010 that it was 'very much seized' with fighting piracy and restoring law and order in Somalia. Given that the TFG had no maritime assets it is difficult to imagine how such worthy aims could have been implemented, although it was clear that the TFG would have welcomed additional funding from the international community. In a statement that must rank high in the annals of optimism, B. Lynn Pascoe, the under-secretary-general for UN political affairs, announced to the Security Council: 'We must also make piracy and robbery off the coast of Somalia costly by addressing impunity and building the capacity of the Transitional Federal Government to expand its authority and deal with law and order.'[53]

Peter Lewis identifies three essential features of an emergent predatory order: first, the concentration of power under coercive auspices, extending repression, killing opponents and removing potential restraints on presidential power; second, material inducements to loyalist officers, civilian cronies and acquiescent politicians; and, third, 'the conscious erosion of central public institutions and the corresponding hegemony of a close circle of ethnic and personal loyalists'.[54] The predatory state, as described by Lewis, hollows out the state.

In other words, a predatory system reduces the economic production of the national economy, but at the same time enriches a small elite, while the mass of the population experiences economic decline. As criminals run the state, and hence control the protective apparatus of the state, the courts and legal system can only be subordinated to this group of criminals. You may feel that this is a long way from the daily attacks on merchant ships off the coast of Somalia, but the concept of predatory government is important, because this is precisely what President Siyad Barre subjected Somalia to until his loss of power in 1990, and this is the model to which most Somali politicians would willingly return, were they ever to regain effective control of the Somali territories.

In Somalia (with the notable exception to date of Somaliland) the aspirant political leaders and their groupings have been rent-seeking, not state-building. The fact that Somali piracy in the past was able to base itself so securely in Puntland said much about the corruption of that territory's leadership and institutions. The TFG was accused of involvement in a number of 'scams' by the UN Monitoring Group. Yet, in March 2010, *The New York Times* reported that the US government planned to offer new support for the TFG, to enable it to control Mogadishu and, in the words of the report, 'to bring a semblance of order to a country that has been steeped in anarchy for two decades'.[55]

The error that international organizations have consistently made in Somalia, and in countries similar to it, is to attempt to build a state and its supporting institutions, by assisting the men who in fact are only the leaders of armed factions, and whose agenda is to exploit the resources of the country for their own ends. By working to limit conflict and create stability, international organizations and outside powers have too frequently achieved the precise opposite of what they have publicly stated as being their objectives. Robert Jackson talks about the creation of 'quasi-states', or internationally enfranchised sovereign states, with governments that are 'often deficient in the political will, institutional authority, and organized power to protect human rights or provide socio-economic welfare'.[56]

Perhaps the idea of a peaceful Somalia will long remain; like the grin on the Cheshire Cat's face, a lingering dream, as it suits so many forces that it remains in its present state; devoid of hope. Despite the gallons of ink and tons of paper used to write reports and recommendations on the future of Somalia, there is at present no obvious solution to the country's problems, although the likely presence of oil in Puntland and the decline of Al-Shabaab in 2011–12 offers some hope for the future. Perhaps we will live to see a triumph of hope over experience.

CHAPTER 4

THE PIRATE COAST

THE KEY ROLE OF PUNTLAND IN THE ORGANIZATION OF PIRACY

Puntland

Like Somaliland Puntland, named after the land of ancient Punt, is partially independent, but it has achieved a high degree of autonomy. It consists mainly of the province of Bari in north-eastern Somalia and adjoins Somaliland on its western border. While not as relatively peaceful as Somaliland, Puntland has avoided many of the problems faced by the rest of Somalia, showing that local governance is a critical factor in ensuring stability.

Puntland's autonomy was established in 1991 by the Somali Salvation Democratic Front (SSDF), which was created by Abdillahi Yusuf with Ethiopian military and financial support.[1] Thereafter, he remained the Ethiopians' man in Somalia. Abdillahi Yusuf was also involved in a number of ventures and continued his close relationship with the then president of Yemen. Abdillahi Yusuf's presence looms large over the development of modern Somali piracy.

President Colonel Abdillahi Yusuf died of pneumonia at the age of 77 in Abu Dhabi.[2] Over 2,000 people attended his funeral; he was laid to rest in Galkayo in March 2012. President Farole of Puntland said at the burial that 'Abdullahi was a patriotic man whose dedication and rigidness will inspire many to come'.[3] Unfortunately, Colonel Yusef's career is likely to inspire people for all the wrong reasons.

Colonel Abdillahi Yusuf and General Mohamed Abshir were rivals who sought to control the territory. Abdillahi Yusuf held the office of president of Puntland from March 1998 to June 2001, after which he attempted, without justification, to remain in office for another three years; a public revolt secured his removal in August 2001. In November 2001 Jama Ali Jama was elected as the new president, but his period in office did not last long, as Abdillahi Yusuf reinstated himself by force, a situation that lasted until 2005, when Madamud Muse Adde was elected.

In 2001 Abdillahi Yusuf, when faced by popular opposition from the people and tribal elders, reacted by raising a militia in his home town and appropriating for his own use the customs revenues from the port of Bosaso, the source of about 80 per cent of Puntland's administrative revenues.[4] Control of the bulk of Puntland's customs and tax base, together with Ethiopian finance, gave Abdillahi Yusuf the ability to do whatever he liked – the personification of predatory government.

Abdillahi Yusuf's election as president of the TFG, which was backed by Ethiopia, gave him a new political base, although he retained great influence in Puntland – as an important leader of the Majeerten sub-clan of the Darod. Puntland's development as a proto-state was therefore dominated by the authoritarian regime of Abdillahi Yusuf and the group around him, and local representatives had little real power. This was in contrast to the more open style of government adopted in Somaliland.

Reno says that 'Puntland ... illustrates the centrality of the political economy of conflict to the establishment of new political communities.'[5] The creation of the Puntland autonomous region was facilitated by the Swedish Uppsala Life and Peace Institute and the UN Research Institute for Social Development War-torn Societies Project. These organizations supported discussions between SSDF leaders and regional elders. However, unlike Somaliland, Puntland has not claimed full independence; it is semi-autonomous, its borders not clearly defined. This ambiguous status in practice served militia leaders and men like Abdillahi Yusuf well; when they wanted to claim the sanctuary of local rights and administration they did so, but they also felt free to play a hand in the larger game centred on the political *mêlée* in the moribund state of Somalia. Ethiopia continued to fund its old allies, such as Abdillahi Yusuf, hence ensuring that Puntland could maintain its relative separation, and that Somalia remained segmented – one of Ethiopia's unstated aims.

The organizational centre of Somali piracy?

The recent history of Puntland is of considerable interest to the students of Somali piracy. Puntland has in the past been the organizational centre of Somali piracy, despite claims to the contrary. The links between the regime in Puntland with the TFG, Yemen and Ethiopia created an environment in which criminals were able to operate freely, supported by sufficient infrastructure and security to enable them to undertake their business without inference or undue risk. Puntland for a period became the modern Barbary coast.

In October 2011 I listened to Puntland's President Abdirahman Mohamud Farole at Chatham House, London, who said, 'Our government's commitment to the anti-piracy effort is very clear.'[6] This was a claim that President Farole repeated at a number of international venues. I must admit that, like many in the audience, I was sceptical, but recent events, detailed below, made me think that he was probably telling the truth. With hindsight we might well see that the burial of Abdillahi Yusuf in March 2012 as marking the end of the expansive phase of Somali piracy. Certainly in Puntland the government appears to be doing all it can to distance itself from that trade, looking instead to the even more lucrative trade in oil to provide for the future. The future is not necessarily a continuation of the past; circumstances change, and we need to allow that Puntland may well have changed – though not completely perhaps.

In April 2010 President Farole, in an interview with Reuters, said that pirates were adversely affecting Puntland, and that piracy had emerged as an industry for a wide range of people, including brokers and facilitators, disrupting the region's traditional economy. He added, 'They have disrupted our economy, which traditionally is based on livestock export and fisheries. No one is fishing on the waters now, [and that, t]hey have spoiled the cultural and religious values, and introduced drugs, alcohol and prostitution.'[7]

In 2011 and 2012 Puntland pressed ahead with the creation of its Maritime Police Force (PMPF). The PMPF has had several successes – for example in May 2012 Reuters reported that 11 pirates, including Mohamud Mohamed Hassan ('Dhafoor')[8] were arrested – though there are suggestions that the force was not been fully trained.[9]

However, the fact remains that Puntland is the place from which piracy is controlled. Peter Eichstaedt, who interviewed a pirate called Abu Suleiman at length, said in 2010 that it was reputed that some top Puntland officials had their own pirate crews.[10] Eichstaedt also noted that, 'The government in Puntland is deeply linked with piracy.' Suleiman had told him that, 'Each payment [from piracy] that comes through Puntland, the authorities get a piece of it...'.[11]

Stig Hansen stressed the concentration of piracy in a few areas, including Puntland, when he wrote: 'Somalia as a whole is not pirate-infested; the pirates operate out of only some regions, using less than a handful of ports to anchor their hijacked ships.' He added that we need to understand the specific local conditions in these pirate areas in order to both curtail and explain piracy.[12] The main pirate havens are Xarardheere, Hobyo, Garaad and Eyl, although other coastal settlements in Puntland have also been used, and there have been attacks from groups based in the southern provinces, using Kismaayo and other bases.

In 2011 the UN Monitoring Group noted that Somali piracy has historically been dominated by two principal networks based in north-eastern Somalia (Puntland) and the Xarardheere and Hobyo districts of southern Mudug region. The activities of a third network, operating from Las Qoray in the eastern Sanaag region, were disrupted in October 2009, when its leader Fu'aad Hanaano was arrested together with several other pirates by the government of Yemen.[13]

Therefore, the two main pirate groups are the Puntland Piracy Network (PPN) and the Hobyo-Haradheere Network (HHN), which cooperate with each other and share resources. The UN Monitoring Group also reported that:

Despite their distinct clan and regional characteristics, there have long been indications of cooperation between the Puntland and the Hobyo-Xarardheere networks: contacts between their leaders, joint participation in some sea operations, the movement of hijacked ships from one anchorage to another, shared negotiators and common suppliers, to name a few. At the end of 2010, such ostensibly ad hoc cooperation was superseded by an agreement to join forces and establish a base at Garacad, where operations would be coordinated and profits would be shared.[14]

According to the UN, this base was subsequently moved to Ceel Dhanaan, a fishing settlement located some 24 nautical miles further south, close to the border of the Jiriiban and Hobyo districts. Other vessels anchored off Hobyo were also moved to another anchorage known as Caduur, located approximately 10 nautical miles north of Hobyo.

The UN Monitoring Group stated in July 2011 that 'Elements of both networks now appear to have merged, operating principally from the largest anchorage at Ceel Dhaanaan, while other elements of the Hobyo-

Xarardheere network continue to operate from Caduur and a pirate camp south of Xarardheere.'[15] The UN Monitoring Group also noted in 2011 that although the number of pirate anchorages was shrinking, that 'engagement in piracy has expanded dramatically. With the exception of Somaliland, pirate operations are now launched from pirate camps all along the Somali coast, from Ceelaayo (west of Bosaso) to areas south of Kismaayo.'[16] They added that pirate activities in the Al-Shabaab-controlled areas, such as Xarardheere, Eel Ma'aan, Baraawe, Merka, Kismaayo and Komaya Island, 'all point to growing tolerance of piracy within Al-Shabaab, which has historically professed its hostility to the practice. This is particularly evident in the coexistence of pirate militias with Al-Shabaab in the Hobyo-Xarardheere area, where Al-Shabaab leader, Sheikh Hassan Afrah ... has reportedly been responsible for ensuring that local Al-Shabaab forces obtain their share of ransom payments.'[17] However, it is important to note from the Monitoring Group's assessment that, although local Al-Shabaab militias obtain a share of ransoms, 'no evidence has been found to suggest any broader or more systematic involvement of Al-Shabaab in piracy'.[18]

The UN in its February 2010 report on Somalia concluded that 'Efforts to restore peace and security to Somalia are critically undermined by a corrosive war economy that corrupts and enfeebles State institutions. . . . The most obvious symptom of the war economy is piracy.'[19] The UN stated that Puntland was at that time still the centre of the piracy industry, and that senior figures in the Puntland administration were involved in the trade:

> Several candidates in the leadership contest of January 2009, which saw Abdirahman Farole accede to the Puntland presidency, accepted significant campaign contributions from pirate leaders. Some notorious pirate leaders remained at liberty in Puntland, and senior officials at times intervened to secure the liberty of kinsmen detained during the course of counter-piracy operations.[20]

The 2010 UN report reflected the most authoritative current source on the organization of piracy within Somalia at the time, other than the research of Stig Jarel Hansen. Ken Menkhaus said, 'There is broad consensus among Somali watchers that the overall findings of this report are right.'[21] However, Robert Young Pelton argued that the UN Monitoring Group reports did not reflect the situation in Somalia completely accurately, as 'the argument could be made that the UN has a conflict of interest in assigning its own people to investigate arms smuggling when it is actually the UN process that allows the unimpeded flow of weapons to al-Shabaab'.[22] He also said that Puntland's PMPF was seen by the Monitoring Group as 'a major source of instability' in the region, on the basis that it was a threat to Somaliland, and that the Monitoring Group also claimed that there had been breaches of the UN's arms embargo by Puntland.[23]

In July 2011 the UN Monitoring Group stated that:

> Puntland has long been a principal hub of piracy, and many pirate leaders and militia are still of Puntland origin. Until late 2010, pirate anchorages were located at Xabo, Bargaal, Bandarbeyla, Eyl, Garacad and a coastal pirate camp was located between Garacad and Eyl. As documented in previous Monitoring Group reports, the attitude of the Puntland authorities was deeply ambiguous, with officials at all levels benefiting from piracy proceeds.[24]

The Puntland authorities did, however, appear to have changed their policies in 2010 and in May they arrested 'Boyah'; at the time of writing in 2014 he still remains in prison. Nonetheless, it is true that in the past many senior pirate leaders and negotiators have in the past operated from Puntland, or have visited with impunity, 'including Mohamed Abdi Garaad, Abdullahi Ahmed Haji Farah (Abdi Yare), Mohamed Saaili Shibin (Ali Jamaa), Abdulkadir Musse Hirsi Nur (Computer), "Bakeyle", [and] Looyaan Si'id Barte (Loyan)'.[25] The Monitoring Group went on to say that convicted pirates have been released on dubious grounds, and cited the case of Abdirashid Muse Mohamed, sentenced to 20 years in prison for the October 2008 hijacking of the MV *Awail*, 'but released in late 2010 by a "presidential pardon" granted to 42 prisoners on the occasion of Eid Holiday'.[26] As always when dealing with Somalia, sorting out the truth from fiction is never easy, if not impossible. It does not seem that the UN Monitoring Group have given Puntland sufficient credit for recent moves against piracy.

The reality, according to reports by the UN and other bodies, is that the Puntland authorities had for many years profited from piracy and human trafficking – that is the smuggling of Somali refugees to Yemen – and the financial problems of the Puntland administration in 2008, when the police could not be paid, served to greatly expand the piracy business. What had been a relatively low-key enterprise, controlled in some measure by the activities of the Puntland authorities, expanded into its full-blown form. Said Shiiq wrote in 2007 that in Puntland, human traffickers, who like pirates have deep connections to the corridors of power, have flourished. In Boosaaso and nearby towns, journalists and other sources sent me the photos of the homes of well-known human traffickers and pirates, whose villas and latest-model Land Cruisers have dazzled me.[27]

The creation of the piracy business model

The development of Puntland's piracy business occurred under Abdillahi Yusuf. It is arguable that the 1989–91 attacks of the SNM, which he controlled, on foreign shipping were the first pirate incidents of recent times off Somalia. The conflict with Jama Ali Jama in 2001–2, which resulted in the removal of the newly appointed president of Puntland and the reimposition of Abdillahi Yusuf in that office, worsened the security situation and ended the collaboration between the British security company Hart Security Maritime Services Ltd and the Puntland authorities, which had started to control fishing using foreign trawlers. Hart did establish the Puntland Coast Guard.[28] After Hart left Puntland, this force became the Somali–Canadian Coast Guard ('SomCan'). Jay Bahadur said:

> There is substantial evidence – including from my own interviews with pirates – that former Hart and SomCan marines turned to piracy. During one of my trips to Puntland, I interviewed a pirate named Ombaali, a sullen and physically stunted youth in his early twenties, who had to be virtually dragged through the door and forced to speak to me. Ombaali, who had served as a 'holder,' or hostage guard, during three pirate operations in 2008, reported that eight members of his extended gang (roughly fifty individuals) had had past histories in the Puntland Coast Guard. 'They were the most experienced at attacking and capturing.'[29]

Bahadur also observed:

> The involvement of ex-Puntland Coast Guard marines in piracy is hardly surprising. The skills and experience possessed by former coast guards – trained to a European standard in sharpshooting, maritime navigation, and boarding and seizure operations – made them perfect employees for the new businesses springing up around the Gulf of Aden.[30]

Abdillahi Yusuf was alleged to be nothing more or less than a warlord who made money through any business opportunity available to him, legal or not. He was only one of many predators, or 'political entrepreneurs', in the Somali environment. Middleton maintained that although men like Abdillahi Yusuf were not directly involved in piracy, they probably benefited from a share in ransom payments, as a 'gesture of goodwill'.[31] Abdirahman Ibrahim, a local academic, made the same point in an interview in 2008: 'You can't have that much money coming in or going out without the top clan people being involved.'[32]

It is an interesting fact that the British government also supported Abdillahi Yusuf financially and medically, by providing him with a house in the United Kingdom, enabling him to have a liver transplant in the Cromwell Hospital in London in 1996, and financing the TFG of which he was head.[33] His stewardship of the TFG saw him and his fellow ministers preside over a brutal and corrupt regime, once the Ethiopian army had cleared Mogadishu. Allegations of torture were commonplace, especially by the TFG's National Security Agency (NSA), which was then headed by General Mohamed Warsame Nur 'Darwiish', a man who until 2006 had earned his living working as a warehouseman in the United Kingdom, at a Tesco depot outside Daventry. It is claimed that the NSA imprisoned hundreds of people on trumped-up charges in the notorious Barista Hisbiga prison, where they were tortured, and that ransoms were demanded in order to secure their release.[34]

In January 2010 Gregory Copley reported that Abdillahi Yusuf was at the time living in exile in Yemen as a guest of President Saleh. His son, and a son of President Saleh, jointly ran a fleet of fishing boats, supposedly seized from their Somali owners by the Yemenis. Copley also alleged that Abdillahi Yusuf and President Saleh had ongoing corrupt business activities. Both men appear to have been effective and successful predatory entrepreneurs.[35]

In November 2008 Abdulaziz Al-Mutairi claimed that 'Piracy, kidnapping and hijacking of ships is the most lucrative profession in Puntland. The leaders of Puntland including Adde Mouse and President of Transitional Government of Somalia (TGS) Abdullah Yousuf [Yusuf] take a lion's share from this illegal business.'[36] He noted that the French forces stationed in Djibouti had arrested six Somali pirates and that 'France confirmed that all six members are kinsmen of Yousuf [Colonel Abdillahi Yusuf] and Moose, and have been identified as former Puntland police officers'.[37] Modern Somali piracy also built on the experience of trafficking people to Yemen from Puntland. Piracy, and the development of Puntland as a criminal safe haven, were planned by leading Somalis, and did not develop because of a reaction of Somali fishermen to foreign trawlers.

Criminal businesses

Piracy is only one facet of the criminal businesses that were based in Puntland: people-smuggling to Yemen was an old-established trade, but immigration fraud also developed as a new venture. The UN Monitoring Group report stated that they were 'aware of several members of a Puntland-based pirate militia who obtained asylum and travel documents in Europe during the course of 2009'.[38] This was more than just another source of income. This was also a security threat to foreign countries. In 2009 the UN Monitoring Group said:

> The activities of Somali armed groups beyond Somalia's borders are facilitated by the widespread practice of immigration fraud. The Monitoring Group has learned that members of Al-Shabaab, Hizbul Islam and pirate militias have taken advantage of this practice in order to gain entry into various European countries, and probably several destinations in North America and Asia also.[39]

In 2009 the UN Monitoring Group reserved its strongest criticisms for developments in Puntland and stated:

> In contrast with central Somalia, where piracy may be accurately described as a product of statelessness and warlordism, in north-eastern Somalia it benefits from the patronage and protection of State institutions.[40]

The UN Monitoring Group confirmed in 2010 that the two centres of pirate activity were the coast of Puntland and the central Somalia littoral east of Xarardheere and Hobyo.[41] They also noted the institutional involvement of the Puntland authorities, saying:

> In north-eastern Somalia, pirate leaders have compromised State institutions at both the local and central levels by co-opting and corrupting government officials.[42]

Without the accommodation of officials in Puntland piracy would have lacked the essential safe haven that allowed the business to operate so successfully. The pirate havens of Xarardheere and Hobyo in the southern Mudug region of central Somalia are less secure, and without the support that was offered by Puntland, it is unlikely that piracy would have developed into such a significant threat to merchant vessels.

Reno said of Puntland in 2003:

> The inability of non-state actors to control political entrepreneurs' access to resources continues to undermine the ability of any single authority to concentrate and control the exercise of coercion. This is reflected in continued incidences of piracy off the Puntland coast.[43]

In other words, predatory warlords in Somalia are beyond control, not subject to law or other sanction. Reno saw the poverty-stricken in the developing countries as being forced into what he called citing Bayart et al., the 'Somali road to development', that is a 'faction based politics centered on violent competition for resources that is incompatible with the existence of a centralized state or expression of a single political community beyond unstable ethnic mini-states and fragmented political affiliations of inhabitants'.[44]

Border disputes and minerals

The borders between Somaliland and Puntland are not defined and the two entities dispute the control of the regions of Sool, Cayn and Sanaag. Somaliland's claim is based on the borders of the old colony of British Somaliland, and Puntland's interest has been in large part driven by the prospect of minerals in these areas, although there are also claims based on clan differences. Conflict has broken out from time to time. In practice, the Warsangeli sub-clan has tried to maintain control of eastern Sanaag, driven by what they regard as exploitive policies by the Puntland leadership who are predominantly from the Majeerten sub-clan. The Majeerten sub-clan is also in conflict with the Sacad sub-clan of the Habargidir clan in the Mudug region, south of Puntland. Fighting was reported in November 2010 in Galkayo town, the capital of the Mudug region, sparked by long-standing disputes over land ownership; 20 people were killed.[45]

The possible impact of oil discoveries in Puntland

Of all the factors that are leading Puntland away from piracy, it is the prospect of becoming a major oil producer that is, in my opinion, the most important. It is difficult to overstate the significance of recent developments – although there is also real concern about the impact piracy has had with Puntland's ability to trade with the rest of the world, as highlighted by President Farole's July 2011 request for help from the UN to free a livestock vessel, and his concern over the hijacking of the UAE tanker *MT Jubba XX*.[46]

In early 2012 there were a series of reports of an oil find in Puntland. In March IRIN published an article referring to the recent discovery of oil deposits in Puntland.[47] African Oil published on its website that it holds 'a 51 per cent equity interest in Horn Petroleum Corp. Horn Petroleum holds interests in 36,168 km^2 (gross) of acreage in respect of the production sharing agreements ("PSAs") in the Dharoor Valley Exploration Area and the Nugaal Valley Exploration Area located in Puntland (Somalia).'[48] The company added that:

> With only 3 wells drilled in the two block areas, this is one of the least explored areas in Africa. Wells that were drilled on the identified structures encountered numerous oil shows; however, the wells Nogal-1 and Kalis-1 did not reach the main exploration target. In the early 1990's civil unrest in the country precipitated the pullout of the oil companies operating in the country at the time including Amoco, Chevron, Agip and Conoco.[49]

However, on 17 May 2012 African Oil announced that it was suspending drilling at its Shabeel well before reaching the planned depth. Horn Petroleum's shares plummeted to less than half their value and African Oil's stock fell 8 per cent.[50] In its 2012 Third Quarter Report, African Oil stated that it had completed a two-well exploration programme in Puntland:

> Both well sites have been restored to original condition and demobilization from Puntland has been completed. While the Company was disappointed that the first two exploration wells in Puntland did not flow oil, the Company remains highly encouraged that all of the critical elements exist for oil accumulations and based on this encouragement the Company and its partners have entered into the next exploration period in both the Dharoor Valley and Nugaal Valley PSC's which carry a commitment to drill one exploration well in each block.[51]

The Puntland government had certainly acted as though it would shortly be an oil producer.

In May 2012 Puntland's president held talks in New Delhi and referred to the recent find in Puntland of a large quantity of oil. *The Hindu* reported that, 'He invited Indian companies to participate in the exploration and sought New Delhi's cooperation for charting out exploration blocks and training Somalis in the petroleum sector.'[52] It seems that his talks were premature. The unresolved question of the role of a regenerated Somali state in controlling Puntland's oil and the extent to which Puntland could retain control in the face of demands from a stronger central government remain.

However, there is no doubt that the possible presence of oil greatly complicates matters when dealing with Puntland. It is a reasonable assumption that President Farole's primary concern was in developing the oil industry, which could bring in billions of dollars. In order to achieve that aim, it is also likely that he was prepared to suppress piracy, and to act in border disputes with Somaliland and with the Warsangeli forcefully. His speeches on the need to control piracy may have therefore been truthful, but he almost certainly had to deal with clan leaders and the other players, who were still profiting from piracy.

Ultimately Farole's struggle (and that of his successor) with the clan leaders, about which we can only speculate, will determine whether Puntland remains a pirate state. In order to achieve this objective, the president requires effective military force, which Puntland has lacked. But military force is a two-edged weapon; it can be used to control piracy and to control disputed territory. The reality is that, unless piracy is controlled, the oil industry will not risk investing the enormous amounts of capital that will be required to develop the capacity to load tankers and pipe the oil from the interior. The port of Bosaso is totally inadequate for its present traffic and there is no way that it can support tankers. Even an offshore loading facility will require massive investment and assured security.

There are a number of interesting possibilities, which actually hold out real hope that the business of piracy could be eradicated from Puntland. The one fact that the leaders of Puntland understand is that oil means money, in vast amounts, and despite the claims of Puntland's former minister for finance, Farah Ali Jama, that any money from oil developments 'will not fall into the pockets of any individual or group. This is for all of the Somali people wherever they may be.'[53] The distribution of oil revenues will be tightly controlled by Puntland's elites.

However, this will create the opportunity to effectively buy out the godfathers of Puntland piracy, as the volume of oil revenue greatly exceeds that from piracy. The problem is that there will be a period between finding oil in commercial quantities and gaining oil revenues. Because Puntland is not a sovereign entity it will, unlike Angola, have difficulty in demanding large advance payments for production agreements and will always need to look over its shoulder at whatever body claims control in Mogadishu. Therefore, it would appear that it is necessary from the prospective of the leader of Puntland and his allies, the PMP or its successor, to become an effective force able to control piracy. Whether this opinion is generally shared is unclear, and it is probable that there are conflicts within the Puntland elites over this policy.

This is all conjecture: how things will actually fall out can only be guessed. However, it is true that there are fundamental issues that will operate within the Somali system at the highest levels. What may happen is that, if oil is found in commercial quantities, struggle will be renewed among Puntland's elites, and that, if the president of Puntland and his supporters are successful, forceful measures will be used to suppress piracy and payments will be made to pirate 'directors' who control the business. In such a case, it would be very likely that conflict with Somaliland could develop for control of the Nugaal Basin, where African Oil and Horn Petroleum hold oil exploration rights. Somaliland will also face pressure to exploit its own possible oil reserves and an additional source of conflict could occur between Puntland and any organization (the successor to the TFG) claiming to represent the government of Somalia.

It is certain that the discovery of oil in commercial quantities in Puntland will be a 'game-changer' in Somali politics, and by enabling elites to replace their income from piracy, it could be the one factor that removes piracy from north-east Somalia. It will also bedevil relationships between the various political entities in Somalia.

Conflict over eastern Sanaag

Alisha Ryu said that 'there has long been a simmering power struggle... for control of Puntland's lucrative commercial hub, Bosasso'.[54] The two oil production-sharing agreements signed between Africa Oil Corporation and their Australian partners, Range Resources Limited, with the government of Puntland on 17 January 2007[55] also encouraged Puntland authorities to move to control eastern Sanaag. The conflict between the Warsangeli and Puntland dates back to 1998 when the Warsangeli declared autonomy. Stig Jarle Hansen, of the Norwegian Institute for Urban and Regional Research in Oslo, said that the situation in eastern Sanaag required extreme caution. He stated that:

The danger is that you could suppress the Warsangeli in a drastic way. Or you could act in a way that mobilizes the Warsangeli to the Shabaab side. So, you can make your predictions come true through your own actions.[56]

In 2006 the Eastern Sanaag Mujahidicen attacked Puntland's security forces over the issue of mineral rights. The Warsangeli, a sub-clan of the Darod, claimed that deals involving its clan territory had been made without their permission. The Warsangeli have also alleged that General Adde and Colonel Abdillahi Yusuf, who were from the Majeerten, another sub-clan of the Darod, were to receive two-thirds of any oil profits generated.[57] Puntland's President Farole also linked the Eastern Sanaag Mujahidicen to Al-Shabaab, and in 2010 said: 'I declare victory over Al-Shabaab terrorists who threaten Puntland's stability.'[58] What is clear is that there has been considerable foreign support over the past few years for Puntland, and the perception that terrorism has been a problem in eastern Sanaag is a major factor in securing this support. By the nature of this type of conflict nothing is in clear sight, but the veil of deception is lifted from time to time. There are allegations of the involvement of mining and oil companies, mercenary companies, rumours of the involvement of the CIA. Alisha Ryu also reported that:

In recent years, the Warsangeli, and other Darod sub-clans in Puntland have complained bitterly about the Puntland Intelligence Service, a counter-terrorism organization created in 2001, and which receives considerable support from the United States. The clan makeup of the powerful service is predominantly Majeerten, and the organization has been accused of working to empower one clan at the expense of others.[59]

It does seem possible that the Puntland administration has pushed local communities out of the Galgala area in order to enable oil companies to operate without constraint: certainly it was alleged by Jaale Cali Justice[60] in 2010 who said that Puntland soldiers burnt farms in Galgala, humiliated women and children in Galgala town, and looted the properties of local people. There are also suggestions that, in addition to oil reserves, there may be large quantities of tin in Galgala.[61]

However, given the stream of misinformation originating from Puntland it is extremely difficult to tell truth from lies. Atom is quoted as denying that he had links to the Islamists groups of southern Somalia: 'I'm neither Al-Shabaab nor [have] links to Islamists groups in southern Somalia, I'm in my home and we are attacked our homes by [the] Puntland president.'[62] In the context of his conflict with President Farole, it appears that the statement that Atom was alleged to have made in July 2010 – 'We shall never stop fighting Puntland. We are part and parcel of Al-Shabaab, we are brothers united by Islamic sharia[63]' – may have been misinformation put out by his opponents; but the likelihood is that Atom is essentially a Warsangeli clan militia leader who has been forced to ally with Al-Shabaab in order to secure the material he needs to fight Puntland's incursions into his clan's territory.

The UN Monitoring Group, in its July 2011 report, mentioned that:

In early 2010, Atom entered into indirect negotiations with the Puntland administration, through the mediation of Warsengeli clan elders. According to a source close to the negotiations, the Al-Shabaab leadership in Mogadishu sent emissaries to pressure Atom to break off the talks. One was Yasiin Kilwe, a Warsengeli associate of Shabaab emir Ahmed Abdi Godane, who was released in 2009 from prison in Hargeysa after having served a six-year prison term; another was reportedly Mohamud Mohamed Nur Faruur, a leading Al-Shabaab figure from the Habar Je'elo clan from eastern Toghdeer region.[64]

In September 2010, Puntland forces captured Atom's base at Galgala. The UN Monitoring Group reported: 'At least one of Atom's senior commanders, Jaama' Osman Du'ale, was killed in the fighting, together with several dozen other fighters, and Atom himself was reportedly wounded in the upper arm/shoulder.' As a result of this setback and Atom's injury, the UN Monitoring Group observed: 'Atom has been driven even closer to Al-Shabaab, travelling to Mogadishu for medical treatment and spent the first half of 2011 between Mogadishu and Kismaayo, seeking military and financial assistance for his forces.'[65]

In January 2011 Puntland's deputy minister of home security, Abdi Jamal Osman Mohammed, told reporters in Bosaso that the Somaliland administration had repeatedly issued hostile public statements regarding Puntland's fighting in eastern Sanaag. He said:

We want to clarify that Puntland Government security forces have duties to defend the state by fighting terrorists, pirates, human traffickers and all forms of organized crime, Puntland government forces are obligated to ensure internal security and stability. Therefore, it is a big surprise that the Somaliland administration sees this security effort as a threat.

He also implied that Somaliland was providing a safe haven for militants by organizing support for fleeing remnants of what he claimed were Al-Shabaab terrorists, who had been fighting in the Galgala area.[66] In other words, the Puntland administration insisted that the Eastern Sanaag Mujahidicen was just a branch of Al-Shabaab, and that by implication Somaliland was supporting Al-Shabaab. Mohamed Abdillahi Omer, Somaliland's minister for foreign affairs, told Reuters: 'Puntland's concern about Somaliland and Al-Shabaab is baseless.'[67] He added that Somaliland is a democratic state with universal democratic values abhorred by Al-Shabaab.[68] In the midst of these conflicts the mineral companies continued their exploration.

It seems as if the conflict in eastern Sanaag could cease to be just a fight between Puntland and the Eastern Sanaag Mujahidicen – though there seem to have been no recent incidents there. Somaliland has a real interest in this area, and the Puntland government has been gearing itself for conflict. In January 2011 the US State Department did try to organize a meeting between President Farole and Somaliland President Ahmed Silanyo in an attempt to defuse tensions.

The role of Saracen in the development of the Puntland Maritime Police Force

Puntland stepped up its military training programme by notably signing a contract in November 2010 with a firm called Saracen International in order to develop the Puntland Maritime Police Force (PMPF). A Puntland press release stated that this force would have 'the mandate to protect the international maritime line off the coast of Puntland as well as the marine

Figure 4.1 The badge of the Puntland Maritime Police Force

resources of the State of Puntland'[69] (Figure 4.1). President Farole referred to Puntland's plan in October 2011, when he announced that:

> Puntland has planned to establish a Maritime Police Force, for which we sought support for almost three years.... Thanks to the United Arab Emirates, we received support to establish a Maritime Police Force mandated to fight pirates and protect marine resources. But it is unfortunate that politically motivated elements have sought to create obstacles against the establishment of our anti-piracy force.[70]

The UN Monitoring Group, in its July 2011 report, was extremely critical of Saracen and its operations in Somalia, including its activities in Puntland developing what was originally known as the Puntland Anti-Piracy Marine Force. The Monitoring Group stated that:

> Between May 2010 and February 2011, Saracen has provided military training, equipment and vehicles to a military force, and deployed armed, foreign security personnel on Somali territory, in the initial phases of an operation that would have become the largest externally supported military activity in Somalia, after AMISOM.[71] [The Monitoring Group] believes that Saracen's operations since May 2010 represent a significant violation of the general and complete arms embargo on Somalia, which prohibits 'all deliveries of weapons and military equipment' and requires that any 'supplies and technical assistance ... intended solely for the purpose of helping develop security sector institutions' be authorised by the Security Council Committee pursuant to resolutions 751 (1992) and 1907 (2009) concerning Somalia and Eritrea. It is also the opinion of the Monitoring Group that Saracen's activities to date have represented a threat to peace and security in Somalia.[72]

The Puntland authorities notified the UN Monitoring Group in May 2011 that the agreements between Puntland and Saracen had been terminated.[73] Sterling Corporate Services then took over the contract until the summer of 2012.

Associated Press quoted a former US government official who, speaking anonymously, said that 'besides targeting pirates, the new force in Puntland will go after a warlord who allegedly supplies weapons to al-Shaba[a]b, Somalia's most feared insurgent group'.[74] This statement appears to confirm the view that one objective of the Saracen contract with Puntland was to fight Atom and secure the disputed territory in eastern Sanaag and Galgala. Other Americans involved in the Puntland operation reportedly include a former US ambassador, Pierre Prosper, and a senior ex-CIA officer, Michael Shanklin.[75]

On 31 October 2010, the MV *Noora Moon 1* delivered approximately 500 metric tons of equipment and hardware for Saracen's Puntland compound at Bandar Siyada, Bosaso, including construction vehicles and also 85 pick-up trucks. The Monitoring Group also noted that: 'Between October 2010 and February 2011, Saracen also chartered fifteen flights to Somalia from the United Arab Emirates and Uganda, involving two Antonov An-32 cargo aircraft operated by Ayk Avia, carrying supplies for the Saracen training camp in Puntland.'[76] Logistical support was provided by the Puntland Development Group, which used a number of ships including the MV *Seafarer* and the escort vessel MV *Eaton* (formerly operated by Blackwater as the MV *McArthur*). There was no doubt that in the period 2011–12 a substantial amount of materiel was delivered to Puntland and that the basis was laid for an effective military force, which had the potential to be the most effective military force under Somali command. It was also clear that the training had only just begun to deliver results and the men were not battle-hardened soldiers. The key to the successes enjoyed by the force in the first half of 2012 was almost certainly the actions of its trainers, who were mainly South Africans. There is no doubt that piracy cannot be eradicated in Puntland without such a force.

Conflict continued to erupt from time to time on the eastern border of Somaliland, including a fight in February 2011 between Somaliland forces and the Sool Sanaag Cayn (SSC) militia. Gaalmudug, Puntland's southern neighbour, also expressed its concerns, and on 6 December 2010, the leader of the Gaalmudug regional administration alleged that Saracen's activities were part of a Puntland campaign to disrupt and destabilize Gaalmudug.[77] The Monitoring Group concluded that: 'Saracen's presence has increased tension in north-eastern Somalia because its operations are perceived as a military threat by Puntland's neighbours, as well as by some parts of the Puntland population.'[78] Their report confirmed that:

It is the Monitoring Group's assessment that Warsengeli apprehension over the Saracen programme has engendered support within the clan for Mohamed Said 'Atom', a Warsengeli militia leader linked to Al-Shabaab' and that 'such concerns are justified. The first units and platoons of the 'Puntland Marine Force' trained by Saracen are intended to serve as an elite land unit for the Puntland administration. Saracen's claim that its personnel and trainees are engaged in 'humanitarian' operations in no way alters the fundamentally military character and role of this force, or the adverse impact of its presence on peace and security in the region.[79]

After the suspension of the Puntland counter-piracy force in February 2011, in the light of critical reaction from several UN agencies, the force engaged in humanitarian work until training resumed by a private security company called Sterling Corporate Services. Some of Saracen's staff worked for Sterling.[80] The PMPF established its own website,[81] which reported on the force's activities, including securing the town of Iskushuban against a force of pirates.[82] On 26 May 2012 the PMPF entered Hafun and captured seven pirates, including Dhafoor, second in command to Isse Yulux, who was in charge of the group who kidnapped the Johansen family in their yacht *SY ING*.[83] This followed on from the PMPF's move into Eyl in February 2012, where they established a presence in a town that was formally a major pirate base.[84] On 6 June 2012 the PMPF attacked Isse Yulux and his gang near Bali Dhidden, but failed to capture him.

It appears that no single company replaced Sterling Corporate Services after its relationship with the PMPF ended in June 2012. Instead a number of South Africans managed the force, but this did not stop it continuing to undertake operations, including its successful operation in December 2012 against the Panama-flagged MV *Iceberg 1* in the coastal town of Gara'ad. The MV *Iceberg 1* had been hijacked on 29 March 2010 and the PMPF rescued all its 22 crew members after an operation, which lasted two weeks. South African Roelf van Heerden commanded the PMPF during the operation.[85]

As noted above, security is a key element of any plans to develop an oil industry, as onshore and offshore operations require protection. This involves an effective, well-equipped and trained force. Piracy needs to be controlled before oil can be exported. In July 2012 the UN Monitoring team also criticized another security force deployed in Puntland, called the Exploration Security Unit (ESU) and formed at the end of 2011. Commanded by Lieutenant Colonel Aadan, it consisted of a force of over 300 armed men and was responsible to the Puntland minister for security, General Khalif Isse Mudan. The ESU was trained by Pathfinder Corporation, a South African company with the involvement of Salama Fikira of Kenya. The personnel in the ESU were hired from among the ranks of the Puntland army and police. ESU's purpose was to provide security for the operations of the company Horn

111

Petroleum and the staff of the firm Canmex, which were in partnership with Africa Oil. The UN Monitoring Team in their July 2012 report[86] stated that

> Pathfinder's transparency and its efforts to comply with the sanctions regime arguably represent 'best practices' for private security companies in Somalia. However, its 'temporary issue' of military equipment and the direct funding of the Exploration Security Unit by Africa Oil (through its subsidiary Canmex Holdings) constitute violations of Security Council resolution 733 (1992).[87]

Puntland's neighbours fear that these forces could equally well be used to extend the territory under Puntland's control.

Robert Young Palton maintains that the UN Monitoring Group reports were not fair in their assessment of the PMPF. He says that the claims that the PMPF were in breach of the UN arms embargo were incorrect and that it was approved by the TFG on 14 December 2011.[88] Certainly the activities of the PMPF in the first half of 2012 bore out the claims made for it by its supporters; it put its training to good effect and was successfully used to suppress piracy. The UN Monitoring Group described the PMPF as a 'well-equipped elite force, over 1,000 strong, with air assets used to carry out ground attacks, that operates beyond the rule of law and reports directly to the President of Puntland'. They then referred to the PMPF as a 'private army disingenuously labelled a "counter-piracy" force'.[89] They added that the PMPF represented a 'flagrant breach of the sanctions regime in Somalia, characterized by a disturbing lack of transparency, accountability or regard for international law'.[90]

It is difficult to see what else the Puntland administration could have done in these circumstances, and in my opinion these statements fail to give credit to the PMPF for its actions against pirate groups, which were becoming increasingly effective. While it is true that such forces could be used against neighbouring political entities, such a local force will be essential to remove piracy from the coast of Somalia. There can never be total clarity in Somalia and the political forces at work in Puntland are complex; nothing is clear cut; pirate backers undoubtedly have had power and probably retain the ability to influence some decisions, but the prospect of oil production has, in my opinion, significantly undermined their power, if not removed it entirely.

Puntland has been the centre most closely associated with piracy, but it does seem to be changing, probably because its leaders understand that oil revenue cannot be realized unless piracy is suppressed. Puntland has jailed Abshir Boyah, an important pirate leader, who was captured in May 2010 in

Garowe. It has also taken an active role in the UNODC Counter-Piracy Programme; working on a two-year advocacy campaign that issues anti-piracy messages and works to develop alternative employment for those who may be drawn into piracy. In collaboration with UNODC Puntland is constructing a new prison at Garowe.[91] It does seem that the authorities in Puntland are working to put their past behind them and that, although it is likely that 'retired' pirate leaders can still be found in the country, the active centres of piracy have been pushed to the south. Certainly it is worth giving Puntland a chance; it has its issues, but nothing in Somalia is risk-free.

The prize is the removal of the main centres of pirate activity in Somalia, something that can only be done by Somalis operating onshore.

PIRACY IN CENTRAL AND SOUTHERN SOMALIA

The key political and economic drivers in central and southern Somalia today are not terrorism, or the actions of patriots seeking to restore law and order, but the activities of criminal gangs and foreign powers. The UN Monitoring Group reported in 2008 that:

> Armed criminal groups are typically self-financing, employing the proceeds from piracy and kidnapping to procure arms, ammunition and equipment. Some of these groups now rival or surpass established Somali authorities in terms of their military capabilities and resource bases.... The evolution of the Puntland and central Somalia piracy networks owes much to the relationships between a small number of key figures.[92]

Two of the three key players were Garaad Mohamud Mohamed and Mohamed Abdi Hassan 'Afweyne', both leaders of the central Somalia network based in Xarardheere. The Monitoring Group also had information that in 2005 Farah Hirsi Kulan 'Boyah' joined them in joint operations.[93] Although this partnership was interrupted by a clash in 2007, by early 2008 the two groups were again cooperating, using Eyl as their main operational base. The UN Monitoring Group said that its sources 'identify Boyah as a principal organizer and financier of pirate activities'.[94] However, since 2010 Boyah has been imprisoned in a Puntland jail.

Afweyne, as of 2012, enjoyed the status of a TFG 'diplomat' and carried a diplomatic passport issued by TFG officials with the authorization of Somali President Sheikh Sharif; which demonstrated that he was protected by the TFG hierarchy.[95] It is also important to note that the central Somalia network always had strong links to Puntland, and one commentator even suggested the initial impetus for the establishment of the pirate network in Mudug was not merely an idea developed by Afweyne, but that the Puntland political elite encouraged such a development outside the area of their direct control in order to divert attention from Puntland and to increase their 'take' of pirate revenue. Such an initiative would of course be 'deniable'. Afweyne's development of Somali piracy into the criminal enterprise that it is today is explained below.

The southern pirate groups

In May 2006 the UN Monitoring Group identified three pirate groups operating in south and central Somalia:

(1) the National Volunteer Coast Guard (NVCG), which 'focuses on intercepting small boats and fishing vessels; it operates close to shore in the greater area of Kismaayo, along the southern coast of Somalia. Its leader/commander is Mohamed Garaad';[96]

(2) the Marka groups, which include several scattered and less well-organized small groups, and is based in the greater Marka area of Lower Shebelle. In the words of the May 2006 report:

They generally have fishing boats and fleets with longer operating ranges than NVCG. Their boats, in some cases, have guns mounted on the decks. These groups intercept a variety of types of vessels. They participate in sea robbery, smuggling and piracy activities and are financed by Sheik Yusuf Indohaadde, warlord and Governor of Lower Shebelle;[97]

(3) the Somali Marines (also known as the Defenders of Somali Territorial Waters), described as follows:

Organizationally and operationally, these are the most sophisticated of all Somali pirate groups. They are organized along military lines, with a Fleet Admiral (Mohamed Ali Hassan), Admiral (Mohamed Osman), Vice Admiral (General 'Gray', head of marine operations) and head of financial operations (Afweyne). They appear to have the capability to operate at a greater distance offshore than the other pirate groups and participate in acts of piracy involving vessel seizure, kidnapping and ransom demands. They operate in areas in the central Somalia coastal region, including off... Haradheere (Xarardheere), their main base area, and Eyl, a satellite location north of Haradheere.[98]

Xarardheere is about 18 kilometres away from the Indian Ocean coast, and its inhabitants are mainly members of the Habar Gidir Saleebaan sub-clan.

The Somali Marines were well-established before 2006, when the UN Monitoring Group reported that the UIC had gained control of Xarardheere, having banned piracy. The UN noted that, in November 2006, since the takeover by the UIC, 'there have been no acts of piracy along the central and southern coastal area.'[99] The removal of the UIC, as a result of the Ethiopian invasion, enabled the Somali Marines to return to their original base.

By 2009 piracy was again in full flow. The UN Monitoring Group considered Somali-based piracy to be a fundamentally criminal activity attributable to specific militia groups and 'families'.[100] In March 2010 the UN Monitoring Group reported that: 'Since October 2009, the main focus of pirate attacks has shifted from the Gulf of Aden to the Indian Ocean. This shift has reinforced the importance of piracy hubs at Xarardheere and Hobyo in the southern Mudug region.'[101]

PIRATE LEADERS

The organization of Somali piracy

In the political economy of modern Somalia a series of different classes of 'predatory entrepreneurs' has emerged – this term is copied from William Reno. At the top are the leaders of major factions, who are either leaders of militias ('warlords'), such as Mohamed Omar Habib (Mohamed 'Dheere') and Muse Sudi Yalahow, or former politicians, and a handful of important businessmen who fund their operations and exploit any opportunity for enrichment, whether it is the supply of food aid by the WFP, piracy, or the supply of funds and arms from foreign states. Abdillahi Yusuf was the stereotypical predatory entrepreneur. As Reno says, his support from the Ethiopians enabled him to loot his own community,[102] and he simultaneously presented himself to international donors as a Somali statesman, becoming president of the TFG. His example is a lesson to those Somalis who have followed in his footsteps: dissembling and falsehood are their watchwords.

Most of the pirate leaders have been solely concerned with the business of hijacking ships, but the wealth generated from ransoms has in recent years enabled the most influential pirate leaders to influence political leaders, for example by funding Puntland politicians campaigns, and even engaging in discussions with the late Colonel Gaddafi. The principal pirate leaders command hundreds, if not thousands, of ordinary fighters, prepared to risk their lives on a daily basis in small boats far out at sea, hoping for a share in a multi-million dollar ransom. Somali pirates are criminals, not the protectors of Somali maritime resources that they sometimes like to portray themselves as. But those who go out to sea in tiny skiffs are desperate and brave men, and many hundreds have lost their lives from thirst and the normal dangers of the deep ocean. Their leaders have been effective and successful organizers and, despite their often humble origins, have run complex businesses with international connections; they should never be underestimated.

In his statement to the UK House of Lords, Rear Admiral Hudson said that piracy,

is like a balloon: it will pop up elsewhere. We have seen the pirates move out into the Somali Basin using motherships, long-range skiffs towing attack skiffs behind them, using things such as the currents which run off the Somali coast to get out into the deep Indian Ocean. They loiter near those north/south shipping routes knowing that distance will always be my constraint and I cannot get to them as frequently as I would like. They have altered their patterns and eased back on the Gulf of Aden, concentrating their efforts in the Somali Basin. The weather has been good for that. I think that, as the north easterly monsoon cuts in, we may see them return to the Gulf of Aden. So these are adaptive organisations. They look at the conditions, they look at where the military forces are and that is how they are able to exploit the weaknesses in our armour.[103]

Mohamed Abdi Hassan 'Afweyne'

Hansen says that the Hobyo-Xarardheere cartel 'set the stage for current day piracy and put Somalia piracy on the international map', and that it was created by one man – Mohamed Abdi Hassan 'Afweyne'.[104] Afweyne is the father of modern Somali piracy, and the key figure in its development.

Afweyne was a civil servant and, according to Hansen, in 2003 he realized that there was real money in piracy and sought investors for his new venture. There is another view of Afweyne's inspiration, that is, that he was actually asked to undertake the work of setting up a new pirate base away from Puntland, but one that was always linked by an umbilical cord with the men who controlled Puntland at the time, particularly the late Abdillahi Yusuf, the man who dominated Puntland's affairs for so long.

A native of Xaradheere from the Suleiman clan of the Hawiye family, he made his home town a major pirate base. From the beginning he showed his skills as an organizer, hand-picked his operatives and 'carefully designed [his pirate group] to keep costs low, profits high and to maximize efficiency'.[105] Afweyne headhunted veteran pirates from Puntland. Garaad Mohamud Mohamed, Abshir Boyah and Farah Abdillahi travelled to Mudug to train Afweyne's new group, thus creating a *de facto* clan alliance with the Majeerten clan. Southern Mudug proved to be an ideal pirate base, relatively quiet and without any strong resident political group that could demand a share of ransom money.[106]

In central Somalia, the Afweyne family has, according to the UN Monitoring Group, 'succeeded in co-opting elements of the local community, mainly from the Habar Gidir Saleebaan sub-clan, through the distribution of wealth'.[107] Afweyne took a leading role in pirate operations centred on Xarardheere and Hobyo. However, in recent years, his son, Abdiqadir, has also led pirate attacks. The UN Monitoring Group said in 2008 that:

> Credible sources have confirmed Afweyne's and Abdiqaadir's involvement, individually or jointly, in the hijackings of at least seven vessels during the course of the mandate: the passenger cruise ship *Indian Ocean Explorer* (2 April 2009), the container ship *Hansa Stavanger* (4 April 2009), the dredger *Pompei* (18 April 2009), the bulk carrier *Ariana* (2 May 2009), the fishing vessel *Alakrana* (2 October 2009), the container ship *Kota Wajar* (15 October 2009) and the bulk carrier *De Xin Hai* (19 October 2009).[108]

He is a man of importance in Somalia and was a guest in Tripoli in September 2009, at Colonel Gaddafi's fortieth anniversary celebrations.[109] During his visit to Libya in 2009 it is reported that Afweyne spoke to Libyan officials and probably also to Colonel Gaddafi. On 23 September 2009, in his statement before the General Assembly of the UN in New York, Colonel Gaddafi, acknowledged that he had met with Somali pirates, spoke in their defence, and 'called upon States to respect Somalia's exclusive economic zone'.[110]

He is now believed to have retired from operational piracy. The Monitoring Group reports this has been taken over by his son Abdiqadir:

'Afweyne nevertheless continues to profit from the piracy business, since he dominates the local *qaad* trade – a highly lucrative enterprise.'[111] In October 2013 Abdi Hassan and his associate Tiiceey were arrested at Brussels Airport after they were lured to Belgium with the offer of acting as advisor to film producers making a film based on Hassan's life. They were put on trial on charges of kidnapping and membership of a criminal organization.[112]

Garaad Mohamud Mohamed

In an interview with *The Globe and Mail* in 2009 Garaad claimed that he undertook piracy with the sole objective of defending his livelihood and that of his fellow fishermen. He comes from the port of Eyl, a well-known pirate base, located in northern Nugaal and in the southern part of Puntland's territory. He began his career as a frontline pirate, participating directly in hijackings and rose through the ranks to become one of the better known organizers and financiers in Puntland. He is a member of the Majeerten/Issa Mohamud/Musa Issa sub-clan, as are Puntland's President Abdirahman Mohamed 'Farole' and Boyah. As noted above, he was one of the original trainers of Afweyne's pirate group. He claims to be poor, but Jay Bahadur says that 'when he took his third bride, the wedding procession included 100 vehicles'. It is also alleged that he was involved in the lucrative hijacking of the MV *Faina*, the Ukrainian ro-ro vessel, laden with tanks, which were later delivered to the South Sudanese.[113]

The UN Monitoring Group said in 2008 that he was a 'well-known figure in Puntland, who in media interviews has described himself as a pirate leader with responsibility for 13 maritime militia groups comprising at least 800 pirates'. The Monitoring Group believes that he is responsible, solely, or with others, for the hijacking of the Panama-flagged, Japanese-operated bulk carrier *Stella Maris* (20 July 2008), the MV *BBC Trinidad* (21 August 2008), the MV *Iran Deyanat* (21 August 2008) and the MV *Bunga Melati Dua* (18 August 2008).

Garaad was also the leader of the pirate group that attacked the *Maersk Alabama* a US-flagged container ship off the coast of Somalia in April 2009. During the three-day confrontation with American forces, Garaad conducted two media interviews by satellite phone, in which he identified himself as the leader of the pirates. After three of his gangs were killed, he threatened revenge against US vessels and crews.[114] He attempted to put his threats into effect by attacking the MV *Liberty Sun* on 13 April 2009; she was a US-flagged vessel carrying food aid to Somalia. In an interview with Agence France Presse, Garaad acknowledged responsibility for the attack and stated that the aim was revenge:

> The aim of this attack was totally different. We were not after a ransom. We also assigned a team with special equipment to chase and destroy any ship flying the American flag in retaliation for the brutal killing of our friends.[115]

It is suggested that Garaad's pirate group may also have been involved in the three-day hijacking of the Togolese-flagged MV *Sea Horse* on 14 April 2009. The *Sea Horse* was en route to India, where it was due to load food for Somalia organized by the WFP. The Monitoring Group stated that it, 'considers Garaad and his militia to have committed multiple violations of Security Council resolution 1844 (2008), which prohibits the obstruction of humanitarian assistance'. The March 2010 UN Report[116] also noted that the Puntland authorities have yet to take any action to apprehend Garaad, or curb his activities.

Hansen says that:

> Garaad Muhammed and Afweyne (and his sons), remain active, enjoying a special position due to their role as coordinators and pioneers. They also seem to play a special role in recruitment where, since they are well known, potential recruits will approach them for contacts among the pirate groups. However, they are less important today than before.[117]

There is some uncertainty about the numbers of men under his command: Garaad claims to control about 800 men in 13 groups, but others rejects this, saying that in 2008 he only controlled a core group of between 20–30. Perhaps the reality is that while his core group is small, he sits at the centre of a much larger network. Garaad is actually one of the best-known and most respected pirates in Somalia: men seek him out and he retains immense influence, although he may not be as active as he was in the past.

Like Afweyne, Garaad appears to have considerable political influence, and Hansen says, 'it has even been alleged that president Farole of Puntland met with Garaad Mohamud Mohamed in Garowe before he met with Hillary Clinton in Nairobi'.[118] At the end of 2010 *Lloyd's List* put him at number four in a list of the 100 most influential people in the shipping industry. The three people ranked above him were China's transport minister, Li Shenglin, chief executive of Maersk Nils Andersen, and the billionaire shipping magnate John Fredriksen. Commenting on Garaad's inclusion, *Lloyd's List* said:

> While the international effort to curb piracy has continued apace, the unpalatable truth is that Somali piracy is running ahead of current efforts to combat it. Where shipping has been struggling in the current market, piracy business is booming – and for every successful ransom payment they become increasingly sophisticated. What was once a cottage industry is now big business and piracy gangs boast quasi-corporate structures with all the trappings of a growing conglomerate. We have even seen evidence of mergers and (hostile) takeovers, as pirate clans seek to dominate the market. In short – the piracy business is booming.[119]

Abshir Abdillahi 'Boyah'

The third most famous pirate in Somalia is Boyah (or 'Boya'). The March 2010 UN Monitoring Group Report said of Boyah that he is, 'Probably the most notorious pirate leader in Puntland'. His full name is Abshir Abdillahi 'Boyah'. He was probably born in 1966 and, like Garaad, is originally from Eyl. Like Garaad he helped train Afweyne's original pirate group, and is one of the recognized founders of modern Somalia piracy. He has a number of aliases and has been known as Farah Hirsi Kulan.[120]

The UN Monitoring Group says that:

> Boyah himself has publicly admitted to being the commander of a maritime militia consisting of approximately 500 pirates. By Boyah's own account, his militia is responsible for hijacking between 25 and 60 shipping vessels since the mid-1990s, including the Japanese-owned chemical tanker *Golden Nori* (28 October 2007) and the French luxury yacht *Le Ponant* (4 April 2008), for which Boyah received $1.5 million and $2 million respectively in ransom payments.[121]

The Monitoring Group noted that Puntland leaders were not only well aware of Boyah's activities, but also tolerated them. In April 2009, a foreign journalist interviewed Boyah, and President Farole's son Mohamed (now the president's media adviser) assisted in setting up the meeting.[122] In order to be interviewed by another journalist, Boyah had to 'cut right through a crowd of Puntland soldiers' to enter a local restaurant.[123] The UN Monitoring Group cites an interview Boyah gave in August 2008, in which he claimed that Puntland leaders received 30 per cent of ransom payments as a bribe.[124] He also made this allegation in an interview with Hansen.[125] Therefore, the reluctance of the Puntland authorities to arrest one of their paymasters is understandable. In May 2009, Boyah attended a ceremony with local government officials in Eyl, where he claimed that, together with 180 of his militia, he had realized that piracy was unlawful and ceased his activities. The Puntland authorities have since made no move to apprehend him and declined to respond to a Monitoring Group request for information concerning measures taken to curb his activities. It was reported in May 2010 that he had been taken prisoner in Garowe and is now serving a term of imprisonment in Puntland.

Mohamed Abdi 'Garfanji'

Mohamed Abdi 'Garfanji' is head of the largest pirate militia in the Hobyo-Xarardheere area.

Fu'aad Warsame Seed, 'Hanaano'

On 23 June 2008 a pirate gang consisting of members of the Deshiishe, Ali Saleebaan and Warsengeli clans, kidnapped a retired German couple in their yacht, the *Rockall*, off the Somali coast in the Gulf of Aden. After 52 days in captivity at the port village of Laasqoray (Las Qoray), which is west of Bosaso, on the north coast of Puntland, the couple was released after a ransom of about $1 million had been paid. The UN Monitoring Group said that the man responsible for the hijacking of the *Rockall* was Fu'aad Warsame Seed, also known as 'Hanaano', a 45- to 50-year-old member of the Warsengeli/Reer Haaji sub-clan who learned the trade of piracy operating from Eyl. 'Hanaano' operates further north than the main pirate groups, and leads the eastern Sanaag pirate militia. The eastern Sanaag is a mountainous area on the north coast of Somalia, between Puntland and Somaliland, populated mainly by the Warsengeli sub-clan of the Harti Daarood, who have a long history of smuggling, transporting refugees to Yemen and trafficking arms.

With the profits of his ventures, Hanaano returned to Sanaag and established a militia of his own, approximately 50–60 men equipped with several gun-mounted 'technical' vehicles, PK general purpose machine guns, RPG launchers, a combination of Heckler and Koch G-3 semi-automatic rifles, AK-47s and SAR-80 assault rifles. Members of this militia include Hanaano's son, Omar Hassan Osman 'Baqalyo', and Ali Dhego-Libaax.

The UN also states that after the hijacking of the *Rockall*, Hanaano and his militia hijacked the Turkish chemical tanker *Karagöl* on 12 November 2008, two Egyptian fishing vessels, *Mumtaz 1* and *Samara Ahmed* on 10 April 2009, and the Italian tugboat *Buccaneer* on 11 April 2009.[126] However, on 29 April 2009, 13 of Hanaano's pirate gang men set out into the Gulf of Aden in two skiffs, in search of a vessel to attack, but suffered an engine failure, and then ran out of fuel. Drifting off the coast of Somaliland these men were arrested by the Somaliland coastguard on 5 May 2009 and taken into custody. On 15 October 2009 Hanaano and seven of his men were arrested at sea by the Yemenis and imprisoned in Sana'a.

The Puntland minister of the interior, General Abdillahi Ahmed Jama 'Ilkajiir', a former military officer, is also a member of the Warsengeli sub-clan. When Ilkajiir returned to Somalia from the United States in 2008 to contest the Puntland presidency, it is claimed that Hanaano contributed over $200,000 to his unsuccessful campaign. Hanaano's investment in Ilkajir had resulted earlier in Ilkajiir reportedly proposing Hanaano for the position of 'Eastern Sanaag Coastguard Commander'. Puntland authorities, in particular Ilkajiir, also successfully pressured Egypt to release members of Hanaano's pirate gang after they were taken prisoner by the Egyptian crew of the *Mumtaz 1* and the *Samara Ahmed* who succeeded in overpowering their hijackers. In September 2009 the pirates were repatriated to Puntland. This was not the only favour performed by Ilkajiir for Hanaano's gang. On 30 November 2009, Puntland security forces reportedly arrested Omar Hassan Osman 'Baqalyo', one of the leaders of the gang, in Bosaso on charges unrelated to piracy; it is said that he was released on 5 December 2009, on Ilkajiir's orders.[127]

Atom and the Eastern Sanaag Mujahidicen

The conflict between Puntland and the Eastern Sanaag Mujahidicen has been dealt with previously. In 2010 the UN Monitoring Group believed that Mohamed Sa'iid Atom's militia group, the Eastern Sanaag Mujahidicen, posed 'a growing threat to peace and security in both Puntland and Somaliland'.[128] As noted above, Atom and his group are a threat to the business and political interests of President Farole of Puntland. Atom continued to import arms from Yemen and to receive consignments from Eritrea, including 120 mm mortars; these arms were almost certainly for fighting Puntland. There were also reports that Atom had completed construction of an airfield near his Galgala base, which enabled him to fly in supplies.[129] Atom appears to be an independent force in the north-east, a threat to the Puntland authorities, and an effective clan leader; his current involvement with piracy is unclear.

THE ORIGINS OF MODERN SOMALI PIRACY

Large-scale piracy is a recent problem in Somalia, which dates back only to 2004–5, although, as noted previously, small-scale piracy off Somalia first occurred before the collapse of Barre's regime. Hansen summarizes the development of Somali piracy as follows:

> Piracy could be said to have started as early as in 1989, but it completely disappeared in 1992. It re-emerged in 1993, and 1994–1995 saw an increase, 1996 again saw a decline, from 1997 and until 2000, there was a slow increase, then it stabilized and increased slightly. Piracy exploded in 2004-2005, putting Somalia on the international maritime security map for the first time, but then it declined in 2006. In 2008 piracy again exploded.[130]

From the perspective of those dealing with Somali piracy today, the key piracy developments were in Puntland particularly after 2004, as Puntland came under greater financial pressure and Yusuf was appointed interim president of the TFG, after a lengthy process sponsored by the international community. In April 2008, after Puntland stopped paying its police force, piracy increased within a month.[131] As noted, the other largest piracy centre in southern Mudug developed because of the work of Afweyne. By 2004 Afweyne created what Hansen calls the first 'golden age' of Somali piracy. The reduction of piracy in 2006 was due to the decision of the UIC to oppose piracy and make it illegal. The invasion of Somalia by Ethiopia, which overthrew the UIC, enabled piracy to re-emerge.

Hansen notes that: 'In the autumn of 2006, the Supreme Council of Islamic Courts (SCIC) decided to end piracy, publicly claiming that piracy was *Haraam* (against Islam).'[132] By spring 2007, the SCIC had virtually eradicated piracy in central Somalia. One of the ironies of the Somali system is that the most effective opponents of piracy (apart from the government of Somaliland, which is not part of the territory we are currently considering) have been Islamic groups. However, the international community has sought to isolate these groups and impose the self-appointed TFG upon the country. In May 2010, another Islamic group, the Hizbul Islam, entered Xarardheere, sending the pirates fleeing from the town. Whether this move was an attack on piracy or part of their ongoing conflict with another Islamic group, the Al-Shabaab, was not clear.[133] The West has too readily seen Islamic groups as potential partners with pirate gangs, but no clear evidence for such assertions has so far been uncovered.

FISHING AND THE JUSTIFICATION FOR PIRACY

One of the recurring myths of Somali piracy is that the pirates originally regarded themselves as an unofficial coastguard protecting Somali waters from foreign fishing boats that were stealing their catch. This is a justification that the pirates are only too ready to repeat, and there is clearly strong feeling within Somalia that Far Eastern trawlers, especially Thai and Taiwanese, and Spanish fleets have stolen millions of dollars of fish from the country. A sense of vengeance is felt when Spanish and French trawlers, together with Far Eastern tuna boats, are hijacked, and there is an edge to such attacks, which needs to be acknowledged. However, Hansen makes it clear that, since modern Somali piracy started, the main targets have been merchant ships, and he says that it should not be forgotten that:

> The name 'Coast Guard' brought pirates advantages during their start-up phase in the 1990s. Several crewmembers of cargo ships falling victim to early acts of piracy claimed that the coast guard term partly came in use for practical reasons; in the early 1990s, it allowed pirates to hail ships and get them to slow down by claiming to be Somali coast guard forces.[134]

It is true that some writers, like Ken Menkhaus, maintain that piracy on the greater Gulf of Aden has evolved as a defensive strategy against exploitation by foreign vessels. Menkhaus says, 'In 1991, foreign fishing trawlers aggressively moved into Somalia's rich and unpatrolled waters, at the expense of coastal fishing villages. Angry Somali fishermen secured weapons and began firing on foreign trawlers.'[135] Hansen contradicts these claims by pointing out that Somali pirates seem to have always hunted for profit, and that 'it is the easiest and most valuable targets, slow-moving cargo ships usually with no ties whatsoever to illegal fishing, that are the most popular victims in the 1980s, the 1990s, as well as in this decennium'.[136]

Under Barre's regime, foreign trawling was licensed and from time to time since 1991 local warlords and authorities, such as Puntland and the TFG, issued their own licences to foreign boats, although a licence issued by one warlord, or authority, would not be recognized by another (such licences were often little more than protection payments). There is no doubt that foreign trawlers have attempted to exploit Somali waters in the past, but since 2008, a few are prepared to risk hijacking, and most have since been taken well away from the Somali coastline. There are other links between piracy and fishing: many Somali fishermen have taken up piracy because of the possibility of riches from ransoms; and some fishing companies, including two lobster companies, have completely converted their business, using all their commercial assets, into piracy groups.[137]

At the beginning of the 2009–10 season, conflict over fishing off the coast of Somalia increased; the Spanish trawler *Alakrana* was taken on 2 October 2009 and the two French trawlers *Drennec* and *Glenan* were attacked north of the Seychelles on 10 October 2009. According to a report by AFP, pirate spokesman Abdi Yare, based in Xarardheere, where the *Alakrana* was anchored, said:

We also demand four million US dollars as a payment for illegally fishing in Somalia. After that we will release the fishing boat. Unless those conditions are met we will not make any deal. The amount of fish they [the Spanish] have stolen from Somalia is more than the amount of the ransom we have demanded.... The ship we are holding is not a commercial vessel, it came to Somalia to steal our marine resources.[138]

Although it is easy to disregard such statements as self-serving, Abdi Yare was reflecting a commonly held view in Somalia; there is a strong dislike, if not hatred, of foreign fishing fleets, which Somalis believe have robbed their country of its fish stocks. However, there is no convincing evidence that opposition to foreign trawlers was the primary cause of Somali piracy. It is important to understand that Abdi Yare, or Abdullahi Ahmed Haji Farah, was one of the major pirate leaders and financiers in the Puntland pirate network. The Monitoring Group stated that Abdi Yare was reportedly involved in at least 15 hijackings between 2008 and 2011, including the hijacking of the tanker the MV *Samho Dream*[139]; his views are therefore not disinterested.

That is not to say that illegal fishing has not been a problem, although the level of pirate activity in recent years has curbed illegal fishing. Johann Hari claimed in 2009 that more than $300 million-worth of tuna, shrimp and lobster were being stolen every year by illegal trawlers.[140] Reuters quoted Mohammed Hussein, a fisherman in the town of Marka: 'If nothing is done, there soon won't be much fish left in our coastal waters.'

In addition, dangerous materials have been dumped in Somali waters, including nuclear and chemical waste. Ahmedou Ould-Abdallah, the UN envoy to Somalia, told Johann Hari: 'Somebody is dumping nuclear material here. There is also lead, and heavy metals such as cadmium and mercury – you name it.'[141] Foreign fishermen, and Italian companies dumping toxic waste, have stolen Somali resources and damaged the environment, although they have (particularly in the case of toxic waste dumping) often paid off local warlords and politicians, including the Barre government; this reasonable sense of injustice and the belief that the international community is not prepared to act against such offenders have given Somali pirates a real sense of self-justification. If Hansen is correct, the real motivation of Somali piracy has always primarily been profit-seeking. However, the international community should ensure that foreign trawlers do not take fish in Somali waters without the agreement of the local communities who live on the coast. It also makes good sense to keep Spanish and French warships from coming too close to the Somali coast, or heading up international fleets; they will not be welcomed in Somalia. The licensing scheme run by Hart for the Puntland authorities until 2002 could be re-examined, as should the work of the Somaliland government. We are not at war with Somalia, not all Somalis are hostile, and if piracy is to be dealt with it will be necessary to agree terms with those organizations that actually control areas of the coastline. A pragmatic approach is the only one that stands any chance of success.

In July 2011 the UN Monitoring Group noted that, since May 2009, four fishing vessels of the Republic of Korea had been observed fishing off the coast of Puntland and delivering their catch to Bosaso port. The Monitoring Group said that:

Notwithstanding Somali pirate rhetoric claiming to protect Somali marine resources, those vessels operate confidently in Somali waters, broadcasting automatic identification system signals and remaining in visual distance from the shore with slow speed, lowered stern ramp and no obvious precautionary measures.[142]

The Monitoring Group has received information that the companies operating the vessels have been issued approved licences to fish in Puntland territorial waters. None of the vessels has ever reported an attack by Somali pirates – a finding that appears to validate the Monitoring Group's previous observation that 'the sale of licences to foreign vessels in exchange for fishing rights has acquired the features of a large-scale "protection racket", indistinguishable in most respects from common piracy'.[143]

THE ROLE OF YEMEN

The Gulf of Aden is an ancient highway and, rather than separating Somalia and Yemen, it links them together. In particular Puntland has a long history of links to Yemen, and the continuing friendship and business relationship between Abdillahi Yusuf, former president of Puntland and of the TFG, and the former Yemen president, Ali Abdullah Saleh, was an important factor in the support for Puntland's piracy industry, according to Kerin Backhaus.[144] Gregory Copley said that 'the western media gained a hint of Pres[ident] Saleh's longstanding linkage with Puntland when, during Yussuf's Presidency of Somalia in November 2008, a Yemeni ship captured by pirates was suddenly freed without ransom being paid'.[145]

Global Security's description of Yemeni corruption is worth quoting at length:

The combination of the absence of strong state institutions and the presence of a fragmented elite in Yemen have given rise to a bandit state in which predatory elites are encouraged to appropriate state resources for private gain. Vast patronage payouts to participating elites are implemented through government mechanisms that are either directly corrupt or have little accountability and oversight attached to them. Grand corruption is not a tangential problem in Yemen. Rather, it is the glue that keeps things in place. Fragmented elites are 'paid off' in various ways in exchange for their political support. Yemen's state structures are so weak that patronage payoffs to disparate elites are a more effective means of social control than institutional measures.[146]

The article also notes that: 'Petty corruption has become so ingrained in popular culture that it is no longer shameful for individuals to prosper as a result of corrupt practices.'[147] This created the ideal environment for the support of Puntland's pirate gangs, and other criminal activities.

In 2008 the UN Monitoring Group noted the key importance of Yemen in arming Somalia: 'Yemen continues to be the primary commercial source of arms and ammunition for Somalia. Weapons from Yemen continue to feed Somali retail arms sales, as well as the needs of armed opposition and criminal groups.'[148] The Monitoring Group added that because there were no regular Yemeni coastguard patrols east of Al Mukalla, the arms traffic from that area to the northern coast of Puntland continued unabated.[149]

The Gulf of Aden is only 170 nautical miles at its widest point and narrows to about 100 nautical miles at other points, ending in the west at the narrow channel of the Bab el Mandeb, which is only 10 nautical miles across. The 30,000 merchant vessels that pass though these waters every year cannot therefore avoid being within easy range of Somali pirates once they enter the Gulf of Aden and, despite the existence of the international shipping channel, many are still attacked, even in Yemen's territorial waters. Although the bulk of pirates appear to be Somali, Yemen does support the activities of motherships at the ports of Al Mukalla and Al Shishr in the Hadramawt, and at Sayhut, Nishtun and Al Ghaydah in Al Mahrah.[150]

There also seems to be a direct link between the business of arms and people smuggling between Somalia and Yemen. The UN Monitoring Group reported in the 2008 that:

[T]here appears to be an intersection between piracy and other criminal activities, such as arms trafficking and human trafficking, both of which involve the movement of small craft across the Gulf of Aden. One sub-group of the Puntland network, based in the Bari region, allegedly uses the same boats employed for piracy to move refugees and economic migrants from Somalia to Yemen, bringing arms and ammunition on the return journey.[151]

In brief ,Yemen is an extremely corrupt and poorly governed state, which enjoys close links with Somalia and Puntland in particular. The fact that Abdillahi Yusuf lived in Sanaa and continued his business relationships with President Saleh of Yemen is an indication of the closeness of the Somali–Yemeni connection.

Without the long-term relationship between the predatory elites of Puntland and Yemen, personified by the friendship of the late Abdillahi Yusuf and ex-President Saleh, piracy would have lacked the organizational and political support that enabled it to survive and prosper. It is impossible to understand the development of Somali piracy without looking north across the Gulf of Aden to Yemen, another predatory state. The root of modern piracy lies not in terrorism, failed states, or in the failure of Western policies, but in greed and in organized crime. The most important elements in the rise and maintenance of modern piracy are the presence of predatory individuals in charge of states and proto-states, and the existence of effective international criminal networks to supply arms and equipment, to invest and to launder ransom money. In the case of Puntland, these factors came together, in a perfect storm, to support a growing and effective piracy business.

CHAPTER 5

THE GEOGRAPHY OF PIRACY

INTRODUCTION

In this chapter the focus is on the incidence of piracy rather than on the actual operations or the causes. The objective here is to create an understanding of the critical importance of maritime 'choke' points. Aside from the weakness of governance in any particular area, the easy availability of arms and the existence of sea-faring skills, piracy will be of little importance where few ships venture. There are over 75,000 ocean-going merchant ships in the world and most travel along a few shipping lanes between key ports. The most important shipping lanes in the world are those transporting crude oil from the Persian Gulf to markets in Europe, the Far East and North America and those transporting manufactured goods from the factories of the Pearl River and the other industrial areas of eastern China and Japan.

This is the regular route of the *Emma Maersk*, loading cargo at Yantian in Shenzhen and taking Japanese goods from ports like Yokohama to deliver to European ports including Felixstowe, Rotterdam and Bremerhaven. She and her seven sister ships are the largest container ships afloat, nearly 400 metres long, with the ability to carry between 13,000 and 15,000 20-foot containers. She normally transits the Indian Ocean, the Gulf of Aden and the Red Sea, although her speed of over 25.5 knots provides a level of protection from pirate attacks.

In the same way the crude tankers leaving Ras Tanura in Saudi Arabia, and the other oil terminals of the Persian Gulf transit the Strait of Hormuz, between Oman and Iran, into the Gulf of Oman and then sail south-west to the Gulf of Aden along the coasts of Oman and Yemen, or south-east down the coast of India, en route to China, Japan and the other markets of Southeast Asia and the Far East. Nevertheless, the largest transporters avoid the Suez Canal and steer south-south-west to the Cape of Good Hope, via the Mozambique Channel, and then to Europe, or the east coast of North America.

Many types of vessels ply these seaways, including tankers, container ships ('box carriers'), general cargo ships and bulk carriers ('bulkers'). Bulkers are the workhorses of the twenty-first century, typically of 25,000–50,000 tons deadweight (dwt), but a few are as large as 400,000 dwt, and larger ones are planned. Riding low in the water, laden with iron ore, wheat and other dry cargoes, they ply their trade along the sea lanes of the Indian Ocean. They are the tramp steamers of the modern world, carrying the essential supplies on which the global economy depends. Their flags are of countries rarely seen other than on such 'flags of convenience' fleets – Liberia, Panama, the Marshall Islands – their owners are corporations registered in tax havens, and their crew polyglot, speaking a dozen tongues. Their slow speeds, low freeboards and relatively small crews make them favourites with Somali pirates – their details passed, via satellite phones, from Suez, Singapore and Dubai to Eyl, or Bosaso in Puntland – their IMO number, AIS code and transit details, with the insurance value of the cargo. The value of their cargoes ensures their ransoming and eventual release.

Many other vessels regularly sail these seas, including brand new liquefied natural gas (LNG) carriers, taking gas from Qatar to the United Kingdom, product tankers, carrying chemicals and feedstock, oil industry-support ships, ocean-going tugs, and even humble dredgers and small general cargo vessels, operating out of the United Arab Emirates and the Indian ports, able to berth at the small havens along the African coast. The eastern waters of the Indian Ocean are immensely busy, a maritime cross-roads, with broad oceanic freeways full of merchant vessels heading to and from the Bab el Mandeb Strait eastwards into the Gulf of Aden, towards the Strait of Hormuz, or south of Galle, Sri Lanka, en route to Singapore. From the Persian Gulf other seaways lead in all directions and this mass expanse of sea is easily accessible from Somalia, which has the longest coastline of any African country. Somali pirates therefore have access to some of the busiest and most important marine lines of communication in the world. According to the US Energy Information Administration, oil movements through the Strait account for about 40 per cent of all seaborne oil traded in the world – that is between 16.5 and 17 million barrels of crude a day[1]. About 30,000 vessels pass though the Gulf of Aden each year and half of all global container traffic transits the Indian Ocean[2]. Europe is China's largest market and it remains dependent on the Middle East for much of its energy supplies. The Bab el Mandeb and Hormuz straits are therefore key bottlenecks, restricted waters – the navigable width of the Bab el Mandeb Strait, at the southern end of the Red Sea, is less than 10 nautical miles, and the Strait of Hormuz is only 21 miles wide.

There are few other maritime choke points of compatible importance. The Strait of Malacca is the most important one, guarding the route to the South China Sea; the English Channel is another, providing access to most of Europe's major ports; and the approaches to the Panama Canal. The Torres Strait is key for Australia. The Taiwan Strait and the Bashi Channel, respectively north and south of Taiwan, are critical transit points for the Far East trade, and the Mozambique Channel is essential for the east African trade. The Korea, La Pérouse and Tsugaru-kaiko straits are vital for the countries bordering the Sea of Japan – the Koreas, Russia and Japan. The waters of the Caribbean, another old pirate centre, have passages and channels between the numerous islands – like the Windward Passage and the Straits of Florida. Otherwise, ships are free to steam out into the open ocean, away from capes and straits. The lack of such a choke point restricts the impact of piracy off West Africa and most of South America. Conversely, the many islands of the Philippines and Indonesia with their innumerable channels, straits and reefs, such as the Balabac Strait and the Makassar Strait, adjoining South China Sea, have the potential to once more become important centres for piracy. The closed seas of the Mediterranean and the Baltic, which also have many channels and passages, have also been important pirate centres in the past; the Barbary Pirates had a profound impact on commerce until the middle of the nineteenth century. Piracy is not wholly unknown in the Mediterranean; the *Tiara*, a super-yacht, was robbed off the coast of Corsica in August 2008.

Because choke points funnel ships through narrow passages, they give a tremendous advantage to pirates, by concentrating targets in a small area. Therefore, it is not surprising that, apart from the Indian Ocean, the most active pirate centre until the recent rise of piracy off West Africa, was the South China Sea and the Strait of Malacca.

Piracy grew off the coast of West Africa in 2012 because of the extension of onshore criminality into the maritime environment, with ships being robbed for their valuables, although some tankers have been seized and then used for carrying bulker (illegal) oil from the Delta. If, in a world that enjoys worse security than today, we were to see an extension of piracy, then the restricted waters of the Far East, the Mediterranean and the Caribbean would be strong candidates for such an increase, because of their geography.

THE NORTH-EAST INDIAN OCEAN AND THE RED SEA

Background

The public awareness of modern piracy is almost entirely focused on the threat from Somali pirates, and there is good reason for this; waters off the coast of Somalia have been the most dangerous in the world and Somali pirates have continued to extend their area of operations. Vessels have been attacked only a 100 nautical miles off the coast of India, less than 50 nautical miles off the coast of Oman, into the Mozambique Channel and the southern waters of the Red Sea.

The original areas, in which Somali pirates operated, were off the coast of Somalia and in the Gulf of Aden, where large numbers of merchant ships are forced into the choke point of the Bab el Mandeb Strait. As the UN Monitoring Group reported in 2008, in the Gulf of Aden and off Mogadishu, 'motherships', larger fishing boats and dhows were normally based in Bosaso and Mogadishu in Somalia, and at Al Mukalla and Al Shishr in Yemen.[3] Until 2009 there were few very long distance attacks, but a pattern of extending the attack area could be seen; as the exclusion zone for merchant vessels was progressively extended away from the Somali coast, the pirates reacted immediately by moving beyond the edge of the boundary between the exclusion zone and the safe area. The present exclusion area includes virtually all the north-west Indian Ocean, except for a corridor along the Indian coast. The attack on the Bahamas-flagged and US-owned cruise liner *Seabourn Spirit* in November 2005, about 100 nautical miles off the Somalia coast and well outside the then recommended 'safe' area, was an early example of this pattern. Somalis are avid internet users; if any information is available on the internet, one must always assume that Somali pirate groups will have read and acted on that information. In 2008 the UN Monitoring Group drew attention to sophisticated use of the media, including the internet, by Somali armed groups.[4] Somali pirates run a sophisticated and well-organized operation; never under-estimate them.

Figure 5.1 Suspected pirate mothership

However, it was the arrival of international naval forces in the Gulf of Aden, and in particular the establishment of the Internationally Recommended Transit Corridor (IRTC) in 2009, that really pushed pirate groups eastwards and south into the Mozambique Channel and the many islands of the Seychelles. Somali piracy is also seasonal, avoiding the summer monsoon, which normally starts in July, and lasts until late August or early September. In the same way, the winter monsoon, which is less severe, also reduces attacks, or moves them into the southern Red Sea, where sea conditions are calmer than in the Gulf of Aden. Monsoons increase the height of waves in the Indian Ocean and the Gulf of Aden. If the swells are a metre or more, it is very difficult to board a moving ship from a small skiff, and the rough seas are also a threat to pirate skiffs transiting from the Somali coast. It is known that bad weather has drowned many Somali pirates, although the tactic of carrying skiffs on board motherships and only deploying them for an actual attack reduced this risk. However, there are reports that attacks have occurred with a three-metre swell (sea state 5), so poor weather conditions do not necessarily guarantee safety for seafarers.

The 2009–10 piracy season

It is informative to look in some detail at the events of the 2009–10 piracy season. This was the period that saw the Somalis greatly extend their area of operations. The remarkable feature of the 2009–10 season was the way in which pirate attacks took place so far from the Somali coast. There were a cluster of attacks to the north-east of the Seychelles, up to 1,000 nautical miles east of Somalia, and in a second area, far to the south of Somalia, in the northern part of the Mozambique Channel. On 5 November 2009, the MV *Delvina* was taken 146 nautical miles north-east of the Comoros Islands. Attacks also occurred along the Omani coast and far to the east, close to the coast of India, developing patterns that became stronger in 2010–11.

However, the shipping industry had been misled by suggestions that international naval forces had a grip on piracy and failed to prepare adequately. One US naval officer, Rear Admiral Bener, claimed in August 2009: 'We have already decreased pirate activity in the Somali Basin and we are hoping to see a decrease in the Gulf of Aden.'[5] To say the least, his words were optimistic. One of the effects of such remarks was to discourage shipowners from taking the necessary anti-piracy protective measures. Training, already arranged, was cancelled[6] and the industry, which had always been reluctant to spend the money necessary to protect its ships, had a cast-iron excuse for doing nothing; arguably some ships were unnecessarily hijacked.

The vast expanse of ocean targeted by pirates could not be effectively protected by international naval operations. The area affected by piracy in 2009–10 had become so vast that, as General 'Buster' Howes, then Commander EU NAVFOR, made clear in 2010, hundreds of warships would be required effectively to cover the area, not the handful actually at sea at any one time[7]. The area in which pirate attacks could occur had expanded to include the whole of the western Indian Ocean, from the coast of India to the shores of Africa, and north into the Arabian Sea. The Gulf of Aden and the southern section of the Red Sea were seen as relevantly secure, though all the vessels transiting this area needed to ensure that their crews were trained and equipped to deal with pirate attacks. Vessels that did not follow the official recommendations, while transiting the Gulf of Aden, remained vulnerable.

The 2009–10 Somali pirate season effectively started on 15 October 2009, the summer monsoon period having ended, when the 24,637 dwt, Singapore-flagged, container ship *Kota Wajar* was hijacked in the Indian Ocean, at 01°.33S 54°.52E. In the next few weeks a total of four bulk carriers and a container ship were hijacked, including the MV *Filitsa*, a Greek-owned vessel taken on 11 November 2009. At this time major hijackings were taking place approximately once every five days. In addition, the husband and wife crew (the Chandlers) of a small British yacht, the *Lynn Rival*, were kidnapped, and a small UAE cargo vessel, the *Almezaan*, and two trawlers, the Thai *Union III* and a Yemeni trawler, the *Al Hilil*, were hijacked. In addition, the Spanish tuna boat *Alakrana* was hijacked on 2 October. Two more vessels were also attacked at about the same time – the bulk carriers MV *Full Strong* and the MV *Feng Li,* off the eastern coast of Yemen.

The 2009–10 piracy season proved to be the most dangerous yet; the attack zone was extended virtually to the Indian coast and south into the Mozambique Channel. Somali pirates were able to take ships despite the presence of record numbers of international naval vessels, even hijacking ships in the Gulf of Aden and off the coast of Oman, which many had thought to be safe. For example, on 8 May 2010, the 13,000 ton MV *Marida Marguerite* was hijacked 120 nautical miles south of Salalah on the coast of Oman, at 14°.58N 054°.47E. The ship was approached by a pirate skiff firing automatic weapons and rocket-propelled grenades. The crew radioed that they had seen the pirates boarding their ship. The Marshall Islands-flagged general cargo ship carried a crew of 22, including 19 Indians, one Ukrainian and two Bangladeshis. The ship was finally ransomed at the end of December 2010, after the payment of $5.5 million to pirates in Garaad.

The key points to bear in mind as regards the 2009–10 season are:

- International naval forces pushed pirate activity eastwards, and south-wards, away from the Gulf of Aden and the southern Red Sea.
- The use of lethal force by international forces, particularly by the United States and France, raised the stakes, as far as the pirates were concerned.
- At the start of the season there were large losses of Somali pirates at sea, due in part to intertribal conflict, as well as weather problems.
- The Somalis exhibited a particular hatred for foreign trawlers, especially for those from Spain, France and Taiwan, which they accused of 'illegally' fishing off Somalia.
- Interpol reported the increasing involvement of organized criminal groups in piracy. There was considerable 'investment' in piracy by high net worth individuals from the Middle East and elsewhere. This resulted in growing sophistication, and the deployment of better navigation equipment.
- From October 2009 the area from which pirates operated was no longer confined to Somalia; the southern coast of Yemen and some uninhabited islands in the Seychelles archipelago were also 'pirate territory'.
- The continuing social, climatic, political and economic pressures within Somalia and Yemen made piracy an extremely attractive proposition for young men.
- The use of large merchant vessels as motherships (large pirate support vessels – LPSVs), which extended their operational range, greatly

increased the numbers of pirates that could be deployed in a pirate action group (PAG). There were reports of over 50 pirates on one mothership, and this allowed them to overcome monsoon problems off Somalia. Bulk carriers and general cargo ships with cranes also allowed skiffs to be taken on board, rather than towed.

There were a large number of actors involved in Somali piracy at the time, and each of these groups could potentially cause conflict with the others. The tribal nature of Somali society and the readiness, with which inter-tribal conflicts are settled by violence, was now intermingled with struggles between criminal groups, as well as with business, political and terrorism factions. The situation was further complicated by the involvement of foreigners – including those fighting for factions within Somalia, intelligence agents, criminals and businessmen. For those who needed to visit Somalia on 'business', they could fly into a number of destinations on Jubba Airways out of Sharjah or Dubai. The regular arms shipments took the normal Ilyushin Il-76 flights. However, once in Somalia any visitor would require their own armed guards and safe passes from the groups through whose territory they passed.

It is important to distinguish between attacks on local trading vessels, which can arise from local disputes, and attacks on commercial merchant vessels in transit. The attacks on bulkers, tankers and product carriers are the underlying business of Somali pirates; the ransoms for these vessels generate the cash flow that sustains the piracy business.

As far as the 'business' of hijacking commercial shipping is concerned, the rich pickings has attracted a host of unpleasant characters. Jean-Michel Louboutin, executive director of police services at Interpol, said in October 2009 that the pirates operating off the coast of Somalia were being controlled by crime syndicates, including foreigners, lured by the multi-million-dollar ransoms. Interpol also stated that the pirates had acquired sophisticated weapons and tracking devices allowing them to extend their reach. As previously noted, pirate motherships were supported from Yemeni ports, despite the fact that an attack on a bulk carrier was thwarted on 20 September 2009 by an embarked Yemeni coastguard unit.

The continuing danger in the Gulf of Aden
The Gulf of Aden is the area that has seen the greatest international naval cooperation to combat piracy; there are normally around six warships on station at any one time. The establishment since 1 February 2009 of the

IRTC and the regular escorted convoys though the Gulf of Aden have been important factors in protecting ships. However, the potential financial rewards for pirates are very high and any vessel that chooses to sail independently of the convoy system is vulnerable. Even in the Gulf of Aden there are insufficient warships available to ensure the safety of all vessels, and the pirate gangs effectively cover the area. Apart from escorted convoys, which require a vessel to be booked in advance, 'group transits' in the Gulf of Aden are organized by the Maritime Security Centre – Horn of Africa (MSCHOA). Vessels register on the MSCHOA website[8] before joining a transit, and then submit via email a booking request for a specific transit time at least 72 hours before the transit time. Vessels are advised to conduct their passage in groups through the IRTC based on their transit speed. This way, a vessel travelling west at 10 knots (nautical miles per hour) joins the IRTC at 1800 local time, one doing 12 knots joins at 0001, one during 14 knots at 0400, one doing 16 knots at 0830 and one doing 18 knots at 1000 – with the objective of all meeting in the middle of the IRTC. If a ship joins a slower group and increases speed, for example it is capable of 14 knots and joins the 12-knot group transit and then increases speed to its maximum, this will increase the risk to the vessel, because warships do not expect it to arrive earlier in any particular area.

A group transit allows the naval forces to know approximately where ships will be and at what times. The difficulty is that warships do not always escort these group transits, but are tasked to use their resources to deter and protect against any pirate attack. The IRTC has two lanes, each five nautical miles wide, with a two nautical mile buffer zone between them: the southern lane, which is on a heading of 052, is for vessels heading east, and the northern lane for vessels heading west. The western end of the IRTC is opposite Aden and the eastern end is approximately on the line from Socotra Island to Haswayl, in Al Mahrah province, Yemen. The IRTC is nearer the Yemeni than the Somali coastline. The original IRTC was even nearer the Yemeni coast than the present one, and it was moved to avoid local fishing fleets, which are too often confused with pirates, and also to take vessels out of Yemeni mobile telephone coverage, as it was thought that the pirates' informants on board were passing course and position information via Yemen.

The middle passage of the IRTC to the south of Al Mukalla, Al Irqah and Shaqra in Yemen is the most dangerous area and transits are timed to place all vessels at roughly the same point within an hour of sunrise, the most common time for an attack. Vessels from any country can also use UKMTO, the UK Maritime Trade Organisation run by the Royal Navy in the United Arab Emirates, as this service compliments the work of MSCHOA. On a voluntary basis any ships can report to the UKMTO team, once they have passed the Suez Canal, through the Red Sea to as far south as the Seychelles, up to the Straits of Hormuz, and east out to 78 degrees east. UKMTO are responsible for tracking vessels through the limits indicated above and are a vessel's first point of contact in the case of an incident.[9] UKMTO liaise very closely with MSCHOA and international forces when incidents occur, advise the master and attempt to organize help where possible.

There are also national convoy systems for vessels from particular countries, and in some cases where the shipmaster is a national of the protecting state. France, Russia, China, India and Japan have offered such services from time to time. In addition, certain high worth, or special cargoes, are given naval escorts, including oil platforms, ammunition and weapons cargoes, and nuclear fuel shipments. Attacks in the Gulf of Aden are from groups who have also operated from forward-operating bases (FOBs) in the small islands west of Socotra, such as Abd Al Kuri.

Until the end of 2009 it appeared that the measures put in place were working effectively, but on 18–19 December 2009, the Yemeni freighter *Al-Mahmoudia 2* was taken, shortly after it left Aden. Two weeks later, on 28 December 2009, the British chemical tanker MV *St James Park* was hijacked in the Gulf of Aden, south-west of Al Mukalla, in the southern corridor of the IRTC,[10] followed three days later by the hijacking of the MV *Pramoni*, another chemical tanker. The attack on the *St James Park* seems to have been made without warning, as there was no radio telephone call for help; only the activation of the SSAS signal by the crew, after the ship was hijacked, alerted the authorities that it had been taken. It is an interesting coincidence that both the *St James Park* and the *Pramoni* were chemical carriers, relatively small vessels (14,000 and 20,000 dwt respectively), with limited freeboard, which normally carry very valuable cargoes. It is possible that both were targeted as the result of an intelligence assessment by the pirates. The maximum speed of the *St James Park* is only 13 knots.

These attacks made it clear that the statements made in August 2009 by Admiral Gary Roughead, chief of naval operations for the Bahrain-based US Fifth Fleet, that, 'The Gulf of Aden is safer for shipping than it was a year ago', and 'The maritime environment is much more peaceful because of the international cooperation',[11] were not justified by events. While many believed that the Gulf of Aden was effectively protected by warships, the 2010 new year hijackings shattered this feeling of confidence. The *St James Park* was in an area where she should have been safe, as was the *Pramoni*.

These hijackings were followed in March by the taking of the MV *Iceberg 1*, a small Panama-flagged, roll-on roll-off vessel with deadweight of 4,500 tons, which was hijacked ten nautical miles outside the Port of Aden, bound for Jebel Ali, in Dubai. However, the *Iceberg 1* was not transiting the IRTC, nor was she in a national escort convoy, and she had not registered with MSCHOA. The *Iceberg 1* and her crew were destined to remain captive for two years and nine months, until December 2012. In the words of Mohamad Abdirahman, the PMPF director, 'Our forces started the operation on December 10, when they went to the coast and laid siege to the ship with the approval of the Puntland government.' Three pirates were killed, three were captured in the operation and nine fled the *Iceberg 1*, which subsequently went aground near the village of Gara'ad in the Mudug region.[12] In May 2010 there were two more major hijackings in the Gulf of Aden, which showed that the new year events were not isolated incidents. The tanker MV *Moscow University* was hijacked on 5 May – an attack that is considered in more detail below, because it involved the recapture of the ship by the Russian navy; and the MV *Panega*, a small Bulgarian chemical tanker was hijacked 68 nautical miles south of Irqah, Yemen and 100 nautical miles east of Aden at 1535 GMT on 11 May.

Figure 5.2 Pirates in skiff surrendering

The Gulf of Aden is therefore not a safe area for merchant shipping. Even where vessels stay in the IRTC they have still been attacked, and others have been taken, although without naval support the situation would have been much worse. The reality is that there are no safe havens in the north-western Indian Ocean and that merchant vessels sailing anywhere in the area are at risk of pirate attacks and capture. They are rather like ducks in a shooting gallery: most get through, but some get hit. The expensive international operation to protect shipping has been unable to secure any area completely, although naval forces stopped many attacks, detained many pirates and destroyed much equipment. Naval forces have done an excellent job with the resources available to them, given the constraints of their rules of engagement, which have had an effect on piracy (Figure 5.2).

The threat along the Omani coast

One of the striking aspects of the 2009–10 piracy season was the extension of piracy attacks along the Omani coast, a progress that continued into 2011. On 19 March 2011 the mothership MV *Sinar Kudus* was taken while sailing about 50 nautical miles north-east of Muscat[13] well within the Gulf of Oman, the first time that any pirate vessel had sailed so close to the Straits of Hormuz. This was a potential game-changer for the authorities in the area. Previously there had been few attacks in Omani waters, except near the border with Yemen. The extension of attacks into Omani waters and the Arabian Sea placed all vessels leaving and entering the Persian Gulf squarely under threat.

The hijacking of the MV *Charelle* on 12 June 2009 south of Sur, Oman, was an early indication of the problem. Attacks continued: on 22 March 2010, mid-afternoon local time, a tanker, the MV *Knock Muir*, a Liberian-flagged and German-managed Aframax, was attacked about 125 nautical miles south-south-east of Salalah; the master and crew were able to beat off the attack successfully. The next day another group hijacked the 11,055 dwt MV *Talca*, a refrigerated cargo vessel, Bermuda-flagged and British Virgin Island-owned, 180 nautical miles south of Mazera Island in eastern Oman. The ship, with a crew of 23, was en route to Bushehr in Iran from Sokhna in Egypt and had passed through the IRTC. She was finally released from Somalia on 11 May 2010, after a ransom, reportedly $2.5 million, was paid.

Omani waters continued to be dangerous, and on 21 April 2010, a cargo ship, the MV VOC *Daisy*, Panama-flagged, was hijacked at around 0600 GMT, about dawn local time, 180 nautical miles west of Salalah, Oman.

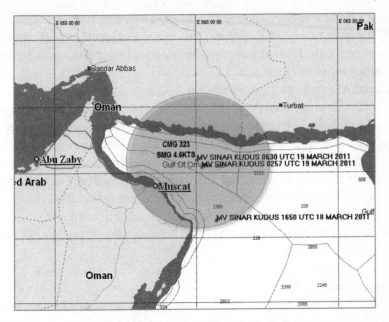

Figure 5.3 The voyage of the MV *Sinar Kudus*

Then on 8 May, the MV *Marida Marguerite*, a Marshall Islands-flagged cargo ship, was hijacked 120 nautical miles south of Salalah. She was approached by a pirate skiff firing automatic weapons and rocket-propelled grenades and the crew reported that they saw the pirates climbing on board. Four days later, at dawn on 12 May 2010, the 72,119 dwt bulk carrier MV *Elini P* was taken 390 nautical miles south-east of Salalah. The *Elini P*, with her crew of 24, was en route from the Ukraine to China and was over 400 nautical miles east of the IRCT. Incidents continue, and the hijacking of the MV *Samho Jewelry* on 15 January 2011, about 350 nautical miles south-east of Muscat[14], was remarkable only because she was retaken by South Korean commandos.

Piracy off the Omani coast had become a routine event by the end of 2009, and successful hijackings of large merchant vessels a commonplace. The main reason was that once vessels left the relative protection of the IRCT they transited north-east along the Omani coastline, or east towards India, and this became a prime operational area for a number of PAGs led by men like *Yellow Can Man* and *White Dhow Man*. The Royal Navy of Oman, which is an effective fighting force, lacked the resources to protect its extremely long coastline and the waters of the Arabian Sea, and international forces had few assets to spare to protect vessels in this area. However, the

Gulf of Oman is the entrance to the Strait of Hormuz and all Persian Gulf shipping had to run the gauntlet of these PAGs. The only way that shipowners could protect their vessels, cargoes and crews was by making their ships more resilient.

Dryad Maritime reported that:

> The MV Sinin, a Maltese flagged and owned 52 466 ton bulk carrier was hijacked 310 NM east of Masirah, Oman. The vessel which has a crew of 23 (13 Iranians 10 Indian) reported coming under attack on Saturday 12 February. An aircraft from the Combined Maritime Force was sent to the vicinity and spotted two skiffs onboard the vessel. Communications with MV Sinin have been lost and there is no information on the condition of the crew. The vessel has altered course and heading towards the Somali Coast.[15]

The Seychelles

The Seychelles territory covers a large area, as far south as the Aldabra Islands and the Farquhar Islands. The authorities in the Seychelles were initially accused of being afraid to deal firmly with pirates, because of the threat they represented to the country's vital tourism industry. It appeared to be the case that the authorities initially thought that a robust approach to piracy would result in Somali pirates retaliating against tourist facilities.

In September 2009 the Seychelles government was also said to have exchanged 23 suspected pirates caught in its waters for three of its own citizens; the seamen arrived home on 13 September 2009. It was said that the pirates had threatened to kill the Seychelles seamen. On 12 October 2009 the Seychelles then released a suspected Somali pirate ship, and its 11 crew, which had been captured after the attack on the French trawlers, *Drennec* and *Glenan*.

However, the Seychelles government took an increasingly hard line in 2010; it improved its acquisition of intelligence, encouraged foreign governments to assist in anti-piracy patrols, allowed maritime patrol aircraft and drones to operate from its territory and acted aggressively towards any pirate attack groups found in its waters. At the beginning of 2011 an unsuccessful attempt by the Seychelles coastguard at freeing the crew of the *Beluga Nomination*, which resulted in the death of a pirate, led to the reported execution of a seaman by Somali pirates and the 'punishment' of two of his comrades in an act of brutal revenge;[16] it is said that all three men died.

Somali pirates were clearly prepared to kill their hostages in order to discourage rescues, which created a moral dilemma for commanders, and underlined the fact that pirates are ruthless criminals, who are in effect at war with 'all mankind'.

Expansion of the piracy threat into the Mozambique Channel

The Mozambique Channel, located between Madagascar on the east and Mozambique on the west, forms an important shipping route from southern Africa and the south Atlantic to and from the Indian Ocean. It is particularly attractive because this route avoids the reefs and island chains to the east of Madagascar.

The Channel is wide and deep, and consists of island groups that are considered strategically important from the standpoint of maritime security. All the countries in this region are fragile, corrupt, and have weak economies and poor maritime security. The coast of Tanzania borders the north-western part of the Channel, the Kenyan coast lies just to the north and Mozambique is on its south-western side. It is a major maritime choke point, like the Gulf of Aden, and the many small islands along the Channel make ideal havens for pirates. At the end of the seventeenth century and beginning of the eighteenth century, English pirates – including William Kidd, Henry Every, John Bowen and Thomas Tew – used Antongil Bay and Nosy Boraha (St Mary's Island), an island 12 miles off north-east Madagascar, as their base. From there they attacked merchant ships in the Indian Ocean, the Red Sea, and even in the Persian Gulf.

In 2009 Somali pirates took a leaf out of their eighteenth-century predecessors' book. On 5 November the MV *Delvina* (a bulk carrier, 53,629 dwt) was hijacked, about 380 nautical miles south-east of Dar es Salaam, and 65 nautical miles due west of Aldabra Island, in the northern part of the Mozambique Channel[17]. The *Delvina* was sailing from the Mediterranean to the port of Mombasa, with a cargo of wheat, and a crew of seven Ukrainians and 14 Filipinos. The attack on the Marshall Islands-flagged *Delvina* was not an isolated incident. About 175 nautical miles to the north-east, the *Jo Cedar* was attacked on 10 November 2009; and on the same day the *Felicitas Rickmers* was attacked, 100 nautical miles north-east of the position of the *Jo Cedar*. Fortunately both vessels avoided capture.

On 22 October 2009 there was another attack on a bulk carrier 360 nautical miles due east of Dar es Salaam; again this was rebuffed. Further north and due east of Mombasa unsuccessful attacks occured on the MV *Harriette* (on 2 November 2009) and the MV *Jolly Rosso* (on 22 October

2009). On the same day, at a point 800 nautical miles due east of Mombasa, the 38,305 dwt bulk carrier MV *Al Khaliq* en route to Mombasa was taken. Shipowners had been told in the past that the area was safe; it proved not to be so. In many ways the Mozambique Channel is similar to the Gulf of Aden, in that it has many small islands and sheltered anchorages where pirates can establish forward-operating bases. The states of the area lack effective coastal defences and there is little maritime surveillance capability. Madagascar has a corrupt and disorganized government.

Piracy continued in the northern Mozambique Channel in 2010. On 5 March the Norwegian-owned product tanker MV *UBT Ocean* was hijacked. This area remained dangerous and the East African ports of Mombasa and Dar es Salaam were virtually blockaded by Somali pirates at enormous expense to the economies of East Africa and those central African states that relied on imports from the Indian Ocean. The cruise liners that used to call at Mombasa were only a memory.

Developments in the Indian Ocean: deep ocean attacks

The area that saw the greatest activity at the end of 2009 was the area north-east of the Seychelles. On 19 October 2009 the Chinese bulk carrier *De Xin Hai* was hijacked 350 nautical miles north-east of the Seychelles;[18] at the time this was the furthest east of Somalia that any vessel had been hijacked. This hijacking was followed by the capture of the MV *Filitsa* on 11 November 2009. A Greek-owned and Marshall Island-flagged bulk carrier, the *Filitsa* that transported a cargo of bulk urea from Kuwait to Durban was hijacked far out in the Indian Ocean,[19] a position that until the hijacking of the *De Xin Hai*, had been regarded by many as a safe point.

On 9 November 2009 the *BW Lion*, a VLCC, was attacked 400 nautical miles north-east of the Seychelles and 1,000 nautical miles east of Mogadishu. The following day the container ship MV *Nele Maersk* was attacked in the same area. The attack on the Hong Kong-flagged *BW Lion* occurred when she was laden with 281,390 metric tons of crude oil en route from West Africa to India – she is a 298,567 dwt vessel built in 2004[20]. The attack is described in detail in Chapter 9.

As a result of the extension of Somali pirates' activities far out into the Arabian Sea there were no 'safe' areas in the northern waters of the Indian Ocean, and the vessels that had felt relatively secure after transiting the Gulf of Aden felt unprotected by then. Crews complained about the lack of precautions and training, which resulted in mutinies, including one known on a German-owned vessel, whose crew were afraid to face Somali pirates – although news of these incidents was quickly hushed up by owners, and crews were easily bought off with extra pay.

The extension of the campaign would have been impossible without the use of motherships, normally long-distance trawlers taken in earlier attacks. These vessels were generally well-equipped and designed to stay at sea for long periods. Once a target had been identified the pirates made their attacks in a determined and vigorous manner. The attack on the *BW Lion* occurred far from any warship and the master was very much isolated. This illustrates a common problem: after a vessel had travelled safely in a group transit, via the IRTC in the Gulf of Aden, it was very much on its own.

Captured trawlers, like the Taiwanese *Win Far 161*, the *Thai Union III* and the Yemeni trawler *Al Hilil* taken on 11 November 2009 were pressed into service as long-range motherships, capable of remaining on station for long periods and deploying skiffs, once their radar and AIS had identified suitable targets. Some longer-range pirate groups may even have targeted particular ships, identified from their AIS[21] tracks and the information on routes given when they leave port – However, it was the opinion of one Royal Navy Commander, who I spoke to, that most pirate groups are opportunists and don't plan ahead.

It is likely that pirates have an effective intelligence system, having access to information from sources in shipping and insurance offices around the world, and spotters based in Suez and other choke points. One tanker owner described to me the checking process in the Gulf of Aden:

A skiff, with a tarpaulin covering most of the hull, draws parallel to our ship about 100 metres away, looks at our ship's name with binoculars, then makes a satellite telephone call for a couple of minutes, after which the skiff speeds away.[22]

However, there is one report that suggests that older methods of divination have also been pressed into service by pirates. It is claimed that the Bahari men of the Somali river areas, now known as 'antennas' or 'satellites', who are said to have magical powers, give guidance to pirates. Abdi Musse Hersi, known as 'the computer', is one the most famous Somali seers in Puntland, and lives in Eyl on the Indian Ocean coast. He has helped pirates to plan their missions and it is said that he has received a cut from ransoms. However, some of the intelligence assessments given to pirates originate from western-trained Somalis, who understand geospatial intelligence gathering, as well as the operation of radar and AIS.[23] There are also stories circulating in maritime circles of masters being warned by criminals not to stray from their planned routes, with threats to their families if they do; but this can never be proven. If this was true, it would confirm the idea that piracy is a global criminal enterprise.

It is interesting that four of the five major ships hijacked at the end of 2009 were bulk carriers, vessels with relatively low freeboards and with low maximum speeds, and these have proved to be the pirates' bread and butter, a reliable source of revenue. It is also clear that the 9 November attack on the tanker *BW Lion* was carried through with great determination, the pirates no doubt wishing to repeat the success associated with the taking of the *Sirius Star*. They did not have to wait long: by the end of November 2009 they hijacked the MV *Maran Centaurus*, which they ransomed for a figure comprised between $5 and $10 million in early January 2010. They repeated their success when they took the South Korean-flagged 319,300 dwt VLCC MV *Samho Dream* on 4 April 2010, 565 nautical miles north-west of the Maldives. A spokesman for Samho said that the vessel was, 'in an area not prone to pirate activity'. Unfortunately he had not looked at the latest pattern of attacks; his ship was sailing in very dangerous waters. Some tankers did escape attacks, including the Indian ship *MT Maharaja Agrasen*, referred to below, and the Kuwait vessel MV *Album* on 30 December 2009; but their slow speeds and low freeboards, when laden, make these huge ships very vulnerable. Their masters also have a reasonable fear of fire onboard when RPGs start exploding on the decks.

It is usually considered that vessels that have a high maximum speed are reasonably safe, which probably accounts for the success of the container ship MV *Nele Maersk* in avoiding capture on 10 November 2010 – although there are reports of ships being attacked even when they are steaming at 18 knots. Bulk carriers and other slower merchant ships are very vulnerable. Once they enter the western Indian Ocean, unless they are prepared and equipped to defend themselves, they can only rely on the presence of naval vessels.

The extension of the threat eastwards towards India

Late on 21 December 2009 the Indian-flagged 147,467 dwt oil tanker *MT Maharaja Agrasen* en route from Mina Al Ahmadi in Kuwait to Visakhapatnam in India, laden with over 950,000 barrels of oil worth about $75 million, reported a pirate attack in the Arabian Sea. The reported attack was by three unlit pirate boats about 366 nautical miles west of Ratnagiri on the west coast of India.[24] Later reports say that the three boats attacked the *Maharaja Agrasen* with machine guns and RPGs. The general secretary of the National Union of Seafarers of India, Abdulgani Y Serang, told the Press Trust of India that the master tried to ram one of the pirate boats.

The Indian Directorate General of Shipping was contacted by the vessel's owners and alerted the Indian coastguard and Indian Navy. The Indian authorities remained in contact with the master and the owners, and were informed that the pirates had not been able to board the vessel because of the evasive manoeuvres undertaken by the master. The owners then ordered the vessel to head directly for the Indian coast. By 0025 on 22 December, the nearest pirate boat was about four nautical miles from the vessel and by 0247, four hours after the alarm was raised, the authorities were informed that no boat was following the vessel. No injury or damage had been reported and the *Maharaja Agrasen* proceeded to Visakhapatnam. Neither UKMTO nor MSCHOA reacted to this attack. The EU NAVFOR website said that the attack on the *Maharaja Agrasen* 'was well outside the normal EU NAVFOR operating area' – a case of EU NAVFOR not anticipating pirates' response to increasing pressures in their western operating areas.

Although there was at first disbelief that an attack would occur so close to India, it is clear that this was a genuine attack. It is important to remember that on 1 December the Greek oil tanker, MV *Sikinos*, was attacked approximately 345 nautical miles south-west of the position of the attack on the *Maharaja Agrasen* and another vessel was attacked on 5 December 2009 approximately 640 nautical miles south-south-west. On 30 December the MV *Album*, a Kuwait oil tanker, was attacked at virtually the same position as the earlier attack on the *Sikinos*, about 650 nautical miles west of the Indian coast. On 2 January 2010 a large ro-ro vessel, the UK-flagged MV *Asian Glory*, laden with cars for Saudi Arabia, was hijacked in the same area.

The 21 December attack on the *Maharaja Agresen* did occur much further north (nearly 17 degrees north) and much further east (about 67 degrees east) than any previous attack, but the earlier attacks to the south-west should have warned shipowners and international forces that there was a potential threat in this area. One interpretation of these attacks in the first three weeks of December was that pirate groups supported by at least one long-range mothership (probably a trawler like the *Win Far 161*) were operating in the area. The *Asian Glory* was taken on one of the busiest ship lanes in the Indian Ocean, where vessels travelling to and from the Far East transit via Galle on the southern tip of Sri Lanka to the Gulf of Aden. Using AIS the PAGs could have picked their targets easily, well out of range of their radar, and would have probably approached the targets from the stern, where most merchant vessels have no radar coverage.

There were a number of surprising factors. First, it would appear that the masters of the vessels attacked in the Indian Ocean had no intelligence reports on previous attacks in the area. Second, the vessels' watchkeepers failed to give sufficient advance warning of attacks. And third, it is not clear whether the *Asian Glory* was steaming at her top speed of over 18 knots, while transiting a very dangerous area. As regards watch-keeping it is a fact that most merchant vessels are undermanned – some smaller ships have a crew of only eight people – and that once they leave the Gulf of Aden there is an apparent tendency to stand-down extra watchkeepers. It is also surprising that very few vessels have any radar coverage aft, or thermal imaging cameras, not only to warn of pirate attacks from the stern, but also for collision avoidance.

It became clear by the end of 2009 that the Arabian Sea was another area in which pirate attacks were regularly occurring and that the zone within a triangle formed by Socotra, the Gulf of Oman and the northern Maldives was by that time a threat area. This triangle covers approximately 600,000 square nautical miles, an immense area of sea and one that cannot be effectively protected by international naval forces. In fact, the former British foreign secretary, David Miliband, made the point that ships using the Indian Ocean would not receive the same level of naval protection from pirates as those transiting the Gulf of Aden, because military resources were limited. The merchant vessels transiting the Arabian Sea were no longer able to assume that they were 'safe', but few had trained their crews, undertaken effective anti-pirate drills, put procedures in place and embarked effective anti-piracy equipment. In fact, some ships disembarked security teams at Salalah, after transiting the IRTC and before steaming east into far more dangerous waters. As a result of these attacks, Lloyd's extended their exclusion zones.

On the morning of 23 March, the Maltese-flagged and Turkish-owned bulk carrier, the MV *Frigia*, 35,000 dwt, was hijacked just over 500 nautical miles off the coast of India. She was proceeding east and had passed the Gulf of Aden in a convoy escorted by the Turkish frigates *Gediz* and *Gelibolu*. The hijacking took place one and a half days after she left the convoy. The *Frigia* was en route to Thailand from Port Said in Egypt with a cargo of fertilizer; her crew consisted of 19 Turkish and two Ukrainian sailors. An EU NAVFOR official expressed concerns that the fertilizer could be used to create explosive devices; but arms supplies have never been a problem in Somalia, and pirates are running the most successful commercial enterprise in Somalia; they can import all the explosives they need, or buy from plentiful local stocks.

The only effective response to these attacks was for merchant ships to become more resilient, to rely on their own resources, and not depend on naval forces. By the end of 2010 pirates had rapidly adapted to the pressure from the international naval forces deployed, at great expense, in the Gulf of Aden and the western Indian Ocean. The result was an explosion of activity across the Indian Ocean, with greater success than ever and steadily increasing ransom payments. This was the time when Somali piracy came of age and became a major threat to maritime lines of communication throughout the Indian Ocean. The scale and seriousness of this threat to international trade is difficult to exaggerate.

SOUTHEAST ASIA AND THE SOUTH CHINA SEA

Historically the South China Sea and the islands of Indonesia and the Philippines have been infested with pirates. Young says: 'The roots of contemporary maritime piracy in Southeast Asia lay in the cultural, economic, and political environment of states in the region, and their inability to effectively control or regulate this environment.'[25]

For nearly 300 years, between 1520 and 1810, China experienced a great age of piracy, and for about half that time pirates held sway over large parts of the south coast of China. There were three great pirate cycles: the merchant pirates of the mid-Ming dynasty (1520–1575); the rebel pirates of the Ming–Qing transition (1620–1684); and the commoner pirates of the mid-Qing dynasty (1780–1810).[26] At the end of this period, in 1805, seven pirate leaders formed a confederation that dominated southern China for the next five years. In 1807 one of the confederation's fleets consisted of 300 junks and had between 20,000 and 40,000 men available; under the confederation, piracy became a major organized business, and the pirates even threatened Canton.[27]

Piracy is therefore a criminal enterprise with a long history in the region, a history that has been unbroken. At the end of the twentieth century the South China Sea and the islands of Indonesia and the Philippines represented the greatest threat to international shipping from piracy, not Somalia. In the

1990s the pattern of attacks was two-fold: local robberies at sea off Indonesia and the Philippines, a problem that continues to this day, and the seizure of merchant ships and their cargoes by organized criminal gangs. As is the case in Somalia, the more serious pirate attacks have involved local predatory elites, including Chinese officials and senior businessmen. Piracy, which involves complex transactions, the need to sell large cargoes and to transfer millions of dollars, cannot be undertaken by small groups of fishermen, unless the objective is merely to rob the crew; the involvement of organized criminal gangs is an essential element in the process. It is difficult to overemphasize this point: like drug smuggling and human trafficking, piracy is a branch of organized crime and needs to be treated as such. Ultimately, success in dealing with piracy requires that those organizing, investing in and managing the business are dealt with: the best means available is to follow the money trail.

The attack on the UK-owned tanker MV *Valiant Carrier* off the Indonesian coast in 1992 was, according to John Burnett, the incident that was in part responsible for the creation of the Piracy Reporting Centre.[28] Unlike Somalia, professional piracy in Southeast Asia focuses on stealing cargoes and sometimes ships. Because of the rapid expansion of Somali piracy over the last five years little attention has been given to Southeast Asian piracy, but it is important, and ongoing. Because of the benefits that the geography of the region avoids pirates, with its many islands and narrow straits, and the endemic corruption of its coastal states, the region has perhaps the greatest potential as a pirate haven. When Somali piracy is just a distant memory, the chances for Southeast Asian piracy to be booming are high. The pirates of the area suffered a setback after the 2004 Asian tsunami, which destroyed many of their boats and villages,[29] but they are now re-equipped, in part due to the generosity of international donors, and they have learnt valuable lessons from the success of their Somali colleagues.

It is clear that political, or predatory, elites are the main organizers and beneficiaries of piracy. Burnett sees organized crime as the main driver of Southeast Asian piracy, and he has identified four main crime organizations that control piracy in Southeast Asia: the Singapore syndicate controls the southern part of the South China Sea and Malacca Straits; Bangkok controls the Andaman Sea; Hong Kong triads control the northern part of the South China Sea; and Jakarta triads control the Java Sea and parts of the South China Sea to Borneo. He adds that there are syndicate branches in Vietnam, Malaysia, Sumatra, Cambodia, the Philippines, Burma and mainland China.[30]

In Southeast Asia ships and their cargoes are stolen, ships' crews can be killed or thrown overboard, ships renamed and used to transport drugs and illegal immigrants to Europe and the United States. Burnett describes how the MV *Petro Ranger* was hijacked in 1998, north of the Horsburgh Light in the Malacca Straits. It was carrying diesel and jet fuel worth $2.3 million. The ship was renamed the *Wilby* and taken to Hainan Island in south China, where the cargo was unloaded. The pirates were arrested by a Chinese patrol boat, but if it had not been stopped it would have become a 'phantom' ship.[31] Piracy in Southeast Asia, as in Somalia, is a business, a violent one in which human life is of little importance.

Attacks in the old pirate havens of the South China Sea and the waters around Indonesia have recently increased. In the first half of 2009 attacks in Southeast Asia and the Far East doubled, from ten in the first quarter to 21 in the second quarter, confirming a similar trend seen in 2008. IMB Director, Captain Pottengal Mukunda, said:

> This is a clear indication that piracy and robbery in Southeast and East Asia has the potential to escalate and shipmasters should remain alert and be aware of the risks involved in the seaway and ports transited during the voyage.[32]

The South China Sea and the many islands of the Indonesian archipelago have been a home to pirates for centuries. In the nineteenth century Rajah Muda Hassim informed Captain Henry Keppel of *HMS Dido* that:

> This is to inform our friend that there are certain great pirates, of the people of Sarebus and Sakarran, in our neighbourhood, seizing goods and murdering people on the high seas. They have more than three hundred *war-prahus*, and extend their ravages even to Banjarmassim; they are not subject to the government of Bruni (Borneo); they take much plunder from vessels trading between Singapore and the good people of our country.[33]

There may no longer be 300 *war-prahus* operating off the coast of Borneo, but the descendants of these pirates still operate, robbing ships at sea, as their forbearers did. Carolin Liss of Murdoch University in Australia argues that five factors are of particular importance in shaping piracy in Southeast Asia: 'over-fishing, lax maritime regulations, the existence of organised crime syndicates, the presence of radical politically motivated groups in the region, and widespread poverty'.[34] She believes that a successful anti-piracy policy must address most, if not all, of these problems and issues. Arguably there is a sixth factor; a tradition of piracy, which goes back thousands of years in these waters.

Local conflicts in Southeast Asia provide the environment in which lawlessness occurs, which enables piracy to flourish. In Indonesia there have been violent confrontations in Aceh, Ambon and Halmahera, the latter two involving intra-religious strife. There is also continuing unrest in Kalimantan and there has been conflict in Sulavesi and Irain Jaya, although that area is away from the main sea lanes. The situation in the Philippines is also chaotic: the island of Mindanao in the southern Philippines experienced murders, bombings, fleeing refugees, guerrillas, government-armed militias in 2008, a virtual civil war, and in the last few years fighting has also taken place between government forces and Muslim MILF[35] insurgents in the mixed Muslim/Christian provinces of Maguindao, Sharriff Kabunsuan and North Cotabato. In southern Thailand, it is claimed that there have been 2,500 deaths over the past decade in the violent conflict between the Thai armed forces and a rebel separatist group in the three Muslim-dominated southern provinces. Added to this mix are the Indonesian Islamic terrorist groups with links to Al-Qaeda, responsible for a number of bombings, including the Jakarta attack of July 2009 and the Bali bombing of October 2002. There is not necessarily direct causation between any of these individual conflicts, or active groups, and piracy, but that there is a situation in which the rule of law, and the control of territory, is insecure in many areas of Southeast Asia. This, together with the high levels of corruption among officials, widespread poverty and the existence of organized crime in the area makes Southeast Asia an environment in which piracy can flourish. China is not immune from a range of problems, notably widespread corruption among officials[36] and links between the Communist Party of China and the triad gangs. Deng Xiaoping, the leader of the Communist Party of China, said in October 1984 that many of the triads were good and many of them were patriotic.[37] Carlyle Thayer says that Vietnam 'suffers from endemic corruption, rising inflation, environmental pollution and other social ills'.[38] Except in Singapore, corruption is a major problem in the region. The connections between sophisticated organized crime, business and politicians have created a perfect setting for piracy.

The capture of vessels, either by pirates, or by corrupt officials using state's resources, has been a feature of Southeast Asian piracy for a number of years. On occasions the crews have been murdered; sometimes they have been detained by police. In 1997 the container ship MV *Vosa Carrier*, en route to Haiphong, was detained by Chinese officials, who then confiscated all of its cargo. The officers and crew were interrogated and beaten by police. The shipowners had to pay $100,000 to secure the release of the vessel.[39]

Stefan Eklof says that tugs and barges, especially with cargoes of palm oil, have become the new target and that, 'Between September 2001 and September 2005 there were 22 reported hijackings of tugs and barges in Southeast Asia. Mainly the incidents were concentrated in the southern Malacca Strait region, where 17 of the reported incidents occurred.'[40] This trend has continued. On 6 April 2009 a Malaysian flagged, tug *Astaka* and barge *Astaka 5* were hijacked off Can Tho in Vietnam; as the IMB report notes, what happened was a classic act of piracy:

Three pirates wearing hoods and armed with guns boarded the tug. The tug had eleven crewmembers onboard including the Master and the barge was loaded with sand. The pirates took hostage four crewmembers, tied their hands and locked them in the Master's cabin. They could hear the sound of the main engines and footsteps outside the cabin. After some time, they felt the tugboat jolt and could smell burning in the cabin. The main engine of the tug had stopped. The crew managed to free themselves and later launched and abandoned the tugboat in a liferaft. They did not see the rest of the crewmembers. Once the four crewmembers reached ashore, they complained to the Vietnamese Authorities who investigated the matter. The tug was later found in the coastal waters of Can Tho and the barge was found with the cargo off Con Dao Island. The other seven crewmembers are still missing.[41]

This is even worse than the situation off Somalia. There the crew, once taken, will eventually be released; in this case it is a reasonable assumption that the seven crew members were murdered.

On 19 February 2009 another tug and barge were attacked in the Malacca Straits, the master and the chief officer were kidnapped and equipment was stolen. Yet another tug and barge, en route from Singapore to Vietnam, was hijacked in the South China Sea off Palawan, Borneo. This time the IMB reported:

Twelve pirates armed with small firearms and long knives boarded [and] ... took hostage 10 crew members, blindfolded and tied them up using masking tape and hijacked the vessels. On 13 April, pirates instructed the crew members to lower and board their life raft. Then, they sailed the tug and barge to an unknown location. A passing ship rescued the crew members on 14 April.[42]

In 2010 there were further incidents involving tugs. On 6 February 2010 a tug towing an empty barge was hijacked north of Tioman Island, Malaysia.[43] Then, during April 2010, a tug and barge were hijacked on the South China Sea; on this occasion the crew were lucky enough to survive and a Malaysian maritime patrol boat located the barge, which had been cast off by pirates.[44] On 27 April 2010 the tug *Atlantic 3* was reported as being hijacked approximately nine nautical miles east of Pulau Bintan en route from Tanjung Ayam, Malaysia to Kintap, Indonesia.[45]

Other ships have been hijacked for their cargoes, including a cargo ship off the Lingga Islands, Southeast of Singapore, which was seized on 22 April 2005; its cargo of tin, valued at $4.6 million, was unloaded at Pasir Gudang in Johor State, Malaysia. Various other cargo ships, tankers and bulk carriers have been successfully boarded and valuables stolen, such as the chemical tanker robbed off the Mangkai Islands in April 2010.[46] There seems to be no reason why larger ships will not also be hijacked, the pirates copying the tactics of the Somalis, although a safe haven for hijacked vessels would need to be developed. In future years the shipping industry will need to be prepared for a major escalation of the piracy problem in the South China Sea.

WEST AFRICA

In January 2010 an ex-US ambassador to Nigeria, John Campbell, said: 'Nigeria cannot be a reliable ally if it is consumed by its own corruption and political machinations', adding it 'is rapidly becoming more like Somalia – a failed state with no real government to cooperate with'.[47] It is difficult to judge the true level of maritime crime off west Africa, in part due to massive underreporting of attacks and robberies at sea. The level of actual attacks may be four or five times the reported levels. It is of course difficult to prove such claims, but having spoken to shipowners whose vessels have been attacked it is clear that it is common not to report such incidents to insurers and cargo-owners; as there is no wish to pay increased premiums, and there is a fear of losing existing business.

The nature of piracy off the coast of West Africa is predominantly a Nigerian problem. Whereas the Ghanaian navy has acted effectively against piracy, there seems to be little will in Nigeria to deal with the frequent robberies at sea and the occasional hijacking of ships. There are two main drivers behind maritime crime in Nigeria; the high incidence of crime in that country and 'bunkering', or the sale of stolen crude oil. The bunkering trade requires oil tankers, or oil barges, and these have often been taken at sea, and in some cases their crews murdered. The dangers to merchant vessels sailing in Nigerian waters are high and attacks are characterized by extreme violence. The attackers are normally associated with militancy in the Niger Delta and Bakassi peninsular, and it is claimed that these militant organizations have links to politicians and military leaders. For example, the US intelligence supplier, STRATFOR, claims that MEND is not an ordinary militant group, and that:

> Its fighters are also given protection by politicians to carry out attacks against energy infrastructure targets within designated territories that largely have been found in the country's oil producing Niger Delta region. Monies generated from MEND attacks (such as ransom payments and revenues from illegal bunkering operations) flow back to PDP (Nigeria's ruling People's Democratic Party) politicians.[48]

Bunkering, which is worth about $1.5 billion a year, appears to be the main source of funds for Nigeria's predatory elite. It is no coincidence that Nigeria's federal government faces a widening fiscal deficit.[49] A Nigerian newspaper, *Vanguard*, quoted a Nigerian security official, who said of the illegal bunkering trade:

> Look here, we have arrested some of these vessels in the past, only to be told to release them immediately by some big shots in the military. In fact now, they do not even wait for us to arrest any vessel. We are warned in advance to expect these vessels and not to interfere with them. Some of those we had accosted in the past had mentioned names of notable retired military Generals who you least expect to be involved in all of this and when we called to verify, it turned out to be true.[50]

There is nothing new about such claims. Writing in 1996 Peter Lewis said of Nigeria:

> The involvement of military leaders in large-scale petroleum smuggling, and imputations of narcotics trafficking, point to further illicit gains. This

157

largesse, supplemented by 'rents' from finance and real estate, has been shared among an élite stratum of loyalist officers, civilian cronies, and acquiescent politicians. Blandishments offered to the military rank and file and the political class were strategically allocated to facilitate personal rule.[51]

Nigeria is an archetype of the predatory state. The disappearance of the *MT African Pride* from Lagos naval yard, after its arrest in August 2003 for carrying illegal crude oil, illustrates the involvement of the country's elites; it exposed the involvement of the chief of naval staff in the bunkering trade. In his testimony to the Nigerian House of Representatives Committee on the Navy, given on 24 November 2004, Captain Peter Duke, accused the chief of naval staff of attempting on several occasions to interfere with his job as commanding officer:

> Any time we arrested and he had interest, he would call me and insult me and bang the phone on me. We had arrested several ships and senior Naval officers would call to say that they should be released. The Chief of Naval Staff had called the Flag Officer Commanding, Western Naval Command that we should release a ship we arrested named M.T. *Molab Trader* chartered by one chief who is a friend of the CNS.[52]

In January 2005 Rear Admirals Francis Agbiti and Samuel Kolawole were demoted to the rank of commodore and dismissed from the Nigerian navy for their negligence in allowing the arrested tanker *African Pride* to escape from navy custody in Lagos harbour in August 2004. Rear Admiral Antonio Bob-Manuel was found innocent of all charges. Prosecutors also alleged that Agbiti and Kolawole were responsible for the 'simultaneous alteration, destruction and removal of documents' following the ship's disappearance. Two junior navy officers, Jonathan Ihejiawu and Suleiman Atan, told the court-martial they were paid 250,000 naira each ($1,850) by Lieutenant Commander Mohammed Abubakar on 31 October 2003, to escort the *MT African Pride* from Lagos harbour to the high seas, where its cargo was transferred to a waiting ship, and replaced by seawater. The court heard that Abubakar had told the two junior officers the payment was from the 'big boys' in the navy. [53] In the light of these events it is not difficult to see why calling the Nigerian navy may not be a good idea if you are attacked. To quote Peter Lewis again:

[T]he military leadership and a small circle of civilian cronies largely circumvented the formal economy through unprecedented corruption, including large diversions of oil stock and revenues, systemic commercial fraud, and intensified drug trafficking. These parallel activities offered refuge from a declining economy to a narrow, predatory élite.[54]

Two incidents in 2009 illustrate the problems faced by merchant ships. On 23 November 2009 the Liberian-flagged oil tanker, the *Cancale Star*, was hijacked off the coast of Benin, to the west of Lagos; at least one of the seven hijackers was Nigerian; a Ukrainian member of the crew was killed. The ship had just loaded 89,000 cubic metres of crude oil from Nigeria. Two days later the Nigerian-owned product tanker, *African Prince*, was hijacked off Nigeria, but was recaptured by the Ghanaian navy on 25 November 2009; one crew member was killed by the hijackers.[55]

As your ship approaches the coast of Nigeria be very careful; you are on your own.

SOUTH AMERICA AND THE CARIBBEAN

Historically the Caribbean was the pirate haven. Its many islands and narrow channels and the eighteenth-century competition between European states made it an ideal environment for piracy. Today crime at sea in the area is mainly about drug-running from Latin America into the United States; human smuggling is largely a land-based operation.

However, there are signs that the region could develop into the fourth major piracy area. There have been a number of attacks on yachts sailing off South America, particularly off Venezuela. There was the strange case of the *Spirit of Cologne*, a German yacht discovered off the coast of Venezuela with the owner's body on board, while his wife was picked up from a life raft in April 2010. Ships are regularly robbed while at anchor off ports, and occasionally people are killed. The common type of maritime crime in South America is robbery from a ship at anchor, or alongside. The International Maritime Bureau reported that in 2009 there were 37 incidents of piracy, or maritime robbery, in South America, compared to 14 in 2008. Twelve of the reported incidents in 2009 occurred in the anchorage, or port, of Callao in Peru.[56] A container ship was robbed on 9 May 2009; the IMB report states that 'Despite having four shore watchmen and extra lighting, the robbers managed to steal ship's rescue boat's engine and escape.'[57] This is typical of the problems faced by mariners in the region. Similar reports from Puerto

Bolivar anchorage on 7 February 2010 and from Conchan Terminal, Peru, on 28 March 2010 record the theft of ship's stores from merchant ships. In 2000, at a time when Somalia was not considered a major problem, Jack Gottschalk and Brian Flanagan considered that 'Brazil is the capital of piracy in the Americas', second only to the waters off Thailand and Indonesia for pirate activity; they also referred to the extent of organized crime there, and said that 'pervasive criminal activity exists that runs from the bustling docks of Rio de Janeiro, the anchorages of Santos, and the Alamoa Terminal, and high into the structure of law enforcement, the labour unions, and elsewhere.'[58]

The danger is that the organized criminal gangs, and narco-terrorists like the FARC, who are deeply embedded in South and Central America, could come to see maritime hijacking based on the Somali model as a new and interesting supplement to their income from drugs, prostitution and human trafficking. If the current global economic problems further weaken states in Central America and the northern part of South America, secure pirate havens could become available for such operations. The United States would face pressure to become involved; but in an era where the major powers are reducing the size of their naval forces and are showing a reluctance to spend money on foreign adventures, such pirate havens may survive. For the moment South America and the Caribbean remain places that yachtsmen should sail with caution, avoiding the coast of Venezuela and Guyana if they can, and where all seamen must take precautions against being robbed when at anchor, or berthed, especially in Peru or Ecuador. However, it would be a mistake to ignore the threat to yachtsmen; Somalis learnt their trade by attacking smaller craft such as fishing boats and tugs. South American pirates may be in the process of learning their craft, but they have an excellent support network of corrupt officials, international criminal networks, and a ready source of investment capital from the drug cartels.

We may not yet have full-blown predatory states in South America, although Peru has in the past met many of the requirements, but the strength of organized crime endures. The index of failed states gives a clue to the countries in the region that may provide future support for piracy; in the 2010 index Colombia ranked 46, Nicaragua 66, Ecuador 69, and the Western Hemisphere's clear winner in this race to the bottom was Haiti, in 11th position in the world, just behind Pakistan.[59] Stephan Feris also notes that the effects of climate change will put additional stresses on countries already ill-equipped to cope with economic problems – Peru and the Andean states being the obvious examples – and will further weaken these states.[60]

Although it is likely that the main growth in piracy in the next ten years will come mainly from the South China Sea, the potential of South America to develop a full-blown pirate industry should not be ignored. There may well come a time when the hordes of tourists, boarding that vast armada of cruise liners at Fort Lauderdale, select their vessel on the basis of its security, rather than on the size of its swimming pool or other onboard entertainments.

CHAPTER 6

PIRATE OPERATIONS

INTRODUCTION: THE BUSINESS OF PIRACY

Modern piracy is not a matter of a few fishermen deciding that it would be a good idea to supplement their income; it is an organized criminal business. Some of the attacks in ports and anchorages are the work of opportunistic thieves, but this is not the normal situation.

Somali pirates, or *sea-shifta*, for example, are organized in separate groups, selected by their leader, often a local businessman, with a clear hierarchy and with clear responsibilities. They are selected and trained, and sport a distinctive gang mark, like a coloured scarf. The word *shifta* derives from the Somali word *shúfto*, which means bandit, rebel, outlaw or revolutionary. In the nineteenth century *shiftas* were a sort of local militia in the mountainous areas of north-east Africa, but they developed into freelance outlaws, rustlers and highway robbers, somewhat in the same way as the reivers on the English–Scottish border in the middle ages.[1] But the meaning of *shifta* or *shiftinnet* (the role of *shifta*) is complex. For English speakers, 'outlaw' is the nearest equivalent – where Robin Hood was one of the good guys and Ned Kelly was a hero. But for many Somalis there is ambivalence about pirates; they can be both heroes and villains.

The larger pirate gangs also appear to have close connections to local politicians, who may themselves be directly involved in the business, and the main pirate groups typically have sub-groups, or companies. Jay Bahadur has described how one group has a range of positions, including supplies officer (responsible for food and '*Khat*'), an accountant, an interpreter, cooks, guards (for defending a captured ship), in addition to the actual attackers.[2]

Given the lack of alternative employment in Somalia, and the possibility of gaining wealth, piracy is an attractive option for many young Somalis. The UN has recorded the recruitment of children into pirate attack groups operating from Puntland; ten cases were recorded in January and February 2010. Some had escaped from militias, only to sign up as pirates. According to the UN: 'During 2010, several cases were documented of children escaping from Al-Shabaab and joining the pirate groups in Puntland.'[3] Most recruits though are slightly older. Reuters reported in April 2010 that hundreds of youths in Haradheere were desperate to sign up as pirates. However, before they can be of any use they normally have to undergo training. Reuters quoted one recruit, Adam Shine, who had waited for months for the chance to join a pirate group in Haradheere. He told Reuters:

I came here with my friends. They had a gun and were immediately recruited and joined companies. But I've never had a gun so, after a fairly long process, I was told to take part in training for a month and now I can join.[4]

After Shine completed his training with guns, boat-handling and global-positioning, he was ready to be deployed. Training is a major issue for pirate groups, and there was a report, citing a Canadian intelligence document, that Al-Shabaab has been providing weapons, combat training and local protection – a complete training package – to the Mudug pirates of southern Somalia.[5] In other words, as in any equivalent military unit, it is essential that the foot soldiers of Somali piracy can fight, navigate and maintain their boat; we should never underestimate the planning and preparation of the pirates. It also appears that some men are forced into piracy, according to the testimony of US Office of Naval Intelligence counter-piracy chief, Brian P. Green, during the American trial of the five Somalis who attacked the USS *Nicholas* on 1 April 2010.[6] In the same way that the Royal Navy used to press-gang seamen, men with seagoing skills are extremely valuable members of any pirate group. Certainly Yemeni fishermen have been press-ganged and hostages are forced to operate motherships.

Like a military unit, which it resembles, a pirate gang has a standard set of tools, procedures and methods. The tools they use are small fishing skiffs, motherships and above all weapons. The larger PAGs, those that are able to range across the Indian Ocean, also invest heavily in intelligence, planning and navigation equipment.

THE ATTACK CRAFT

The basic tactics of piracy have changed little over thousands of years; pirates must possess a nimble vessel that is significantly faster than their prey, a good sea craft able to carry sufficient armed men to overwhelm the ship being pursued. In the age of sail and manpower fast galleys were frequently the answer, although each region produced their own pursuit craft – from the *prahus* of Borneo to the dhows of the Persian Gulf pirates, the *brigantines* favoured by Caribbean pirates, and the most famous pirate craft of all, the *Xebec* used by the Barbary pirates. The most common pirate craft today is a small coastal fishing boat, typically a form of 'skiff' (Figure 6.1a). A skiff is a flat-bottom open boat of shallow draft, with a pointed bow and a square stern. Traditionally such craft were propelled by oars, or sail, but today the main form of propulsion is the outboard motor, and the unit most commonly used in Somalia is the Yamaha Enduro 40 hp model, commercial outboards that are only available in Asia, Africa and parts of Australia. They are cheap (about $2,200) and basic, have two cylinders and a single carburettor. With no sophisticated electronics they can be easily maintained within Somalia and even repaired at sea (Figure 6.1b).

The standard Somali skiff, of glass-fibre construction, 5–7 metres in length, was first used in Somalia in the 1980s as the result of a Swedish development project aimed at helping coastal fishermen. This craft is called a *Leila Alawi* after a famous blonde Egyptian singer and film star because the Yamaha outboard 'sings' when under power. A second larger craft was also produced, called the *Volva*, a 10–12-metre fishing boat with an inboard Volo Penta diesel. This is often used to support the smaller rate skiffs by carrying supplies, but it is not a true mothership.

Skiffs normally have one outboard, although two can be fitted, and are usually tracked travelling at around 26 knots, when in attack mode. The UN Monitoring Group on Somalia noted in 2010 that 'With the exception of the outboard motors, most equipment and weapons found on pirates are [is] outdated and in poor condition. [...] All seized outboard engines were Yamaha Enduro types, fairly recent models and in good condition.'[7] The skiffs used by Somalis vary slightly in design, but have a family resemblance. There are reports that new models of skiff are being developed

Figure 6.1a Somali attack skiff – UN Monitoring Group

Figure 6.1b Yamaha Enduro outboard motor

and enhanced versions may be given deeper hulls, to improve their seaworthiness. This is a matter of some importance to Somali pirates, as it appears that hundreds of them may have drowned at sea, overcome by rough waters and high winds. The craft used off Nigeria and in the South China Sea are similar, although rigid inflatable boats (RIBs) have been used by West African pirates; but there are no reports of their use by Somalis yet.

MOTHERSHIPS

One unusual feature of Somali piracy has been the widespread use of motherships – large pirate support vessels, or LPSVs – to carry skiffs and to provide support for operations far from Somalia. The importance of the mothership is that it has allowed Somali pirate gangs to operate far out in the Indian Ocean and into the Arabian Sea. An ideal mothership is a Far Eastern tuna boat, such as the *Win Far 161*, equipped with long-range fuel tanks and the latest electronic equipment, including radar, AIS tracker, GPS navigation aids and good radios.

One recent development has been the use of merchant ships as motherships, vessels like the MV *Sinar Kudus*. General cargo ships and bulkers have good cranes and can carry several attack skiffs. There are also reports that over 50 pirates have embarked such ships. These LPSVs have excellent sea-going capabilities, long range, good speeds, and are indistinguishable from other merchant ships; they can therefore get near to target vessels without arousing suspicion, especially at night when it is impossible to read their names. In the last quarter of 2011 the use of LPSVs was rapidly expanding, and this development had allowed PAGs to extend their radius of operations greatly. There were reports of PAGs being sighted south of Sri Lanka. There were also unconfirmed reports of LPSVs being equipped with heavy machine guns.

It seems that motherships are often deployed to predetermined positions, either a waypoint or an intercepting position, waiting for their prey; they may also be used to resupply other PAGs. The intelligence available to such operations must be assumed to be comprehensive and effective. The AIS system broadcasts the position, heading and speed of a ship fitted with it, to anyone with access to the internet and a standard vessel tracking service. Strangely many ships have 'technical problems' with their AIS equipment once they enter the Red Sea, or pass west of India: this seems to be very sensible, no point in broadcasting information to the enemy.

Motherships may be controlled by Somalis, but normally the original crew is forced to man the vessel, while it undertakes its pirate patrols. Some pirate commanders have even put the hostage crew against the ship's rails and threatened to shoot them if an attack is launched against the vessel. Foreign navies have not always understood that not all the men on board motherships are pirates, and have not always been able to distinguish between a mothership and a hijacked vessel. The worst case was the sinking by gunfire of the Thai fishing boat the *FV Ekwat Nava 5* by the Indian navy ship *INS Tabor*, killing 15 of the 16 original crew who remained on board after the Somali pirates, who had hijacked the vessel on 18 November 2008, fled.[8]

Smaller craft, including Yemeni fishing boats, coastal trading craft and the Somali fishing boat *Volva* are also used as support boats by PAGs operating near the Somali coast and in the Gulf of Aden. Larger motherships can support the PAGs operating across the Indian Ocean, in the Arabian Sea and the Mozambique Channel. Somali *sea-shifta* have a two-fold interest in capturing tuna boats. First, there remains a strong feeling in Somalia that these vessels are illegally taking Somalia's fish (although many are hijacked far away from Somali waters). Second, they make ideal motherships. The arguments over illegal fishing have a lot to do with the public justifications for piracy and the attempt to gain support within the Somali diaspora. Members of the Somali diaspora certainly have the capacity to invest in piracy and support these business operations, thus being an important constituency – although it is important to stress that the majority of Somalis living outside the country are law-abiding. Psychologically it is also useful for the average Somali pirate to feel that his job is not only about blackmailing foreigners into ransoming their ships and crews; the sense that he is also protecting the national interest is a useful pretext for his activities. The myth that Somali piracy emerged from a reaction to illegal foreign fishing also surfaces from time to time, whereas the truth is that piracy has always been a money-making scheme and most foreign boats have obtained some form of licence from someone in Somalia. But of course as Somalia has no true national government, it is rather difficult to show that your licence came from the 'right' authority.

The tuna boats hijacked by *sea-shiftas* are often abandoned by their owners, as they carry no insurance and the boat is worth less than the ransom being demanded. There is frequently no consideration by the owners for the welfare of the crew. The case of the Taiwanese tuna boat *Win Far 161* is one of the saddest. After ten months in the hands of Somali pirates she was finally released on 11 February 2010, after payment of a small ransom, with two or three of her crew dead: their bodies were pickled in barrels (though reports vary); it was reported that these men died of malnutrition, disease and neglect.[9] The *Win Far 161* was used extensively as a mothership, after being hijacked 160 nautical miles north of the Seychelles on 6 April 2009; its owner, Hseih Long-yan, has been accused of doing nothing to secure the vessel's release. Another Taiwanese fishing boat the *Jih-chun Tsai 68*, was hijacked on 30 March 2010. The *Jih-chun Tsai 68* was sunk by the frigate *USS Stephen W Groves* on 12 May 2011, approximately 100 nautical miles off the Somali coast; the Master died and two crewmen were injured.[10] A NATO Press Release, issued on 18 May 2011 stated that,

'During an engagement between the USS STEPHEN W GROVES and the Taiwanese fishing vessel Jih Chun Tsai 68, a known pirate mothership, shots were exchanged before the pirates surrendered. Subsequently a boarding team from the STEPHEN W GROVES was able to access the fishing vessel where they found 4 dead and 2 injured people. The dead were identified as the master/owner of the fishing vessel and 3 pirates and the injured were 2 of the pirates.'[11]

Figure 6.2 The hijacking of the *Tian Yu 8*

169

On 13 November the fishing vessel *Tian Yu 8* was hijacked, and the crew were photographed huddled under the guns of pirates (Figure 6.2).[12]

The Taiwanese fishing vessel *Tai Yuan 227* was used as a mothership after its capture, having been hijacked north of the Seychelles on 6 May 2010. Other small vessels that may have been used as motherships in 2010 include the Yemeni coastal freighter MV *Scootra 1*, hijacked on Christmas Day 2009, the *FV Sakoba*, hijacked in February 2010, the MV *Iceberg 1*, hijacked on 29 March 2010 and reportedly sighted by the USS *McFaul* with the new name *Sea Express* on 19 May 2010. Ecoterra reported that as the owners, Azal Shipping of Dubai, refused to ransom the ship, the sailors were not given food, water or medicine and were starving and sickening.[13] As noted previously, the crew were finally freed after a Puntland government operation in December 2012, one man having died in captivity and the master was missing. A number of other vessels were also hijacked in April 2010, including three large Thai fishing boats taken off the Maldives on 18 April 2010: the *FV Prantalay 11*, the *FV Prantalay 12* and the *FV Prantalay 14*. Two Yemeni fishing boats were also taken at the beginning of April 2010 in the Gulf of Aden.

Yachts have also been used as motherships and one is thought to have been used in the hijacking of the product tanker, MV *James Park*. Only the most foolish yachtsman would now venture into the western Indian Ocean, so it is unlikely that new victims will be readily found.[14] On 30 March 2010 India banned Indian-flagged motorized sailing vessels (i.e. dhows) from sailing west of Salalah, Oman or south of Malé, in the Maldives. This probably reduced the number of small Indian vessels being hijacked. However, as it will be readily understood from the long list of suitable vessels held by the Somalis in 2010, there is no shortage of suitable motherships, and the Far Eastern tuna boats, in particular, are ideal long-distance support vessels – good sea boats, with long range, well-equipped, with large amounts of storage, and with the ability to deploy small boats from their decks. Too often, these boats and their crews were abandoned by their owners and their half-starved crews were forced to sail as part of a Somali PAG.

THE ARMS TRADE

The hijacking of the Panama-flagged MV *Almezaan*, in-bound to Mogadishu on 7 November 2009, appeared to lift a corner of the veil, which obscures the arms trade to Somalia. The *Almezaan* regularly sails from the United Arab Emirates to Somalia and it was alleged that the ship was carrying light arms, ammunition, as well as RPGs, in addition to other general cargo.[15] A report in *Lloyd's List* on 10 November 2009 said that the vessel may have also been carrying short- and medium-range missiles, when its cargo was offloaded at Garacad, near Eyl. It is unclear precisely what the exact content of the cargo was, or who it was intended for – suggested recipients vary from Al-Shabaab, to the African Union, to the TFG. It is also unclear who loaded the Dubai-owned ship, which appears to have transited from the Persian Gulf.

The *Almezaan* was released on 19 November, only 12 days after being captured, for the tiny amount of $15,000. It had been hijacked earlier on 1 May 2009, taken to Haradheere and released less than a week later without any ransom being paid. The *Almezaan* certainly had powerful supporters in Somalia, and the allegations of gun-running (denied strongly by its owners) have to be taken seriously; but of course in Somalia all is smoke and mirrors, and nothing is ever certain. In March 2009 the master was prepared to take life to defend the *Almezaan*, even though previous hijackings had been short-term and cost little. The ship was attacked twice by a gang of at least seven pirates in a pair of fast skiffs 60 miles south of Haradheere, while in transit to Mogadishu. During the second attack the *Almezaan's* security guards shot and killed one member of a group of pirate attackers and their skiffs were riddled with bullets.[16]

Another mystery vessel is the MV *Rim*, a North Korean-flagged rust bucket, 37 years old, Romanian built, 3,500 tons, owned by a Libyan company, White Sea Shipping, and with a crew of ten men – nine Syrians and one Romanian. The MV *Rim*, hijacked in the Gulf of Aden on 3 February 2010, north of the IRTC, was taken to Somalia. According to the filed transit report the ship was sailing from Mariupol in Ukraine, and was on its way to Kandla, India with a cargo of kaolin china, after which it was going to be scrapped. However, it is alleged by some that the MV *Rim* had actually stopped in Libya and Eritrea, and was on its way to Yemen. Libya had a continuing involvement in the Horn of Africa, mainly because of its attempts to undermine Egyptian policy in the region. Mesfin says that 'Libya which was not directly involved in territorial or other disputes in the Horn of Africa helped the enemy (Ethiopia) of its enemy's (Egypt) allies, Sudan and Somalia.'[17] Eritrea has a reputation as a transhipment point for arms, and supplies for Yemeni rebel groups are often routed via its ports. But in another version of the story the MV *Rim* was abandoned by the shipping company, various pirate groups bought and sold the ship and crew, and the ransom of $300,000 demanded by the pirates was not forthcoming. The crew were kept on starvation rations and had to collect rainwater and cook in seawater. At this point, on 2 June 2010, when their captors had decided to kill them and sell their organs to make money, a Somali cook called Ahmed gave the crew three AK-47s and, in a confused and bloody 45-minute fire fight, in which the pirates fired on each other, the hostages killed their pirate guards or forced them to jump into the sea.[18] The MV *Rim* made it out to sea, southeast of Garacad, pursued by other pirates in the hijacked vessel MV *VOC Daisy*, but this was too much for the ship's ancient engines, which seized up. A helicopter from the Spanish warship, the *SPS Victoria*, intervened in time to drive their pursuers away.[19] Two days later, with the Dutch warship *Johan de Witt* standing by and assisting, the crew – with Ahmed their saviour – gave up their attempts to restart the engines and abandoned ship. The wreck of the MV *Rim*, it is understood, now lies on the Somali coast, and the stories of its double life continue to circulate; perhaps the truth will finally surface one day. There are no reports on whether the ship was searched before she was finally abandoned. The point is that, although the MV *Rim* probably was not carrying arms, small ships like this, sailing under such flags, are an ideal vehicle for illegal trades. If the reports are correct, which is not certain, it seems that their captors may have been seeking to follow the example of the Kosovo Liberation Army (KLA), who butchered Kosovo Serbs prisoners for their organs.[20] The KLA of course rejects all such claims, as the pirates would certainly have done, had they lived.

The UN imposed a total arms embargo on the territory under UN Security Council Resolution 733 adopted on 23 January 1992. This resolution implemented 'a general and complete embargo on all deliveries of weapons and military equipment to Somalia until the Security Council decides otherwise'. This resolution still stands, but has been mainly honoured in the breach. Since 1992 all the players in the territory of what was once Italian Somalia (we will disregard the independent state of Somaliland in this discussion) have been able to arm themselves at will from a selection of effective, if often rusty, weaponry.

The supply of guns and rockets to Somalia does not merely arm pirates, but it has enabled the various factions in Somalia to carry out a wholesale slaughter of the civilian population and to drive large numbers of the population into refugee camps in Somalia, Kenya and the Yemen. For over 20 years, since the days of President Barre, Somalia has been continuously engaged in internal conflict. In September 2008 Amnesty International published the report 'Blood at the Crossroads: Making the Case for a Global Arms Trade Treaty', which described the impact of modern arms on the people of Somalia:

Amnesty International has documented the toll that the use of artillery, rockets and mortars has taken on the population of Mogadishu, resulting in wide-scale deaths and injuries – sometimes of entire families as artillery shells destroyed their houses – and the displacement of the population of entire districts of the city. Some 6,000 civilians were reportedly killed in fighting in the capital Mogadishu and across southern and central Somalia in 2007.[21]

The slaughter of the innocent continued.

In April 2008 a report by the UN Monitoring Group stated that:

Weapons sent to all parties of the Somali conflict originate in some of the same States as previously reported, namely Eritrea, Yemen and Ethiopia. The routes are, however, more covert, and weapons reach Somalia either by a larger number of smaller vessels, or through remote locations along land borders.[22]

In the same report the Monitoring Group noted that prominent security officials of the TFG, Ethiopian officers and Ugandan officers of the African Union Mission in Somalia were selling arms in the Mogadishu arms markets, including weapons originating from their own stocks and arms seized during battles with insurgents. Arms traders told the UN that the biggest suppliers of ammunition to the markets were Ethiopian and TFG commanders, who diverted boxes officially declared 'used during combat'. In a subsequent report in December 2008 the UN team concluded that:

Somali armed forces and groups remain in possession of fairly limited arsenals, consisting principally of small arms and crew-served infantry weapons. At the low end of this range are AK-47s, pistols and hand grenades; at the high end of the range are anti-aircraft cannons, anti-tank weapons, and medium mortars. There are a small number of functioning armoured vehicles, artillery pieces and rocket artillery, which are rarely used in combat.[23]

Interestingly, from an anti-piracy viewpoint, this report also noted that:

Exorbitant ransom payments [the result of piracy] have fuelled the growth of these [pirate] groups, including the procurement of arms and equipment and the maintenance of militia establishments in violation of the arms embargo. Although there is some evidence of linkages between piracy, arms trafficking, and the activities of some armed opposition groups, the Monitoring Group is currently more concerned about the apparent complicity in pirate networks of Puntland administration officials at all levels.[24]

As the UN Monitoring Group observed, Somali militias received weapons and training from neighbouring states, including Eritrea. Some of these weapons were delivered from Eritrea to Somalia using an Ilyushin 76TD aircraft, which made a number of flights. Other arms supplies were delivered by small boats. The UN Monitoring Group report stated such deliveries 'continue to occur on a fairly regular basis'.[25] However, in 2008, it was Yemen that held the position of primary exporter of commercial arms to Somalia. The UN Monitoring Group reported: 'Weapons from Yemen continue to feed Somali retail arms sales, as well as the needs of armed opposition and criminal groups. Insurgent groups in Ethiopia also procure arms and ammunition from Yemen, which then transit Somalia.'[26]

In 2009 the United States was also publicly identified as a major weapons supplier to Somalia, although, given the interest of the United States in the territory, it is likely that it had been clandestinely supplying arms over a long period. It seems that the bulk of weapons supplied by the United States to the TFG in 2009 came from Ugandan army stockpiles. A US State Department official said in August 2009 that the United States planned to increase supplies of arms and ammunition from 40 to 80 tons. News reports stated that 40 tons of arms were supplied in June 2009, but that within a short period much of that consignment was on sale in Mogadishu's arms markets, the locals keenly buying up new types of weapon available for the first time. US officials obviously had not taken the time to read the UN Monitoring Group's reports, or they would have had second thoughts about supplying the TFG with weapon, and would have anticipated such an outcome. In 2010 The UN Monitoring Group reported on the sale of weapons from TFG stocks, for example AK-47 type assault rifles, which arrived in Puntland markets, still crated, allegedly from TFG stocks: these weapons were known locally as *Sheikh Sharifs*, after the president of the TFG.[27] These weapons undoubtedly found their way on to pirate skiffs. The UN Monitoring Group concluded: 'Although difficult to verify, it is increasingly plausible that the Transitional Federal Government represents a more important source of arms and ammunition than foreign sponsors for its adversaries.'[28] In other words, by supplying the TFG with large quantities of arms the United States had actually become the main arms supplier to Al-Shabaab, the group that US officials often associate with Al-Qaeda. It would appear that the US supplied weapons to the TFG with the idea of fighting Al-Shabaab, but that those organizing these supplies were not informed about the realities on the ground in Somalia. This may well have been the result of an ill-judged political judgement, designed to show that the United States was fighting terrorism in Somalia.

In its July 2011 report, the UN Monitoring Group noted:

An intersection controlled by the Government in Mogadishu, known as 'kilometre four' (K4), is one of the primary locations where the Government [TFG] sells its ammunition, often in exchange for qaad, which is widely sold on the streets of K4. Qaad vendors often serve as intermediaries for arms dealers and brokers in Bakaara market and, in some cases, sell directly to Al-Shabaab.[29]

Nothing had changed. The Monitoring Group also observed: 'The predominant perception in Mogadishu is that the Government and pro-Government forces sell between one third and one half of their ammunition.'[30]

There were also reports that Ethiopia continued to act as a distributor of arms to favoured Somali factions, and that in 2010 it flew arms supplies directly into Somalia. It was known that three Ethiopian flights landed at Dhuusamareeb Airport on 28 June 2010 and that quantities of weapons were unloaded, including AK-47s, RPGs, PKM machine guns and mines, which were supplied to Ahlusunna, a group then heavily engaged in conflict with Al-Shabaab.[31] Small cargo ships, dhows and Ilyushin 76s continue to move tons of arms into Somalia, mostly supplied by foreign governments that wish to support one faction or another. The TFG was in practice just one of these many factions. Bakaara market is the main arms market in Mogadishu, and the part of the market where guns are sold is called *Cirtoogte* – 'sky shooter' – because buyers often test-fire weapons into the air.[32]

Somalia's arms suppliers have included a number of governments, merchants of the Persian Gulf and anyone else who wants to make a quick buck out of misery, or seek to 'influence' the situation in the mess that is Somalia. The UN arms embargo has been a dead letter for many years.[33]

PIRATE WEAPONS

The bulk of the arms used by pirates in Somalia, West Africa and elsewhere have traditionally been from the Soviet era – the Kalashnikov AK-47s and RPG-7s carried by the well-dressed Somali clansman. The AK-47 is a very effective weapon; its 7.62 mm bullet gives it a real killing power, unlike the 5.56 mm NATO standard bullets used by modern Western armies. It is rugged, can be covered in mud, buried, and still fire. Larry Kahaner has called it 'the world's most prolific and effective combat weapon';[34] it kills about 250,000 people each year. The most common version in Somalia is the Chinese-made Type 56. The poor condition of many of the weapons seized from pirates indicates that some of the weapons may be ex-Somali government stock from the 1970s and 1980s.

The RPG launcher is the other weapon most frequently used by Somali pirates. It is another Soviet-era design, which has been in service for about 50 years. The UN Monitoring Group noted in 2010 that most of the RPG grenades observed in Somalia are high explosive anti-tank (HEAT) type PG 7 V, PG 7 VL or PG 7 VM grenades, and that 'the market price per unit of the PG 7 V grenade in Somalia is estimated as US$50'.[35] The effective range of an RPG is around 300 metres, although its maximum range is about 1,000 metres. It is very inaccurate at such ranges, especially when fired from a small fast-moving boat. An impact fuse or a timed fuse can be used and a typical Somali pirate skiff will carry up to four warheads. The RPG 7 grenades are sensitive to moisture and temperature, and need to be properly stored and handled. An RPG round carried in an open skiff can easily develop faults and cannot be relied on. The main function of the RPG during attacks on merchant ships is to make a large 'bang' and frighten the masters and crew of the vessels so that they stop the engines and surrender their vessels. It appears that armour-piercing rounds are of little use at sea, although there are incidents where they have been used, for example off Nigeria.

The UN Monitoring Group also noted that the following types of weapons were regularly found in the possession of captured Somali pirates in 2009: 'AK-47 type assault rifles, SAR-80 and Heckler and Koch G3 assault rifles, Tokarev pistols, RPG grenades and launchers.'[36] Other weapons have been recovered, but heavier weapons, which are available in Somalia, including the PKM machine gun, the B10 recoilless rifle and the Carl Gustav M2 anti-tank weapon, do not appear to be common armament onboard pirate skiffs.

The UN Somalia Monitoring Group then went on to examine the types of weapons being used in Somalia. They noted that improvised explosive devices (IEDs) were being used and that the growing sophistication of these devices suggested that there had been 'the importation of expertise and the transfer of skills through training'.[37] They concluded: 'The conduct of five simultaneous, coordinated suicide bomb attacks in Hargeisa and Bosaso on 29 October 2008 represented a qualitative leap over previous improvised explosive device operations.'[38] Interestingly, in light of the arguments over the cargo of the *Almezaan*, the Monitoring Group noted that there were,

> reports of a small number of more advanced anti-tank weapons', but they said that they had at that time found no evidence of functional wire-guided anti-tank weapons, although there were 'small numbers of man-portable surface-to-air missiles, and the growing use of night-vision equipment.[39]

In recent years things have moved on, but the existence of night-vision equipment, which is an invaluable aid to pirates attacking at night, and man-portable surface-to-air missiles, which can protect motherships from helicopter attacks, highlight the military assets that are potentially available to Somali pirates.

If, and it is a big if, the *Almezaan* was carrying missiles, as *Lloyd's List* suggested, the most likely types would have been ex-Soviet short-range anti-tank wire-guided missiles like the 9K11 Malyutka, also known as the AT-3 Sagger, or the radio-guided 9K114 Shturm, also known as the AT-6 Spiral. Large numbers of the wire-guided Franco–German Milan missile are also available on the international arms market.

On balance, the AT-3 Sagger is the easiest anti-tank missile to acquire – the Soviet-era stockpiles of anti-tank missiles were vast. The Soviet Union produced about 25,000 Saggers a year during the 1960s and 1970s.

Neither the Sagger, nor the Spiral, is easy to use, and prolonged training is required to make use of these weapons effectively. They are far more potent weapons than the RPG-7, having a warhead of over 2.5 kg (5.3 kg in the case of the Spiral). It is possible that there are some Saggers in Somalia and that they have been delivered to the TFG or Al-Shabaab. If this is the case they could theoretically have been deployed on board pirate vessels. They are difficult, if not impossible, to fire from a small skiff, but could be fired from a mothership, or possibly from the *Volvo* craft widely used in Somalia, and with a three-kilometre range they could frighten the life out of any master unfortunate enough to be on the receiving end. It is not clear that they would seriously damage a large merchant ship, but they certainly have a much bigger warhead than the tried and trusted RPG-7 – although they cannot be used as a close-in weapon, because they have a relatively large minimum range of about 500–800 metres. It is to be hoped that the report in *Lloyd's List* is wrong and that the findings of the UN Monitoring Group are still relevant – that there are no operational wired-guided missiles in Somalia.

There is another weapon that it has been rumoured may be deployed by Somali pirates, but for which there is no firm evidence – the Soviet-era RPG29, which is a potent anti-tank weapon. The RPG29 fires two different types of projectiles; the PG-29 V anti-tank/anti-bunker round and the TBG-29 V thermobaric anti-personnel round. The PG-29 V round has a tandem-charge HEAT warhead for defeating explosive reactive armour (ERA). It has been described as the most dangerous adversary of main modern Russian battle tanks, in tests conducted against T-80 and T-90 tanks; it penetrates the tanks over their frontal arcs, despite the reactive armour and the already thick hull.[40] The RPG29 is arguably too powerful for pirate use, as its use can destroy the ships being attacked. It has been suggested that the Liberia-flagged Suezmax tanker *Brillante Virtuoso* was hit by one of these weapons, 20 nautical miles off Aden on 6 July 2011; which led to a fire in the accommodation block and evacuation of the vessel. The reports were confused and could not be relied on, and there was even a suggestion that the Yemeni coastguards may have fired the weapon at the tanker.[41]

From the point of view of mariners, any country that ignores the UN embargo is potentially putting weapons in the arms of pirates. This message needs to be clearly understood. The current military involvement by the international community in Somalia continues to create a threat to mariners that an effective arms embargo on the territory would go some way to reducing. It is worth remembering that some munitions, like RPG rounds, have relatively short shelf lives in Somalia and need continual replenishment. The danger, highlighted by the case of the *Almezaan*, is that even more sophisticated weapons can end up in the hands of pirates, tipping the balance in their favour.

There have also been reports that Somali pirates acquire weapons from Libyan stockpiles. Judith van der Merwe of the Algiers-based African Centre for the Study and Research on Terrorism told Reuters that, 'We believe our information is credible and know that some of the pirates have acquired ship mines, as well as Stinger and other shoulder-held missile launchers.'[42]

Concerns about the trade in Libyan weapons have been stated by Amanda Dory, the US deputy assistant secretary of defense on African affairs; she said that the weapons used by the Libyan rebels are now a threat to the whole region. She added, 'The breakdown of security in Libya has generated a significant flow of militants and weapons and has decreased legitimate cross-border traffic at a time of great economic fragility and turbulence.'[43]

PIRATE TECHNIQUES

The hijacking of a vessel by pirates falls into three phases. First, find a target; second, close with the target; and third, board and subdue any opposition.

Finding a suitable target can be a lengthy and complex task. For the larger Somali pirate groups that operate far out into the Indian Ocean some hijackings may result from intelligence gathered from within the shipping industry, the use of AIS tracking and the correct positioning of the attack group. For operations in the Gulf of Aden, the lower reaches of the Red Sea, off Oman and in the coastal waters of Somalia, it is likely that most targets are hijacked using operational patrolling, although intelligence undoubtedly plays a part even in this situation, and local fishermen act as lookouts for the pirate groups, using satellite phones to call pirate bases.

Closing with the target is normally straightforward: the target rarely has a speed of more than 15 knots, and Somali skiffs can travel at 26 knots. In such a case the skiffs will close at 11 knots or more if they are coming from the target's direction of travel. Actual interceptions vary, but a typical scenario would be for a mothership to deploy two or three attack skiffs ahead of the target vessel just before dawn, and for the skiffs to aim to board the target near the bridge – that is on that part of the vessel forward of the propellers and aft of the bow wake. One skiff crew will often attempt to board while the others provide covering fire from AK-47s and RPGs. The supporting skiff may also make a lot of noise on one quarter, say the port side of the vessel, while the boarding party attempt to board on the starboard side. The attack skiffs carry aluminium ladders with a hook on the end – these are often longer than the skiff. Once hooked onto the ship's rail one man tries to board and, if he is successful, he will be followed by his comrades. The pirate who is the first aboard is normally given a car, such as a Land Cruiser, and a larger share of the ransom (this may be three times the amount given to his colleagues). In giving the first man on board an additional reward the Somalis are copying the Barbary pirates, who used to give an extra slave to the man who first got on board the ship being attacked.

The vulnerability of merchant ships should be assessed by looking at a number of factors. Put simply they need to be able to: first, see the attack and take precautions in time; second protect their crews from the effects of bullets and blast; and third, resist boarding.

The average bulk carrier of around 30,000 dwt has a maximum speed of around 12 knots (far less if her hull is dirty), a low freeboard when fully loaded, and she is as blind as a bat from the stern – no radar, no thermal imaging, no CCTV cameras and little visibility from the bridge, as a huge funnel effectively blocks all views aft. Undermanned, and run on a shoestring, the ship in any case has real difficulty in keeping an adequate watch. A pirate skiff running alongside the stern of such a vessel before daylight may be able to board the vessel before the alarm is raised. It is not surprising that bulk carriers (bulkers) are Somalis' favourite targets.

Merely firing at the bridge can force the master to stop the engines and surrender the vessel even before the ship is boarded; it is said that this is what happened to the VLCC *Sirius Star* (Figure 6.3). James Grady, the ship's second officer, said 'we were forced to allow them on board when the pirates began firing in the air'.[44] Firing an AK-47 into bridge glass makes the bridge a dangerous area, not only because of the bullets, but because of flying glass. Bullet-proof protection is available, but at present few ships have this essential defence.

If the bridge is secure, equipped with bullet-proof glass and with most of the crew in a safe area below deck (a citadel), then the master can attempt to resist boarding. His first step is to call for full speed and then manoeuvre the ship so as to make boarding difficult; he can even attempt to ram the skiffs – anything to make life difficult for the pirates. Because the master is dealing with a well-armed opponent he has to avoid, at all times, exposing his crew to gunfire: that means that the use of crew-directed water-hoses, long-range acoustic devices (LRADs) (which are in any case ineffective), and throwing things overboard, must be avoided. Systems that can be controlled remotely, like automatic water cannon, can be effective, and so can lasers, but some forms of laser require specially trained operatives. Flares and thunderflash-type fireworks carried as emergency stores can also be a useful aid, but their use needs to be in accordance with company policy. A searchlight can also be very effective, especially when used at night, as it can disorient an attacker. As noted later, the deployment of armed guards is not without risks,

Figure 6.3 The *Sirius Star* with pirate skiffs at the stern

and can be an expensive exercise, but from about 2010 it has increasingly become the norm. Insurers offered discounts of up to 75 per cent where vessels carried armed guards.[45] As a result non-lethal alternatives, such as water cannon, were not generally adopted. However, it is clear that the presence of armed security teams and other forms of ship hardening did make ships more resilient and less likely to be hijacked by pirates.

Some shipowners have in the past put great faith in razor wire, partly because they believed that it was a cheap solution. Razor wires are difficult to install properly and, unless done with care, the crew may even find that use of safety equipment such as liferafts on board ship is compromised by having great coils of razor wire everywhere. Somali pirates have in any case developed effective techniques to overcome razor wire as well as the electrified wire used by some shipowners. They overcome the electrical defences by using large metal sticks that cause a short circuit. They also throw blankets over the razor wire and then put surf boards or aluminium ladders on the blankets to enable them to climb over it. While this is going on, their support skiff gives covering fire to discourage any attempt to stop the boarding.[46]

Finally, once on board, the pirates will try and threaten any member of the crew they can grab until the engines are stopped and the other pirates are allowed to board. Admiral Mike Mullen, chairman of the US Joint Chiefs of Staff, said the pirates were well trained. 'They're very good at what they do', he told a Pentagon briefing in Washington. 'Once they get to a point where they can board, it becomes very difficult to get them off, because, clearly, now they hold hostages.'[47] If all the crew members are in a secure citadel, the pirates may have access to the ship without gaining control of its key systems. In such cases naval forces have often been able to board and recover control of the vessel.

CHANGES IN STRATEGY

The 2009–10 pirate season in the Indian Ocean saw a significant change in the strategy of Somali pirates. Because of the presence of international naval forces and the growing capability of Somali pirates, the main focus of attacks moved away from the Gulf of Aden, to the coast of Oman, out into the Arabian Sea, as far east as the Maldives, and south into the Mozambique Channel. That is not to say that the Gulf of Aden was completely safe – attacks and hijackings continued to occur, despite the presence of Western warships and the establishment of the IRTC. The MV *St James Park* was seized in the Gulf of Aden on 28 December 2009, and the MV *Pramoni* was taken on New Year's Day 2010. On 5 May 2010 the Russian-owned tanker MV *Moscow University* was hijacked in the Gulf of Aden; the ship had a secure citadel and this enabled the men from the Russian destroyer *Marshal Shaposhnikov* to retake her the next day. The captured *sea-shifta* were cast off in leaky boats, never to be heard of again. At the start of the 2010 summer monsoon the Gulf of Aden, which is protected from some of the worse effects of the weather, again became popular with the pirates; on 28 June the *MT Golden Blessing*, a Singapore-flagged product tanker was seized, even though a naval helicopter was in the area, and on 4 July the *MT Motivator*, a small tanker, was taken in the southern part of the Red Sea, north of Bab el Mandeb.

In fact in the first quarter of 2010, within the Gulf of Aden and the adjacent sea areas of the Red Sea and Arabian Sea, four vessels were hijacked, and in the same period in 2009 five were hijacked – only a 20 per cent reduction; the international naval presence was not as effective as some would have liked to believe, and arguably represented a very poor return on investment. Although the number of attacks in the Gulf of Aden area did, according to the IMB, fall from 41 to 17 when comparing these two periods, the key test remains avoidance of hijackings.

Somali pirates have shown themselves to be resourceful and well-organized. Larger pirate groups have invested in motherships and developed the ability to deploy their attack groups as far as the Indian coast. In doing so they have also further enhanced their intelligence capacity and improved their ability to intercept target vessels at sea by using GPS navigation devices and night-vision equipment. At the higher end Somali piracy is a well-financed, sophisticated and organized criminal business; and should never be underestimated. In contrast there are also small pirate groups with little training and ability, who end up with no-hope cases like the MV *Rim*, which the larger groups could see would generate no ransoms.

Jean-Michel Louboutin, Interpol's executive director of police services said in Lyon that maritime piracy was 'a criminal phenomenon with a global magnitude' which required countries to combine and co-ordinate their law enforcement efforts to identify those responsible and their modus operandi.[48]

At an INTERPOL Conference in Singapore in 2009, Mick Palmer, Australia's Inspector of Transport Security, said that, 'There's clear evidence of increasing organization in the activities of the pirates. Their weaponry continues to get more sophisticated, and their attacks are happening further out to sea.'[49]

The two hijackings in the middle of October 2009 served to confirm Mike Palmer's analysis. On 15 October the Singapore-flagged *Kota Wajar* bulk carrier was hijacked at 01°.33S 54°.52E and on 19 October a Chinese bulk carrier, the 40,892 ton panamax *De Xin Hai*, was taken at 01.53°N and 060.05°E. Port Victoria in the Seychelles lies at 4.37°S 55.27°E, so both vessels were taken approximately 5 degrees north of Port Victoria and on a longitude track between 54 and 60 degrees east. The fact that the *De Xin Hai* was the first ship to be taken east of the 60 degree line of longitude by Somali pirates was a major development and showed that the Indian Ocean between the Seychelles and the Maldives had become a danger area.

As noted above, the international naval presence in the Gulf of Aden reduced, but did not remove, the threat of piracy in that area, but it did encourage larger pirate groups, or 'companies', to move their main operating areas eastwards, outside the patrolled area. The size of the Indian Ocean is such that there are not sufficient naval vessels available to provide adequate protection outside the Gulf of Aden area. It is interesting that neither of the two bulk carriers hijacked at that time were routed via the Gulf of Aden: the *De Xin Hai* was en route from South Africa to China with a cargo of coal, and the *Kota Wajar* was en route to Mombasa from Singapore. Both masters would have thought that they were well away from any threats.

These hijackings also confirm a second aspect of Mike Palmer's claims, that the pirates have the capability to track and locate big trading ships at sea. The most likely means by which they are tracking their targets is the AIS fitted on most ships. Since 2004 AIS has been mandatory for all vessels over 300 tons and the system broadcasts information about each ship, including its name, position, course, speed and destination. Ships in the area receive this information and can track each vessel in their vicinity. There are a number of programmes available that enable AIS information to be read on a standard PC or on an electronic chart system. The larger modern tuna boats hijacked by the Somali pirates may have this equipment on board, or it could have been installed in Somalia. AIS receivers are freely available, such as the RADARPLUS SM1610-2A manufactured by Shine Micro, Inc. in the United States and which is sold for US$4,400; this 'demonstrated long range performance'.

It is relatively easy to find AIS information on public websites, which, even if a few days out of date, could be of value to pirates. VesselTracker.com is one well-known example. I believe that the IMO should now reconsider the mandatory use of this technology, which the United States pressured it to introduce after the 2001 attacks on New York and Washington DC. It seems that no one seriously considered the disadvantages of introducing this system. Anecdotal evidence is that many masters, aware of the dangers, are disabling their AIS equipment and removing the whole system when transiting dangerous waters.

There are different types of AIS technology; larger vessels carry Class A AIS which is based on SOTDMA technology. Each Class A AIS system consists of a 12.5 W VHF transmitter, an integral global navigation satellite system (i.e., GPS) receiver, two VHF TDMA receivers, one VHF DSC receiver, and standard marine electronic data interface to shipboard display and sensor systems. Class A AIS can tune over the whole 156.025–162.025 MHz VHF maritime band. According to the US coastguard AIS has a range similar to that for other VHF applications, essentially depending on the height of the antenna. Its propagation is slightly better than that of radar, due to the longer wavelength, so it is possible to 'see' around bends and behind islands if the land masses are not too high. A typical range at sea is 20 nautical miles, and a pirate mothership can therefore cover an arc of 40 nautical miles, using an AIS receiver. Assumingly, pirate groups have the ability to operate in packs, each mothership covering an arc of 40 nautical miles; two motherships cover 80 nautical miles, and so on. Any vessel crossing this line are then identified and followed, and the tracked ship is unaware of the threat. Pirate operations could mirror German Second World War U-boat tactics in the north Atlantic.

AIS is not the only problem. There is a second tracking system that is mandatory under IMO regulations. This system is known as Long Range Identification and Tracking (LRIT) and, as its name suggests, is long range. It uses Inmarsat C equipment to broadcast a signal to satellites every six hours. There is no evidence of any use by pirates of LRIT data, although corrupt individuals government agencies could theoretically make such information available. Even if LRIT information is not generally available there is a system, AISLive, that coordinates data from AIS feeds; this service offers a state-of-the-art tile-based mapping system, full access to all the global charts on AISLive.com, five-day weather forecast, dynamic vessel searching, up to 16 levels of zoom on nautical charts and coverage of circa 25,000 live vessels at any one time. It also covers over 2,000 ports, terminals and anchorages.[50] Obviously this service is only available to companies operating in the maritime industry, but it only takes one employee to search the database regularly to provide a number of possible targets to pirates. In dealing with organized crime at this level of sophistication it must be assumed that pirates have penetrated any insurance company, shipping line, or port authority, and security measures should reflect this. It is no longer the case that the threat is from a corrupt port official in some Middle Eastern port; pirates are as likely to be getting information from London, Europoort or Hamburg. AIS data, including data derived from satellites, is now freely available from Websites including VesselTracker.com and FleetMon.com.[51] In short any pirate with an Internet enabled Smartphone will now have all the information on potential targets that he needs.

There is one incident in June 2007 that appeared to confirm that pirates have been using AIS to identify and track a vessel, and that occurred in the hijacking of the Danish bulk carrier, the *Danica White*. According to the official Danish report on the hijacking, the vessel saw on its AIS screen a 220-metre long pilot ship with a fishing licence:

The ship was named NAUTICA + another name. The Master thought it looked odd. He was able to see the ship visually and the length was less than 100 meters. They spoke of this on board. It was sailing in the opposite direction at about 2 nm.[52]

In conclusion 2009 marked a new stage in the Indian Ocean piracy campaign. In the same way that German U-boats evolved new tactics, Somali pirates have adapted quickly to the threat from international naval vessels. Somali pirates also show the ability to use automatic tracking devices to identify and track targets, and probably to select them long before they enter the area between the Seychelles and the Maldives. And, as noted previously, there is no shortage of weapons in Somalia. There are reports from masters that the more sophisticated Somali pirate groups assess likely targets before they enter the danger zone in the Indian Ocean. There is an obvious preference for bulk carriers and product tankers, relatively slow ships with low freeboards and small crews, but which often carry valuable cargoes. Smaller pirate groups operating off Somalia take old rust buckets, often overdue for the breakers' yard, but the long-range groups go for valuable ships that they can be certain will be quickly ransomed, although they are not above hijacking tuna boats that can be used as motherships, or anything else, if they are running low on food, fuel and water.

The taking of very large ships, such as VLCCs like the *Sirius Star*, is unusual and such vessels need to be carefully guarded. It seems that only the more sophisticated groups can deal with such ships.

The most likely course of action is that a list of possible targets is selected, that they are tracked and that spotters use satellite phones to confirm the details of the vessel and its defences to Somalia, from where it is decided whether to continue to target it. The attack group then only needs to wait just off the normal vessel track, say from the Gulf of Aden to southern Sri Lanka, in order to intercept it.

It might happen in this way. At 0400 local time, just before sunrise, while the ship, a South Korean-built bulker of 40,000 tons carrying wheat, is travelling in what the master thinks are reasonably safe waters only 450 nautical miles west of the Indian coast, two skiffs approach the stern at a closing speed of 15 knots, unseen by radar, their wakes shining bright in the phosphorescence of the typical seas, covering a sea mile every four minutes. By the time the watchkeeper sounds the alarm the first pirate has swung on board and the ship is lost. 7.62 mm AK rounds smash the bridge glass and the master signals 'stop engines'. Abdul has won his Land Cruiser. The next day EU NAV announce that the ship turned round and appeared to be heading for Somalia.

THE USE OF INTELLIGENCE BY SOMALI PIRATES

The idea that Somali pirates use intelligence to the degree suggested above is not mere speculation. In addition to the statements by Interpol, referred to above, there are other reports that indicate that this is the reality for contemporary pirate operations. Somali piracy is no longer, if it ever was, based on the activities of a few fishermen attacking foreign vessels just off their coast. Somali pirate groups are long-range hunters, looking for specific types of prey. One of the more interesting indications of how things may work was a report from *Cadena Ser* in Spain, quoted by the *Guardian* newspaper in London. The Spanish journalist who filed the story told AFP that it was based on a military report from a European country. While there is no way to confirm for certain that the story is correct, it is worth consideration.

According to the report from *Cadena Ser*, at least one of the four or five major Somali pirate groups has London-based 'consultants', who provide intelligence to help them choose their targets. It was also claimed that the hijacking of at least three vessels – the Turkish freighter *Karagöl*, the Greek cargo ship *Titan* and Spanish tuna trawler *Felipe Ruano* – took place after tipoffs from this London-based network of informers and that in each case the pirates had full knowledge of the cargo, ports of call, nationality and course of the vessel. Andrew Mwangura, who heads the East African's Seafarer's Assistance Programme, in Mombasa, Kenya, was quoted as saying, '… for many [other] ships, the negotiations involve people in London'.[53] The *Guardian* article also describes how the *Karagöl*, a Turkish chemical tanker, was hijacked in the Gulf of Aden, and taken to Somalia, where it was held for two months while ransom negotiations were concluded. It claims that the ship had been singled out as a target by London-based informers who gave the attackers, who had spent several days practising the assault, details of its layout, route and cargo.

Haldun Dincel, general manager of Turkey's Yardimci shipping company, who was the company's negotiator with the pirates, said: 'They made regular calls from the ship to London',[54] and other centres, using satellite phones, once the ship was moored off the Somali coast. Dincel added that 'Every day the chief of the pirates got in touch with people from London, Dubai and some from the Yemen.'[55] The report also pointed out that the national flag of the vessel is taken into account when choosing a target. Some of the negotiators that Dincel dealt with had lived in the United

States, and one had a US college degree; in other words some of the people involved in piracy are educated men.

When Graeme Gibbon-Brooks of Dryad Maritime Intelligence Ltd was interviewed he confirmed that 'We have heard [about] this a lot. It strikes me as plausible. They are getting more sophisticated because they are funded by criminal gangs from outside of Somalia.'[56] He warned, however, that while pirates might receive information on individual targets from London and elsewhere it was still difficult to locate a ship in mid-ocean. He added that pirates were more likely to receive lists of potential targets so they could identify one ship from the list, if they came across it.

What is clear is that Somali piracy involves people living outside Somalia and that information is flowing into larger pirate groups. It is not essential that the pirates' informants actually work in the shipping industry, although it is likely that some do. Any pirates with access to an AIS tracking service and a subscription to *Lloyd's List* will have a comprehensive set of information on ship movements and cargoes. Although a source within a shipping company or ship's builders will normally be required to obtain plans of the internal layout, there is a high probability that pirates also have contacts on the Suez Canal and at other key ports on the Persian Gulf, and the Gulf of Oman, such as Fujairah, where many ships bulker, and in East Africa.

For Somali pirates and their colleagues overseas, piracy is a business, and a very well paid one. They are obviously using every means at their disposal to enhance the success of their business, and are well connected with the rest of the world. This is modern global organized crime, not the *Pirates of Penzance.*

THE PIRATE BUSINESS MODEL

There is some debate about the Somali piracy 'business model'. The smaller groups remain local and clan-based, but the major pirate groups have continued to evolve their management structures and business methods. Information that was correct two or three years ago may no longer be relevant. As the UN Monitoring Group reported in February 2010:

> The success and expansion of pirate militias has necessitated new organizational arrangements and practices. Although leadership of pirate networks remains anchored in Puntland and central Somalia, participation in maritime militias and investment in pirate operations is

open to a broad cross-section of Somali society. The refined business model guarantees every participant in the operation, if successful, a well-defined percentage or share of the ransom money.[57]

Although pirates operate a network in which various clan-based, and sub-clan, groups cooperate, the larger pirate companies have clear structures and a chain of command. Jay Bahadur described the structure of one pirate company in some detail.[58] There were 35 men, made up of friends and relatives from Eyl and the nearby city of Garowe. The gang included four 'officers': the businessman responsible for funding the operation, an interpreter who negotiated the ransom, an accountant to keep track of costs and payments, and a logistics officer, known as 'commander of the *khat*', who was responsible for getting supplies of food, drink and the *khat* leaves that Somali men chew all day. The next group were the attackers, which consisted of nine men. There were also two cooks and, finally, 20 men known as the 'holders' who guarded hijacked ships. The hierarchy was reflected in the shares of ransom money handed out, in a similar way to the distribution of prize money in the Royal Navy in Nelson's day. According to Bahadur the pirate group responsible for hijacking the MV *Victoria* on 5 May 2009 in the Gulf of Aden split the $1.8 million ransom, after deductions for expenses of $230,000 in maintaining the vessel at Eyl, with 50 per cent going to the investor, known as the commander-in-chief, and $9,000 going to the junior cook. The rest got various sums, from the $150,000 and Land Cruiser that Mohamad Abdi received for being the first attacker to board the *Victoria*, $41,000 each for the other attackers, and $12,000 each for the 'holders'. Bahadur estimates that the other three officers received sums from $30,000 to $60,000 apiece. It is not clear from his account how the local elders and Puntland politicians were paid, but some of the expenses while at Eyl probably went to the tribal elders and the commander-in-chief (aka 'Computer') who paid the various Puntland politicians and others from his 50 per cent share. Computer, according to Bahadur, also paid for the $40,000 initial costs of skiffs, weapons, fuel and other supplies. Like British sailors of 200 years ago, the ordinary pirate appears to let his ransom money slip quickly though his fingers; paying double for cars and houses in advance of the pay-out.

The UN Monitoring Group described a very similar set-up in February 2010. They said that a pirate company required a minimum of eight to 12 attackers prepared to stay at sea for extended periods of time. Each team were equipped with a minimum of two attack skiffs, weapons, provisions, fuel and preferably a supply boat. The costs of the operation were usually borne by investors, some of whom may also have been pirates. According to the Monitoring Group a pirate should already possess his own firearm for use in the operation, and for this 'contribution' he receives a 'class A' share in any profit. Pirates who provide a skiff or a heavier firearm, like an RPG or a machine gun, may be entitled to an additional A-share. The first pirate to board a vessel may also be entitled to an extra A-share, as the description of the *Victoria*'s hijackers shows. This way of dividing the spoils is not set in concrete, but is just a general guide. Outsiders may also have purchased shares in the pirate company; like the Somali woman who made $75,000 after investing an RPG launcher in one company. The bigger (and well-hidden) investors may even take their share directly, via banking channels, before the cash is dropped onto the deck of the hijacked ship; all is secrecy and investigative reporters few on the ground.

The Monitoring Group estimated that holders normally receive about $15,000 each, and say that investors take 30 per cent of the ransom, local elders 5–10 per cent and, after paying the holders and the cooks, that the remainder is divided among class-A shareholders, including the attackers. Obviously, there will be other payments, including the bonus for the first man on board the hijacked ship, and money to the senior tribal and politician leaders, over and above the payments to local elders for the right to anchor. The other people who profit are the suppliers who advance supplies to the hijacked crew on credit.[59]

On occasions, for example, where the attackers have captured more than one prize, the guarding of vessels may be sub-contracted to other groups. Somalis are traders by nature and flexible in their business dealings. Each group is therefore likely to have its own business processes and model. The principle that is clear is that the majority involved get relatively small sums (though large by the standards of the local economy) and the investors and businessmen organizing pirate companies can make very large sums of money indeed, which accounts for their investments in houses in Kenya, and elsewhere. What is successfully obscured is the amount of money being paid to predatory politicians in Somalia and Yemen. Overall these are the men who make most from the misery of kidnapped seamen, not the teenagers with rusty AKs, who risk all to board a ship in the open sea.

RANSOMS: THE PROCESS

Ransoms and tribunes are as old as piracy and were the main revenue source of the Barbary pirates; in 1795 alone the United States was forced to pay nearly $1 million in cash, naval stores and a frigate to ransom 115 sailors from the dey of Algiers. Annual gifts by the United States were settled by treaty on Algiers, Morocco, Tunis and Tripoli.[60]

Ransoms are the primary revenue-generating method of Somali pirates. In this they are unique; in other regions, robbery and stealing cargoes are the main focus of the pirates. Rear Admiral Hudson told the House of Lords in January 2010 that in 2009 'somewhere in the region of $80 million'[61] was paid in ransoms to Somali pirates.

The kidnapping of crews has also been on the increase off West Africa. On 2 July 2010, 12 crew members were taken from the freighter *BBC Polonia,* which was three nautical miles south of Bonny Island, near Port Harcourt, Nigeria. The master and senior engineer of the MV *Northern Spirit* were also kidnapped from their ship in the Port of Douala, Cameroon on 16 May 2010. On the same day, in Douala, the master of the MV *Argos* was also kidnapped by armed men. However, these cases tend to be settled quickly for relatively small amounts of money. West African pirates have merely extended their kidnapping criminal business model, widely used on shore, to seafarers. They currently lack the ability to hold ships and their crews for long periods, and appear to lack the sophisticated infrastructure of the larger Somali pirate groups. However, piracy has continued unabated off Nigeria, and oil tankers are targeted for their cargoes, which are off-loaded and sold like the oil stolen onshore as part of the Nigerian 'bunkering' trade. In September 2012 the *MT Abu Dhabi Star* was seized for a short while before the crew were rescued by the Nigerian Navy.[62] A few days earlier West African pirates had stolen more than 3,000 tons of fuel from the *Energy Centurion* – a Greek-operated oil tanker that was hijacked off Togo.[63]

At present the same is true in Southeast Asia, although until China clamped down in the late 1990s a number of ships and their crews were taken to Chinese ports and held until payments were made. Alternatively the ship was renamed and reflagged and sold to new owners, or used by the triads to take drugs and illegal immigrants into the United States and other countries. The criminal groups in that area have not yet copied the Somali pirate business model.

Somali pirates have developed sophisticated and effective methods for establishing and negotiating ransoms. As previously noted, the Somali piracy business has networks of supporters in other countries to deal with the movement of that part of the ransoms that are not parachuted onto the decks of ships. Given that a proportion of the ships hijacked have been selected in advance by an intelligence assessment, there is also an appreciation of the relative value of cargoes and types of ship, and the size of ransoms demanded has been steadily increased to better reflect the worth of the vessels and their cargoes.

As the hijacking business has grown and the size of ransoms increased it seems that the involvement of business figures outside Somalia has also grown. Martin Murphy says that 'the bulk of the money goes elsewhere', not to Somalia, and that there has been a growing sophistication in dealing with payments. After 2005 payments were, according to Murphy, 'increasingly made in Mombasa and then in Dubai where intermediaries became used to doing business with a smartly-dressed Somali woman who once the payment was secured, made a phone call authorizing the ship's release'. He added that this indicated that non-Somali business interests were 'almost certainly' linked to senior Somali political figures.[64] Murphy also quoted Andrew Mwangura, who said that apart from being used to buying cars and drugs, the ransom proceeds were invested in Somali businesses, including human trafficking, charcoal, minerals and *khat* growing.[65]

None of this is surprising. Somalis have a long tradition of trading and there are large expatriate Somali communities in Saudi Arabia, Arabia, Kenya, the United Arab Emirates and Yemen. In addition, Somalis have established communities in the United States, Australia, the United Kingdom, Norway, Sweden and other parts of Europe. This is a powerful network of individuals bound together by connections of clan and self-interest. While most Somalis are not involved in piracy, there are doubtless many Somali businessmen who see it as an opportunity.

The process of ransom negotiation typically involves a number of parties. First, there is the negotiator appointed by the Somalis, whose name will change with each hijacking – Ali one day and Mohammed the next. He represents the pirate group who have seized the ship and will need to deal with his principals. Second, there is the shipowner, who will normally have no idea of how to deal with the situation. Third, there will be the shipowner's kidnap and ransom underwriter. And, finally, there will be the specialist negotiator appointed by the underwriters. A shipowner normally ends up appointing a specialist negotiator at great expense. Specialist kidnap and ransom negotiators are a particular breed: their work is highly dangerous, especially if they have to visit the country where the kidnapping occurred, and most have a special forces background – British SAS and the like. The dangers are illustrated by the fact that Felix Batista, a US kidnap negotiator, was himself kidnapped and then almost certainly murdered in Mexico, while participating in a kidnapping seminar.[66] Kidnap and ransom insurance is illegal in some countries, like Italy, as it is regarded as rewarding crime. But underwriters at Lloyd's of London provide such cover for many clients, as the alternatives for kidnap victims are all much worse than the payment of money.

A kidnap negotiation follows a set formula, which is as true for a kidnapping onshore as at sea. Evidence of the condition of the victims is normally provided at regular intervals, and the kidnapped crew may be allowed to make telephone calls to confirm the details of their capture. As a concession, if negotiations are proceeding well, they may also be allowed to talk to their family; this can add to public pressure on a shipowner to settle the ransom payment. A recent variation is that crew members are ill-treated, or even tortured, and then made to beg for help from their families, who in some cases in India have also been asked by the pirates' local associates for money to buy food for the hostages.

The initial demand will be exorbitant, and it is at this point that the shipowner will panic and deny that he will be able pay the demand under any circumstances. The process is the same as bargaining in a Middle Eastern bazaar: both sides will have expectations as to the settlement figure and will have knowledge of the actual amount of recent ransom payments, numbers that are carefully hidden from the public. If a small cargo carrier is taken the initial demand may be for $10 million – but the negotiators will be well aware that the 11,055-ton Bermudan-flagged MV *Talca* was ransomed for $2.5 million in May 2010.[67] So for the Somali negotiator, while he is aiming to get $3 million, $2.5 million would be acceptable, and for the kidnap and ransom negotiator and the underwriters he represents he will be trying to make a case for a lower final ransom, say $1.5–2 million, given that the ship taken is much older than the MV *Talca*, has a smaller crew and is only carrying a cargo with low value, or was in ballast. The amounts paid have also tended to increase significantly over the last five years.

The kidnap and ransom negotiator will start with a low number and point out that his client is bankrupt and lost millions in the last year. Each negotiator will move their position towards a compromise in stages, trying to appear reasonable and each having to keep their principals informed and engaged in the process. In fact even in the best-run negotiation, this process of offers and counter-offers will need about eight weeks at the minimum; the release of the MV *Talca* after just under two months (she was hijacked on 23 March 2010, 120 nautical miles off the coast of Oman and 180 miles south of Mazera) showed that the negotiations were dealt with professionally. For comparison, the ransom paid at the beginning of 2010 for a slightly larger cargo ship, the 23,709 dwt MV *Filitsa*, was $3 million.[68] For the professional dealing with ransom payments this is a business transaction, but where a ship has full kidnap and ransom insurance the underwriters know the drill and the process can be compared with motor insurance – companies settling claims after argument over the details. In fact, all insurers expect to pay out for a percentage of the policies written and for them this is a normal part of their business. It is too easy to argue that claims should be settled earlier, and that crews are under stress while being held, but the evidence shows that where professionals deal with matters there is the minimum of pressure on crews and ships have normally been released after about eight weeks, although this period has tended to increase in 2010–11 as higher ransoms are demanded.

Being held hostage is never going to be easy and shipowners need to do everything that they can to avoid their vessels being taken. But at the end of the day their overriding consideration should always be for the safety of their crews, and dealing with ransom demands promptly is the best policy. Recent US pronouncements on the non-payment of ransoms for Americans have shown a lack of insight into the practicalities of Somali piracy. The worst cases are of Taiwanese fishing boats and small rust buckets of no value owned by African and Asian people, with no insurance: these crews are often abandoned and left literally to starve, or even, if the reports cited above concerning the MV *Rim*, and other vessels, are correct, threatened with being butchered.

THE COST OF A HIJACKING

The UN Monitoring Group in their July 2011 report gave a breakdown of the costs of the hijacking of the MV *Victoria*. The total cost of the hijacking was calculated as €3,219,885.80, broken down as follows:

The direct costs of the hijacking were €2,585,161.27:

- company costs (travel, communication, hotel, meetings, etc.);
- cash stolen by the pirates on board the hijacked vessel;
- communications from the vessel;
- lawyers;
- private security risk company (negotiations, ransom delivery, debrief etc.);
- ransom payment;
- charter of a tug boat after the hijacking;
- port and agent's fees;
- repairs (hull, machinery, equipment, computers, etc.);
- medical costs.

In addition, indirect costs deriving from the loss of hire of the vessel were €634,724.53.[69]

Media reports said that the ransom paid was $1.8 million (€1.27 million at August 2011 rates), although it is alleged that the negotiation and the pirate commander took an additional $150,000, bringing the ransom to $1.95 million (€1.38 million), which was about 60 per cent of the total cost incurred by the owners and underwriters. The additional (non-ransom) costs can be considerably higher, as additional payments to the crew and the costs of healthcare have not been included in this list.

THE RANSOMING OF THE MV *MARAN CENTAURUS*

The ransoming of the MV *Maran Centaurus* on 18 January 2010 set a new record for the award paid to Somali pirates for the release of a ship and its crew. The ease with which this vessel was hijacked, and the relative lack of interest shown by the world's media in its hijacking, illustrates with force the extent to which the taking of a super-tanker on the high seas had become almost a common event, in contrast to the interest that was generated only a year before by the hijacking of the *Sirius Star*. The taking of the 319,000 dwt South Korean VLCC MV *Samho Dream* on 4 April 2010 went out of the public spotlight even more quickly; by then interest in such events had truly waned.

The Greek-flagged VLCC *Maran Centaurus* left Mina Al Ahmadi in Kuwait en route for the Louisiana Offshore Oil Port, in the Gulf of Mexico, the United States. On the evening of 24 November it headed into the Straits of Hormuz, between Oman and Iran, and less than five days later it was boarded by Somali pirates 570 nautical miles north-east of the Seychelles. This huge 299,900 dwt, 1,090-foot long (330 metres) vessel had a crew of 28 when taken. On board the *Maran Centaurus* carried a cargo of nearly two million barrels of crude oil, worth over US$150 million at the then current market price of about $75 a barrel. By 2 December the tanker was anchored 30 nautical miles south of Hobyo, Somalia, and it remained on the Somali coast until it was released 47 days later, on 18 January 2010. The fact that it was freed so quickly points to the professional nature of the ransom negotiations. In contrast, the MV *Samho Dream* was held for over six months before being ransomed in November 2010, which shows the increasing difficulties as larger ransoms are demanded; the ransom for the MV *Samho Dream* was said to be $9.5 million.[70]

Figure 6.4 Ransom dropped on the deck of the *Sirius Star*

The *Maran Centaurus*, owned by Maran Tankers Management Inc., was only the second VLCC to be hijacked, the first being the *Sirius Star*, owned by Vela International, which was taken on 15 November 2008, 450 nautical miles south-east of the Kenyan coast. The *Sirius Star* was released after 55 days, on 9 January 2009. The ransom, reported to be $3 million, was dropped by parachute onto the deck of the hijacked tanker (Figure 6.4).

There is some dispute about the amount of the ransom actually dropped on to the deck of the *Maran Centaurus*. Reuters says that it was $5–7 million; it was probably nearer the lower end of that estimate, say $5.5 million. But this sum was still the largest ransom ever paid to Somali pirates and leaves open the question whether additional sums were paid to the pirates' organizers, via more conventional routes. Ecoterra International, a Somali 'environmental' group based in Kenya, which has good links with the pirates, claimed that the ransom was over $7 million in cash and that another $2 million was transferred via the banking system, a total of $9 million. Although Ecoterra often have information that other websites lack, there is no way of checking this claim. It is likely that their figure for the amount of cash is too high, although the additional $2 million may be correct, giving a possible total of $7.5 million, slightly higher than Reuters' largest estimate.

In Haradheere, on the coast of Somalia, the size of the ransom created tension even before it was delivered. Reuters reported that rival pirate gangs fired shots at each other on 17 January in a dispute over how to split the ransom. The pirates who had hijacked the vessel, who came from Puntland, refused to share the ransom with gangs from Haradheere, where the vessel was moored. However, the *Maran Centaurus* was under the control of gunmen from Haradheere, not the original hijackers. It is said that the Puntland pirates had threatened to set fire to the ship, although this threat seems to have been merely a negotiating tactic, rather than a statement of intent. At this point, in a totally bizarre move, the pirates on board the tanker called for assistance from the international anti-piracy force. It is reported that two helicopters from an international warship (probably from the Greek warship *FS Salamis*, which was in the area) hovered over the attacking skiffs using the downdraft from their rotors to frighten off the attackers, but did not open fire. The Puntland gang was outnumbered and overwhelmed, when the hundreds of well-armed pirates from Haradheere boarded the ship.

After the pirates announced that they had resolved their problems, two aircraft appeared overhead and the enormous ransom in cash was parachuted from one of the aircraft; a delivery to a Somali cargo cult from John Frum.[71] However, the arguments had not been completely settled; two pirates were killed in a gun battle with a rival gang, as they returned to the shore from the *Maran Centaurus*. In addition, Reuters were told that four pirates were killed and three others injured ashore, when one group attacked another one on the evening of 18 January, because they had not yet had their share of the ransom. It was also reported that piracy financiers were involved in the fighting. The ransom was then held in a heavily guarded house in Haradheere and there was great tension in the town while the gangs waited for the sharing of the loot.

Reports of intra-pirate conflict may be of little importance in the wider scheme of things, but they do highlight the difficulties faced by shipowners, and their agents, in negotiating ransom payments. It is difficult enough trying to ensure that crews are safe and that they are removed from Somalia without delay, but when owners have to deal with two, or more, conflicting groups, this makes negotiations very complex. There was also confusion when the *Sirius Star* was freed; five of the pirates were reported to have drowned when their small boat capsized in a storm after leaving the *Sirius Star* with their share of the ransom. The situation around the *Maran Centaurus* was unprecedented – an armed stand-off by two pirate groups and threats to a laden supertanker. If the tanks of the ship had been breached, the spillage of two million barrels of crude oil it carried would have represented an environmental disaster on a vast scale, which would have destroyed ecosystems and fisheries along the Somalia coast, with no prospect of any help to clean up the coast.

Maran Tankers Management Inc., owner of the *Maran Centaurus*, said in a statement from Athens that it was 'delighted' the ship, its crew and cargo had been freed. They added:[72]

Maran Tankers Management Inc. will not be releasing any details of the talks which led to the release of the vessel, as they do not wish to provide any information which might in any way encourage further criminal acts of this kind.

The *Maran Centaurus* left Somalia, en route to Durban in South Africa, with its full cargo of oil.

PIRATE NEGOTIATORS

There has been increasing interest in the role of Somali pirate negotiators. The UN Monitoring Group lists Ali Hassan Sharmarke, Looyaan (Loyan) Si'id Barte, Mohamed Saaili Shibin and Ahmed Saneeg as important negotiators during 2009 and 2010. As the Monitoring Group notes, as negotiators must speak foreign languages, especially English, they are usually recruited from outside pirate networks, and operate essentially as specialist 'consultants'. Many of the negotiators had lived aboard. Some, like Loyan, have travelled aboard recently. It is also common for them to deal with more than one set of negotiations at a time.

The negotiators are becoming increasingly important within the pirate hierarchy. The UN Monitoring Group states that in a number of cases 'negotiators have also extracted additional, secret payments from shipping companies either for themselves, or in concert with the pirate militia leader, in some cases giving instructions for funds to be wired to a foreign account'.[73] Some negotiators have also become investors in pirate operations, reinvesting their gains.

One of the most important pirate negotiators is 'Loyan'. Between January 2009 and April 2011 the UN Monitoring Group estimated that he was involved in negotiating 20 Somali hijacking cases for ships, including the MV *Samho Dream*, the MV *St James Park* and the MV *Hannibal II*. The Monitoring Group added that he, 'tries to remain as anonymous as possible, calling himself "Loyan", "Leon" and "Ali", or sometimes using pseudonyms like "Blue Moon", "Red Sun", "Seabird" or "Bluefish"'.[74] Loyan's full name is Looyaan Si'id Barte and, although he worked mainly for the PPN, he dealt with at least six negotiations on behalf of the HHN.

This is a well-paid job. The Monitoring Group estimated that, in the period of just over two years from January 2009 to April 2011, Loyan received at least US$500,000 for his services as a principal negotiator. He speaks good English and the UN Monitoring Group says:

He is a skilled communicator and negotiator who often manages to finalize the ransom agreement at close to the amount he has targeted from the outset. Shipping company negotiators have described him as generally polite, straightforward, and determined, but also capable of being threatening when he feels the need.[75]

THE CONDITION OF HOSTAGES: THREATS, ABUSE AND RUSTY WATER

There is a view that Somali pirates treat their captives well, because this guarantees that they will survive to be ransomed. While it is true that most Somali pirates take great care to avoid killing hostages, because a live captive is worth money, reports of the experiences of those unfortunates held in Somalia show that this can be an extremely unpleasant, and even life-threatening, experience. It is important to understand that ransoming hostages is a business and, if you are unable to be ransomed, either because you have no money, or you are abandoned by your employer, then your outlook will be bleak.

When the French yacht Le Ponant was hijacked in 2008 the pirates used a manual that stressed good treatment of their captives. Captain Patrick Marchesseau said: 'There was no physical abuse at all, no mistreatment.'[76] However, seamen taken in 2010 and 2011 had very different experiences, which, in part, was probably due to the knowledge that threats serve to increase the size of ransoms, and also to the emergence of a group of brutal and sadistic pirate leaders, who enjoyed abusing their prisoners. Abuse and torture have become commonplace, and are now the norm. Major General Buster Howes, Commander of EU NAVFOR, said that Somali pirates have begun systematically using hostages as human shields and torturing them – the methods used including tying hostages upside down and dragging them in the sea, locking them in freezers, beating them and putting plastic ties around their genitals.[77] There are also reports of worse treatment, including the burning and mutilation of seamen.

Far Eastern fishermen whose employees refuse to negotiate have been denied all essentials, including food and water, and some have died of neglect as a result. Somali pirates are also capable of using threats, including the threat to kill hostages, taking their organs for sale, and actual violence, if they believe that this will increase the likelihood that captives are then ransomed, and that possible rescue attempts will be discouraged. Hostages on motherships have also been used as human shields to discourage attempts to retake those ships.

Seamen captured by Somali pirates have been routinely abused, 'examples of serious abuse included one crewmember's fingers being squeezed with pliers, seafarers being hung overboard and immersed in the sea up to their shoulders, and some even being taken by boat a few miles away from the main vessel, thrown overboard, and abandoned in the water for a period of time.'[78] If you are captured by some pirate groups torture is routine. This goes far beyond psychological pressure to hasten negotiations and secure larger ransoms. Captain Prem Kumar, the well-respected master of the MS *Rak Afrikana*, was so badly treated during his 320 days of captivity, forced to stay on the bridge for the whole period, beaten, ill-fed, that he succumbed to a paralytic stroke caused by his ill-treatment; he died within days of being released.[79] The British press and television made much of the captivity of the Chandlers, a retired couple who were misinformed enough to try sailing from the Seychelles to East Africa. They were decanted from their yacht, *The Lynn Rival*, into a pirate vessel, under the eyes of the *Wave Knight* RFA. After payment of nearly $1 million they were released in November 2010.[80] It is, however, just as important to remember the fate of all those other unfortunates held captive by Somali pirates, most of whom are Asian, and who are too often ignored by the international media.

It is not true that Somali pirates will not kill or injure their captives. On 25 May 2007 at approximately 0600 Somali pirates tied Chen Tao, a Taiwanese fisherman on the *Qingfenghua 168* (hijacked on 18 April 2007) to a post and shot him six times. This murder was undertaken with the express purpose of forcing the owner of the vessel to pay a ransom, with the threat that more seamen would be killed if he did not agree to their terms. The owner had previously refused to pay the pirates $300,000. Prior to the murder of Chen the seamen on board were beaten up three to four times a day; this violence continued until their release.[81] The reported execution of a seaman abroad the *Beluga Nomination* in 2011, referred to above, shows that this was not an isolated incident. Although the full story of what happened on the *Beluga Nomination* is still not known, in a statement Beluga said that three crew members had been killed while attempting to escape.[82]

The Taiwanese tuna fishing boat *Win Far 161*, which was taken on 6 April 2009, was finally released after ten months, on 11 February 2010, and three of its crew are reported to have died during their captivity from malnutrition, disease and neglect.[83] The *Win Far 161* had a crew of 30: its master and first engineer were Taiwanese, five others were Chinese, 17 were from the Philippines and the other six were from Indonesia. The *Taipei Times*, on 7 September 2009, questioned whether the Taiwanese foreign ministry actually cared about the crew of the *Win Far 161*. The *Win Far 161* was used as a mothership in attacks on other merchant ships. The US navy said, on 27 August 2009, that Somali pirates had used the *Win Far 161* and that they had fired a rocket at a US navy helicopter from the vessel. They added that the *Win Far 161* was involved in the first attack on the *Maersk Alabama*. The *Win Far 161* is a large, long-range boat, well equipped with radar and also AIS. It was an excellent command vessel for long-range pirate missions of the type carried out in 2009–10 north-east of the Seychelles, with the vessel able to track target vessels and to deploy fast skiffs near the victim.

Another ship's crew that endured appalling conditions was the Greek and British-owned MV *Ariana*, which was hijacked on 2 May 2009. The MV *Ariana* was seized north of Madagascar, en route to the Middle East from Brazil, with a cargo of soya beans. The ship was released on 12 December 2009, but the owners forced the master to continue the voyage to Iran once it was freed, without stopping at any port en route for replenishing supplies and assisting the crew. The MV *Ariana* had a crew of 24 Ukrainians including two women and a girl – Natalia Loss, the wife of the chief engineer, was travelling with her 12-year-old daughter.

The ship's crew could be as violent as the pirates. The other woman on the ship was Larysa Salinska, the ship's cook, 39 years old, who suffered a miscarriage during her sixth-month pregnancy while in captivity. She urgently needed medical help, but received no assistance. Larysa said: 'I was bleeding like a tap. I thought I would die from bleeding.'[84] It was alleged that the miscarriage was the result of Larysa being beaten by the Ukrainian ship's engineer; the pirates offered to evacuate Larysa and the other females off the ship but the master, Genadiy Voronov, kept them on board.[85] In a telephone call to *The Kyiv Post*, Captain Voronov described the conditions on board as atrocious: 'We are not allowed to move around the ship. The whole crew is in one cabin.'[86] He added: 'They [pirates] give us some rotten rice and that's all we eat here. A couple of kilos a day for 24 people. No fresh water to drink or to wash up.'[87] Voronov also said that the ship's engineer, Volodymyr Streshniy, had been beaten up and 'may have had a concussion. He was nauseous, lacked coordination and was generally weak. For two or three days, he could not get up from the deck.'[88] It is claimed that the pirates wanted to shoot the ship's engineer for beating up Larysa Salinska and that his injuries were the result of their anger over his actions.

Larysa Salinska also said that the water and food were extremely bad:

When you are hungry, you will eat anything – rotten rice or rusty water, but I can't. The boys eat it though. The water provided is red. We try to filter it through cotton wool or any way we can. It's a savage life.[89]

The *Ariana* was without power for a long period, after it ran out of fuel. The extended lack of power further worsened conditions on board.

Threats are routinely made by Somali pirates to kill hostages if any rescue attempts are made. The crew of the Chinese bulk carrier *De Xin Hai* were threatened in this way, as were the crew of the Spanish fishing boat, the *Alakrana*, who spent 47 days as the prisoners of Somali pirates. They recounted the horror of their abduction by pirates. In a press conference, machinist Victor Bilbao said: 'We were frightened because at any moment they might have shot us.' During their appearance before the judge, the crew members of the *Alakrana* broke down in sobs and could barely speak of the trauma they suffered. Speaking for the crew, machinist Bilbao affirmed that the pirates drank alcohol constantly. He said: 'They are animals and they treated us even worse [than animals].'[90]

It does appear that the treatment of hostages has been getting steadily worse over the last few years. The treatment of Indian seamen by Somali pirates is causing the greatest concern. Siddharth Srivastava said that 'Freed or rescued [Indian] seamen say they have been tortured mercilessly.'[91] Then in April 2011 Somali pirates refused to release some Indian members of the 15-man crew of MV *Asphalt Venture* when their colleagues and the ship were released on payment of a ransom. A pirate called Abdi, speaking to Reuters by phone from Haradheere said: 'We are holding eight of *Asphalt Venture* crew. It was a joint understanding among us not to release any Indian citizens. [...] India hasn't only declared war against us, but also it has risked the lives of many hostages.'[92] At that time India held over 100 pirates captured by the Indian navy and the pirates were attempting to exchange hijacked Indian seamen for these pirates. This was a dangerous development for all seamen, because the same principles, if accepted by India, could be applied to any country that caught Somali pirates. Unfortunately, Egypt and the Seychelles have both succumbed to similar threats in the past.

Mariya Vijayan, from Tamil Nadu in India, who spent six months as a hostage in Somalia, said:

It's my second life. They are not human beings; they are like animals. We have undergone every kind of torture, both mental and physical. They captured our vessel by posing as the Mogadishu Navy. For the first ten days, there were no facilities for communication. Then, they started limiting the food supply. There were days we survived with just two potatoes and some chillies. It is horrible to recall what we underwent. Sometimes they fired shots near us just to frighten us.[93]

Choi Jin-kyung, a South Korean seaman captured in 2011, mentioned 'The pirates frequently beat the captain and other senior crew while shouting "kill".'[94]

Pirates captured by the Indian Navy in 2011 told their captors that they were justified in committing crimes because they came from very poor backgrounds.[95]

To be a captive in Somalia today is to be placed in constant fear and stress, to be subject to threats and actual violence, and to be uncertain when this state of affairs will end. No shipowner should ever want to risk that its crews end up in such a situation.

Unfortunately in 2012 the situation had not changed. On 14 August 2012 the Somali Report[96] highlighted the following situation:

- eight merchant ships were held by Somali pirates;
- 28 hostages on land were held by Somali pirates;
- 222 hostages on ships were held by Somali pirates;
- $29.2 million were paid in ransoms to Somali pirates in 2012.

Activity was relatively quiet at that time; the summer monsoon ensured that the sea state remained high. However, on the MV *Orna*, a bulker that was hijacked on 20 December 2010, negotiations over the payment of a ransom stalled, and the pirates killed one man and wounded another as a 'protest' over the delay. Hassan Abdi, pirate spokesman, said that the killing was a message to the ship's owners.[97]

The remaining crew of the MV *Albedo*, which was hijacked in November 2010, all drowned in July 2013 after the vessel sank in rough seas. A EU Naval Force press report said that a 'Maritime Patrol Aircraft sighted two life boats on a Somali beach approximately 14 miles north of the position of the Albedo. No members of the MV Albedo crew or pirates were sighted in or near the lifeboats.'[98] The mother of one of the crew, Aman Kumar, had described the conditions experienced by the crew in August 2012: 'Three days ago I got a call from my son, who was literally crying. He was saying the pirates are not giving him food and threatening to kill him if their demands of $1 million ransom and release of 61 Somali pirates held by the Indian Navy were not accepted.'[99]

In July 2012 it was reported that 7 of the MV *Albedo's* crew were released after a ransom of $1.2 million was paid, but that 15 hostages were returned to the vessel by the 'investors', following a dispute between pirate groups over the sharing of the ransom.[100] Of all the loss of life that occurred as a result of Somali piracy, the pointless deaths of these seamen on the MV *Albedo* is probably the worst incident. These men drowned after suffering a wretched period of captivity, during which they were tortured physically and psychologically, according to Jawaid Khan, one of those crew members who was fortunate enough to be released.[101]

CHAPTER 7

THE IMPACT ON THE SHIPPING INDUSTRY

THE GLOBAL SHIPPING INDUSTRY

The global shipping industry is characterized by its very high level of internationalization. Shipping, with few exceptions, is no longer a 'national' business, where the owner registers ships on its national register, carries goods to and from the home country and looks to crew ships with that country's nationals. There are exceptions, like the US Jones Act (the Merchant Marine Act of 1920), which restricted shipping and passenger trade within the United States to US-owned or US-flagged ships, and stipulated that 75 per cent of a ship's crew must consist of US citizens.

Like international banks, shipping companies will swiftly change the domicile of their assets when there is a tax advantage to be gained. Ships may be registered with a flag of convenience, owned by an offshore company, registered in somewhere like the Isle of Man, and this company may itself be owned by a series of shell companies and the ultimate owners may live in Monaco, Switzerland, or anywhere in the world. Ships will be built by whichever yards offer the best current combination of price and performance; if you need a bulk carrier, this will probably mean a Chinese yard like Rongsheng Shipbuilding & Heavy Industries' Nantong facility, at the mouth of the Yangtze River. The ships will typically be officered by men and women trained by academies in Europe and Asia and the crew will be provided by manning agencies in countries like Bangladesh, Ukraine, India and the Philippines. English will probably be the ship's operating language, although it may not be the mother-tongue of anyone on board.

Apart from a few shipping lines, like the Danish shipping line Maersk, which maintains a high profile, the majority of shipping fleets are relatively small and rarely well known. Maersk is really a supply chain company, owning interests in port facilities and dominating the high end of its market in the transhipment of containers around the world; ships are merely the obvious part of this supply chain. Many vessels are placed on long-term charter, for example to the oil majors, and in turn many owners use ship management agencies to run their vessels and organize charters. The majority of merchant vessels are 'tramps', in that they will go wherever the cargo owner directs them.

For most of the time, unless you look out from the Harwich ferry at Felixstowe, or glimpse the ranks of container ships in Hamburg, after driving south through the Elbe Tunnel, or glance down from your seat on a plane en route to Dubai, on the lines of 300-metre long VLCCs, looking like toy boats, loading at Ras Tannūrah on Saudi's Eastern Province, the global fleet is virtually invisible. These ships carry around 90 per cent of the world's cargoes by volume, and are the arteries of the global economy. In their holds are the food, fuel and goods we rely on, from the Chinese Christmas toys in a giant container ship, the Qatari natural gas delivered to Milford Haven and fed into the UK grid from ships like the *Al Oraiq*, huge car carriers loaded with Japanese SUVs, Brazilian iron ore carried in a Valemax very large bulker, the grain that we bake our bread from carried in another bulker and the gargantuan supertankers, hull-down, like the *TI Europe*, 441,561 dwt, 380 metres long, laden with over 3 million barrels of oil. At $120 a barrel that is a cargo worth around $360 million, although a container ship full of electronics and computer components may be carrying five times that value.

Until the world economic crisis hit the shipping market in 2008 the amount of cargoes carried had risen steadily year on year. The ease of financing and the economies of scale encouraged the ordering of massive new fleets, which the owners believed would make them even richer. In 2008, as we will see, the bubble burst.

The identity of ships can also change rapidly – a new owner, a new name, and a new flag – but the IMO number remains and is the only way that the true identity of the ship can be tracked. There is an innate fluidity about the whole shipping industry.

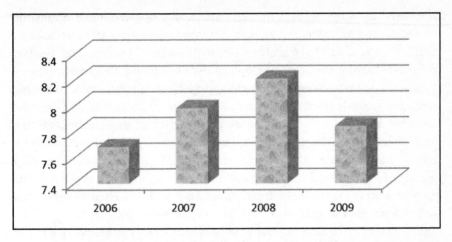

Figure 7.1 World seaborne trade ton-miles (billions)

FLAG STATES AND OWNERSHIP

According to the UN Conference on Trade and Development (UNCTAD)[1] nearly 95 per cent of the world's fleet by tonnage is owned by the nationals of just 35 countries. Greece has the largest controlled fleet by tonnage, with Japan second, followed by China, Germany, South Korea and Singapore. These six countries actually own over 57 per cent of the global fleet,

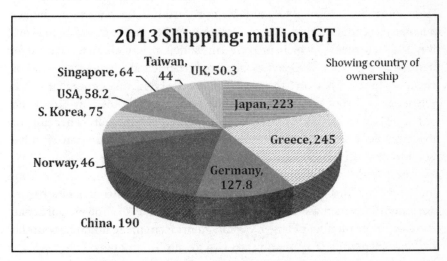

Figure 7.2 The largest fleets by million dwt in 2013, showing country of ownership

calculated by tonnage, and the next six countries, the United States, the United Kingdom, Norway, Taiwan (China), Denmark and Bermuda own nearly 17 per cent of the global fleet, by tonnage. These twelve countries therefore account for 74.61 per cent of the global fleet, by tonnage.

UNCTAD calculates that in 2013 there were 41,215 ships of 1,000 gross tonnage, or above, in the global fleet.

While ships may be controlled by the nationals of one country, they are often registered (or flagged) in another jurisdiction. In January 2013 73 per cent of the world's fleet was 'flagged out'. The greatest tonnage of ships is registered in Panama: 21.5 per cent of the world total dwt, Liberia is second by tonnage with 12.2 per cent of the world total dwt and the Marshall Islands third with 8.6 per cent of the world total dwt. Registration in a foreign jurisdiction used to be about tax advantages, but things are more complex today, with many owners preferring a flag state with a good reputation for enforcing regulations; as a result about 50 per cent of UK-flagged vessels have foreign owners.

THE ECONOMIES OF SCALE

Over the last 200 years the shipping industry has developed on the basis that the larger the ship the cheaper the costs per ton of cargo carried. The principle of the economy of scale is fundamental within the shipping industry, the only restrictions being those imposed by geography. The limitations on size of ships have been the ability of shipyards to build very large ships, the availability of suitable port facilities, deep enough channels and canals (and the depth of natural waterways like the English Channel and the Malacca Straits, which provide fundamental limitations). One of the main drivers towards larger vessels is that, generally, the larger the vessel the cheaper the cost per dwt from the shipyards. UNCTAD quoted $433 as the price per dwt of a 300,000 dwt tanker at the end of 2009, only 46 per cent of the $941 cost per dwt of a 45,000 dwt tanker.[2] For the shipowner this was the equivalent of 'buy one get one free' in the supermarket – an offer too good to pass up.

And a vessel with greater carrying capacity offers the prospect of making more revenue. In a rapidly expanding market for cargo, this leads inevitably, not only to an increase in the number of ships, but to a disproportionate increase in the number of larger vessels. Apart from the relative cheapness of building bigger, once at sea a vessel like the 397-metre long *Emma Maersk* (170,974 gross tons) needs only the same size crew as a vessel a fraction her size, and is therefore far more economical to run than two smaller ships with the same total cargo capacity. The *Emma Mærsk* has seven sister ships in the same 'E' class. These ships have a cargo capacity of up to 15,000 teu (20-foot equivalent units), a measure of the number of standard containers they can carry. The Maersk Triple E class, the lead ship of which is the MV *Mærsk Mc-Kinney Møller*, which entered service in the summer of 2013, is even larger, with a capacity of 18,340 teu and a tonnage of 165,000 metric dwt.[3]

The Triple E class effectively represents the current Suezmax limit, the largest size of vessel that can transit the Suez Canal, with their draft of 14.5 metres, 400 metres long and 59 metres wide. The current maximum depth of the Suez Canal is 20 metres.

In the past the upper limit for container ships was around 5,000 teus – the 'Panamax' threshold. A Panamax is a ship that can transit the Panama Canal, although in 2014 improvements to the Panama Canal will create a 'New Panamax' standard, enabling container ships with up to 13,000 teu to use the canal. The Maersk E and Triple E class ships will, however, be too long for the new Panama locks; they are designed for the China to Europe route.

One of the limitations on these very large vessels is that they are too large for many ports, which either lack the depth of channel required, or have inadequate loading facilities. This has meant the development of a hub-and-spoke distribution network for containers, with the largest ships calling at super-ports like Hong Kong, Shanghai, Bremerhaven and Rotterdam, and smaller vessels distributing containers to other ports. Interestingly, in 2013 no US port could handle the Triple E class, although six European ports could.[4] Similar problems apply to very large crude carriers and to the Valemax class of 400,00 dwt bulk carriers. VLCCs and ULCCs (ultra large crude carriers), like the TI class of 441,500 dwt, are too large to transit the Suez Canal fully laden.

THE SIZE OF THE GLOBAL MERCHANT FLEET

According to the figures produced by UNCTAD, there were 47,122 seagoing commercial ships over 1,000 GT in service at the beginning of 2013, with a combined tonnage of 1,613 million dwt. Of this total oil tankers made up 490 million dwt and dry bulk carriers 684 million dwt – an increase of 4.5 and 9.9 per cent respectively over the 2012 figures. At the same time the total tonnage of container ships was 206 million dwt in January 2013 (an annual increase of 4.9 per cent) and the general cargo fleet reduced

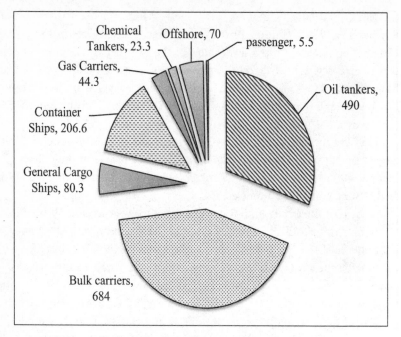

Figure 7.3 World fleet by vessel types (millions dwt)

slightly to 80 millon dwt, but significantly less than the 2010 figures of 109 million dwt.[5]

A PERFECT STORM CAUSES MARKET COLLAPSE

The fall in the Baltic Dry Index

The global shipping industry carries the bulk of the world's goods and much of its food and fuel. The amount of cargo transported by sea virtually doubled in the 18 years from 1990 to 2008, and grew by approximately 43 per cent between 2000 and 2008. However, the global economic crisis had a dramatic effect on the shipping industry in 2008 and 2009, from which it has yet to fully recover. In October 2008 the average earnings for bulk carriers (the Baltic Dry Index, or 'BDI') were 80 per cent lower than the levels in April 2008. In fact on 20 May 2008 the BDI was 11,793 and by 5 December 2008 it fell to 663, a fall of 94 per cent. Jeremy Penn, the Baltic's chief executive said: 'The violence of the movement, the violence of the correction are unprecedented, particularly in the Capesize market .... The sudden and extreme lack of demand for freight has left everybody stunned, I suppose is the best word to use.'[6]

Figure 7.4 The collapse of the BDI (May–July 2010)

The volatility of the BDI continued into 2009 and 2010, although it did not match the extremes of 2008. On 15 July 2010 the BDI reached 1,700, whereas it had been 4,209 on 25 May 2010. In other words, the index dropped to 40 per cent of its previous value in less than eight weeks. There was a small recovery, a 'dead-cat bounce', in early August, when the BDI stood at just under 2,000.[7]

The BDI continued its roller-coaster performance into 2011, reaching a high of 2,995 on 10 September 2010, but falling to a new low of 1,043 on 4 February 2011. By 20 April 2011 it was still only 1,262, well below the level of July 2010. The index declined further in 2012, reaching 662 on 1 February 2012 and 707 on 30 August 2012.

By 8 February 2013 the BDI had returned to the same level as the 2012 summer lows, and stood at 748, down from 1,097 on 27 November 2012. Like a heart rate monitor the BDI records the underlying state of the patient, in this case the world economy. Even though it had rallied to 2,330 on 16 December 2013, after starting the year at 698, the BDI was very far from the heights reached in 2008. It will be a long time before it trades at over 11,000.

In such conditions it is virtually impossible for shipowners to plan, and it is very tempting for charters to renege or renegotiate contracts and thus impose severe losses on shipowners. The massive over-ordering of capacity made the world economic crisis a particular disaster for sections of the shipping industry, especially for the bulk carrier fleets. In 2007, 312 new bulkers were delivered (average size 78,526 dwt) and, in 2008, 355 bulkers left the yards, with an average size of 81,408 dwt. A fall in the BDI in 2008 was therefore unavoidable; cargo rates would have fallen even without the global economic crisis; with it they fell off the Tarpeian Rock. Jeremy Penn may have been stunned, but he should not have been surprised. The bad news was that the shipping industry entered the downturn having placed large orders. In January 2009 the order book for bulk carriers was 324.7 million dwt, although this declined to 136.7 million dwt in January 2013.

Commercial pressures also encouraged the construction of ever larger ships in a bid to reduce the cost of transportation. In 2008, Vale, the Brazilian mining company, placed orders for twelve 400,000-ton Valemax ships to be constructed by Jiangsu Rongsheng Heavy Industries in China (see Figure 7.5) (although the full order may not have been completed due to contractual arguments)[8]. In addition, on 2 November 2008, the Oman Shipping Company signed a framework agreement with RSHI for the construction of four 400,000-ton vessels to transport iron ore from Brazil to the port of Sohar in Oman: the *Vale Liwa, Vale Sohar, Vale Shinas* and *Vale Saham.*[9] Other ships of the same size have been ordered from South Korean yards. These giant vessels transform the costs of moving ore, in the same way that the MV *Mærsk Mc-Kinney Møller* has transformed the economics of container shipment.

The global economic crisis: The collapse in world trade

The underlying reason for the collapse in freight rates was the reversal in global economic production that occurred as a result of the global economic crisis, and the resultant dramatic drop in the volume of goods shipped. The fact that the industry had massively over-ordered capacity would not have been a major issue if world trade volumes had continued to grow at the rates seen in the early years of the twenty-first century. For the G7 countries in the first quarter of 2009 trade volumes fell over 27 per cent on a year-on-year basis. This fall came on top of earlier falls and an upturn in global trade in the immediate future is unlikely. In the period 2008–9 global trade fell by a large percentage, probably around 30 per cent. The OCED, in a report issued on 15 July 2009, said that:

The unprecedented and largely synchronized drop in merchandise trade volumes of the Group of Seven (G7) countries of the last quarter 2008 continued in the first quarter 2009. When compared year-on-year, the steep rate of decline already observed for Q4 2008 reached two-digit levels in Q1 2009 for almost all countries.[10]

The figures were bad both on an annual basis and in comparison with the previous quarter. On a quarterly basis, G7 exports fell by 13.6 per cent while imports were down 10.5 per cent in the first quarter of 2009. On an annual comparison of 2009 and 2008, G7 exports dropped by 22.8 per cent and imports fell 16.8 per cent in the first quarter 2009. Some countries were more affected than others. Japan experienced a 26.7 per cent slump in quarter-to-quarter exports and a drop in imports of 12.9 per cent. On a year-on-year basis, the value of exports and imports of goods and services plunged, by 27.1 per cent for exports and by 27.9 per cent for imports in the first quarter. The sharp drop observed in Q4 2008 continued in Q1 2009, albeit less steeply. The OECD also noted that, both on an annual and a

Figure 7.5 Bulk carrier *Vale Dongjiakou* under construction in China, photograph by Christopher Ledger

quarterly basis, the trade in goods fell at about twice the rate for those of services. Although the OECD saw signs of the steep drop in trade easing at the end of the first quarter for some countries, the general trend remained downwards.[11]

By the summer of 2010 the OECD reported some easing in the G7 trade position:

> Merchandise trade volumes for the G7 countries as a whole continued to grow in the first quarter of 2010, but at a slower pace than in the fourth quarter of 2009. Based on seasonally adjusted monthly data, merchandise trade values remain approximately 20 per cent below pre-crisis levels in April and May.[12]

In other words, trade recovered compared to the very low volumes of the first quarter of 2009, but not vigorously, and rates of recovery had slowed in the first quarter of 2010, compared to the last quarter of 2009. The May-to-July 2010 fall in the BDI indicated that trade volumes were still weak and that the hoped-for recovery in world trade did not happen in 2010. The continued low levels of the BDI in 2011 and 2012 indicated that the trade in basic raw materials remained depressed.

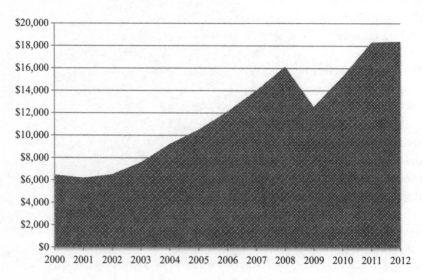

Figure 7.6 World exports by value (billions of US Dollars) World Trade Organization database

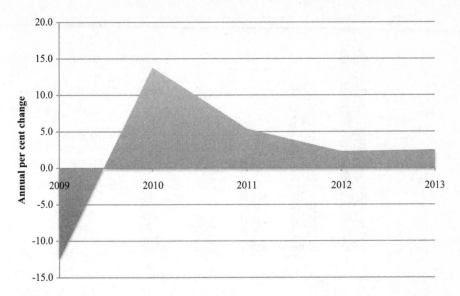

Figure 7.7 Annual percentage change in the volume of world merchandise trade (WTO figures)[13]

As Figures 7.6 and 7.7 show, there was a substantial drop in world trade in 2008–9, which recovered in 2010, but subsequent growth has been slow compared to the period 2000–8, and the outlook is not dynamic. It is therefore likely that the shipping industry will have to cope with difficult trading conditions for some years.

The rush to build and the hangover

The demand for all vessel types reached a peak in demand between mid-2007 and the end of 2008. Thereafter demand fell away and prices for new builds plummeted, reflecting the savage drop in freight rates. Like the sorcerer's apprentice who could not stop the magic once he had conjured up the spell, the world's shipyards, having geared up for massive increases in production, continued to complete new, and often unwanted, vessels. Because the lead time for ship-building is measured in years, there was no effective way to stop all this unwanted production – many shipowners having accepted, in the good times, severe restrictions on their right to cancel. But even where owners did cancel, yards often completed the ships, because the additional costs were marginal, compared to the costs of writing off half-finished vessels.

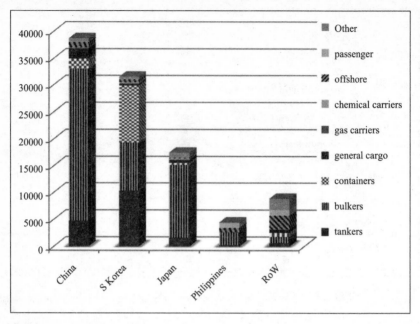

Figure 7.8 World ship production by country and type – 2012 (UNCTAD)

In 2008 nearly 3,000 vessels of an average size of 27,443 dwt were delivered.[14]

The recent cycle of ship-building has mirrored in some way the 'die-off' cycles of herd animals, like reindeer, which have overgrazed their pasture. Over time a large number of older vessels will be broken up, until the numbers are reduced to a level at which freight rates make shipping once again a profitable industry.

As yards tried to gain new orders in this chaotic market, prices for new builds fell by 22 per cent in the period 2007–8 for a 72,000 dwt bulker, and by 46 per cent for a 4,000 teu container ship, although prices for some types of vessel held, and the prices for the largest LNG carriers actually increased by 11 per cent in the same period. However, few new orders were received and in March 2009 only 13 new orders for ships larger than 1,000 gross tonnage were signed.[15] As Figure 7.8 shows, ship-building recovered by 2012 in part because of the need to reduce the cost of ship operation by using larger vessels, which do not require larger crews and utilize modern fuel-efficient engines. The total tonnage available in 2012 also increased significantly, UNCTAD reporting that while 95 million dwt were built in 2012, only 36 million dwt were scrapped; an additional 59 million dwt entered the market.[16]

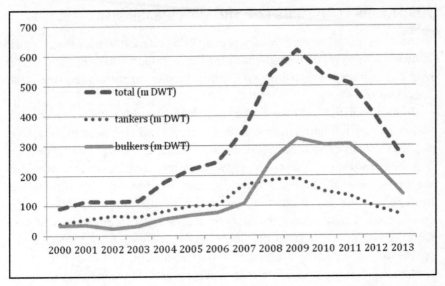

Figure 7.9 World shipping orders (millions dwt) – UNCTAD

As Figure 7.9 shows, World orders for shipping tonnage peaked in 2008 (UNCTAD records the maximum of 644.3 millions dwt on order in October 2008), and there has been a steady decline in the order book ever since. But, as noted, scrappage rates remained relatively low and the overall world tonnage continued to increase. The increase in world tonnage is also due to the time-lag between order and delivery, and it was only in 2012, for the first time since 2001, that the fleet that entered into service during that year was less than that delivered during the previous year. By January 2013 the world fleet was 1.63 billion dwt, more than double the 2001 figure.[17] Because of the long lead times involved in acquiring new ships the industry has been forced to react slowly to the impact of the 2008 recession.

According to UNCTAD, the last ten years have also seen two important trends, firstly ships are becoming larger and the number of shipping companies is falling. This has reduced competition in some markets, and enabled the larger companies to improve their profitability.

POST-CRISIS ECONOMICS AND THE SHIPPING INDUSTRY

In the years following 2008, which was really a perfect storm for the shipping industry, cargo rates fell dramatically and new builds came onto the market in large numbers at exactly the wrong time, further depressing revenue, while operating costs rose.

Bulk carrier fleets, in particular, but also other shipowners, had to deal with a massive reduction in world trade volumes and the resultant collapse in the rates available from charterers. As world trade dropped, large numbers of new, bigger ships came down the slipways. Added to these obvious pressures shipowners also had to deal with uncertainty over fuel prices, additional war insurance cover for piracy in the Indian Ocean and the demand for compensation from near mutinous crews afraid of being hijacked. In such extreme conditions it is hardly surprising that they resisted pressures to spend money on anti-piracy precautions. Bankruptcies became a normal occurrence in the industry. International pressures on the industry to reduce its CO_2 output and to burn low-sulphur fuel are also on the horizon, which will put additional financial pressures on shipowners.

The impact of the global financial crisis was felt in the container shipping market, as well as in the bulk dry cargo market and the tanker market. The buoyant growth of the previous 20 years ended abruptly in 2008, and the industry, which had ordered new capacity before the crisis, faced over-capacity in its market for some years to come, with an inescapable impact on profitability. In September 2009 Simon Parry described 'the ghost fleet' of around 500 idle merchant ships anchored near Singapore, what he called, 'An armada of freighters with no cargo, no crew, and without a destination between them.'[18]

At the end of April 2009, 506 container ships, or 10.6 per cent of the total world capacity, were idle.[19] However, in 2010, the container ship sector saw a dramatic recovery, due to the scrapping of nearly 300 ships in a two-year period, the renegotiation of deliveries and the cancellation of orders and slow-steaming by two-thirds of the global fleet. In addition, no new orders for container ships were placed for a period of nearly two years, although some orders were placed in the second half of 2010.[20]

Of especial importance for the readers of this book is the fact that piracy has imposed additional costs on the industry at the worst possible time. As Somali pirates have extended their area of operations out from the Somali coast, towards India, the Arabian Sea and the Mozambique Channel, insurers have extended the area where shipping is deemed to be at risk and required that shipowners pay for additional war risk cover before transiting these 'exclusion zones'. In 2008, Frank and Osler estimated that the increased cost of war risk insurance premiums for the 20,000 ships transiting the Gulf of Aden could reach as much as $400 million, at $20,000 per transit.[21] A US study for Congress in February 2009 referred to additional premiums from Lloyd's underwriters being between $10,000 and $20,000 per transit.[22] There is one important difference between Lloyd's hull insurance policies and those written by US insurers: Lloyd's policies explicitly cover the peril of piracy under the London Institute hull form, whereas US insurers generally exclude coverage for piracy, reserving it for a separate war risks policy.

There are also pressures to bring down kidnap and ransom (K&R) insurance rates as more insurance companies enter that market. The cost of coverage under these policies halved in the two years since 2008, with $5 million of cover costing about $15,000 a transit in the summer of 2010.[23] But K&R policies are an optional extra, and many shipping companies do not buy such cover, relying on their hull and war risk policies. Even so kidnap and ransom premiums climbed to $100 million in 2009, as companies, including Aspen Insurance Holdings Ltd, Ascot Underwriting Ltd, Griffin Underwriting and Chubb Corporation, developed new marine K&R policies. A typical K&R policy covers the ransom of the ship and its crew, including negotiations with pirates and hiring ex-special forces teams to deliver the ransom. But, as noted elsewhere, ransoms are normally paid under sue and labour,[24] although K&R cover does make the process somewhat easier – especially given that specialized negotiators and the associated security team who delivers the ransom can charge up to $2.5 million. K&R policies also covers the situation where people are taken off a ship, as happened in 2010 in West Africa, and undoubtedly speeds up the negotiation process.[25] K&R underwriters can also expect to recover some of their expenditure under general average from the hull, cargo and war risks underwriters.

However, as the exclusion zones were extended, vessels needed war risk cover for longer periods, and there are now few routes in the Indian Ocean that completely avoid exclusion zones. Tankers sailing south out of the Persian Gulf, via the Cape of Good Hope, will now transit an exclusion zone, even when they do not sail through the Gulf of Aden, and war risk cover is now needed in the Mozambique Channel and along the coast of Oman.

The insurance industry is obviously reluctant to disclose sensitive information relating to the charges for cover, but Frank and Osler's 2008 estimate of $400 million in additional premiums would seem to be too low for the purposes of calculation of 2011 costs. It is probably wise to add in $100 million for K&R cover, and to assume at least another $200 million in premiums arising from the massive extension of exclusive zones. Although this is a guess, without any basis in published data, if they are correct the total additional burden imposed on the shipping industry for additional insurance in the Indian Ocean, the Gulf of Aden and the Red Sea is in the order of $700 million, or approximately ten times the sum paid in ransoms in 2009. You can draw your own conclusions, but it does not seem that underwriters' profitability is currently threatened by the claims arising from Somali piracy.

Shipowners who decide to avoid the Gulf of Aden and sail around the Cape of Good Hope[26] may not completely remove their exposure to pirate attacks, especially if they sail to the Persian Gulf or Pakistan. However, a ship on a voyage from the Far East to Europe could well avoid exclusion zones by taking the southern route. The problem is the additional sailing time and fuel burning. It has been estimated that rerouting 33 per cent of cargo via the Cape of Good Hope would cost shipowners an additional $7.5 billion per annum, money that would pay for a lot of anti-piracy measures and additional insurance.[27] Maersk did reroute their AE7 service via the Cape of Good Hope for a while, but they announced a rethink and now transit the Suez Canal. In early 2009 Maersk said the logic of the southern route was that it saved Suez transit costs of about $600,000 per voyage for an 11,000 teu vessel, but added seven to ten days to the passage.[28] Even though the number of pirate attacks fell dramatically in the Indian Ocean, on 12 June 2013 Lloyds Joint War Committee listed in JWLA021, JWC Hull War, Piracy, Terrorism and Related Perils, the following Listed Areas:

'The waters enclosed by the following boundaries:

(a) on the north-west, by the Red Sea, south of Latitude 15° N
(b) on the west of the Gulf of Oman by Longitude 58° E
(c) on the east, Longitude 78° E
(d) and on the south, Latitude 12° S

excepting coastal waters of adjoining territories up to 12 nautical miles offshore unless otherwise provided.' The shipping industry is still carrying the cost of piracy due to the burden of additional insurance premiums and the security measures.

Shipowners face a range of other costs that are outside their control, including port charges, pilot fees, and bunkering in particular. Prices for maritime bunker fuel, which were $361 a ton in the second quarter of 2007, climbed to $667 a ton in the third quarter of 2008, but fell back to $263 in the first quarter of 2009; by August 2010 they climbed again to $465 on the US west coast.[29] In December 2013 the price of IFO180 was $616 at Singapore, $640 at Fujairah and $667.50 at Houston.[30] In other words, nothing is certain as far as the shipowner is concerned: key costs can yo-yo in months and it is virtually impossible to predict future profits (or losses).

There are almost unprecedented pressures on the shipping industry today, bearing comparison with the Great Depression. Shipowners are very often operating at the edge, taking risks, keeping costs to the minimum and reducing crew numbers. Their ships are too often unable to keep adequate watches for long periods and have not received the equipment (such as water cannon) that they need to resist pirate attacks. Piracy was the last thing the industry needed and in its weakened state it found it difficult to cope with a new set of demands.

THE THREAT TO CRUISE LINERS

The danger

As I have made clear piracy is a real and present danger to merchant ships transiting much of the Indian Ocean, Red Sea, South China Sea and the Gulf of Guinea. The attacks on bulk carriers and product tankers became routine, and rarely made the television news or the front pages of newspapers. However, I believe that it is important to highlight the threat to one particular class of ship – cruise liners – because the political impact of the hijacking of a cruise liner filled with US and European passengers would be immense. It would make any other event associated with piracy pale into insignificance. Whereas I tend to discount some of the concerns about the level of the terrorism threat, it is undoubtedly the case that cruise ships are a potential terrorism target.

To understand the likely impact of any hijacking or terrorist attack on a cruise ship, we need to go back to 1985 and the hijacking of the *Achille Lauro*. On 7 October 1985, four men from the Palestine Liberation Front (PLF) took control of the ship as she was sailing from Alexandria to Port Said. During the hijacking the Palestinians killed Leon Klinghoffer, a disabled Jewish-American passenger, and threw his body overboard. After negotiating their safe passage to Tunis with the Egyptian authorities, the Americans intercepted the

Egyptian aircraft in which they were travelling and forced it down in Italy. This was followed by an unpleasant US–Italian confrontation at a US air base in Italy, particularly when the Americans tried to remove the hijackers from Italy, ignoring Italian jurisdiction. Finally, the Italian courts tried and imprisoned the hijackers. All this drama was closely followed by the world media and the hijacking was on the front papers of newspapers for days. Today, with many 24-hour television news channels desperate for stories, and new broadcasting technology, such a story would have massive implications. The *Achille Lauro* was also, by modern standards, a small to medium-sized cruise liner, able to take 900 passengers. The *Achille Lauro* hijackers were only in charge of the ship for two days, but at the time the story was of global importance. If 2,000 passengers, many of them elderly, were kidnapped and kept at sea, the pressures on the international community would be immense. Special forces would probably be deployed if possible, but inevitably there would be civilian deaths and, if US citizens had been hijacked, the president of the United States, in particular, would be under strong pressure to send ground troops.

If a medium-sized cruise liner with 1,500 elderly Britons and Americans was hijacked, some of whom were subject to a medical condition, requiring constant medication, the media would see this as a threat to life and limb, not as a case of kidnapping for ransom. If such a ship were to be held for any length of time, and was subject to the appalling conditions experienced by the crews of vessels like the *Ariana*, then it would be difficult for the ship's doctors to maintain many of their elderly passengers alive.

We have to be prepared for the possibility of attacks and cruise liners need to be very well protected if they venture into regions experiencing conflict and piracy. If terrorists, rather than pirates, were to attack a cruise liner then their purpose would be to maximize the media coverage that the attack generated and, in such a case, the aim would probably be to kill and injure passengers, particularly Americans and Israelis. The ramifications of such an event would be incalculable. However, it is difficult to see what the international response would be, but a special forces boarding of any liner taken is high on the list of possibilities.

In recent years there has been an upsurge of terrorist activity in Yemen, with al-Qaeda in the Arabian Peninsula being especially active, in Somalia Al Shaabab remains active and is able to undertake attacks outside Somalia, as it showed with its September 2013 attack on the Westgate Mall in Nairobi, and in Lebanon, conflict between Hezbollah and Sunni groups has created a difficult situation in the eastern Mediterranean. It would therefore be a mistake to discount the possibility of such a high-profile attack.

The idyllic Indian Ocean?

For many people cruises in the Indian Ocean are an idyllic experience. However, the upsurge of pirate attacks on merchant vessels, particularly in 2008 and 2009, in the Gulf of Aden and the Indian Ocean, focused attention on the possibility of more pirate attacks on cruise liners. Since 2005 there have been confirmed attacks on cruise liners, and the hijacking of the French sail cruising vessel, *Le Ponant*.

Pirate attacks on cruise liners

The six incidents that have been reported off Somalia and Yemen are:

(1) *5 November 2005* The *Seabourn Spirit*, which was carrying 151 passengers, was attacked at 0550, 115 km off the Somali coast, by two skiffs supported by a mothership. RPGs and guns were fired at the ship. The crew used LRADs and fire-hoses, and sunk one skiff by ramming it. Assistance was given by the *USS Gonzalez*.

(2) *4 April 2008* The French sailing cruising vessel *Le Ponant* was hijacked by two skiffs in the Gulf of Aden. Thirty crew members were taken hostage and were freed on 11 April 2008 after a $2 million ransom was paid. The crew did not appear to resist the attacks.

(3) *30 November 2008* At 0930 local time, the *MS Nautica* was attacked in the Gulf of Aden in the IRTC by two skiffs. One skiff closed to 300 yards and rifle shots were fired at the ship. No damage was sustained by the ship.

(4) *5 March 2009* The MV *Balmoral* was subject to a pirate attack, while sailing in the Gulf of Aden. A spokeswoman for Fred Olsen said:

Balmoral encountered suspicious activity by two small craft, closing at high speed. The ship's master requested passengers to assemble in safe havens as part of a pre-planned safety procedure. Aggressive manoeuvring was implemented and contact was made with the EU Coalition Task Force (which patrols the Gulf of Aden in an effort to combat piracy).[31]

(5) *25 April 2009* The Italian cruise ship *MSC Melody* was attacked 200 nautical miles north of the Seychelles archipelago, while on a 22-day

cruise from Durban, South Africa, to Genoa, Italy. According to reports from the passengers, initially no one noticed the ship was being attacked; a woman leaning over the ship's rail in semi-darkness gave the first warning after she noticed that there was a small boat next to the ship. Jules Tayler, a passenger on the ship, and others rushed to the railing and saw five or six men sitting in a roofless pirate boat. One of the pirates started climbing a rope to the deck beneath them. Tayler said that 'He was already halfway up', and another passenger screamed: 'Pirates!' David Nelson, an Australian passenger, said: 'The night-time raid started about 2330 when pirates attached a rope ladder to the ship.' He added: 'The pirates actually had ropes attached to the port stern side of the ship and were climbing.'[32]

The passengers began throwing tables and deckchairs at one pirate on a rope. He was hit and fell into the sea, and the skiff turned around. This incident lasted for a few minutes and then the pirates opened fire. Jules Tayler counted three salvos of 25 to 30 rounds each. The pirate skiff approached the *Melody* repeatedly; it would disappear under the stern, only to re-emerge. The passengers continued to throw chairs although they were being fired on; one passenger was shot in the leg, and a bullet grazed a crew member's head. After about 6 ship's security staff arrived on the scene and fired shots, this convinced the pirates to withdraw. Jules Tayler and Rolf R., another passenger, were certain that throwing chairs and tables at the pirates saved the ship. Six hundred passengers were listening to a classical music concert in another part of the ship at the time of the attack and could easily have been taken hostage if the pirates had boarded. Rolf R., in an interview with *Spiegel Online* said: 'The crew was totally overwhelmed and no one knew how to ring the alarm.'[33] It was thought that two skiffs were probably involved, but because this was a night-time attack, and there was a lot of confusion, no one was certain.

Mr Vago, the chief executive of the ship's owners, MSC Cruises, said afterwards that he was shocked by the pirate bands. Journalists had told him that a Somali, who claimed to be the head of the pirates, bragged about the attack by phone. The caller allegedly said that cruise ships were a new target for pirates, but this time, they had failed due to technical reasons.[34]

At the time of the attack the *Melody* had no lookouts posted, the captain received no warning from the ship's radar, and there did not seem to be any clear anti-piracy drill. The company cancelled a later cruise by the *MSC Symphonia* in the same waters.

(6) *About 3 May 2010* The Japanese cruise ship *SS Oceanic* was attacked off the coast of Yemen with grenades fired by an RPG launcher. The ship escaped by adopting zig-zag manoeuvres and using high-pressure water-hoses. It is thought that the pirates were later apprehended by NATO forces.[35]

The six attacks described above, particularly the attack on the *Melody*, show how close the pirates did come to taking a cruise ship. While pirate activity has been reduced off Somalia, planning for vessel security should never be neglected, the threat to cruise ships can equally come from terrorist groups, as from pirates.

Dealing with the threat

While it is clear that all the major operators have security plans in place and that passenger drills are undertaken, I doubt that reliance, as in earlier incidents, on fire-hoses and LRADs alone is sufficient given the sophistication of the pirates' operation. It is also clear that crew members on board these vessels should not be exposed to incoming fire from pirate boats, as was Michael Groves. Furthermore, if the reports are true that the crew of one vessel prepared fake wooden guns to wave at attackers, it is important for masters to understand that anyone displaying such items would be the first to be shot by any attackers.

Any cruise liner entering the Indian Ocean needs to be fully equipped to resist pirate attacks, to have trained its crew, to maintain proper anti-pirate watches, and to undertake regular anti-piracy drills involving both crew and passengers. In particular small cruise liners should avoid the southern part of the Red Sea and the coasts of Eritrea, Yemen and Oman, as the risks are simply too high.

Threats in the Seychelles and the Maldives

The Seychelles and the Maldives are both attractive and popular tourist destinations. However, in recent years, there have been a series of pirate attacks in the Seychelles and a few near the Maldives. In March 2009 pirates hijacked the *Indian Ocean Explorer*, a tourist boat popular with British diving enthusiasts, near the Seychelles' island of Assumption with seven locals on board. A few weeks' earlier pirates had seized the yacht *Serenity* off the Seychelles, with three people on board.[36]

There have been a number of attacks and hijackings off the Seychelles, including the four-hour long attack on the German-owned *Felicitas Rickmers*, 420 nautical miles west of Victoria, Seychelles, on 10 November 2009 (the crew were so traumatized that it is said that mutiny was in the air). On 22 October 2009, about the same time that Paul and Rachel Chandler were kidnapped from their yacht *Lynn Rival*, while sailing from the Seychelles to Kenya, pirates seized control of the Panama-flagged MV *Al Khaliq*, which was hijacked 550 nautical miles north-east of the Seychelles. Earlier, on 2 May 2009, the bulk carrier *Ariana* had been seized just 180 nautical miles west of the Seychelles.

Pirate activity in the Seychelles continued in 2010, although the Seychelles coastguard had greater success in combating the problem. In March 2010 the Seychelles patrol vessel *Topaz* repelled a pirate attack, when one pirate mothership and two pirate skiffs opened fire on her. The *Topaz* returned fire, sinking one skiff; while the mothership exploded and caught fire, a third skiff managed to escape. Earlier the *Topaz* had rescued six Seychellois and 21 Iranian hostages from a large dhow which had been hijacked by Somali pirates.[37] In the same month, armed guards on the Spanish tuna boat the *Txori Argi* fired several warning shots at pirates, about 80 miles from Victoria; this PAG was then intercepted by the Seychellois coastguard patrol boat *Andromache*, about 100 nautical miles north-west of the Seychelles and eight pirates were detained.[38] The *Topaz* was in action again on 29 May 2010 when she caught three suspected pirate boats, destroying two attack skiffs, disarming nine suspected pirates and allowing them to go free in their mothership.[39] Although the Seychelles' authorities are clearly doing all they can to combat piracy, with the aid of EU NAVFOR patrol aircraft, the seas around the islands continue to see pirate operations.

The eastwards extension of pirate attacks in the 2009–10 season raised the potential of the threat to the Maldives, and on 21 May 2010 eight pirates in a skiff attacked a tanker only 105 nautical miles west of those islands, which, like the Seychelles, are a tourist magnet. It would seem that the days of cruise ships anchoring off a remote Indian Ocean island, while their passengers are shuttled to and fro to the beaches on the ship's tenders, are past. The dangers are now far too high. The great advantage of cruise liners is their relatively high speed – 20 knots is not an uncommon top speed, fast enough to throw most pirate attacks off, if the master has sufficient warning. But once these vessels are anchored they are very vulnerable to direct assault and attacks on their tenders.

The real threats to cruise liners are the more obvious ones; the transits of the Gulf of Aden and the southern Red Sea. Cruise ships on the ever popular 'round-the-world' cruises still transit the Gulf of Aden en route to India, and other vessels continue to offer cruises to the Persian Gulf via the Gulf of Aden. It is interesting that in December 2008 shipper Hapag-Lloyd took the precaution of flying the passengers, and many of the crew, of the *MS Columbus* from Hodeidah in Yemen to Dubai, in order to avoid the possibility of a hijacking in the Gulf of Aden.

The ramifications of a successful hijacking

Had the pirates not been seen by the woman on the *Melody* looking out on the night-time sea, and had a group of passengers not taken risks throwing deck furniture at gun-firing Somalis, the 1,600 passengers and over 500 crew of that ship would have been involuntary guests, moored off the Somali coast – their meals somewhat different from the 'Italian treats of tiramisu and cannolis' and 'your favourite cakes, pastries and tarts', promised by the shipping line.[40]

Once the news of their seizure had been announced, the world's 24-hour news services would have carried continual reporting on the incident, interviews with distressed relatives, and with anyone who had ever been to sea in the Indian Ocean. Special forces would have been deployed to Djibouti, politicians given news conferences, retired naval officers and other experts on piracy wheeled out on breakfast television. In the secret rooms of defence ministries there would have been near panic: briefings would be organized in Washington, Rome, Paris and London, ministers would have assured the public that everything was under control and the military would have told them that in a fire-fight off Somalia they would expect to lose at least 20 or 30 hostages, but that the casualties could be greater and they would also expect to lose a number of the special forces operatives. Two options might be put forward: first, that special forces retook the ship before it could make landfall off Somalia; and second, that the ransom that had already been demanded should be paid without delay. To support the action plan, a group of US Navy Seal and British Special Boat Services operatives would be sent to Djibouti and two USAF AC-130U Spookies and an RAF C5 Special Forces Hercules would be deployed to Camp Lemonnier to deliver them to the target. Naval assets would steam at maximum speed towards the hijacked vessel.

In such a case Western politicians would be under the most extraordinary pressure and, unlike the case of the Chandlers, the two British pensioners kidnapped from their yacht, or the approximately 400 seamen held hostage at the end of 2010, this issue would remain centre stage until the problem was resolved. It would also undoubtedly be the catalyst for military intervention on the Somali mainland, with the objective of 'taking out' pirate havens. Some governments would take the view that this was an act of terrorism, rather than an act of piracy, and this perception would guide their responses. Recent responses to other perceived 'threats' show that governments normally take action to improve perceptions at home, rather than because of a detailed assessment of the complexities of the situation. The outcome of any such response could be messy for all concerned.

In short, although hijacking a cruise liner may appear attractive and desirable to Somali pirates, in reality this is almost certainly an enormous 'own goal', as virtually unlimited military resources would be deployed against them. There is, however, no certainty that the final outcome will have a happy ending.

CHAPTER 8

LEGAL AND INSURANCE ISSUES

THE ROLE OF INSURERS

It is a requirement that before a ship can enter the ports of the world it is insured. The maritime insurance market is dominated by Lloyd's of London, a market of underwriters that developed originally at Edward Lloyd's coffee house, known as 'Lloyd's'. Mr Lloyd first opened for business at Tower Street in the City of London, about 1688, the year that William and Mary became the King and Queen of England. By 1774 Lloyd's had become the Society of Lloyd's based in the Royal Exchange and today Lloyd's occupies a striking building at 1 Lime Street, designed by Sir Richard Rogers.

Lloyd's is not the only marine insurance market and Lloyd's underwriters have effective competitors, but Lloyd's still dominates the market for marine insurance. Over the last 300 years the development of the London insurance market has led to the standardization of insurance policies, and further developed marine insurance law; English law and practice have therefore formed the basis for modern maritime insurance law and policy terms. Lloyd's has also seen the gradual introduction of measures that increase seaworthiness of vessels. The most famous was the load line, or 'Plimsoll Line', named after Samuel Plimsoll MP, who championed its introduction: this eventually became an international standard. Lloyd's surveyors played an important role in defining the standard load line, which was finally made compulsory for British ships, and for foreign ships leaving British ports,

229

under the British Merchant Shipping Act 1890.[1] It was finally adopted by 30 countries who signed an international convention in London in 1930.

Insurance underwriters (Lloyd's syndicates) 'write' the insurance policies that set the terms of the contract and take the risk (which they may reinsure). Brokers act on behalf of the shipowners to arrange the best policies, and different underwriters may be responsible for the different policies (hull, cargo, war risk, PandI, etc.) taken out for a vessel and its cargo. Shipowners cannot do business directly with Lloyd's underwriters and use Lloyd's brokers as intermediaries. Each syndicate has a 'box' in the underwriting room at Lloyd's from which business is transacted with Lloyd's brokers. Each box includes a couple of benches and desks at which the syndicate's underwriters sit, and the visiting Lloyd's brokers agree business with them.[2] Because of the interaction of the difference types of insurance and the variation between provisions in insurance contracts there can be significant differences between the insurance contracts for different vessels.

SEAWORTHINESS

The adventures and perils of the sea

A seaworthy ship is a ship that is fit for any normal perils of the sea, and includes the fitness of the vessel itself, its equipment, and the skills and health of its crew. The ship need not be in perfect condition, but the ship must be fit for the purpose for which it is being used and offer reasonable safety on the high seas. As the UK Marine Insurance Act 1906 stipulates in section 39(1): 'In a voyage policy there is an implied warranty that at the commencement of the voyage the ship shall be seaworthy for the purpose of the particular adventure insured.'[3] Section 39(4) of the 1906 Act adds: 'A ship is deemed to be seaworthy when she is reasonably fit in all respects to encounter the ordinary perils of the seas of the adventure insured.'[4] And section 39(5) states:

> In a time policy there is no implied warranty that the ship shall be seaworthy at any stage of the adventure, but where, with the privity of the assured, the ship is sent to sea in an unseaworthy state, the insurer is not liable for any loss attributable to unseaworthiness.

So an insurance policy will not cover an unseaworthy vessel, that is a ship that is not fit 'to encounter the ordinary perils of the seas of the adventure insured'.[5]

The adventures and perils of the sea are described in the First Schedule to the 1906 Act as follows:

> They are of the seas, men of war, fire, enemies, pirates, rovers, thieves, jettisons, letters of mart and countermart, surprisals, takings at sea, arrests, restraints, and detainments of all kings, princes, and people, of what nation, condition, or quality soever, barratry of the master and mariners, and of all other perils, losses, and misfortunes, that have or shall come to the hurt, detriment, or damage of the said goods and merchandises, and ship, &c., or any part thereof.[6]

The 1906 Act is quite clear: where a ship undertakes 'an adventure', and the perils of the sea that are foreseeable during that adventure (or voyage) include piracy, or the threat of 'rovers, thieves' and the like, then that ship is not seaworthy if it is not prepared to deal with such threats.

In practice marine policies normally follow policy wordings from Lloyd's committees and the Institute of London Underwriters. There is also the International Hull Clauses wording, which was introduced in 2002.[7] However, it can still be argued, exclusions in policies excepted, that if you transit the Gulf of Aden and fail to take anti-piracy precautions your ship is not seaworthy and your insurers may be able to avoid liability for losses resulting from pirate attacks and hijackings if the policies follow the terms of the UK Maritime Insurance Act 1906, or similar legislation enacted by other states. Jonathan Steer wrote that in considering the risks from piracy, 'a comparison could be drawn with fire-fighting and fire-detection equipment and procedures. The absence of these could very easily render a vessel unseaworthy. Fire is a statistical risk, a potential danger – and so is piracy in some areas.' Steer concluded that 'a shipowner who sends his vessel to the Gulf of Aden ... would be well advised to make sure that he has properly trained and equipped officers and crew to deal with piracy'.[8] As Steer said, 'Whilst it would not be easy to show that the loss was "attributable" to the shipowner's failures, it seems almost inevitable that, faced with sufficiently large claims, insurers are going to start looking quite hard at these questions.'[9]

Peter Tribe, a partner at the same law firm as Jonathan Steer, Elborne Mitchell, also said that it is possible that insurers could treat a vessel as unseaworthy if it was sent through a known pirate area with an insufficiently trained crew and without adequate anti-piracy equipment.

INSURANCE CLAIMS

Given the importance of the insurance market in determining the behaviour of the shipping industry and in paying ransoms where ships are hijacked, it is worth briefly looking at some specific issues that affect that market, in particular the justification for the payment of ransoms and the process by which liability for ransoms is shared between different classes of underwriter. The insurance market, like all professions, has its own language, but in order to understand its operations it is useful to understand terms such as 'sue and labour' and 'general average'.

Sue and labour

It should be noted that the actual course of events in any insurance claim is determined by the specific terms of the contract, and that these terms may vary widely. Therefore, I am not suggesting that the processes described below are always followed. But rather I am attempting to give an indication of what may happen in a typical claim, to guide the general reader, for whom the workings of Lloyd's are a mystery.

Ransoms will initially be paid out by the shipowner. Some shipping companies may have K&R cover for their crew and vessel, in addition to the normal hull, war risks and protection and indemnity. The main advantage of K&R cover is that such a policy typically insures any ransom payment up to an agreed sum, and provides for the costs of negotiation and other costs arising from a hijack. Most K&R underwriters also offer access to specialized negotiators and support staff, taking some pressure off the shipowner. However, even if the shipowner does not have K&R cover, the vessel's insurers will indemnify it for the ransom payment under the terms of 'sue and labour' provisions.

It is important to remember that ransoms can also be paid under 'sue and labour' provisions by hull and war risk underwriters. Sue and labour clauses are normal in maritime insurance contracts and state the duty of the insured to seek to minimize any loss and recover detained property, such as a hijacked ship. In other words, sue and labour clauses encourage and bind the assured to take steps to minimize a loss for which the underwriter would be liable, and then to take steps to reduce the amount of the loss. The payment of ransoms to recover a hijacked ship and its cargo (which is normally insured separately) is therefore normally a sum and labour issue, as it reduces the prospect of a total loss of the hijacked ship by the payment of a lesser sum. Claims for sue and labour are treated separately from claims for general loss, because the intention is that the shipowner will be compensated for money spent attempting to avert or minimize loss, over and above the value of the insured value of the ship if it is a total loss.[10]

General average

Where there is a claim, the underwriters for the various policies – hull, war risks, cargo and K&R – will normally seek contributions from one another under a process known as 'general average', unless such right is excluded under the terms of one, or more, of the policies, or the insurers waive recourse. According to insurance broker Marsh:

> Attack by pirates (or any violent theft attempt) is likely to be covered by the ship's war insurers, both in relation to any hull damage and to crew injury/death, while payments to avoid both (ransoms) will be typically addressed as if a general average sacrifice. Since *Hicks v. Palington* (1590) it has been assumed that ransom payments are a subject for general average payments.[11]

The English courts have long accepted that shipowners are entitled to recover contributions for such general average sacrifice from cargo underwriters and other interests.[12] However, there are some areas where this principle is not entirely clear. Jonathan Bruce says 'So far the legal liability of P&I interests to contribute to ransom payments by way of general average has not been tested in the English Courts, but such a dispute cannot be far off.'[13] 'P&I' or 'Pandi' means protection and indemnity insurance, which is covered in respect of third party liabilities and expenses arising from owning or operating ships. Bruce explains that there could also be problems where hull and war risks underwriters argue over liability and where the shipowner may have accepted different warranties under each policy. In many situations the position will not be clear.[14] He adds that there is another potential area of dispute where a hull underwriter could try to rely on the malicious acts exclusion, putting this risk onto war risks, another point that has, at the time of writing, yet to be tested in the English courts.[15]

If general average is agreed, and subject to the provisions of the insurance contract, cargo owners will normally have an obligation to contribute to a ransom demand. There is also the possibility that charterers may have such an obligation, unless excluded in their insurance, or they are indemnified by

233

the shipowner. Owners and hull underwriters will initially deal with ransom demands, rather than cargo or P&I underwriters. Broker Marsh says:

> In the event that the crew or master is specifically held hostage (the ship then not being 'in peril'), historically the shipowner's Protection and Indemnity (P&I) Club, or other crew liability insurer, would treat the ransom as a 'sue and labour' expense, but high ransoms may not be protected by this treatment.[16]

K&R policies should also cover the costs of ransoming crew members.

Detention of a vessel

There are a number of other insurance issues that can also arise with hijackings. For example, there can be problems if the vessel has been chartered, as a long period of detention by pirates during a relatively short charter period could result in a claim for frustration.[17] In addition, there may be a dispute as to whether hire charges are payable during a period of detention; this will be determined by the precise wording of the charter. There is also the possibility that the shipowner may have a claim against the charterer, where the charterer required the ship to transit a known piracy risk area; but the converse may be true if the charterer is indemnified against all liability under the contract for hire. The precise terms of the contract will need to be examined with care, and there is the potential for further disagreement and claims, where shipowners refuse to transit dangerous areas, or deviate around known threats.

The issue of detention was considered before Mr Justice Steel in the Commercial Court in London in December 2009, in the case of *Masefield* v. *Amlin Corporate Member Ltd.* The case related to the *Bunga Melati Dua*, a chemical/palm oil tanker, which was hijacked by Somali pirates on 19 August 2008 in the Gulf of Aden during a voyage from Malaysia to Rotterdam. The owner of two parcels of bio-diesel on board the vessel claimed that on the capture of the vessel by the pirates and its removal into Somali waters the cargo became an actual total loss under section 57(1) of the Marine Insurance Act 1906, as the owner had been 'irretrievably deprived' of the cargo. The owner alternatively claimed that there had been a constructive total loss under section 60(1) of the 1906 Act, because the vessel and cargo had been reasonably abandoned on account of its actual total loss appearing to be unavoidable. The *Bunga Melati Dua* was actually ransomed quickly and freed at the end of

September 2008 after 41 days. Mr Justice Steel declared '[I]n my judgment, is that an assured is not irretrievably deprived of property if it is legally and physically possible to recover it (and even if such recovery can only be achieved by disproportionate effort and expense).'[18] He also said that the vessel and its cargo had not been abandoned: 'To the contrary the shipowners and the cargo owners had every intention of recovering their property and were fully hopeful of doing so.'[19] Accordingly, there was no reasonable basis for regarding an actual total loss as unavoidable and he concluded that 'the claimant has not made out its claim for a total loss whether actual or constructive.'[20] In this case the shipowners commenced ransom negotiations promptly and the ship was released in less than six weeks. However, where the owner refused to enter into negotiations with the hijackers, as was the case with the MV *Iceberg 1*, or where the detention of the vessel continued for a long period, like the bunker barge *Al-Nisr-Al-Saudi*, hijacked on 1 March 2010 and still held eight months later,[21] it is likely that the courts would find that the owner had been irretrievably deprived of its property and thus entitled to claim that a constructive total loss had occurred. In current circumstances the decision in *Bunga Melati Dua* may not be applicable. Where there is no prospect of a recovery of the vessel or its cargo, or where the cargo has deteriorated, then cargo owners will claim a total loss, a process helped by the fact that many charter contracts allow such claims after a fixed period of detention.

The need for effective cover

In short, a number of areas are potentially cause for disputes between underwriters of different classes of insurance, and it seems likely that a number of these disputes will be tested in the courts. Although the principles of insurance law, as it applies to piracy, have been known since the eighteenth century, piracy claims at current levels are a new problem as far as twenty-first century underwriters are concerned. The variation in hull and war risk policies, the need to ensure that cover against piracy is clear, and questions as to the effectiveness of K&R policies mean that shipowners and their brokers will need to be very careful to arrange effective cover against the threat of piracy.

Premiums should reflect the preparedness of the vessel

In January 2010 Rear Admiral Hudson announced to the House of Lords that he would like to see insurers give a discount for those ships 'that fully participate' in anti-piracy measures.[22] This is a suggestion that I have been making for some time. Where a ship is 'fit to transit', war risk and other policies should reflect the preparedness of the vessel and the level of actual risk.[23] It is desirable to set out the minimum prudent requirements for vessels transiting a high risk area, acknowledging that the situation of individual vessels will vary to some extent. Clearly, much depends on a vessel's size, speed, and manning levels, among other factors, but the basic rules remain broadly the same.

I actually believe that the time is fast approaching when an owner whose vessel is hijacked will be called to account if it has failed to take certain basic precautions for the protection of the crew, passengers and cargo. And if the owner's or management company's failure has led to the death or injury of persons on board, they will leave themselves vulnerable to civil and criminal liabilities. In assessing the vulnerability of a vessel it is necessary to consider its 'resilience', or capacity to resist attacks. It is to be hoped that the insurance market will eventually adopt such measures, if only to ensure underwriters of unprepared vessels do not bare unreasonable risks.

SAFETY OF LIFE AT SEA (SOLAS)

The Safety of Life at Sea (SOLAS) Convention of 1914 introduced measures designed to minimize the risk of sinking and the improve fire protection; for example, watertight and fire-proof bulkheads were made mandatory. The Convention was agreed following the sinking of the *Titanic* with the loss of more than 1,500 lives, although implementation of its terms was delayed by the First World War.

Since 1914 there have been four other SOLAS conventions: the second was adopted in 1929 and entered into force in 1933; the third was adopted in 1948 and entered into force in 1952; the fourth was adopted (under the auspices of IMO) in 1960 and entered into force in 1965. The present version was adopted in 1974 and entered into force in 1980.

The SOLAS conventions cover many aspects of safety at sea. The 1914 Convention included chapters on safety of navigation, construction, radiotelegraphy, life-saving appliances and fire protection. The current version deals with the same safety concerns. The 1914 Convention was, as the title implies, concerned primarily with the safety of human life; before 1914 the annual loss of life from British ships alone averaged between 700 and 800 people.[24] The 1914 Convention required merchant vessels to carry an adequate number of lifejackets and lifeboats, which had to provide protection against the elements. In addition, stability standards, fire-resistant bulkheads and the installation of a public address system were included.

Later SOLAS conventions have widened the requirements for safety equipment; for example, improved lifeboat-release mechanisms are now required. Under the 1974 Convention port officers are empowered to take action if there are clear grounds for believing that the condition of the ship or of its equipment does not correspond substantially with the particulars of any of the ship's certificates. The officer can take steps to ensure that the ship does not sail until it can do so without endangering passengers, crew or the ship itself. While there are no plans at present for a replacement convention, there are regular amendments. Incidents like the *Herald of Free Enterprise* tragedy have resulted in the rapid introduction of amendments – in that particular case the new amendments came into force on 29 April 1990 just over three years after the disastrous loss of 193 passengers and crew.

It would therefore be possible for the IMO to recommend new safety standards to protect both new and existing vessels against piracy. The mechanism to impose anti-piracy requirements exists and I believe that in the near future the IMO will need to discuss such changes. In 1992 amendments to the regulations were introduced for ro-ro car ferries, following the sinking of the car ferry *MS Estonia* in the Baltic on 28 September 1994, when its loading doors failed; 852 people drowned as a result. These changes were applied to the existing fleet, some of which had to be modified at great expense, or even withdrawn from service, rather than just applied to newly built vessels. Where the safety of life at sea is an issue, the IMO can, if it wishes, act relatively quickly and decisively.

Unlike the general duty of seaworthiness the SOLAS system is based on agreed international standards and inspections. However, it could also be argued that under English law, over and above the duty to comply with the 1974 Convention, a shipowner owes a general duty of care to their crew and passengers.

PAYMENT OF RANSOMS

There are three separate legal issues that need to be addressed before paying a ransom under English law: first, whether the payment of a ransom is itself legal; second, whether there are money laundering issues to be considered; and, third, whether the ransom is being paid, in whole, or in part to terrorists, in which case it cannot be paid under current English law. English law is particularly important in that Lloyd's market plays a major role in the settlement of maritime ransoms, and London lawyers, agents and British security companies are prominent in this field.

The actual payment of ransoms to criminals has, in principle, been legal under English law since the repeal of the 1782 Ransom Act. In 2009 the British House of Lords, in a report entitled 'Money laundering and the financing of terrorism', concluded: 'We have received no evidence to suggest that the payment of a ransom should be made a criminal offence, and we do not suggest that the law should be changed.'[25] In the same report the House of Lords also expressed concerns that ransoms could fund terrorism and said:

> In every case of piracy where a ransom has been demanded and the payment is being assembled in the United Kingdom, those involved have in our view a duty to seek consent for the payment of the ransom. Not to do so is likely to result in the commission of a criminal offence.[26]

The reason why they believed that consent should be sought was to ensure that money laundering legislation was being complied with. In their report the House of Lords also expressed concern about a statement by the Home Office, which said that they 'have no legal instrument to prevent companies from [paying ransoms] or for requiring them to report their activities, unless a link is established between piracy and terrorism.'[27] The House of Lords disagreed and said:

> [C]onsent may be required when assembling money in order to provide a defence to the money laundering offence under section 328(1) of POCA [UK Proceeds of Crime Act 2002]. A decision by SOCA [the UK Serious Organised Crime Agency] to grant consent is a decision to confer a defence to a prosecution for a money laundering offence, and not to judge the propriety of the planned ransom payment.[28]

As regards the payment of ransoms that may reach terrorists, the United Kingdom, Canada and the United States have all designated Al-Shabaab as a terrorist organization. It is an offence under the 2000 UK Terrorism Act to raise funds or launder money for the benefit of terrorist organizations, or if the payee had reasonable cause to believe that the payment of a ransom would result in money passing to a terrorist organization. The payment of a ransom to a terrorist organization is therefore illegal under UK law.

However, by July 2009 the British authorities had not found any evidence that pirate ransoms were being paid to Al-Shabaab. It is now necessary to quote at some length from the House of Lords report, because what they said is important and cannot really be paraphrased – particularly when it comes to the statement about the lack of evidence of a direct link between piracy and terrorism:

It seems to us that there is a serious risk that a significant proportion of money paid to pirates as a ransom could be used for the financing of terrorism. When we put this to Ian Pearson MP, the Economic Secretary to the Treasury, he told us '... there is no direct evidence of the proceeds of piracy being directed towards terrorism'. But he added: 'I have been careful not to say that it is not going to terrorism. What I have said is that we have not found a direct link to that.' (Q 479–480) Subsequently the Home Office conceded that in the case of Somalia the existence of terrorist groups in the area was well known, but added that it was not thought at the present time that Somali pirates were connected in any systematic way to those terrorist organisations.[29]

The House of Lords added that the UK government had a duty to establish the facts, something that an individual shipowner could not do:

In our view the likely reason no link has been found between piracy and terrorism is that no link has been sought. We concede that in the case of a failed State like Somalia, almost devoid of law enforcement authorities, with a minimal banking system and large ungoverned areas, it is extremely difficult to trace what happens to a ransom once it is paid. However it is important to know whether the proceeds of piracy are being used for terrorist financing, and if so the order of magnitude of the sums involved. The Government must take the initiative, if possible in concert with other interested States.[30]

The House of Lords report is worth reading in full – it makes a series of excellent points. For example:

We are struck by the sharp contrast between the naval efforts being deployed by the Government, the EU and NATO to deter and eliminate the threat from the rise of piracy off the Horn of Africa, and the lack of any concerted action to inhibit the transfer of the proceeds of these criminal acts, or even to establish whether they might be helping to finance terrorism.[31]

The Lords urged the UK government to raise this issue with their EU partners, and suggested that the countries best placed to help find answers to these questions are those in that area, including Saudi Arabia, Yemen, Kenya and the Seychelles.[32]

On 7 December 2009, in a House of Lords debate, Lord Brett said:

The Government regularly examine all available intelligence for evidence of links between piracy and terrorism. I have to say that, to date, we have found no evidence. I sympathise with the view that one cannot see vast sums of money being passed around in Somalia without believing that some of it could be going to terrorist organisations in one form or another. However, we have found no evidence of any operational or organisational links. There is much open-source speculation – we are all a part of it. The noble Lord, Lord Skelmersdale, asked what we are doing to try to establish whether it is true. It has not been possible for any of our or our partners' intelligence agencies to corroborate it. Therefore, it is a question not of a country having a view, but of intelligence that we have been able to glean from allies, as well as from our own endeavours, failing to find any organisational or operational link.[33]

So at the end of 2009 the government of the United Kingdom and its allies, which it is reasonably safe to say included the United States and others, had 'no evidence of any operational or organisational links' between the payment of ransoms and terrorism in Somalia, and Lord Brett discounted 'open-source speculation'. In dealing with ransoms it is important to keep reviewing the situation and to take advice from governments, because at the end of the day they are the only organizations with the ability to assess adequately whether money may be flowing to terrorism; for the rest of us, all is essentially speculation.

By being subject to the observance of money laundering requirements, there seems no legal reason why UK companies and their insurers cannot continue to pay ransoms to Somali pirates; although, as discussed below, the US and EU orders of April 2010, implementing the work of the UN Sanctions Committee, complicated the situation. If a link between any pirates and Al-Shabaab is shown, all bets will be off and the payment of any ransoms to pirates with links to Al-Shabaab will be illegal under UK law (and under the laws of most other jurisdictions).

US PRESIDENTIAL ORDER ON THE PAYMENT OF RANSOMS

On 12 April 2010 the UN Security Council Committee on Somalia and Eritrea issued a 'List of Individuals Identified Pursuant to Paragraph 8 of Resolution 1844 (2008).'[34] This list included eight individuals and one organization, Al-Shabaab. Resolution 1844 (2008) introduced financial sanctions against those persons designated by the relevant UN Sanctions Committee as:

(1) engaging in or providing support for acts that threaten the peace, security or stability of Somalia, including acts that threaten the Djibouti Agreement of 18 August 2008 or the political process, or threaten the TFIs or African Union Mission in Somalia (AMISOM) by force;
(2) having acted in violation of the general and complete arms embargo imposed by Resolution 733 (1992);
(3) obstructing the delivery of humanitarian assistance to or access to, or distribution of humanitarian assistance in, Somalia.

The next day, on 13 April 2010, US President Obama signed a presidential order dealing with the payment of ransoms by US persons, which implemented the UN sanctions, but which also added an additional three individuals and implemented the sanctions in a different way from the original UN provisions. Since it was published there has been a real concern that the effects of the order are that anyone providing Somali pirates with financial support, for example by paying ransoms, could be subject to fines and criminal sanctions in the United States. Given the wide definition of US person to include any organization or individual with US links, the tendency of US courts to claim universal jurisdiction, and the ease of extradition from the United Kingdom to the United States, a number of people have become very uncomfortable. It has also been said that the effect of the order will be to restrict the ransoming of seafarers. The International Chamber of Shipping and the International Shipping Federation said: 'The US does not appreciate the potentially life-threatening impact of the order on the lives of over 250 seafarers currently [April 2010] being held captive.'[35]

The order actually stipulates that a US person may not transfer property, pay, export, withdraw, or otherwise deal with persons listed in the annex to the order and any person determined by the secretary of the Treasury, in consultation with the secretary of state, to have engaged in acts that directly or indirectly threaten the peace, security or stability of Somalia. In other word, the presidential order gives a list of people whom Americans, and people and organizations with US connections, cannot deal with, but it is not a blanket ban on the payment of ransoms – although it does say that 'among other threats to the peace, security, or stability of Somalia, acts of piracy or armed robbery at sea off the coast of Somalia threaten the peace, security, or stability of Somalia.'[36]

However, there is real concern that insurers and shipowners could be caught by US courts' interpretations of the order, which is broadly drafted. Only when there are a few incidents will it become clear whether this order in practice has an adverse effect on the payment of ransoms by any party with US connections. At present it would be wise for those involved in any hijack case with US connections to consult with the Office of Foreign Assets Control (OFAC) of the US Department of the Treasury, before making any ransom payments in Somalia – though ultimately this may not be sufficient to absolve them of responsibility. The drafting of section 1(b), the determination that 'acts of piracy or armed robbery at sea threaten the peace, security, or stability of Somalia', and the prohibition on the making of 'donations', by which it appears the order means ransoms, for the benefit of any person who is listed under section 1(a), needs to be carefully considered. As yet, there is no defence of acting reasonably, or any procedure for checking with the US authorities.

There is also a real concern over the correct interpretation of section 4 of the order, as it appears to suggest that individuals and organizations can be added to the prohibited list without prior notice: 'there need be no prior notice of a listing or determination made pursuant to section 1(a) of this order'.[37] Therefore, it would be possible to be in breach of the order without knowing it. This has created an impossible situation for the insurance and shipping industries; there can be no certainties.

Two of the individuals prohibited by the United States (but not by the UN) are important pirate leaders, a factor that really complicates the situation. Let us hope that this order is reissued in a clearer form, possibly with a procedure for seeking juridical or US government approval for the payment of ransoms. By contrast the European order (see below) is better drafted and includes a defence, where those who provided financing, or financial assistance, did not know, and had no reasonable cause to suspect, that their actions would infringe the prohibition.

In this situation insurers and shipowners will need to seek the best legal advice and also work closely with their governments before paying any ransom demand. This is a complex state of affairs and there are no easy answers. The US order heightens the uncertainties faced by the insurance and shipping industries and may mean that insurance policies written by US companies and international companies with US offices will need to be reassessed; in particular many K&R policies are written by US insurers, who may now refuse to make payments because of the possibility that they are in breach of this order. The US government now needs to bring in procedures and processes so that the insurance and shipping industries (and their professional advisors) know what they can and cannot do.

The hijacking on 10 December 2010 of the MV *Panama*, a Liberian-flagged cargo/container ship, 177 metres in length, operated by a US-based company, Ship Management Services Inc. of Coral Gables, Florida, and owned by Eurus Berlin LLC, appeared to show that the US authorities dealt with the problem of ransoming a US-owned ship in the same way as other countries. The MV *Panama* was sailing from Dar es Salaam, Tanzania to Beira, Mozambique when hijacked about 80 nautical miles off the East African coast. The MV *Panama* was released in September 2011 after a ransom of $7 million had been paid.[38]

It is clear that the United States acted unilaterally by adding individuals over and above those in the UN list; the United Kingdom asked the UN in April 2010 for a 'technical hold' to be placed on a US proposal to add Abshir Abdillahi and Mohamed Abdi Garaad to the list of people subject to sanctions under UN Security Council Resolution 1844, a fact that highlighted the very different concerns of the UK and US governments. Michael Peel wrote in the *Financial Times*:

> The proposal is contentious in the UK because it widens sanctions aimed at those allegedly behind the conflict in Somalia to include the pirates, amid concern in some quarters internationally that ransoms could be used to fund al-Shabaab. . . . Britain's dilemma is that criminalising ransoms would cause problems for the many shipping industry interests in London, including lawyers and private security companies that have played a leading role in freeing kidnapped ships and crews.[39]

EUROPEAN UNION COUNCIL ORDER NO. 356/2010

On 26 April 2010, shortly after the US presidential order was issued, the European Council issued an order 'imposing certain specific restrictive measures directed against certain natural or legal persons, entities or bodies, in view of the situation in Somalia'.[40] The order, after referring to the UN arms embargo imposed on Somalia and UN prohibitions on certain named individuals, stated:

> The restrictive measures [in the Order] are aimed at individuals and entities designated by the United Nations (UN) as engaging in or providing support for acts that threaten the peace, security or stability of Somalia, including acts that threaten the Djibouti Agreement of 18 August 2008 or the political process, or threaten the Transitional Federal Institutions (TFIs) or the African Union Mission in Somalia (AMISOM) by force, as having acted in violation of the arms embargo and related measures, or as obstructing the delivery of humanitarian assistance to Somalia, or access to, or distribution of, humanitarian assistance in Somalia.[41]

The European Union therefore put into force measures, which applied to all member states of the European Union, to restrict dealings with those persons, entities or bodies designated by the UN Sanctions Committee.[42]

The language used was very similar to that in the US presidential order, which says that it applies to those who:

> have engaged in acts that directly or indirectly threaten the peace, security, or stability of Somalia, including but not limited to:
>
> (1) acts that threaten the Djibouti Agreement of 18 August 2008, or the political process; or
> (2) acts that threaten the Transitional Federal Institutions, the African Union Mission in Somalia (AMISOM), or other international peacekeeping operations related to Somalia.[43]

However, unlike the US presidential order, the European order makes no direct reference to piracy, although the general terms referred to above are wide in their scope, being aimed at those who threaten the peace, security or stability of Somalia. It is clear that the release of the US and the European orders was coordinated and that the primary objective of both was to stop the flow of funds to Al-Shabaab, and other persons listed by the Security Council or the UN Sanctions Committee.

The European order, by article 2.1, therefore freezes all funds and economic resources owned, or controlled by, those persons and organizations listed in the order, and says in article 2.2 that no funds or economic resources shall be made available, directly or indirectly, to those listed. Article 2.4 also prohibits activities 'the object or effect of which is, directly or indirectly, to circumvent the measures referred to in paragraphs 1 and 2'. However, article 2.5 does create a defence where funds or economic resources are made available, but the person or organization concerned 'did not know, and had no reasonable cause to suspect, that their actions would infringe this prohibition'.[44] The European order, which is far more detailed and precise in its drafting than the US presidential order, also prohibits technical assistance related to military activities or to the supply, sale, transfer, manufacture, maintenance or use of military supplies and technology and the financing of military activities, or arms sales.

The European order was put into force under English law by a HM Treasury Financial Sanctions Notice on 28 April 2010.[45]

THE LIST OF PROHIBITED PERSONS AND ORGANIZATIONS

The US presidential order included the eight individuals and Al-Shabaab listed by the UN, and three additional men – Mohamed Abdi Garaad, Abshir Abdillahi and Yemene Ghebreab. In an article in the *Globe and Mail*, Jay Bahadur described Mohamed Abdi Garaad as the 'Pirate King of Somalia'.[46] On 8 April 2009, pirates under Garaad's command attacked the MV *Maersk Alabama*.[47] The second individual listed only by the United States as having pirate connections is Abshir Abdillahi, otherwise known as 'Boyah'. The UN report added, 'By Boyah's own account, his militia is responsible for hijacking between 25 and 60 shipping vessels since the mid-1990s.'[48] It is no surprise that the Americans are keen to deny him the fruits of his labour. In addition, the Americans included Yemene Ghebreab, head of political affairs and presidential adviser at the PFDJ, the only political party in Eritrea. Eritrea had been heavily involved in arming groups in Somalia and opposed the former TFG, largely because of the support given to it by Ethiopia.

The UN list of eight individuals included Fares Mohammed Mana'a, who was described by Jane Novak as a 'leading regional arms smuggler', and noted that he had also been 'the Yemeni government's prime negotiator with the Houthi rebels'.[49] There is one man with alleged pirate connections in the UN list, Mohamed Sa'id 'Atom', who commands the militia group known as the Eastern Sanaag Mujahidicen. The UN press statement issued on 12 April 2010 said:

> Mohamed Sa'id 'Atom' has engaged in acts that threaten the peace, security or stability of Somalia. Atom has directly or indirectly supplied, sold, or transferred to Somalia arms or related materiel or advice, training, or assistance, including financing and financial assistance, related to military activities in violation of the arms embargo. Atom has been identified as one of the principal suppliers of arms and ammunition for Al-Shabaab operations in the Puntland region. He is described as the leader of a militia that emerged in 2006 in the eastern Sanaag region of northern Somalia. ... Atom's forces were implicated in the kidnapping of a German aid worker, in the kidnapping of two Somalis near Bosaso, and in a bombing of Ethiopian migrants in Bosaso on 5 February 2008, which killed 20 people and wounded over 100 others. Atom's militia may also have played a secondary role in the kidnapping of a German couple captured by pirates in June 2008.[50]

As previously noted in Chapter 4, there is an amount of special pleading and disinformation connected with Atom. The Puntland administration is certainly very keen to remove him and his militia from eastern Sanaag, probably in order to control natural resources, including oil.

Of the other six people on the UN list, all were seen as threats to the TFG. Two are members of Al-Itihaad Al-Islamiya. Hassan Abdullah Hersi Al-Turki is believed to have terrorism connections, and is one of the leaders of Al-Itihaad Al-Islamiya, as is Hassan Dahir Aweys. Three on the UN list were leaders of Al-Shabaab. Sheikh Ahmed Abdi Aw Mohamed was the emir of Al-Shabaab, Fuad Mohamed Khalaf had raised money for and worked for Al-Shabaab, Bashir Mohamed Mahamoud was a military commander of Al-Shabaab and was a member of its leadership council. Finally, Yasin Ali Baynah was accused by the UN of attacking the TFG and rejecting the Djibouti Agreement.

UNCERTAINTIES

It is surprising that the United States does not coordinate its policy on sanctions against Somali interests with the European Union. The European Union has at least produced a well-drafted document, with reasonable safeguards, but the United States has produced a badly-drafted document, which appears to say that some organizations and individuals can be added to the prohibited list without anyone being told in advance. In addition, the United States has added three other individuals not included by the UN or the European Union. All is confusion and uncertainty. This does nothing for the cause of Somali peace and certainly nothing for the shipping and insurance industries, which are now worried that by paying ransoms they could unwittingly commit an offence under US law.

Because Garaad and Boyah, who are included in the US list, control so many pirates, shipowners and insurers will have to be particularly careful when paying ransoms for any ships held off Somalia in the future. The negotiation process with pirate gangs is complex and difficult, but insurers and shipowners now have almost as hard a time dealing with the legal problems at home, and ensuring that they have not broken any domestic legislation. These issues add yet another layer of complexity to negotiations and are a factor that can further delay securing the release of ships and their crews. In the worst case crews could be stuck off the coast of Somalia for many months at end, as has happened to Asian fishermen, without adequate food and water, slowly sickening in the heat and dying of neglect; all because the insurers and owners could be denied the opportunity to ransom them.

A FATAL CONFUSION

Aside from the failure of the United States to coordinate its Somali sanctions with the UN and the European Union, the basic problem with the original 2010 UN sanctions list is that it was an attempt to protect the Somali TFG.

US policy in Somalia, since 2001, appears to have been primarily focused on extending the 'War on Terror' into Somalia. And in a self-fulfilling prophecy, the pronouncements by Al-Shabaab of its links with Al-Qaeda and the 11 July 2010 bombing in Kampala have given all the justification that is needed for the continuation of a deeply flawed policy in Somalia. At the heart of US and UN policy is the idea that the TFG is actually a functioning government with the ability to make decisions that bind Somalia, and to use military force to remove its opponents. Phillip Carter of the Bureau of African Affairs of the United States State Department said on 22 July 2009: 'We work with Somalia's neighbours, particularly Uganda, to provide the TFG with the resources it needs to combat rebel and terrorist forces.' He added: 'Supporting AMISOM and the TFG should be central to the international community's strategy of stabilizing Mogadishu and supporting the Somali peace process.'[51]

This leads to the idea that those opposing the TFG are all 'Islamists' with potential, if not actual, links to 'terrorism', particularly Al-Qaeda. The TFG politicians were keen to promote this view of the world – a view that Ambassador Carter reflected, when he said:

> Foreign terrorists operating out of the country pose a danger to the region and beyond, jeopardizing peace and good relations between Somalia and its neighbours. On 29th February 2008, the US Secretary of State designated al-Shabaab as a Foreign Terrorist Organization (FTO). Al-Shabaab is a violent and brutal extremist group whose leadership maintains links with Al-Qaeda operatives. Al-Shabaab enjoys safe haven in Somalia. Some of its senior leaders are believed to have trained and fought with Al-Qaeda in Afghanistan, and foreign fighters are among the al-Shabaab rank-and-file currently fighting against the TFG and other moderates in Somalia.[52]

Al-Shabaab is an unpleasant organization, which undoubtedly has links with Al-Qaeda and has the ability to undertake acts of terrorism in Somalia and the region. It is clear that foreign extremists now control Al-Shabaab.[53] Terrorist attacks by Al-Shabaab accounted for the murder of 22 people, including graduating medical students at the Shamo Hotel in Mogadishu in December 2009 by a suicide bomber and the Kampala bombings of 11 July 2010. There does, however, appear to be mileage in attempting to separate the moderate Somali Islamists in Al-Shabaab and elsewhere from the foreign extremists. International opposition to Al-Shabaab expands its influence, increases the flow of funding from the Arabian Peninsula and encourages other foreign extremists to flock to its banner. In the end it will become gradually more difficult to remove the non-Somali elements. It needs to be remembered that US and Ethiopian pressure on the Islamic Courts Union destroyed the popular movement, and enabled Al-Shabaab to emerge from its ruins, a case of creating something far worse than the original problem.

Before August 2012 the US and UN were faced with the difficulty that the TFG was totally ineffective and, according to the UN Monitoring Group, it was corrupt, lacked competence, and suffered from having a weak and indecisive 'president', Sheikh Sharif. It was dependent for its survival on a small African Union force, AMISOM, which was originally too small to defeat Al-Shabaab, and had a habit of mortaring civilians in Mogadishu in response to attacks on it and the TFG. Time will tell whether the new regime in Mogadishu will fare better.

The UN sanctions list appeared to have no clear logic; in practice it was a collection of people or organization such as Al-Shabaab disliked by the United States and other UN members. It included a Yemeni arms dealer, an Eritrean politician and Yasin Ali Baynah, who seemed to be on the list simply because he was an Islamist opposing the TFG.

The impression is also given that international policy-makers are doomed to repeat their past failures, because, in the words of Sir Winston Churchill, 'Those who fail to learn from history are doomed to repeat it.' The failed policies of the past are being recycled. International policy in the Horn of Africa seems to be first and foremost about 'terrorism', and that there is no interest in any other agenda, including the stabilization and stability of Somalia. The UN's sanctions of 12 April 2010 therefore had little or nothing to do with the interests of mariners.

Writing shortly before the US presidential order was published, Stephen Askins of the London maritime law firm Ince and Co. said:

> Fundamentally it cannot be in anyone's interest to criminalise the victims of a hijacking. The effects of a US move to introduce these Regulations could have serious consequences for those that are affected by piracy, while doing little to address the issue of preventing piracy and dealing with those responsible.[54]

Askins also quoted Mr Justice Steele who in *Masefield* v. *Amlin Corporate Member Ltd*,[55] a case that involved the hijacking in 2008 of the *Bunga Melati Dua*, commented on the payment of ransom:

> So far as harm is concerned it is truth that payments of ransom encourage a repetition, the more so if there is insurance cover: the history of Somali piracy is an eloquent demonstration of that. But if the crews of the vessels are to be taken out of harms way, the only option is to pay the ransom. Diplomatic or military intervention cannot usually be relied upon and failure to pay may put in jeopardy other crews.[56]

In these few words lies the pith and essence of the argument.

Given the increasing importance of Al-Shabaab, it is likely that more individuals and organizations will be added to the UN prohibited list and the EU and US lists, and difficulties for insurers and shipowners will be on the increase.

PIRATES AND JUSTICE

Escaping justice

International naval fleets sail the waters of the Indian Ocean and press releases describe their successes, while remaining quiet about the huge costs of keeping such a large fleet at sea off Somalia. Having captured some pirates they are frequently unable to prosecute them, because the warship's state is often reluctant to imprison Somalis who may claim asylum on their release. A case in point was the capture on 3 August 2010 of seven Somalis by the Spanish warship *SPS Victoria*, after her helicopter had stopped an attack on the Norwegian product tanker MV *Bow Saga* in the Gulf of Aden. After the intervention by the *Victoria*'s helicopter on 3 August the pirates stopped their attack and tried to flee. They stopped after warning shots were fired, first from the helicopter, and then from the warship *Victoria*. A boarding team from the *Victoria* found weapons in the skiff.[57] All seven individuals were returned to Somalia. The statement issued by EU NAVFOR explained that 'Due to the legal framework and timelines encompassing piracy and criminal activity at sea, the prosecution of the seven individuals in this specific case could not be initiated with confidence.'[58]

Policy by different nations towards captured pirates has varied tremendously, but having been caught there is a good chance that most pirates will be disarmed and sent on their way after a medical check-up and regular meals. After French special forces in April 2008 captured six of the pirates involved in the hijacking of the luxury yacht *Le Ponant*, and apprehended six more pirates in September 2008 who had hijacked the yacht *Carré d'As IV*, the French authorities were not clear how to treat them. Although the European Union and 160 nations have ratified the UN Convention on the Law of the Sea (UNCLOS) 1982, articles 100–107 of which deal with piracy, many countries have not enacted the necessary domestic legislation to enforce these provisions. It has also become clear that the recent upsurge in piracy requires even greater cooperation than that envisaged by UNCLOS. On 28 April 2010 Recommendation 1913 (2010) was adopted by the Parliamentary Assembly of the Council of Europe.[59] The Assembly also recommended to the Council of Ministers the preparation of 'a code of conduct on how to deal with suspected pirates in full compliance with international human rights standards'.[60] The Assembly also recommended that the Council of Europe States

'seek appropriate ways in which the existing international legal framework can be adapted to face current needs of policing at sea and consider creating, provided all existing disadvantages in this field are removed, a special mechanism (either international, or with international participation) for the prosecution of persons suspected of piracy.'[61]

There has been a reluctance to transfer large numbers of Somalis to the jurisdictional systems of the navies participating in the international fleet, particularly as the attacks are often on the vessels of third-party states and there are fears that the Somalis would never leave their new homes, claiming asylum if acquitted, or that their human rights would be in danger if they were forced to return to Somalia after serving prison terms.

Because of the lack of a clear legal process and concerns about importing asylum seekers, most pirates and suspected pirates, including many who have been caught red-handed, have been freed to return to Somalia. In March and April 2010, EU naval forces captured 275 suspected pirates but released 235 of them (more than 85 per cent) after taking their weapons. Of the 40 who were detained, 11 were sent to the Seychelles for prosecution, ten who attacked a German container ship *Taipan* went to Hamburg after being transferred by the Dutch, and 19 were handed over to Puntland; it likely that they were then freed. During the same period, out of 39 suspects captured by US naval vessels, 18 (more than 46 per cent) were released. The US government has decided only to prosecute pirates who attack US vessels.[62] From August 2008 until early July 2010 the international naval forces encountered 1,129 pirates. Of these, 638 (56.5 per cent) were arrested, but later released; 478 were detained; and 13 were killed. During the same period, 78 pirate vessels were destroyed and 20 were confiscated, and a large number of weapons were destroyed, or thrown overboard before the craft could be searched.[63]

Addressing the UN sixty-fourth General Assembly, Informal Meeting of the Plenary on Piracy, Antonio Maria Costa, executive director at the UNODC said:

There were some 500 pirates under detention, about half outside Somalia, but there was a limit to the number of pirates who could be imprisoned outside of the country. Court proceedings in the countries of seized vessels was impractical, given the distance and jurisdictional arguments. The cost of patrolling the seas of Somalia was enormous. The annual budget of all 44 vessels operating in the Indian Ocean stood at $1.5 billion, while the Anti-piracy Trust Fund had a budget of $3 to $5 million.[64]

Apart from his comments on trying pirates, Mr Costa's point on the relative costs of anti-piracy measures was instructive. If the cost of additional insurance premiums is now around $400 million, add the $1.5 billion and the additional costs incurred by the international community in dealing with piracy – probably at least $100 million – that gives an annual cost of $2 billion, against a probable cost of ransoms of $75 million, less than 5 per cent of the anti-piracy costs currently borne by the international community. It would be cheaper to pay the Somali pirates $100 million a year and not ask any questions about how they spend it. In this age of political correctness, this may not be widely accepted and, of course, having been offered $100 million the recipients could become greedier and ask for more; that is always the potential problem when you deal with criminals. However, this was the time-honoured method of dealing with the Barbary pirates.

Trials in third countries

One solution, which has been reasonably successful, is to hand pirates over to the courts of third countries in the area in which the pirates are caught and to compensate the authorities in those countries for the costs associated with trying and imprisoning them. Kenya has been a popular destination. On 11 December 2008 the United Kingdom reached agreement with Kenya that the Kenyan authorities would accept and prosecute suspected pirates who were detained by UK forces. This formalized early *ad hoc* arrangements by which Kenya had tried eight alleged pirates captured in November 2008 by *HMS Cumberland*.[65] The United States transferred ten suspected pirates to Kenya in January 2006 as a result of a similar arrangement, which was made permanent on 16 January 2009.[66] Agreements were also signed between Kenya and China, Denmark and Canada and with the European Union, the latter agreement being signed on 6 March 2009.

Early in 2010 Kenya refused to accept more suspects. But following a meeting with an EU delegation led by Baroness Catherine Ashton, vice president of the European Union, Kenya's foreign affairs minister, Moses Wetang'ula, announced that Kenya would resume accepting suspected pirates.[67] Increased funding and security guarantees were a critical driver in Kenya's change of heart. Alan Cole, the UNODC Counter-Piracy Programme Co-ordinator, based in Nairobi, reported on 15 June 2010 that Kenya and the Seychelles would receive $9.3 million over the next 18 months, which would cover the cost of securing the attendance of witnesses at trials, and would also be available for equipment and other improvements to the countries' criminal justice systems. In June 2010 a new high security court room opened in Shimo la Tewa in Mombasa, built by the UNODC Counter-Piracy Programme with international funding.[68] This facility opened on 24 June 2010 and was built by the UNODC Counter-Piracy Programme with contributions of its donor states: Australia, Canada, the European Union, France, Germany and the United States.[69]

In addition, the Seychelles Coastguard is receiving assistance from the European Union, India, the United Arab Emirates, the United Kingdom, the United States and China in its fight against maritime piracy. The president of the Seychelles announced the signing of a $15 million agreement with the United Arab Emirates to improve the local coastguard service by the construction of a new base and the provision of five more patrol boats.[70]

On 30 October 2009 the European Union agreed with the Seychelles that the Seychelles authorities would try suspected pirates, and agreement in principle was also reached with Tanzania in May 2010; on 12 June 2010 Mauritius announced that it too would prosecute suspected pirates.

But Kenya remains the main centre for dealing with Somali pirates. In July 2010 it was holding the highest number of piracy suspects in the region, 105 on trial and 18 already convicted, with sentences ranging from seven to 20 years. At the beginning of July 2010 the first cases where heard at the new Shimo la Tewa high security court room, ten miles north of Mombasa.[71]

Trials in home countries

Abduwali Abdukhadir Muse, the one pirate who survived from the attack on the *Maersk Alabama* on 8 April 2009, was prosecuted in the United States and, having pleaded guilty on 16 February 2011, he was sentenced to over 33 years in federal prison.[72] He has promised not to fight his deportation back to Somalia when his term ends.[73] The United States also planned to try 11 other suspected pirates in Norfolk, Virginia.

On 17 June 2010, the Rotterdam District Court sentenced five Somalis, each to five years' imprisonment for attacking the Dutch Antilles general cargo ship *Samanyolu* in the Gulf of Aden on 2 January 2009. However, the Somalis being prosecuted in the Netherlands are quite content. Willem-Jan Ausma, the lawyer who represents Farah Ahmed Yusuf declared:

> When I first spoke to my client, he said being here was like heaven. For the first time in his life he didn't feel he was in danger, and he was in a modern prison with the first modern toilet and shower that he'd ever had.[74]

Further trials are taking place in France and Spain. Yemen also tries pirates captured by its own forces and those handed over by other navies. On May 2010 a court in Yemen sentenced six Somali pirates to death for hijacking the *Qana*, a Yemeni oil tanker in April 2009, killing one Yemeni crew member, with another missing. In addition six other pirates were sentenced to ten years in prison for the hijacking, which also wounded four crew members.[75] Yemen has received a number of suspected pirates from other countries, including seven suspects who had been located in December 2008 by the Danish warship *HDMS Absalon* drifting in a boat with a failed engine. On 12 February 2009 the Russian cruiser *Peter the Great* captured ten suspected pirates who had been in speedboats approaching an Iranian fishing trawler; these were also handed over to Yemen.

But a few countries choose to try pirates in their own jurisdiction, if they cannot be transferred to Kenya. Somalia or the Seychelles, as Nick Hopkins reported, more and more of the suspected pirates are being freed. The Somalis can hardly believe their luck. 'When I have told them [the pirates] that we are putting them back to shore they are more or less celebrating', said Commander Anders Friis, captain of the Danish warship Absalon. 'They are very, very happy.' Of the 58 suspected pirates captured during a six-month patrol, only eight were tried.[76]

Human rights issues

There have been genuine concerns about the human rights of pirate suspects tried in the Indian Ocean region after being captured by international forces. The same problem also occurs when terrorist suspects are deported from European states to Asia, Africa and even the United States.

In January 2009 the then UK secretary of state for defence gave an assurance in the House of Commons that where the United Kingdom transfers prisoners to third-party states it will do so 'in accordance with its international law obligations and will always seek assurances of fair treatment and international standards of human rights'.[77] The 6 March 2009 Agreement between the European Union and Kenya provides that no pirates who are transferred there will suffer a death sentence, that they will have a fair trial and will not suffer torture and cruel, inhumane and degrading treatment or punishment.

There are also international agreements that limit the ability of states to hand pirates over to other states for trial and punishment, including the UN Convention Against Torture and other Cruel, Inhuman or Degrading

Treatment or Punishment (UNCAT 1984), and the European Convention on Human Rights (ECHR 1950). However, it is possible to go too far with concerns for the pirates' human rights. In 2008 the British Foreign Office issued a directive to the Royal Navy not to detain any pirates, because doing so could violate their human rights. The Royal Navy was advised that captured pirates could claim asylum in Britain and that those who were returned to Somalia faced beheading for murder or having a hand chopped off for theft under Islamic law.[78] A balance needs to be set between fair treatment and the prevention of piracy, or there will be strong pressures to discard the international conventions on human rights.

THE USE OF ARMED GUARDS, LEGAL AND PRACTICAL ISSUES

Background
Many shipping companies and security advisors have recently seen the deployment of armed guards, contracted from private maritime security companies (PMSCs), as the best solution to the problem of piracy. While it is the case at the time of writing that no ship carrying armed guards has been captured off Somalia, a number of serious issues relating to the use of armed guards on civilian vessels remain to be considered. The role of PMSCs also needs to be examined here, as the use of armed force by private companies raises real concerns since there have been a few close calls, where armed guards have run out of ammunition or nearly been overwhelmed by attacks. These incidents are not publicized for obvious reasons.

The issues relate to the legality of the carriage of weapons onboard ships; the potential legal liability of the shipmaster and the owners where armed guards kill or injure third parties, or cause damage to the ship and its cargo; the cost of deploying armed guards; and the consequences of over-reliance on armed guards at the expense of other protective measures. I will also look at the emerging international guidelines and the need to establish effective rules of engagement for the use of armed guards.

Legality of carrying firearms under international law
UNCLOS 1982 regulates activity on the high seas generally, rather than the carriage of weapons in particular. Instead, article 94(1) of UNCLOS stipulates that each state must exercise jurisdiction and control over vessels flying its flag. Accordingly, it is up to each individual state to legislate on this matter. So the regulations governing the carriage of weapons are those laid down by the flag state, but a vessel must also comply with the law within the

waters of each coastal state it enters. A state may prohibit the carriage of any weapons into its territory, even though there is no contravention of the law of the ship's flag state. In February 2012 states such as France, Spain (which also asked for a licence to be provided), Saudi Arabia, Kenya and Brazil demanded that prior notice be made when a ship was carrying weapons. Australia required registration with a number of government agencies. In South Africa all firearms must be registered, which in practice means that foreign vessels cannot bring guns into the country; within the same week in 2011 two masters were arrested and charged under the South African Firearm Control Act.[79] Although national requirements change, and this is far from being a comprehensive list, it does highlight the fact that the carriage of weapons on board merchant ships is not straightforward. Indeed, some armed response teams have illegally hidden weapons on board a ship, creating a potential legal problem for the master and the ship's owners; while some others have been forced to ditch their weapons overboard before entering national waters, in order to avoid problems.

A recent development, by which PMSCs seek to avoid the problems of landing weapons, is the deployment of floating armoury ships, which are stationed in international waters. According to *The National* (Abu Dhabi) about 12 armoury ships operate globally, at least four of which are located off the coast of Fujairah, one off the United Arab Emirates. On 1 October 2012 the Sri Lankan-flagged vessel *Sinbad*, operated by Avant Garde Maritime Services, was boarded by the UAE coastguard after it strayed into national waters.[80] Some PMSCs have also sought to overcome the restrictions placed by many countries on landing weapons by leaving weapons caches in remote spots. In 2011 'An Eritrean Foreign Ministry report said that former British Marines employed by a British company, Protection Vessels International Ltd., had 'offloaded "countless amounts" of arms including 18 different types of snipers, ammunition and night vision equipment on an island 30 nautical miles off the mainland' of Eritrea.[81] The men were held in an Eritrean prison for six months before they were released.[82]

PMSCs too often appear to operate like freebooters, despite attempts by many in the industry to present a responsible image. The UN Monitoring Group on Somalia and Eritrea reported that 'In mid-2011 ... a PMSC offered a shipping company, in return for hard cash, to rescue a hijacked crew and vessel by use of force, engaging in a firefight with pirates if needed.'[83]

Some countries, like the United States, have actively encouraged the use of armed guards. US Coast Guard Maritime Security Directive 104-6 (series) requires US-flagged vessels operating in the Horn of Africa and Gulf of Aden regions to provide additional armed or unarmed security as needed. However, other countries were, at least initially, reluctant to endorse such measures.

The International Ship and Port Facility Security (ISPS) Code requires all vessels flagged in a signatory state of SOLAS 1974 to put in place a safety plan specific to each vessel. These measures are not prescriptive, and so the carriage or use of firearms for self-defence is not prohibited. The IMO initially strongly discouraged but did not prohibit the carriage and use of firearms by seafarers for the purpose of defence from piracy. According to its secretary-general, Koji Sekimizu, the IMO is increasingly moving towards the adoption of an international regime to be established that will provide a framework for flag states that decide to allow vessels to deploy arms on board. Mr Sekimizu dismissed the current industry schemes, and said: 'What is clear now is that the way forward is not industry self-regulation on a voluntary basis.'[84] The IMO has issued guidelines to security companies and shipowners.

There are serious concerns about the dangers of carrying weapons. In particular, there is concern as to whether some of the armed guards deployed have sufficient competency and skill to use weapons, and apprehension that the use of weapons may escalate an already dangerous situation. It is also the case that some PMSCs do not operate according to any reasonable guidelines and are merely hired guns. Rumours abound of guards just killing men in small boats, pirates or not; the few cases that have surfaced are all most certainly the tip of the iceberg. It is not only the Somalis who operate outside the law.

Criminal sanctions

If someone is killed or injured in the territorial waters of a country or in a port, the perpetrator of the killing may be subject to the criminal laws of that country. States are also likely to claim jurisdiction where their citizens are killed in unlawful circumstances in international waters. India did so in the case of the killing of two Indian fishermen by Italian naval guards Latore Massimiliano and Salvatore Girone, who were onboard the MV *Enrica Lexie* in February 2012. Italy claimed that the vessel was in international waters when the incident took place, outside the jurisdiction of Indian courts. India disputed this, arguing the incident occurred in a 'contiguous zone' where Indian law applies.[85]

In a previous incident off Oman in April 2010 shots were fired, without any warning or provocation, from a cargo ship at a group of nearly 75 fishermen, mistaken as pirates, who had set off in 25 boats from Salalah.[86] One fisherman, Raju Ambrose, 34, was declared 'dead on arrival' by doctors at the Sultan Qaboos Hospital in Salalah on the south-western coast of Oman, and another was injured. I believe, from conversations with maritime officers, that there have been many similar incidents, and most have gone unreported because the victims were killed far out at sea. It does appear that many security guards are virtually untrained and are not operating with any rules of engagement, and that seeing a man in a small boat they will shoot him without asking questions. What is surprising about the incident off Kerala is that the Italians were trained military personnel, who would have been expected to fire warning shots, not fatal rounds.

There are likely to be criminal and civil law implications for the guards, the master and the shipowner under most flag state national laws if death or personal injury is caused by the use of a firearm. Not all states exonerate the user of the firearm on the basis that he has acted in self-defence. Seafarers may therefore find themselves facing unforeseen penal consequences under foreign laws. The International Tribunal for the Law of the Sea, in its *M/V Saiga No 2* judgment, which related to naval personnel, said that:

> international law ... requires that the use of force must be avoided as far as possible and, where force is inevitable, it must not go beyond what is reasonable and necessary in the circumstances. Considerations of humanity must apply in the law of the sea, as they do in other areas of international law.[87]

The judgment further suggested that practices that were normally followed before resorting to force must be used. These included both visual and auditory signals, such as firing shots across the bows and a variety of other measures.

Insurance issues

Shipowners must concern themselves with a number of insurance issues: the first set of issues relates to insurance against damage, death or injury, caused by the armed guards; the second relates to compliance with the provisions of the insurance contracts that cover the vessel and its cargo.

Section 41 of the UK Marine Insurance Act 1906 implies a warranty into every contract of insurance that the voyage is lawful and that, so far as the assured can control the matter, the voyage will be carried out in a lawful manner. If the assured decides to undertake self-defence by involving lethal weapons, this can amount to carrying out the voyage in an unlawful manner. For public policy reasons, a breach of the implied warranty of legality cannot be waived by underwriters. If the shipowner's self-defence measures are not lawful, then underwriters will be automatically discharged from liability under the policy from the breach onwards. As a further point, many contracts contain provisions that oblige owners to waive their right of recourse against the security company, should they have caused damage or loss to the vessel. In view of this, hull and war risks underwriters need to review and approve the ship's insurance contract when armed guards are carried.

The cost of using armed guards

It is normally estimated that a shipowner will pay around US$5,000 or more per day for a team of three to four armed guards. For a ship that regularly transits the Gulf of Aden and/or the Indian Ocean they may carry armed teams for around 100 days a year, at a cost of US$500,000 a year. For an industry that is suffering from depressed freight rates, particularly for bulk carriers which were badly affected by the collapse in the BDI in 2008, this represents a severe financial burden. Other measures, including hardening the ship and the use of water cannon, can normally be undertaken at a reasonable fixed cost, and represent a real alternative to the use of armed guards. It is also the case, that just because armed guards are used, this does not mean that other protective measures are not also required. I have read at least one confidential report from a ship's officer in which he said that the pirates nearly overwhelmed the guards, and the ship had no other defensive measures in place to fall back on; the defence against the attack had been a very close run thing.

At the minimum a ship transiting the Indian Ocean, the Gulf of Oman and the Gulf of Aden, with or without guards, armed or not, needs to have effective razor wire in place, a citadel and armouring for the bridge and preferably the accommodation decks. Best Management Practices Version 4 (BMP4) says that 'If pirates are unable to board a ship they cannot hijack it.'[88] BMP4 adds that 'if armed Private Maritime Security Contractors are to be used they must be as an additional layer of protection and not as an alternative to BMP.'[89]

The management of armed guards

The management of armed guards on ships raises a number of problems. Article 34-1 of SOLAS Regulations provides that:

> The Owner, Charterer, the Company operating the ship as defined in Regulation 1X/1 or any other person shall not prevent or restrict the Master of the ship from taking or executing any decision which, in the

Master's professional judgment, is necessary for the safety of life at sea and protection of the marine environment.[90]

This is reiterated in the ISPS Code, which requires that the master of the ship must have the ultimate responsibility for the safety and security of the ship. So legally the master of the ship must be in charge. However, security companies often demand that the master does not have full control over their operations, nor take the final decision as to whether or not weapons are deployed and used. That decision may rest with the security team, on terms that the master only need be consulted 'if there is time'. The justification is that, if faced with a lethal threat, the right to self-defence outweighs the master's overall responsibility to his crew and the environment. This means the master may not have full control of a key area of the vessel's security, which in turn may affect the safety of the crew and vessel. Further, there may be a contractual obligation with the security company to follow 'security' instructions from the guards, which may even extend to the rerouting of the vessel, which in turn may result in a breach of contractual obligations to charterers and/or cargo interests.

In all circumstances the use of weapons on any ship must be governed by clear rules for the use of force (RUF) agreed by the owner and the security company. At present there are no generally accepted standards for RUF. The RUF should reflect the laws of the flag state. They should also make clear that lethal force is only used when there is serious and imminent threat to life, and only where use is proportionate. The use of armed guards places a serious responsibility on the shoulders of the master and the shipowner and, in particular, on the company's directors, who may be held to be personally liable where death or serious injury results. The shipowner should also have a process in place to review the proposals for the provisions of armed guards, to have knowledge of the personnel used, of the weapons deployed and their licensing and for training the ship's crew how to react in case of an engagement. A failure to put such processes in place creates major risks for the shipping operator.

Some relevant factors for consideration when hiring a security company include:

- references;
- the place of registration and business, how long they have conducted business and the size of the organization;
- the background, experience and qualifications of the management and personnel;

- whether the company has specific marine experience;
- whether sub-contractors are permitted;
- whether the company is a member of any industry organizations such as the BAPSC (British Association of Private Security Companies) or SAMI (Security Association for the Maritime Industry);
- whether the company has signed or is willing to follow the IOCC (International Code of Conduct for Private Security Companies);
- whether the law and jurisdiction provided for in the contract are acceptable to the shipowners and their underwriters;
- whether the company offers additional services beyond that of security;
- whether they are independently audited; and
- whether they have implemented a 'no drug, smoking and alcohol' policy.

International guidelines

In May 2011 the IMO approved interim guidance to shipowners, ship operators and shipmasters to use private armed security personnel on ships. This guidance was revised and issued by the IMO as MS.1/Circ. 1405 on 25 May 2012. Other guidance documents were also issued to flag states. The IMO did not endorse the use of armed guards but said that,

> The absence of applicable regulation and industry self-regulation coupled with complex legal requirements governing the legitimate transport, carriage and use of firearms gives cause for concern. This situation is further complicated by the rapid growth in the number of private maritime security companies (PMSC) and doubts about the capabilities and maturity of some of these companies.[91]

The IMO added:

> The use of PCASP [privately contracted armed security personnel] should not be considered as an alternative to Best Management Practices (BMP) and other protective measures. Placing armed guards on board as a means to secure and protect the ship and its crew should only be considered after a risk assessment has been carried out. It is also important to involve the Master in the decision making process.[92]

The IMO's guidelines stress the importance of undertaking a risk assessment and, if it is decided to use armed guards, of undertaking a full evaluation before selecting a supplier. It also declared that,

As the quality of the service delivery depends to a very great extent on the quality and experience of the individuals that make up the onboard PCASP team, the quality of the selection and vetting of that team is essential. PMSC should demonstrate that they have verifiable, written internal policies and procedures for determining suitability of their employees.[93]

The guidelines also deal with insurance issues, the licensing and control of firearms, the composition of the armed team, command and control issues, training, record-keeping and RUF. These guidelines represent a logical and sensible approach to the deployment of armed guards, although it will be a long time before all shipowners follow them.

At present large numbers of untrained and unsuitable men act as armed guards – the bad, the worse and the downright awful. I have heard stories of bus drivers, middle-aged prison officers and other similar 'adventurers' going to sea with guns, of ex-soldiers spending weeks being sea-sick, of men from the Far East being paid less that $100 a day and having no weapons training, and of teams of three (four should always be the minimum, two on watch at any time) who would stand little chance if a surprise attack caught them unaware. Unfortunately it is only a matter of time before an armed team is overwhelmed; the aftermath can be bloody as revenge is taken, and the consequences do not bear thinking about. To repeat BMP4: '[I]f armed Private Maritime Security Contractors are to be used they must be as an additional layer of protection and not as an alternative to BMP.'[94]

I do not argue that armed guards should never be used. For slow and vulnerable vessels like cable layers, tugs, oil rigs and the like, there is no alternative, but for modern fast vessels in full compliance with BMP4, and possibly with additional protection from effective water cannon, guards are an option, not a necessity. It all depends on the vessel and the security assessment undertaken by the shipowner. Local regulations can also limit the use of armed personnel, for example off West Africa, so armed guards can never be a universal answer to ship security. India's attempts in 2012 to try two Italian marines for murder also highlight the risks that armed guards and their employers run; there are no easy solutions.

CHAPTER 9

VESSEL DEFENCE

MERCHANT VESSELS: THEIR ADAPTIVE CAPACITY

Merchant vessels have been attacked by pirates for thousands of years and, as a result, they have reacted to the threat by developing defensive measures; in other words, merchant vessels have an adaptive capacity. East Indiamen often carried heavy cannon and could cope with attacks from warships; in 1804, a fleet of East Indiamen and other merchant vessels, under Commodore Nathaniel Dance, fought off a French squadron at the Battle of Pulo Aura.

Over the last 150 years piracy has not been a major threat, except in parts of the South China Sea, but the rapid growth of Somali piracy has changed this picture, and vessels now need to develop systemic resilience, that is the capacity to survive attacks by adopting a systemic approach to a range of interrelated tactical problems. There was a natural unwillingness by most shipowners to react quickly to the Somali threat, and many were encouraged to believe that international naval forces would deal with the problem. However, pirates have traditionally proved very difficult to deal with, notably the Barbary pirates to whom Great Britain, and the other European powers, were long forced to pay a large annual tribunes in order to avoid their merchant ships being captured. In 1784 the US Congress agreed to pay the Barbary states a tribune, and did so for the next 15 years, at a rate of up to $1 million per annum, an enormous sum for the period.[1]

Increasingly the resilience of a ship requires that five separate areas are dealt with:

- training and procedures;
- intelligence (situational knowledge) and communication;
- watchfulness;
- protection of the crew;
- active defensive measures.

The shipowner has a duty to protect his crew at all times; a duty referred to as SOLAS.

NATURE OF THE THREAT TO SHIPS: LESSONS AND BEST PRACTICES

The nature of the threat to merchant vessels is simple: that, despite the best efforts of the master and his crew, well-armed pirates will board the vessel or force the master to heave to under the threat of armed force, and allow the pirates on board. Good intelligence will, of course, help the master to plot a route away from known pirate groups, from the scenes of recent attacks, and reported PAGs.

As with any attack the best ally of the attacker at sea is surprise – if the attackers can approach the vessel without being detected by radar, or being seen by the watchkeepers, the master will have no time to prepare his defensive measures and to send the crew to a safe area (a 'citadel'). It has been noted elsewhere that many merchant vessels, particularly bulk carriers, are totally blind aft from the bridge – their radar is too often masked by a large funnel, and their watchkeepers must be stationed on the bridge wings in order to be effective. In most cases there is no attempt to remedy the situation by the use of CCTV, or thermal imaging cameras, covering the stern. Some masters have undoubtedly had a rude awaking on finding that the first pirate already puts his unshod feet on the deck, and his comrades are ready to open fire on the wheelhouse from a few metres away. At this point rapid surrender is the only option, and the owner will wake up the next day to receive a telephone call from EU NAVFOR asking why his ship is heading for Somalia.

An alert ship can prepare and change course to double-check that they are under attack – and not just crossing the path of local fishing skiffs, as Captain Mattijssen of the MV *Album* did. With non-essential personnel out of the way and all crew off the deck the master at least has a chance. Exposing crew to incoming fire by operating fire-hoses, LRADs and throwing things at the pirates greatly increases the risk that someone will be killed or injured. But the worse thing is waving replica guns at the pirates; the crews may be happy that they have spent many hours making realistic wooden copies of AK-47s, but once they show such toys the crew members holding them will immediately be seen as a lethal threat and the pirates will respond by shooting at the holders of these imitation firearms in an attempt to kill them. Fake guns are a suicide device, and increase the likelihood that the pirates will aim to kill, even those not holding them. Using shotguns is also to be avoided for the same reasons, while a shotgun loaded with very heavy gauge shot can be a man-killer at close-range, it is not the weapon to use against human targets some distance away; the rifle will win this uneven contest every time. Seamen are also rarely combat-trained, whereas the Somalis have been using AK-47s from a very young age, and live in an environment where few have ever known peace.

HOW VESSELS DEALT WITH ATTACKS

The importance of learning from experience

While it is possible to train and plan, to equip a ship with protective devices, to surround it with razor wire and electric fences, only the actual experience of being attacked can show who will escape and who will be taken. In practice many masters will surrender their ship if the pirates succeed in boarding and can bring their guns to bear effectively on the bridge from the deck or walkways, or if the show of fire-power is so great that the master and his crew have a reasonable belief that their lives are under threat.

Vulnerable vessels, that is those that are slow, and/or have a low freeboard, are unlikely to be able to put up much of a fight, unless they are well-equipped, or have an effective armed response team. Vessels with small crews, or that have been surprised and unable to prepare to defend themselves, are also likely to surrender quickly. However, in the accounts that we have seen it seems that the character of the master is the single most important factor in avoiding capture; the other key factors are the level of anti-piracy training, ship hardening and the crew's confidence in the master. If the master can avoid the pirates actually boarding the ship, by manoeuvring it as Captain Mattijssen of the MV *Album* did so successfully, or by throwing obstacles in their path as Captain Stapleton of the *Boularibank* did, and he is prepared to take the risk that his crew may be injured by bullets or grenades, then the ship will probably escape. The fight may be long, lasting several hours, but eventually the pirates will acknowledge their defeat and break off the engagement. Some masters, like the captain of the *Maharaja Agrasen*, actually took the fight to the pirates by trying to ram their craft, a difficult manoeuvre with an oil tanker, but one calculated to intimidate the attackers.

In dealing with the threat from pirate gunfire and grenades the master has to balance the undoubted dangers that await hijacked ships off Somalia: crew members have been killed or died of neglect; the experience is deeply unpleasant and can cause long-term physiological damage to some individuals, similar to the impact of war on soldiers. People have also been shot dead by pirates, high on *khat* and exhausted after a long period at sea. A master's primary duty is the safety of the lives of his crew, but in the scheme of things no course of action can be risk-free. If the owner of the vessel has a poor reputation for looking after his ships, and has not taken out K&R insurance, the master will be justified in taking greater risks to avoid capture. Captain Mattijssen's actions were textbook; he cleared all non-essential personnel into a safe area, radioed a distress call and notified the owner and then turned to the problem in hand. Captain Stapleton's decision to allow his passengers and non-essential crew members to remain on the bridge in harm's way was, in my opinion, questionable, to say the least. There have been hundreds of attacks and each master has dealt with them differently, but it is important to learn from these invaluable experiences, and to be honest about decisions, made on the spur of the moment, that should not be copied.

The attack on the BW *Lion*

In the autumn of 2009 there was a spate of pirate attacks in the Indian Ocean and the Gulf of Aden. Between 15 October and 16 November six large merchant ships were hijacked, together with other smaller craft, including two trawlers, a yacht and a small merchant ship trading with Somalia. For every successful hijacking in this period, at least two vessels are reported to have escaped a pirate attack, and none fought a longer and harder battle than the crew of the tanker *BW Lion* on 9 November 2009.

As the EU NAVFOR website reported, around noon local time, the *BW Lion*, a Hong Kong-flagged VLCC of 298,567 dwt, IMO No. 92,58519, carrying 281,390 metric tons of crude oil from West Africa to India,

> was attacked by pirates in two fast attack skiffs in the Indian Ocean, 400 nautical miles North East of the Seychelles and 1,000 nautical miles East of Mogadishu, the capital of Somalia. Automatic weapons and Rocket

Propelled Grenades were fired at the bridge during the attack. There were no casualties.[2]

EU NAVFOR reported that the master, Captain Sunil Fredrick Mani, was in contact with UKMTO (Dubai) throughout the attack, 'which lasted nearly two hours'. The master and his crew were able to prevent the pirates boarding,

Through a combination of evasive manoeuvring, vessel maintaining full sea speed, the effective use of water hoses and anti-boarding measures against the pirates attempting to board the vessel, the master and crew were able to prevent the pirates getting a foothold onto the ship and taking control.[3]

This attack took place at 1°10S 61°32E, further from Somalia than any previous attack, in an area regarded by many as being outside the danger zone. It is obvious that the officers and crew of the *BW Lion* showed enormous courage and professionalism. The fact that Captain Mani had over 24 years' experience at sea, including 12 years with VLCCs, and enjoyed the full confidence of his crew were undoubtedly important factors in the successful defence of the vessel.

At the November 2009 price of around $145 a barrel, the *BW Lion*'s cargo was worth over $290 million; in comparison the four-year-old *BW Lion* was probably worth about $60–80 million, and the total assets at risk, over and above the lives of the crew, were therefore around $350 million. For such ships the ransoms paid to date therefore do not represent a high percentage of their actual value. This would not be the case for a small cargo vessel loaded with sand, or scrap, which was at the end of its useful life, where the ransom demanded could exceed the value of the assets. Given the fact that the owner of such vessels had avoided the additional costs of K&R insurance and might be unable, or unwilling, to pay the Somalis, it is possible to see why VLCCs are normally ransomed within weeks and the crews of rust buckets may spend many months, or even years, enjoying the uncertain delights of the Somali coast – dirty rice and rusty water.

In the same way, the crew of the MV *Sikinos*, a 150,709 dwt oil tanker, took determined action when their vessel came under automatic gunfire from pirates; they fired flares and also used high-pressure hoses to repel the attack.

In contrast, at 1213 GMT on 29 November 2009, the 14-year-old VLCC *Maran Centaurus* was boarded 570 nautical miles north-east of the

Seychelles. This 1,090 foot (330 metres), 299,900 dwt vessel left Mina Al Ahmadi in Kuwait en route for the Louisiana Offshore Oil Port in the Gulf of Mexico on the evening of 24 November. It then headed down the Persian Gulf and into the Straits of Homuz, passing the United Arab Emirates on its starboard, and within less than five days it was hijacked. From the reports available it appears that the ship was quickly overwhelmed and its 28-man crew of Filipinos, Greeks, Ukrainians and a Romanian were unharmed. It was soon en route to Somalia, shadowed by the Greek frigate *Adrias*. On board the *Maran Centaurus* carried 275,000 metric tons or nearly 2 million barrels of Kuwaiti crude oil: at the then-current market price of about $75 a barrel, the cargo was worth over $150 million. By 2 December the tanker had anchored 30 nautical miles south of Hobyo, Somalia.

Outwardly this incident appears to be similar to the hijacking of the Saudi Aramco (Vela) tanker the *Sirius Star* on 15 November 2008. The hijacking took place about 450 nautical miles south-east of the coast of Kenya at 04°41S 48°43E. The ship was released on 9 January 2009, after a reported ransom of $3 million had been paid. There is, however, no comparison between the circumstances of the two cases. When the *Sirius Star* was hijacked no vessel of its size had ever been taken and the ship was well outside the 'normal' risk areas. This was not the case with the *Maran Centaurus*, because ever since the hijacking of the *Sirius Star* it had been obvious that Somali pirates were keen to take another similar prize. The *Maran Centaurus* was transiting an area that had seen a number of recent attacks and successful hijackings in the previous six weeks. The attack on the *BW Lion* occurred about 125 nautical miles south of the position where *Maran Centaurus* was hijacked and the MV *Filitsa* had also been hijacked on 11 November, about 190 nautical miles south-east of the position where the *Maran Centaurus* was seized.

It appears that the *Maran Centaurus* was unprepared for this attack and there is no sign that it was equipped with any defensive measures. Outwardly she was very similar to the *MW Lion*, which successfully resisted an attack for two hours. In other words, a well-run ship can resist attacks and it seems obvious that the better trained, equipped and prepared the crew are, the lower the likelihood that their ship will be successfully hijacked. Another tanker that successfully resisted a prolonged attack, which lasted four hours, was the Indian-flagged oil tanker, *MT Maharaja Agrasen*, en route from Mina Al Ahmadi in Kuwait to Visakhapatnam in India, laden with over 950,000 barrels of oil worth about $75 million. She was attacked in the Arabian Sea, by three unlit pirate boats about 366 nautical miles west of

Ratnagiri on the west coast of India, at 17°11N 66°05E. The pirate boats attacked the *Maharaja Agrasen* with machine guns and RPGs. The general secretary of the National Union of Seafarers of India, Abdulgani Y Serang, told the Press Trust of India that the master tried to ram one of the pirate boats.

The Indian Directorate General of Shipping was contacted by the vessel's owners and alerted the Indian coastguard and Indian navy. The Indian authorities remained in contact with the master and the owners, and were informed that the pirates had not been able to board the vessel because of the evasive manoeuvres undertaken by the master. The owners ordered the vessel to head directly for the Indian coast. By 0025 on 22 December, the nearest pirate boat was about four nautical miles from the vessel and by 0247, four hours after the alarm was raised, the authorities were informed that no boat was following the vessel. No injury or damage was reported and the *Maharaja Agrasen* proceeded to Visakhapatnam. The length of the attack was unusual, but not unique; German-owned and Marshal Islands-flagged *Felicitas Rickmers* was also attacked for four hours on 10 November 2009, 530 nautical miles east of Dar es Salaam, an unpleasant experience for the ship's crew. Masters have to be prepared to defend their ships over long periods; Somali pirates are persistent and tenacious.

Neither UKMTO nor MSCHOA reacted to the attack on the *Maharaja Agrasen*, largely, it appears, because it occurred in what they regarded as a safe area. However, previous attacks had shown that pirates were actually operating in the area and the authorities appear to have failed to understand the importance of the earlier incidents. Three weeks earlier, on 1 December 2009, the Greek oil tanker, the MV *Sikinos*, had been attacked approximately 345 nautical miles south-west of the position of the attack on the *Maharaja Agrasen* and another vessel was attacked on 5 December approximately 640 nautical miles south-south-west. On 30 December a Kuwait oil tanker, the MV *Album*, was attacked at virtually the same position as the earlier attack on the *Sikinos*, about 650 nautical miles west of the Indian coast.

The attack on the MV *Album*

The attack on the MV *Album* is interesting for two reasons: first, the owners tried to deny that it had happened, apparently worried that it could affect their business; and, second, Job Mattijssen, the ship's Dutch captain, recorded the attack in detail in an interview with RNW (Radio Netherlands Worldwide).

At 0915 on 30 December 2009 the helmsman of the MV *Album* sighted a fishing boat:

> Somali pirates use fishing boats as motherships. This allows them to work 600 miles off the coast. The fishing boats are equipped with a so-called skiff, a polyester speedboat measuring five to six metres with a powerful outboard motor, which can make 25 knots in a calm sea.[4]

Captain Mattijssen said:

> In less than ten minutes we see the skiff heading for us, but because of the waves it isn't making much headway. To be on the safe side, I change course by 90 degrees, so I'm sailing directly into the waves.[5]

This makes it harder for the pirates to draw alongside. 'On both port and starboard they then have to deal with around two-metre waves.' He then sent all non-essential crew members to the galley and started the extra generator, allowing him to use two steering engines which gave him a faster response from the ship's rudder. The first helmsman came up with the idea of opening the ballast tanks. He also started the ballast pump and within a few minutes seawater from the tanks was pouring over the deck. Captain Mattijssen told RNW: 'The water is meant to deter the pirates – not because they don't like getting wet, but because their skiff is an open boat and they don't want it full of water.'

The master then ordered the transmission of distress signals and informed the shipping company in Cairo; but the person at the other end spoke poor English, so the master turned his attention to the ship. Because the *Album* kept going, the pirates fired a grenade over the ship. Captain Mattijssen said 'Because I didn't stop, the game starts in earnest.'[6] The pirates fired more grenades and their AK-47 rifles. Captain Mattijssen said, 'They get closer and closer. Now it's down to my helmsmanship and even more to pure luck.'[7] Twice the master ordered the rudder turned hard, to make the waves rougher on the side the pirates were trying to board, although, as he said, 'when you turn the ship this quickly you lose a lot of speed, and the lower your speed the easier it is for the pirates to get on board'.[8] After 45 minutes the pirates gave up. Captain Mattijssen concluded:

> I have the feeling the pirates only fired to intimidate us. They could easily have fired on the wheelhouse windows with their AK-47, but they didn't.

It's my impression that they weren't out to hit people, that they deliberately avoided it.[9]

In the 2009–10 Somali pirate season attacks took place along the line from the Seychelles to the Maldives, into the Mozambique Channel, and throughout the Arabian Sea. The zone within a triangle formed by Socotra, the Gulf of Oman and the northern Maldives became a threat area. This covers approximately 600,000 square nautical miles, an immense area of sea and one that cannot be effectively protected by international naval forces. In fact the then British foreign secretary, David Miliband, made the point that ships using the Indian Ocean would not receive the same level of naval protection from pirates as those in the Gulf of Aden because military resources were limited.

The attack on the *Boularibank*

In two radio shows, one with the BBC World Service and another with BBC Radio 4, Matthew Bannister and Fergal Keane interviewed Peter Stapleton, the English captain of a British container ship, the *Boularibank*, crewed by Russians, that fought off Somali pirates in the Gulf of Aden on 28 April 2009. However, in comparison with Captain Mattijssen, Captain Stapleton took greater risks.

He failed to clear the bridge of non-essential personnel, and in fact his passengers stayed there throughout the attack, keen to see what was going on. He also sent his crew on deck to throw lengths of timber into the sea to discourage the attackers. In both cases it is arguable that the individuals concerned were exposed to the danger of being shot or hit by grenades – although, it is clear that Captain Stapleton remained calm and in control during the whole incident; he was awarded the Merchant Navy Medal for his bravery.

It is very important that crews of merchant ships keep out of harm's way. When *Seabourn Spirit* was attacked by pirates in November 2005, Michael Groves, the master-at-arms of the cruise liner, was hit by shrapnel, while operating an LRAD. Groves and his colleague Som Bahadur both received bravery awards from the Queen in 2007 for their work in defending the ship.

The *Boularibank* was returning to Hull from Malaysia with a Russian crew and 11 passengers, including the captain's wife. To the east of the Gulf of Aden a blip was seen on the radar screen, and from the bridge, the captain saw two attack skiffs being launched from a trawler, which was being used as a pirate mothership. Like Captain Mattijssen, Captain Stapleton looked to his seamanship, manoeuvring the ship to make the skiffs change course. As he told the BBC, manoeuvring,

> does create a bit of a lumpy wash that these small boats have got to cross over all the time so it means they've got to do some work to catch up with you, it's not just straight alongside and bang on board.[10]

However, in a surprising move, Captain Stapleton summoned his passengers to the bridge, some of whom were viewing the attacking pirates almost as if they were a tourist attraction. As for the Russian crew Captain Stapleton said, 'They were prepared to defend the ship as best they could. They knew that I wanted to defend the ship. I wanted to get back home and they want to go home.'[11]

Once the attackers realized that the ship was not going to heave to they fired their guns and an RPG was fired, fortunately without injuring anyone. Captain Stapleton then ordered that three-metre lengths of heavy timber be thrown over the port side; this made the skiff back off. He told Fergal Keane:

> My bottom line was I don't want to kill anybody but I want to put them off boarding my ship so if you drop them in the water in front of a speed boat he has got to pull away from you, he cannot go over it. So that was the thinking all the time. Passive defence.[12]

The timber defences had been rigged up as a last-ditch method of protecting the ship, but having downed two lots of wood he had exhausted his reserves. Fortunately at that point the attackers withdrew, possibly because their reserves of grenades and ammunition were also running low.

As a result of a distress call from the *Boularibank* the Russian destroyer *Admiral Panteleyev* subsequently arrested 29 pirates and sunk their mothership.

The case of the *Maersk Alabama*

On 8 April 2009, four Somali pirates boarded the *Maersk Alabama* when it was 240 nautical miles south-east of Eyl on the Somali coast. There is an email from one of the ship's engineers, Matt Fisher, to the first engineer on the *Maersk Arkansas*, sent at 1358 on Friday, 10 April 2009, that is two days before Captain Phillips was rescued and the day after the

Maersk Alabama was freed. This was reproduced on a maritime blog, gCaptain.com,[13] which was quoted by CNN on 20 April 2009,[14] and which has a wealth of detail that rings true. According to Fisher's account, he wanted to tell his friend the lessons they had learnt so that he could help to better prepare his ship against pirates. His advice is important for all mariners, so it is worth quoting at length. According to Fisher, the only men captured by the pirates – Captain Phillips, the third mate and two able seamen – were all on the bridge. He said: 'I don't really know why they stayed on the bridge until the pirates got up there.'[15] He also said:

> The pirates got up to the bridge very quickly once they were onboard. We had a locked cage door over the ladder well from main deck, but it only took a second for them to shoot it off. They then got to the bridge up the outside ladders.[16]

By gaining access to the bridge the pirates also got hold of the keys to everything on the ship. The rest of the crew had then taken control of the engine and steering so that the bridge controls were no longer effective. Mike Parry stayed in the engine control room and the chief mate, Shane Murphy, stayed on deck tracking the pirates' movements. Fisher said, 'We kept swinging the rudder side to side. The pirates' boat capsized, though I'm not sure exactly when or what caused it.'[17] It was this event that forced the pirates to use a ship's lifeboat to escape.

Fisher recorded that after about 20 minutes the ship's engine was stopped, but he did not know who did it. He then shut off the air bottles and Mike Parry, the chief engineer, switched off the electric power. Parry was also able to get outside and trip the fuel shutoff for the emergency diesel generator (EDG). The ship was therefore stopped dead in the water with no electrical power. Fisher said that he thought that cutting power was critical, and that, 'The pirates were very reluctant to go into the dark.'[18] He added that they would want to be able to shut off the EDG from the engine control room in the future. The crew, not held by the pirates, then retreated to a secure area in the fantail[19] by the steering gear, which was their citadel. Fisher said that they had previously welded a padeye,[20] or fairlead,[21] on the inside of the hatch to the fantail, so that it could be secured from the inside. He said that because the pirates did not have grenades the crew felt secure there; however, in a similar case, a crewman was shot through a citadel door while welding it shut, so some type of armoured protection would have been an added insurance. While the crew felt safe, they lacked water and the space was very hot. Fisher told his friend: 'In the future we will store food and water in various spots for emergency usage.[22] ... I think we will also run a fresh water line into the steering gear.'[23] The crew left the citadel and filled some bottles with water and got some supplies from the galley. The pirates sent the third mate off on his own to look for crew members, so he was able to escape. After this one of the pirates, Abduhl Wal-i-Musi, with an able seaman then went into the engine room searching for the crew. Mike Perry 'was able to jump him in the dark and we took him prisoner in the steering gear'.[24] After this, no other pirates went down into the engine room.

The pirates were in an impossible situation: the ship was immobile and powerless, their skiff was sunk, and the crew were hiding in the darkness of the engine room and the compartments of the ship. They had no option but to leave the ship. Fisher then said that Captain Phillips talked them into taking the ship's rescue, or MOB, boat. The three remaining pirates, with Captain Phillips, got the boat into the sea. The crew opened negotiations by radio, dropping food, water and diesel down; they also restarted the ship's power. There was a further complication when the boat failed to start. Two of the crew got into the lifeboat and dropped it, exchanging the lifeboat for the MOB boat. They also planned to trade the captured pirate for Captain Phillips, but that did not work out. The pirates and Captain Phillips went off in the lifeboat followed by the ship for several hours, until the US navy in the form of the destroyer *USS Bainbridge* (DDG-96) and the frigate *USS Halyburton* (FFG-40) took over early on 9 April. Under the command of the chief mate, the ship set course for Mombasa with a US navy escort, arriving on 11 April.

Fisher's concluding advice should be read by anyone transiting dangerous waters:

> Have a well fortified location with food and water supply. Kill all the lights. Leave the alarms going, the noise helped cover our movements through the house. Flashlights and radios are very handy, as well as the sound-powered phone.[25]

He added that in this stressful situation he was impressed with the way in which the entire crew responded: 'We didn't have anybody who wanted to give up'; and that: 'I assume the company will be forced into taking some kind of action to assure our security from now on.'[26]

The standoff and rescue of Captain Phillips was reported in full. The lifeboat ran out of fuel and negotiations continued for three days between the pirates and Commander Frank Castellano, the captain of *USS Bainbridge*. At 1919 local time (1619 GMT) the order was given for US navy Seal snipers to shoot once they had all three pirates in their sights; the three pirates in the lifeboat were all killed, the fourth, who had been on board the *Bainbridge*, was the only survivor. Vice Admiral William Gortney, the head of the US Naval Central Command, said in a Pentagon briefing from Bahrain: 'The on-scene [US navy] commander determined that the captain was in imminent danger.'[27] There are unofficial reports, which cannot be substantiated, that the order to fire would have been given much earlier, but for the insistence of President Obama that he determine the course of negotiations and give approval. In the event naval officers on the scene determined that the threat to Captain Phillips' life was immediate and initiated action.

Matt Fisher's account of the incident is one of the most important records we have of an actual hijacking, and all mariners who read it owe him a debt.

After the attack some of the crew formed the Alabama Shipmates LLC.[28] According to a report by CNN, 16 of the 19 crew members of the *Maersk Alabama* claimed that Captain Phillips, 'ignored explicit warnings to stay well off the coast of Somalia before his capture by pirates in 2009'. The ship's chief engineer, Mike Perry, told CNN, 'It's almost like he wanted to be captured'. The ship's third engineer, John Cronan, also told CNN that Phillips 'was advised to change course by competent deck officers and he overruled them.' It is also claimed that the vessel received an email stating that, 'Vessels should consider maintaining a distance of more than 600 nautical miles from the Somali coastline,' from a security company, Securewest, the ship was attacked approximately 380 miles off the Somali coast.[29] It appears that these claims will finally be tested in the American courts, and that nine of the original crewmen are sueing the ship's owner, Maersk Line Limited, and the operator, Waterman Steamship Corporation.[30] It is likely that the Court will hear a complex story of genuine heroism by Captain Phillips and his crew and disagreements over some of the actions taken at the time. The account of Colin Wright, the third mate, given to the *Houston Chronicle*, suggests a very complicated situation. Wright says that Captain Phillips went voluntarily into the lifeboat 'to show the pirates how to operate it.'[31] The Alabama Shipmates stated:

> While the Alabama Shipmates are disappointed with Richard Phillips' actions in the days preceding the attack, as well as his actions over the past year, their primary concern has been and remains ensuring the safe passage of merchant vessels off the coast of Somalia. The Alabama

Shipmates have had no substantive communication with Richard Phillips and are therefore unable to comment on his upcoming book or its contents.[32]

Richard Phillips' book is *A Captain's Duty: Somali Pirates, Navy SEALs, and Dangerous Days at Sea*.[33] The disagreement between Captain Phillips and his crew surfaced again in 2013, when the film *Captain Phillips* was released; the nine crewmen who are still involved in litigation appear to disagree with Captain Phillips' version of events.[34] This is unlikely to be the last time that shipowners are sued by crew members who have been attacked at sea.

The hijacking of the MV *CEC Future*

When Captain Andrey Nozhkin of the MV *CEC Future*, a Danish ship owned by Clipper Projects, saw that pirates were alongside and aiming their second RPG round at the ship's bridge, he decided that further resistance was pointless. He had prepared fire-hoses and was in constant touch with international naval forces as his ship entered the Gulf of Aden, and when the pirate skiff was spotted he had at first manoeuvred the ship to try and make boarding difficult.

Having allowed the pirates to board he was directed to Eyl on the Somali coast, where the vessel remained for two months before finally being ransomed. The ransom paid was between $1 and 2 million, but one of the pirate leaders saw nothing from it; he was shot dead by his men when he reached the shore, in a quarrel over the division of the ransom money. One of the other leaders was also killed in the months that followed.[35]

The retaking of the tanker *Moscow University*

Finally, there is the strange story of the *Moscow University*, a Russian-owned oil tanker, that was seized on 5 May 2010. According to EU NAVFOR:

> The Liberian flagged (Russian operated) oil tanker, *Moscow University*, was hijacked approximately 350 miles east of Socotra. It was reported that the crew had locked themselves into the 'rudder compartment' and a Maritime Patrol aircraft made contact with the crew a few hours later to confirm that they were safe. A Russian warship, *Marshal Shaposhnikov*, was reported to be heading at full speed towards the hijack position. EU Naval Forces and other units from the multinational forces in the area

offered support to the Russian ship and a German Maritime Patrol aircraft from CMF 151 were put on alert to support any operation.[36]

The next day the *Marshal Shaposhnikov* arrived at the scene and launched a helicopter, which was fired on by the pirates. Fire was returned, as the crew were safe in their citadel. The pirates surrendered after Russian forces stormed the ship, killing one pirate, and injuring three others. The Russian naval boarding party then took control of the tanker, released the crew and secured the pirates.[37] In other words, to this point the Russians had given a textbook example of the importance of using a citadel and not leaving the crew in the hands of pirates.

This was not the first example of such a recapture – a month earlier, on 5 April 2010, the Dutch warship *HNLMS Tromp* recaptured the MV *Taipan*, a German-flagged and owned container ship of 12,612 dwt. Marines from the *Tromp* boarded and retook control of the ship. Another similar incident was the successful rescue of the crew of the *Falcon Trader II* by the US navy, after they were boarded by Somali pirates 300 miles north-east of Masirah, Oman, in March 2011 and went into their citadel.[38] The crew of 13 were released unharmed and ten pirates were taken into custody (Figure 9.1).

After having announced that the pirates would be tried in a Russian court, the Russians apparently changed their minds. The blog, 'Flags of Convenience' quoted an unnamed high-level Russian Defence Ministry

Figure 9.1 The rescue of the *Falcon Trader II*

official who said that the pirates who boarded the tanker *Moscow University* never made it to shore and were likely dead. He added that they were stripped of their weapons and navigation equipment and, about 300 nautical miles offshore, were put into one of their own skiffs.[39] However, Russian shipping expert Mikhail Voitenko told AFP that reports about the pirates being set free in a boat could just be a cover story and that they may have all been killed when the *Moscow University* was recaptured.[40] The truth will probably never be known, although a photograph, released at the time, appears to show a number of live pirates lying on the deck of the tanker. But piracy can be a dirty game, on both sides of the equation.

PRACTICAL DEFENSIVE MEASURES

Preparation and training

In order to defend a ship the owners and the master need to develop an effective 'ship security plan' (SSP). This is in any case a requirement under the ISPS Code, but for any vessel that is planning to transit waters where piracy, or attacks in port, are a potential threat the normal SSP requires to be modified, and kept up to date. The booklet issued in 2009 by the Oil Companies International Marine Forum (OCIMF), *Piracy – The East Africa/Somalia Situation*, is a good starting point.[41] It is worth complementing this with other material, such as Captain Corbett's *A Modern Plague of Pirates*,[42] and taking advice from a marine security consultancy.[43]

The basic rule is that a ship's crew must be trained and properly equipped before transiting any danger area. As the experience of seafarers shows, at some point the attackers will break off their attack if they can be thwarted in their attempts to board a vessel, although this may take several hours. If there are warships within reach, any delay will buy time for them to intervene; helicopters can be very effective, especially if they fire on the attackers. In drawing up defensive procedures the company security officers and masters need to decide whether to surrender the vessel once it is boarded, or whether to withdraw *all* the crew to a secure and armoured citadel and, like the crews of the MV *Taipan* and the *Moscow University*, wait for naval forces to retake the ship. If the citadel is in a secure area, like the engine control room, protected by locked and secured doors, the master can retain control of his ship, disabling all bridge controls, before retreating via a secure, pre-planned route to the citadel, and keep communications open to international naval forces and the owner. The crew of the *Maersk Alabama* showed the importance of being able to stop the ship's engines and cut electrical power.

Once their ship was dead in the water the pirates only wanted to leave; she was no longer a prize that they could steer to Somalia. As Matt Fisher noted, it is important to route all controls to a secure area and ensure that there are sufficient supplies there. Once a ship is dark, as the experience of the *Maersk Alabama* showed, pirates are afraid to enter the engine room and the underwater areas of the vessel.

The other lesson from the hijacking of the *Maersk Alabama* is that shipowners need to ensure that they have taken sufficient measures to protect the crew and the ship in order to avoid the threat of litigation from crew members, their families and their unions. Being attacked and being held as a hostage are traumatic experiences that can have long-term psychological effects.

As part of the SSP there should be clear instructions and agreed signals for actions. For example, had the bridge of the *Maersk Alabama* been cleared quickly Captain Phillips and the other crew members on the bridge would not have been taken. Ideally there should be clear stages of alert and action – say yellow alert for a suspicious approach, orange alert for an attack, red alert for the attacking craft within one kilometre and another signal for pirates on board. Sets of bridge cards should always be available to watchkeepers and copies of the piracy instructions should be communicated to all members of the crew. It is also important to hold regular drills and to repeat training before entering a threat area. New crew members need to be integrated into the team and old crew members need to refresh their skills. For most of the crew their instructions will be to go to the citadel.

The ship also needs to be prepared for its transit of a threat area. Razor wire should be placed around the ship's rails, in a properly planned and effective manner, not because it is very effective, but lack of such defences will give the impression to the pirates' reconnaissance teams that the vessel is unprepared. All doors leading into the ship should be secured from the inside – padlocks are not sufficient as they can be shot off easily – escape hatches can be secured with metal grills, and all bridge glass should be covered with blast- and bullet-resistant protective film. Finally, if possible, the ladders to the bridge should be modified to be raised and lowered using a block and tackle, and made secure by also being covered in razor wire. However, at no time should any anti-piracy measure compromise the safety of the ship and all emergency escape routes and access to lifeboats must remain clear at all times. Some ships have been equipped with an electric fence system, like electrocoil, but, as noted previously, Somali pirates now commonly carry a metal bar to short it out when boarding. Some ships also carry dummy lookouts, to give the impression that there are more crew available; such dummies need to be moved frequently if they are to be effective, and a keen observer will notice that there is no movement or reaction by these 'watchkeepers', so their use is of limited effectiveness. In any case once the attackers are close to the ship it will become obvious that these are merely decoys.

Intelligence, watchkeeping and alertness

The most important action that a master can take is to avoid trouble. The first step is to have access to good intelligence, advice on recent attacks and the presence of PAGs. Intelligence is normally supplied directly to the owner, and the company security officer then passes on the information, although it can also be supplied directly to the master, sometimes with recommendations for action.

The second most important action is to have good and intelligent watchkeeping. A ship needs to ensure that watchkeepers and the bridge team have the ability to see threats coming from any quarter, especially from astern, and on far too many ships the stern has little or no coverage by radar, thermal imaging, or the mark one human eyeball: in other words, they are too frequently as blind as bats aft of the bridge. Shipowners must remedy this problem on any vessel sailing in troubled waters, or the master may wake up to find pirates assaulting his bridge. There can be no excuses for not having 360-degree coverage of the sea around the ship.

Watchkeepers need to be rotated regularly, especially at night, and all the available crew needs to be trained to act as watchkeepers, because the more warning the master has of threats the more effective his actions will be. At all times when in troubled waters, especially during the middle watch, between midnight and 0400, when the pirates most like to attack, the ship needs to remain alert.

Dealing with an attack

As noted before, the first action that any master should consider taking on seeing a suspicious approach, which may just be a fishing boat, is to change course. If the approaching craft then follows the ship it is almost certainly an attack, the master should sound the alarm, if he has not already done so, and instigate the agreed set of drills and procedures – finally closing down the ship, putting pressure in any water cannon or water-hoses that he has deployed, starting any auxiliary pumps, sending all non-essential crew to the citadel and alerting the authorities and other ships of the attack. He should light the ship and use the ship's searchlight(s) to illuminate the attacking craft; powerful searchlights can disorient an attacker. If he has lasers he should also target them on the attackers at this stage, before the skiffs come within RPG range. Once the attackers are a mile away water cannon, or hoses, should be put into action and the bulge pumps should also pump water over the side. In darkness or low light the attackers should also be tracked by remote-controlled searchlights and the bridge team should stand by to target water cannon from the bridge using remote controls. No one should ever be allowed out on the open deck: the danger from bullets and explosions is simply too great.

If it appears, despite careful manoeuvring of the ship, that pirates are likely to board, all controls should be routed to the citadel and the bridge controls disengaged. The bridge crew should immediately leave for the citadel (unless company policy is to surrender at this point). The ship, now under control from the citadel, with the electrics, including the emergency lights, switched off in all areas, except the citadel, should then be put on a course towards the nearest warship or safe harbour; the pirates will not want to be passengers in such a case. If all else fails the engines can be stopped and all electrics killed, and the pirates then have no possibility of sailing the ship anywhere unless they can break into the citadel and seize the crew. There are many possibilities for blocking doors and passageways on board and for the pirates the ship will be an uncharted maze. It is of vital importance that the citadel has good radio communications at all time in order to brief warships of the status of the crew and to provide intelligence for rescue forces.

Special equipment

While not every ship will have all the available specialized anti-piracy equipment, it is certainly important that all ships transiting pirate areas have protective film on their bridge glass as this protects against the effect of grenade explosions and bullets. It is also fundamental that the bridge team have effective bullet-proof vests and helmets. Shipowners should consider armouring the steel work of the bridge, to protect vital control and navigation systems, and certainly should always armour the door of the citadel.

Anti-pirate water cannon are another very effective solution, but pumpage must provide sufficient pressure at all times and, if necessary, auxiliary pumps should be fixed. Abundant water cannon must be deployed to cover all parts of the ship where the pirates may board; this generally excludes the bows, as the bow wave makes the water too rough to allow a small craft to keep station alongside the ship. The range of the water cannon needs to be at least 60 metres and the pressure must be sufficient to knock a man down and swamp a skiff. Properly directed and deployed water cannons are a powerful non-lethal defence.

Lasers constitute a second effective long-range deterrent, as they will temporarily blind attackers and make it very difficult to target the vessel. However, their operators require special training. Some lasers on offer are also expensive, although cheaper solutions are available. Other defensive measures are available, including pyrotechnics and loud bangers; these may be useful tools, as they can disorient the pirates and encourage the crew.

Among the 'non-lethal' weapons available to defend ships, one of the best known is the LRAD, which is a very powerful loudspeaker system, and is useful for communicating at long-range distances. However, as a weapon system for use against pirates it presents some problems. It requires a man to hold or direct the device, which increases the danger to the operator. It also suffers from 'windage' where the pressure of the wind moves it. It is commonly agreed that the LRAD is not very effective on the open sea, whereas in urban settings it can work well.

A security team provided by Anti Piracy Maritime Security Solutions (APMSS) of Poole, Dorset, used an LRAD successfully on 14 November 2008 to repel pirates attempting to attack a chemical tanker. However, two weeks later, on 28 November, another APMSS security team used an LRAD to fend off three attempts but ultimately could not prevent the pirates from boarding and taking over the MV *Biscaglia*. The security team jumped into the sea and were finally picked up by a helicopter. As a result *Lloyd's List* questioned the effectiveness of LRADs.[44]

The LRAD is relatively expensive, but is very cheap compared to the US military's Active Denial System which costs around $5 million. This system, which is not yet available in a civilian system, has a range of 500 metres and is capable of causing immense discomfort at that range: the US army calls it the 'pain ray.'[45]

The use of security personnel and arms

Although the US authorities were quick to give their blessing to the carriage of firearms on board merchant vessels, authorities in other countries have in the past strongly discouraged their use. However, attitudes have changed; for example, the UK Department of Transport first issued its 'Interim Guidance to UK Flagged Shipping on the Use of Armed Guards to Defend Against the Threat of Piracy in Exceptional Circumstances' in November 2011, and stated that 'The [UK] government recognises that the engagement of armed guards is an option to protect human life onboard UK registered ships from the threat of piracy, but only in exceptional circumstances and where it is lawful to do so.'[46] This represented a major change in UK policy. The use of armed guards has also been covered previously in Chapter 8.

Vessel resilience

Training, procedures and specialized equipment will increase the resilience of merchant ships. However, it is also important to audit the risk to individual vessels regularly. Some types of ships are so vulnerable that they should not travel unescorted through dangerous waters: they are too low, too slow and so can be easily boarded. Most tugs, oil support vessels and dredgers fall into this category. Merchant ships are not warships, designed to cope with the impact of weapons. While it is possible to make a normal merchant vessel reasonably resilient to gunfire and even to RPG rounds, this does not mean that they can cope with wire-guided anti-tank weapons of the type now reported to be in Somalia, or with other types of heavy weapons, like cannon.

The threat to vessels needs to be monitored and reassessed continually, and the defensive measures that were adequate one year may be less effective the next. Increasing vessel resilience, which also raises crew confidence, is the single most important measure that can be taken to resist vessel hijacking, especially at a time when budget cuts reduce the size of Western navies and inevitably bring pressure to reduce the commitment in the Gulf of Aden. A resilient ship will also be able to cope better with transits of the Gulf of Guinea and the continuing threat in the South China Sea and the Malacca Straits.

There is rarely a permanent answer to any problem of this type. What we have is a form of economic warfare, with organized criminals predating on the maritime lines of communication we all depend on. We cannot surrender; we have to be able to deal with the problem and a large part of the solution is better and more effective defence of merchant vessels. The shipping and insurance industries are slowly facing up to the issues, and legal pressure and insurance industry requirements will at last result in the imposition of new standards for maritime security.

THE ROLE OF NAVAL FORCES

By the summer of 2009 there was a widely held belief in the shipping industry that piracy was under control in the eastern part of the Indian Ocean because of the presence of large naval forces in the area. But the international naval forces, while partly effective in the Gulf of Aden, initially proved inadequate to protect the wider waters of the Indian Ocean.

By the end of October 2009, 27 ships from 16 different nations were assigned for counter-piracy and convey-protection operations off the coast of Somalia, in the Gulf of Aden and the Indian Ocean. They formed part of EU NAVFOR, NATO, CTF 151, or were nationally deployed vessels from Japan, China, India and Saudi Arabia. The Iranian navy also deployed warships in the region, but did not cooperate with other forces. The Omani navy was responsible for the protection of its own coastline and Yemeni coastguards provided support for some foreign vessels.

However, it was likely that the number of naval vessels actually on station and engaged in operations was far lower and there may have been only around five or six naval vessels in the Gulf of Aden at any one time. Precise figures were not publicly available, but the frigates and destroyers, which are the ideal vessels for this work, need to deploy from home bases, often far away – like *HMCS Fredericton*, which departed Halifax, Canada, on 25 October 2009. In addition, once in the region naval vessels require replenishment and may be called on to undertake other duties. The international fleet is also deployed eastwards and along the Somali coast, and assists in patrolling in the area of the Seychelles.

The primary focus of the international naval fleet has been the protection of ships transiting the Gulf of Aden, coming to the assistance of merchant ships travelling in convey, through the IRTC in the Gulf of Aden. This operation reduced the level of attacks in the Gulf of Aden in 2009, although three vessels were hijacked there in the first quarter of 2010 and two were taken in a few days in August 2010. The pirates had therefore adapted their approach and learnt that warships could do little, or nothing (unless the crew were safe in a citadel), once the pirates were on board.

Commander Dow RN, in his evidence to the House of Lords, has stressed that EU NAVFOR is not undertaking operations of war:

The only thing I would add, my Lord, is that this is clearly a law enforcement operation rather than a war against pirate or an armed conflict such as we are engaged in elsewhere. There are constraints imposed by the law of the sea, either in customary international law or under the United Nations Convention on the Law of the Sea, that we follow. The principle is the use of reasonable force, reasonable force being the minimum necessary to impose your rights under those provisions: to board, search, seize, arrest, detain, what have you. Lethal force is available where there is a threat to life, in very much the same way as for any other law enforcement operation.[47]

There is often a misunderstanding of the role of international naval forces, and they have for good legal reasons to acknowledge what could be called the 'fiction' of the TFG's control of Somalia's territorial waters. In 2008 the UN Security Council passed Resolution 1816 that allowed states to cooperate with the TFG for a period of six months to enter the territorial waters of Somalia and use 'all necessary means' to repress acts of piracy and armed robbery at sea, in a manner consistent with relevant provisions of international law. In October 2008 the UN also passed Resolution 1838 under Chapter VII of the UN Charter, which called upon states with naval vessels and military aircraft operating in the area to use, on the high seas and airspace off the coast of Somalia, the necessary means to repress acts of piracy in a manner consistent with UNCLOS 1982. This had the effect of asking states to implement the provisions of Resolution 1816. The provisions of Resolution 1816 were extended beyond the original six months, although the basis of anti-piracy operations on the high seas is not reliant on the resolution, which only refers to Somali territorial waters. One of EU NAVFOR's main tasks has also been to protect the World Food Programme's maritime convoys, taking food to Somali refugees.

It is frequently argued that the presence of the international fleet in the Gulf of Aden has pushed piracy activity into the Indian Ocean. In 2009 there were a series of attacks and hijackings in the Arabian Sea and out as far as the coast of India. But the area that needs to be protected is enormous. The distance from the Gulf of Aden to Victoria in the Seychelles is over 1,000 nautical miles; Victoria is also 730 nautical miles from Mogadishu, over 1,100 nautical miles from Male in the Maldives and nearly 2,000 nautical miles from the Strait of Hormuz. The international force initially lacked first-rate maritime patrol aircraft coverage. In 2009 the Luxembourg government provided two Swearingen Merlin III aircraft operated by CAE Aviation; they were based in Mahé in support of the EU's 'Operation Atalanta', but had a limited range of less than 600 nautical miles. In March 2010 a Swedish coastguard DASH 8-Q-300 was deployed for four months, and in April a Portuguese P3 (Orion) Papa aircraft, an excellent maritime reconnaissance platform and one that upgraded EU NAVFOR's capability, was deployed for the same period. But such assets are only deployed for a limited period and EU NAVFOR needs long-term commitments of long-range maritime reconnaissance aircraft.

One area where international naval cooperation has been effective is in the area of communications and coordination, via the MSCHOA website. Rear

Admiral Hudson explained to the House of Lords how communications with ships work:

> There is the straightforward commercial VHF, speaking on normal communications means, where we pass information and exchange identities, tell them who we are, just exchange information. Yes, any other ships can listen to it – pirates, for instance, would be able to listen to a VHF conversation – but in terms of merchant ships, it is quite difficult to get secure communications on to them. We can pass information through the UKMTO through Inmarsat channels, which are not overt, they are not readily interceptable, and we do do that, when we say, 'Be in position X at time Y' – we pass that through Inmarsat channels – but when we meet the ship we do talk on ordinary VHF channels. In terms of co-ordination, we do have secure means of doing that at an unclassified level. It is based on an Internet, it is the same banking protocols that you and I would use to move our money around over the Internet, so it is as secure as that, and from our security centre we release passwords, we give various companies, shipping agencies, outside organisations, access through password control, and that is where we can identify any specific threats for downward dissemination through their own routes. It is overt ship-to-ship via Inmarsat and radio but a secure area where we pass wider tactical data.[48]

At various times US naval officers, such as US Rear Admiral Terry McKnight in January 2009, have said that naval forces have 'dramatically' cut piracy off the coast of Somalia. He added: 'The pirates can look out and see a lot of navy ships out there and it's been a deterrent... This is a coalition of many nations. We are out there and we are working together.'[49] In August 2009 US Admiral Gary Roughead, chief of naval operations for the Bahrain-based US Fifth Fleet, told a press conference that, 'The maritime environment is much more peaceful because of the international cooperation', and that, 'The situation is better than it was about a year ago'[50] – although he did predict a surge in piracy in the Gulf of Aden. Unfortunately the 2009–10 pirate season served to disprove such optimistic statements.

Despite the $1.5 billion that is said to be the annual cost of the international naval operation, naval operations suffer from a series of limitations. The most obvious limitation is that the forces available cannot cover the whole area of the Indian Ocean subject to pirate attacks. The second limitation is that the rules of engagement and the lack of a unified system of justice for dealing with pirates have restricted the effectiveness of naval forces. Finally, international naval forces cannot operate in territorial waters, which means that they cannot operate in the southern part of the Red Sea and in the Bab el Mandeb between Yemen on the Arabian Peninsula, and Djibouti and Eritrea on the coast of Africa.

The eastward movement of PAGs may be due not only to the presence of naval forces in the Gulf of Aden; the reality is almost certainly more complex. Somali pirates have shown an ability to innovate and expand their operations, and the 2009–10 season benefitted from increased investment and improved planning. It is likely that the PAGs would have gone east, even if the international naval forces had not been sent to the Gulf of Aden, but it is likely that the presence of naval forces encouraged this development.

There are a number of somewhat contradictory forces that are now coming to bear on the international naval presence. First, virtually all defence ministries are under pressure to reduce their costs, and this on its own would lead to a reduction in the number of naval vessels deployed. Second, there is pressure to increase the effectiveness of the naval forces, because they have not stopped piracy. Third, there is a growing perception that Somalia (and Yemen) are becoming bases for terrorist groups and this will increase the pressure to deploy more military forces in the region.

The logical outcome would be to deploy more smaller vessels to deal with the pirate threat: these are cheaper to operate and more capable than large naval vessels for this type of task, although fleet supply ships, like the Royal Fleet Auxiliary ships used by the Royal Navy, are required in order to enable them to stay at sea for longer periods. In fact RFA *Fort Victoria* was deployed off the coast of Oman for periods in 2012 in this role. More maritime patrol aircraft are needed.

CHAPTER 10

ARE THERE ANSWERS?

WHAT THE MARITIME INDUSTRY MUST DO

At some point in the future clan heads and other people of influence within Somalia may decide to pursue a more peaceful way; this did happen in Somaliland, although there remains the threat that that territory may still be forced back into the mess that is the rest of Somalia. The foreign jihadists who currently control Al-Shabaab are not part of the Somali system; it is very probable that, left alone, the Somalis will oust them. Only if they are glorified by Western actions are they likely to stay. It is important to remember that in the past Al-Qaeda was unable to operate successfully in Somalia because of the chaos and the clan-based nature of Somali society; the more structured societies of Kenya and Nigeria remain a more congenial environment for jihadists.

It is now vital that all ships that transit any waters where piracy is a problem, and this includes West Africa and the South China Sea as well as the Gulf of Aden and the waters of the western Indian Ocean, are properly equipped, and the crew trained and able to thwart attacks.

WHAT DOES NOT WORK

It is no longer sufficient to rely on the presence of navies in dangerous waters. They have not been the whole answer, although in many instances they have been able to assist merchant ships under attack. The scale of the problem is so great that there are just not enough warships available to provide universal protection over such a vast area of sea. The force requirements for this sort of a missions would exceed 100 warships actually at sea. EU NAVFOR and other naval forces have done the best that they can within the limits imposed by their resources and their rules of engagement, and without their presence the situation would undoubtedly have been far worse. EU NAVFOR have also suffered from a lack of long-range reconnaissance aircraft.

It is of course true that more aggressive rules of engagement, a greater willingness to shoot (not a problem the Russians appear to suffer from) and the deployment of more aircraft and warships would make the international naval forces more effective.

Somali pirates proved adaptable and responded to the presence of naval forces by increasing the numbers of attack skiffs (for example, 15 were used during one attack in September 2010) and by varying their operational areas. By September 2010 the attacks on convoys in the Gulf of Aden were becoming continual; pirates were launching a series of attacks, and the presence of warships often made little difference, unless they opened fire on the skiffs.

The political conditions in Somalia and the failure of previous international attempts at imposing a solution on the warring parties through a confusion of objectives with the 'War on Terror' has made a bad situation even worse. This has given rise to what Hoehne describes as the 'binary logic' of conflict, as Al-Shabaab and the United States have moved to 'mutually reinforcing "arrogance" and [an] unwillingness to compromise'.[1]

The UN Monitoring Group said in 2011, 'Since the disintegration of Hisbul Islam in December 2010, Al-Shabaab remains the principal threat to peace and security in Somalia.'[2]

The danger is that Al-Shabaab moves from being a Somali nationalist Islamist organization to one that supports terrorist attacks on Western states. If Somali nationalist elements within that organization regain control from foreigners, this danger would be dramatically reduced. Without a settlement of the conflict within Somalia, which involves Al-Shabaab, piracy will continue to be a threat to civilian maritime traffic.

RESILIENT SHIPS

Defence in depth

As the navies of the world cannot alone provide the answer and there is no sign of peace on shore, then the merchant fleets of the world are left to cope on their own, which means that merchant ships have to be better protected, making their hijacking a much more difficult task. I am a director of a company called Idarat Ltd. and we offer advice on securing ships and other assets against attack; we talk of 'systemic resilience', that is of looking at all the different aspects that can make ships 'resilient' against attacks. By looking at the different elements as a system it is possible to look at the interactions of different pieces of equipment and to develop a set of procedures and training that integrates them. In this way the master of a ship has a clear set of processes that he can use when his vessel is threatened.

In our experience there is not one 'magic bullet' that provides defence against pirate attacks, but a range of interlocking products and services that creates systemic resilience. The first objective is to make it very difficult for pirates, terrorists and others to board a vessel at sea. The possibility that any defensive system can be overcome will always remains, but the chances of this happening can be greatly reduced. We base our procedures on the principle of defence in depth, otherwise known as 'elastic' defence. A ship is therefore protected by a series of defences and, if one fails, the attackers still have to overcome others layer of defences. Medieval castles were designed according to the same principles; the attacker is delayed and uses a large part of his resources in overcoming the various defensive systems, giving more time for help to arrive. This protects the crew and allows naval forces time to deal with the attack. If you rely on one layer of defence, for example guards, then if that layer fails, the whole ship is lost. The Maginot line, built by the French before the Second World War, is often cited as an example of static defence. In fact, when the Germans attacked France in May 1940 they outflanked it by using the Ardennes as an invasion route. The reliance of the French army on the line's effectiveness meant that France had in practice lost the habit of mental flexibility, which is the cornerstone of any successful military response to an attack. In defending a vessel only a combination of measures used with flexibility will be truly effective, and those measures need to be continuously reviewed in the light of the changing threat, the vessel's operations and changes to the crew. The defence of the vessel needs to allow the crew to withdraw into safe areas, or citadels, as the defensive rings are breached, having delayed and weakened the attack.

Given the availability of effective services and products today, there should be no easy pickings for pirates.

The danger is that, because the principles to be applied are essentially military principles, the shipping industry will have difficulty in grasping them and will instead seek a simpler but inefficient solution to a complex problem. In some cases there are also management issues and problems in communication of policy from the head offices of shipping companies to their masters and officers, and a failure to transmit information from ships to management.

Advice to shipowners

This section is based on Idarat's advice to shipowners and insurers, and reflects the author's work as a director of that company.

First, a shipmaster needs to be supported by good intelligence, as this may enable him to sail around or away from potential threats. Merchant ships have no interest in confronting pirates: it is far better that they avoid trouble if they can. The aim must be to thwart attacks, not to go into battle. That is the job of navies.

Second, the crew and officers of a ship should be trained in anti-piracy drills and understand how to operate any anti-piracy equipment carried by the vessel. In short, they must know how to respond to any emergency. For most of the crew this implies going to the ship's citadel, out of danger, as soon as the attack is launched. Training and procedures are the key to creating good crew morale and confidence. These procedures and drills, which should always be tested prior to entering dangerous waters, also include basic security measures, such as the use of alarm signals, razor wire, securing doors and blocking access to the bridge.

Third, the vessel needs to be 'hardened' to protect the crew from the effects of RPG blasts and rifle bullets; bridge glass in particular must have a level of protection from blast and bullets, and the bridge team should also have personal protective gear. In addition, an effective citadel should always have a bullet-proof door.

Fourth, the ship requires effective watchkeeping and sensors that can detect small craft heading towards the vessel from all directions. Slow ships and smaller vessels have particular problems, and for some vessels additional personnel in the form of guards may be necessary.

Fifth, the bridge team needs to know how to identify and respond to a threat, using a searchlight if it is dark, or otherwise visually determining that there is a genuine attack and not just a local fishing craft approaching the stern. The master needs to report the attack, and his position, to the authorities and his owner, in accordance with company procedures, and to remain in contact while under attack.

Sixth, the master needs to manoeuvre the ship to make boarding difficult and also to deploy any defensive measures, including water cannon and lasers, with which the ship is equipped. If armed guards are on board, they should be ready to respond to gunfire from the pirates on the master's orders and in accordance with previously agreed rules of engagement.

Finally, if the ship is boarded, the bridge team, including any security personnel, must leave the bridge via a secure route, well before any pirates can obtain access, switching off all engine and other controls, which should be routed to the citadel. As the *Maersk Alabama* hijacking showed, a ship dead in the water, which pirates cannot control, is of little use to them. Ideally, a vessel should be capable of being controlled from the citadel.

Citadels or safe areas

Great care needs to be taken with the construction of a citadel. It must be armoured so that gunfire, or blast, cannot wound those inside. Its position should not be obvious. It needs its own water supply, drainage, electricity circuits, satellite phone and AC, with its own air supply. There must also be clear procedures for the use and provisioning of the citadel. If all else fails there should also be a procedure for surrendering control of the vessel to the pirates. As pirates become aware of the increased use of citadels it is likely that they will make greater efforts to locate and break into them; passageways leading to the citadel need to be blocked and lights need to be cut, and crews must all locate to the citadel; no man should be left outside, or he/she is likely to be forced to give information on the crew's plans. Fire-suppression systems must be disabled within the citadel in order that the crew are not suffocated by CO_2 or halon gases. No documents dealing with anti-piracy procedures should be left in the ship where the pirates may find them. Bridge cards should be kept on an individual's person.

A citadel should be installed on all merchant ships transiting the Gulf of Aden and the Indian Ocean. In 2010 a number of crews were able to take refuge and emerge after pirates had left their ship, or when marines had taken control of the ship. One example, among many, is the rescue of the crew of the MV *BBC Orinoco* in the Indian Ocean. According to Indian reports, at about 0600 on 11 November 2010 the ship was about 450 nautical miles west of Mumbai, when it reported being attacked by pirates. According to the Indian navy's spokesman, the crew of 14 (five Ukrainian and nine Filipinos) 'locked themselves in the ship's engine room and the steering compartment and communicated with their agents, UKMTO Dubai via email'. The Indian Navy despatched, *INS Veer*, a Vidyut-class missile boat, and *INS Delhi*, a guided missile destroyer, with a team of marine commandos (MARCOS). An Indian Navy long-range maritime patrol aircraft was also deployed and the Indian coastguard was put on standby. The Indian Navy arrived at the scene at daybreak: 'MARCOS slithered onto the merchant ship from a Sea King helicopter and took the crew, who were locked in compartments, to safety, while the helicopter provided airborne fire support', according to the Indian Navy spokesperson.[3]

Each stage of the defence of the vessel must be planned and recorded, and the crew must learn the standard responses and practice regular drills.

It has been claimed that the taking by pirates of the *Beluga Nomination* in January 2011 revealed that citadels are not an effective defence, after the crew spent nearly two days in a citadel.[4] The reports are unclear, but it seems that the pirates cut through the ceiling of the citadel with a gas torch. This would indicate that the citadel may have been in the accommodation area, which is not the ideal place to locate it, and much easier to breach than a citadel located below decks. Had a warship come to the rescue at an earlier stage the use of the citadel would have been effective. It is also clear that the pirates used cutting equipment that had been on board the ship to breach the citadel, pointing to the fact that gas bottles and cutting equipment should be properly secured when transiting a high threat area.

The crew of another ship also escaped without incident, after British-flagged chemical tanker *CPO China* was boarded by pirates on 3 January 2011, about 365 nautical miles south-east of Salalah, Oman. The ship's crew of 20 took refuge in a safe area from where they had control of the ship. When men from the Australian frigate, *HMAS Melbourne*, boarded the *CPO China* the next day, the pirates had left and the crew were safe.[5] Citadels are the last means of defence, but can be very effective. As the commander of *HMS Cornwall* said, 'citadels give us options'[6]; in other words, no citadel, no naval intervention.

SETTING STANDARDS: THE ROLE OF FLAG STATES AND MARITIME ORGANIZATIONS

Seaworthy vessels

It is of vital importance that effective anti-piracy standards are established by each fleet, and that a fleet-wide policy is implemented. Effective international standards will come, but agreement will take time. As previously explained, in order to be seaworthy a ship must be fit for the purpose for which it is being used and offer reasonable safety on the high seas.

As noted above, the UK Parliament passed the Marine Insurance Act in 1906. This still governs English law and has dominated international marine insurance law over the last 100 years. The 1906 Act says that there is an implied warranty that at the start of a voyage the ship shall be seaworthy for the purpose of that voyage, and the definition of 'seaworthy' is that the ship is reasonably fit in all respects to encounter the ordinary 'perils of the seas' during that voyage. In other words, a ship must be 'fit to transit' and take measures to deal with those threats that are foreseeable during the planned voyage. The perils of the sea include pirates, rovers, thieves, and takings at sea, among other threats and dangers. This piece of legislation, which codified the established practices of the shipping industry, remains relevant today and it is on this foundation that all subsequent regulations and codes are based.

The International Safety Management Code (ISMC), which is incorporated into chapter IX of the SOLAS Convention, also requires that the shipowner 'must also make sure that it is able to respond at any time to hazards, accidents and emergencies involving its ships'.[7] It is therefore arguable that underwriters are justified in refusing claims where a vessel's crew was not trained, or the vessel was not equipped to a reasonable standard, to deal with piracy, which has normally been regarded as an ordinary peril of the sea, both under the provisions of the 1906 Act and under the provisions of the ISMC.

It is also to be expected that the IMO will at some point amend the ISMC to clarify the position on anti-piracy standards for new-build ships, and possibly even for existing vessels that transit dangerous waters. But it is likely that the IMO will act only once the insurance market and one or two flag states have acted to introduce their own standards, building on existing best management practice.

This is an area where insurers can also have an enormous influence, as can the various P&I clubs, war risk committees, national maritime organizations and international bodies. There is currently no generally accepted standard for anti-piracy protection, although some recommendations have been published, including the OCIMF's excellent 'The East Africa/Somalia situation, practical measures to avoid, deter or delay piracy attacks'.[8] One of the reasons for the slowness of response is that setting such standards for all ships is extremely difficult. The vulnerability of ships varies enormously: a fast container ship with a high freeboard, capable of travelling at over 20 knots, is in a much better situation than a laden bulk carrier, wallowing along at 10 knots, with only a three-metre freeboard, and a small crew. Tugs, cable layers and oil rigs have their own special problems, and yachts should normally be excluded from certain areas, as there is virtually nothing that can be done to protect them. In other words a lot of work will be required to establish an effective system of anti-piracy standards for all ships.

It is, however, possible for underwriters to require their own minimum standards from shipowners, with a method of dealing with different classes and types of ship. By so doing they will be developing an approach that will be further refined and eventually accepted as a general standard for the world fleet.

Codes and minimum best practice

We can see in the advice produced by OCIMF, in conjunction with the IMB, Intercargo, ICC, BIMCO, SIGTTO, INTERTANKO and IGP&I, an initial outline of the necessary steps – although much more needs to be done. In January 2010 Rear Admiral Hudson told the House of Lords:

> Our estimation is that about 70 per cent of the ships that move through the Gulf of Aden, east or west, participate in our security centre, contribute and actively engage at any one time. We have got a sizeable minority, about 30 per cent, who do not, for whatever reason, take our advice.[9]

These figures were confirmed in September 2010 by Major General Buster Howes, the operational commander of EU NAVFOR, when he said that approximately 30 per cent of owners, operators and managers were putting their ships and crews at risk off the coast of Somalia by failing to follow industry guidelines, including failure to register their vessels with MSC in Dubai prior to transiting the Gulf of Aden and by failing to provide adequate lookouts.[10] What was particularly surprising was that Buster Howes said that a significant minority of northern European-flagged, or owned, ships were not complying with the minimum standards. There is also a large gap between the vessels that meet the minimum best practice and the vessels that are fully equipped and trained to thwart pirate attacks; and it is of great importance to seafarers that the level of protection is raised across the merchant fleet. Reports from security personnel embarked on merchant ships in the area are that few ships have effective security procedures to combat piracy and that the problem of inadequate crew numbers means that watchkeepers are under great pressure. There is also a high level of fear on many vessels, and mutinies (rarely officially reported) are common among crews who do not want to transit the Gulf of Aden. The situation at the end of 2010 was that few merchant ships were fully trained and protected against piracy, a situation that the naval forces in the region were very keen to greatly improve.[11]

It also seems likely that the ISMC and the ISPS Code will both eventually be updated to include piracy, that ship's security officers will in due course be required to attend recognized anti-piracy training courses if their vessels are to transit high-risk areas, and that vessels will have to be certified as having met anti-piracy standards in the same way that they are inspected regularly for other safety requirements. Therefore, a vessel proceeding into a known piracy area would be in breach of international maritime regulations. It would not be seaworthy and its insurance cover would be invalid, hence making the shipowner personally responsible for any loss and for the payment of any ransom.

Maritime experience, going back as far as the introduction and enforcement of the Plimsoll Line, or 'load line', has shown that regulations and changes to industry practice are needed to achieve uniform safety standards. The load line was introduced to counter the unacceptable losses of ships and lives that were occurring during the nineteenth century owing to the failure of many shipowners to act prudently. There is now a need for similarly bold measures to counter the unacceptable losses caused by piracy. Let us hope that, unlike the load line, such measures are introduced swiftly.

RED LINES

The level of piracy in the Indian Ocean, Gulf of Aden and Red Sea stabilized and hijackings were much lower in 2012. In 2011, according to EU NAVFOR Somalia, 151 attacks on sizable ships were verified, with 25 vessels being successfully pirated. But in the January to November 2012 period, the number of attacks dropped to 31, with just five ships captured, the last one in May 2012.

Rear Admiral Duncan Potts, the then Operation Commander of the European Union Naval Force (EU NAVFOR), told the BBC in November 2012 that the reduction in the level of attacks was due to four factors:

- the deployment of armed private security guards on board ships who have been 100 per cent successful in deterring or defeating attacks;
- better management practice by shipping companies, such as hardening their vessels or taking evasive action;
- pre-emptive action by combined navies in the region, helping to ensure that pirates do not get out of their anchorages;
- a change in Somalia at national and local level, with Somalis far less tolerant of pirates.

However, he was under no illusion that the problem had already been solved and knew it could still return.[12] There is now an established international naval presence in the area. Navy forces, although they cannot stop piracy, have limited its impact in the Gulf of Aden and have disrupted pirate operations elsewhere in the Indian Ocean. In the last five years Somali piracy has become an established fact of life and at present no one can really imagine that Somali piracy will disappear. As noted previously, the possibility of oil finds in Puntland may force the removal of piracy from that territory, but at the time of writing piracy remained a real threat in the area.

However, acceptance of the status quo, as regards Somali piracy, is actually dependent on the situation not worsening in any significant way. There are a number of 'red lines' that, if crossed, could dramatically alter perceptions and change the way in which the international community is prepared to deal with Somalia. One example would be the hijacking of a cruise ship full of wealthy passengers; it would not be politically acceptable to leave 400 middle-class Europeans in the hands of the Somalis, whereas the world has learnt to turn away from the over 700 seamen of various nationalities held by the Somalis. Another red line would almost certainly be the massacre of the Western crew members of a ship; as there seems to be a racial element in the reaction of the international media to the plight of the mainly Asian crews held by the pirates. There was little reaction to the failure to release Indian crewmen, where the pirates have sought to bring pressure on the Indian government. A third red line would be the withdrawal of EU NAVFOR, and the rest of the international fleet, because of budget restrictions. Other red lines would include a complete ban on the payment of all ransoms, along the lines proposed by the United States, on the grounds that a proportion of most ransom payments are being paid to Al-Shabaab, or a terrorist attack on ships in the Gulf of Aden, making it impossible to distinguish between pirates and potential terrorists.

There are a number of actions that the international community could take in reaction to such game-changing events, depending on what those events are. In the event that seamen are murdered in greater numbers (and seamen have already been killed in cold blood by pirates) then greater force could be employed against pirate havens, and rules of engagement about not endangering hostages could be relaxed, because standing to one side would be shown actually to put the hostages in serious danger of death or injury. Pirate havens could be bombed and the anchor cables of hijacked vessels cut by commandos; special forces could assault captured vessels and use overwhelming force to minimize the loss of hostages' lives. Pirate leaders could be arrested by special forces; pirate supporters and investors in other countries could be hunted down and imprisoned. The links are known and international cooperation could identify and capture many of these people. In other words life could be made even more difficult for the pirates. There were signs that a more aggressive policy was being put into place in 2012, when EU NAVFOR forces attacked a pirate base near Haradhere. Bile Hussein, a pirate commander, claimed that speed boats, fuel depots and an arms store had been destroyed.[13] In December 2012, the storming of the *Iceberg 1* by Puntland forces marked an important increase in pressure on the pirates.

However, such a policy may not be cost-free: more hostages could die and ships and their cargoes might be lost. These costs would actually be significant, and that is why more aggressive policies have not been pursued to date. If ransoms could not be paid, military action to recover the crews and their ships would be the only option. The pirates could try to raise the bar by increasing the levels of violence and increasing the threats to hostages. We have already seen an escalation of violence and the exposure of hostages to greater threats. The crew of the *Samho Dream* were subject to abuse during their seven-month ordeal; Captain Kim Sung-kyu told *Yonhap News* in a phone call that the 24-member crew were living in sub-human conditions. Kim said the abuses got worse and the pirates deprived the crew of sleep and food, and then threatened to kill them one by one, if a ransom was not paid. The situation on the small ro-ro vessel MV *Iceberg 1*, hijacked just outside the port of Aden on 29 March 2010, was even worse. On 27 October 2010 the third officer, Wagdi Akram, a Yemeni and father of four, jumped overboard in a fit of dementia. His body was retrieved and stored in a freezer, wrapped in an orange plastic casing with a few bags of ice to keep it cold, the electric power having failed when the diesel for the generators ran out.[14] The ship's Yemeni captain Abdirazzak Ali Saleh told Agence France-Presse:

Diseases have appeared among crew members, some have haemorrhoids, one has lost his eyesight and another has serious stomach problems.... The water we have is unclean and we have only one meal a day, boiled rice, that's it. The crew is suffering physically and mentally.

The fact that the 24 (now 23) crew had been locked up in a space only five metres square, for nearly nine months, greatly increased their stress.[15]

For several years, Somali pirates have considered motherships an important asset. These were originally large skiffs, dhows or fishing trawlers. However, at the end of 2010 the use of hijacked merchant ships as motherships-large pirate support vessels (i.e. LPSVs)–appeared to have been adopted as standard practice. This was an important and dangerous development. The general cargo ship MV *Izumi* was used as a mothership in attacks on the MV *Torm Kansas* near Pemba Island off East Africa and then, on 6 November 2010, on the EU NAVFOR Spanish warship *ESPS Infanta Christina*, which was escorting an African Union supply ship *Petra 1*. The Spanish warship responded to fire from the MV *Izumi* by firing 'warning shots', rather than using direct fire, because hostages were aboard the vessel.[16] The MV *Izumi* was also used as a mothership in the middle of December 2010, operating in the Somali Basin about 60 degrees east.

By the end of 2010 it had become obvious that the Somalis had learnt from the failure of the *ESPS Infanta Christina* to stop the MV *Izumi* and concluded that whereas Somali-manned fishing trawlers and dhows, when used as motherships, can be easily taken or sunk by international naval forces, larger ships represent a totally different problem for the navies of the world. First, the rules of engagement of most navies preclude firing on a ship that contains hostages; second, where a ship, like the *MT Motivator*, with a cargo of lubrication oil, is used, then there could be serious environmental consequences if it were to be sunk or damaged. The use of an LPG carrier, such as MV *York*, as a mothership carries particular risks, given the potentially explosive nature of its cargo.

There are other advantages in the use of LPSVs; a large merchant ship can carry many more attack skiffs and pirates than a dhow, it normally has excellent cranes and hoists; the accommodation is relatively comfortable and the vessel has a full suite of navigation and radio aids, not to mention an effective radar. The pirates can also save money and manpower, as a separate team of guards does not have to be recruited to keep an eye on the hostage crew, and the sight of the vessel patrolling the high seas puts additional pressure on an owner reluctant to part with a ransom. There have been cases where a vessel has appeared to go to sea purely for this reason, as happened with the South Korean VLCC MV *Samho Dream*, before its release in November 2010. A VLCC is hardly the ideal mothership.

The use of LPSVs will enable pirate groups to put to sea at any time of the year, without bothering about the monsoon seasons and seek calmer areas of sea even further from the Somali coast. In this way the areas of operations could be extended well south of the equator and even east of Sri Lanka. It would also have the advantage of removing the need for pirate havens, although a secure 'support base' will remain essential. As a result we could see this form of hostage-taking adopted off other coasts, in the South China Sea and the Gulf of Guinea, which lack secure 'pirate havens'.

In this way the Somali pirates will also reduce their vulnerability to attacks from Al-Shabaab, and other Islamist groups. In May 2010 pirates abandoned their base at Xarardheere in haste, after Hizbul Islam attacked the town. Witnesses reported: 'several pirate bosses raced out of town in luxury four-by-four trucks, with TVs packed in the back and mattresses strapped on top'.[17] The relationship between pirates and Al-Shabaab has been a complex one; pirates have almost certainly paid protection money to Al-Shabaab in some situations and have been ready to pay for weapons and training. But Al-Shabaab was also a threat to pirates, when it sought to extend the territory under its control. It is also the case that the relative decline of Al-Shabaab could open new opportunities for southern Somali-based pirate groups.

We could even see the hijacking of bunkering tankers in order to refuel these new motherships, although there are reports that Somali pirates are already buying bulker fuel from the sub-continent; of course it is impossible to confirm these reports. There was, however, a report in July 2011 that Somali pirates were using the island of Socotra as a refuelling base, replenishing vessels without having to return to Somalia. It is not clear how the fuel supplies were reaching Socotra: Reuters suggested[18] that Yemeni military personnel may be selling supplies, or it is possible that the pirates were buying supplies from unscrupulous bunkering companies.

On 30 December 2010, NATO reported that the Singapore-flagged LPG carrier MV *York* was being used as a mothership,[19] as were the Panamanian-flagged 24,105 dwt chemical tanker MV *Hannibal II*,[20] the fishing boat *Shiuh Fu No 1*[21] and the Panama-flagged 72,825 dwt tanker MV *Polar*.[22] In addition the 13,065 dwt Marshall Islands-flagged chemical tanker, *MT Motivator*, had acted as mothership during the hijacking of the MV *Ems River* on 27–28 December 2010, and the 20,170 dwt Panamanian-flagged MV *Izumi* had continued its patrols under pirate control into the Arabian Sea, NATO having reported it at 06°30N 052°18E, on a course of 245° with a speed of 13 knots, on Christmas Eve. So, at the end of 2010, it was known that five sizeable merchant ships and one fishing boat were at sea, acting as motherships. In addition, various dhows and larger skiffs were deployed in the same role.

LPSVs represented a much greater threat to shipping than the earlier class of motherships and one of the key tasks of EU NAVFOR and the other international naval forces was to track their whereabouts at all times.

One red line was crossed in September 2011 when a British woman, Judith Tebbutt, from Kiwayu Safari Village on the north Kenyan coast was kidnapped by Somali pirates. This was quickly followed by the kidnapping of a disabled Frenchwoman, Marie Dedieu, from Manda Island, in the Lamu archipelago on Kenya's northern Indian Ocean coast.[23] This had a devastating effect on Kenyan tourism.

THE BIG PICTURE

This book has tried to interweave the theme of Somali piracy with the geopolitical problems of the Horn of Africa. The picture is complex, and goes far beyond the criminal activity of piracy. There is a rawness about seafaring and life in Somalia that is beyond the understanding of the ordinary person in the West. Life on board a 20-year bulk carrier can be unpleasant at the best of times; wallowing in the deep ocean, heavy laden with a cargo of Australian coal, an old, rusty and ill-equipped ship, the plating creaking in a heavy swell, as she reluctantly crests a grey and lumpy sea, and her owner faces bankruptcy because Baltic rates are so low. A far cry from the 'Dirty British coaster with a salt-caked smoke stack, Butting through the Channel in the mad March days,' described by John Mansfield.[24] Her polyglot crew, selected for their willingness to work for virtually nothing, even with 'reduced optimal manning levels', are never sure whether the ship is really seaworthy. As Veeresh Malik says 'Seafarers have always been Giffen goods, replaceable.'[25] Then low on the starboard side, there are rifle flashes and the sound of gunfire, as out of the darkness a pirate's AK-47 rakes the hull plating and shatters the glass on the bridge wing. A pirate in one of two skiffs, he and his fellows all wearing face masks, then readies a grenade launcher.

In the same way it is important to grasp the horrors that the population of Somalia face on a daily basis. It is a country in which young men, many only just in their teens, with guns can take what they want, rape women and avoid any sanction. It is a place where famine and drought is a commonplace, as the failure of the rains in 2011 demonstrated. When food aid is provided, local 'businessmen' steal it from the poorest and then sell it for their own gain. Life is too often 'nasty, brutish and short'. The Somalis are a charming people, intelligent, quick and adaptable, but they live in an appalling environment.

The problems of Somalia are further exacerbated by the fact that its territory is strategically important to its neighbours, and Western policy-makers have too often appeared determined to view it in terms of the US 'War on Terror', the danger being that this is almost a self-fulfilling prophecy. Somalia's factions are therefore supported by a number of different regional powers, each with their own agendas. The US base in Djibouti gives the United States a platform from which to monitor, and interfere in, Somalia's affairs.

If Western policy towards Somalia has often seemed to worsen the situation, the activities of its neighbours have too often deliberately aimed to enfeeble and incapacitate Somalia. In particular, Ethiopia undoubtedly believes that a strong Somali state would once more stir up trouble in the Ogden; Kenya will also have grave doubts about old Somali claims to part of its northern territories, whereas Eritrea and Egypt have interfered in order to cause problems for Ethiopia; using secret proxy campaigns, in place of open conflict. Then there is the real, although normally hidden, conflict between Iran and Israel and that between Iran and Saudi Arabia; Somalia is on the edge of this, but it has the potential to further destabilize the Horn.

Then, as if Somalia was not sufficiently damned, there came the criminal business of piracy. Modern piracy has been a well-run, well-organized business, in the main it has been controlled by a small number of men. The maritime story also reflects the dirty underbelly of the shipping industry; some ships and their crews have been abandoned by owners unwilling to pay any ransoms, although it is said that one Mediterranean man decided to pay up after a visit from the Ukrainian secret service, not an organization to cross. In some cases the shipowners have been as bad as the pirates. Somalia sees life in the raw, shorn of pretence – life and death stand close together.

FAILED STATES AND FAILED POLICIES

Predatory elements in Africa and elsewhere have hollowed out states, taking the wealth of those states for themselves and their followers, and leaving the husks for the common people. Somalia, when it still had a government, pioneered this undermining of the state. What we therefore have in Somalia is not so much a 'failed state' as the remains of a state, which lacks the structural and organizational systems to reconstitute itself. Like Shelley's 'Ozymandias', Somalia is half sunk, shattered. At conferences and during meetings in such places as Chatham House, you meet the troops of Somali politicians, waiting for someone else to sort their country out, so that they can once more take control of power. They do not readily admit to the corruption and the errors of the past, do not admit that Somali elites plundered their country without care for their countrymen; like the followers of the cargo cults of the South Seas, they wait for a solution to be parachuted out of the skies. For them the problems of Somalia are something the 'international community' must solve.

In his book *Collapse* Jared Diamond describes how the Norse colonies on Greenland died out.[26] He lays the blame in part on the behaviour of the elites, and says: 'Norse society's structure created a conflict between the short-term interests of those in power and the long-term interests of the society as a whole. Much of what the chiefs and clergy valued proved eventually harmful to the society.' When the government of Somalia sat down with the Italian mafia and agreed to the dumping of toxic substances on its territory it had abrogated its responsibility to the people of Somalia, and any moral authority that it may have had. Where elites in any society ignore the duties that their privileges in the national hierarchy have given them, then the foundations of any society are undermined, and the centre cannot hold. In the words of W.B. Yeats: 'Mere anarchy is loosed upon the world.'[27]

If Somalia is ever to enjoy a stable and effective government it will be necessary to look carefully at the relative success of Somaliland since its independence in 1991 – although strong forces remain that still wish to submerge Somaliland in the mess that is the rest of Somalia. The one force of national unity within Somalia remains the commitment of the population to Islam, and it is important for outsiders to understand that a nationalist and Islamist group will not automatically be a terrorist group. The mistreatment by Siyad Barre's government of Somaliland's clans helped Somaliland to forge its own identity, and Somalia may be able to use Islam and Somali nationalism to create a similar foundation. But it will be able to succeed only if its elites commit to being part of the solution, rather than part of the problem; this is not yet the case. It is also the case that as the elites have moved their families out of Somalia the new generation in the diaspora will inevitably become focused on life in, say, Sweden or the United States, rather than on Somalia. What is certain is that Somalia will never be able to build a stable state on a commitment to violence and that the foreign elements in Al-Shabaab are currently the largest threat to Somali society, because their fanaticism focuses on conflict elsewhere in the world, not on the needs of Somalia.

Piracy has flourished in the broken society created in Somalia, organized by elites, who are enriched by its successes. Until there is a reassertion of non-criminal values within Somali civil society piracy is likely continue to be a fact of Somali life; although, hopefully, at greatly reduced levels.

PIRACY AND THE PREDATORY STATE: THE PROBLEM OUTSIDE SOMALIA

Somalia has not been unique in Africa, or elsewhere, in being a victim of predatory elites. Many African countries offer examples of elites that choose to exploit their power for personal profit, rather than fulfil responsibilities they have undertaken to honour. The Open Society Justice Initiative (OSJI) remarked in March 2010 on the massive disparity between the incomes of elites and the average person in Equatorial Guinea. Equatorial Guinea actually has a per capita gross domestic product greater than that of Italy, South Korea, or Saudi Arabia, but most of the population is in desperate poverty, and over 60 per cent have less than $1 a day to live on. The OSJI said that Equatorial Guinea was marked by chronic hunger, a crumbling education system, frequent blackouts, poor sanitation, and disease and accused President Obiang, his family members and cronies of being responsible for massive 'spoliation' – the theft of the country's natural resources and wealth. The OSJI briefing added:

> The president and his close circle [the 'Nguema/Mongomo group'] ….
> divert to their own private benefit the overwhelming preponderance of
> revenue from Equatorial Guinea's natural resources, including its land
> and hydrocarbon resources. This gross misappropriation of the nation's
> resources has continued for well over two decades, enriching members of
> the Nguema/Mongomo group and making Equatorial Guinea an almost
> perfect kleptocracy.[28]

Another West African state with a similar name, Guinea, also has a reputation for profound corruption, something that has endeared it to drug smugglers. IRIN said in 2008 that drug traffickers were taking advantage of Guinea's poorly-staffed and ill-prepared justice system, and easily compromised public officials to transit drugs through Guinea to other West African countries, and on to Europe. Their report quoted Professor Barry Saifoulayue from Sonfonia in Conakry who said that, for the right sum, traffickers buy immunity:

> To avoid any risk of arrest or imprisonment … it is enough to have the
> protection of a high-ranking army captain who will lend his help at any

moment. That is the case with certain drug traffickers ... because no one dares arrest them.[29]

Nigeria was an early example of a predatory state, and the situation in the rest of West Africa is little better. It comes as no surprise that maritime piracy is on the increase in the Gulf of Guinea and that national navies, with the notable exception of Ghana's, appear to be unable to do anything to control the problem. Attacks off the coast of Nigeria are a commonplace and many (probably the majority) are never reported. For example, on 22 September 2010 a group of 20 armed men in three vessels took captive one Thai seaman from the *Jacson 30*, a pipe layer. On the same night three French nationals were kidnapped from the *Bourbon Alexandre*. In the same way that the breakdown of the institutions of the Somali state created an environment in which piracy could flourish, the same conditions now exist around the Gulf of Guinea; as a result, piracy off West Africa will become a much bigger problem over the next few years.

The maritime security situation in the South China Sea is also threatening. The factors that influence pirate attacks in that area are the involvement of criminal organizations in the sale of cargoes, the tradition of maritime banditry in the Philippines and Indonesia, and the inability of governments effectively to police the large number of islands in the area. Government corruption is a long-term problem, but does not yet approach West African levels. In September 2010 the IMB said that 27 pirate attacks have been reported in the South China Sea since January 2010, as opposed to only seven in the whole of 2009.[30] Although the South China Sea has what are probably the best geographical conditions in the world for piracy, with large numbers of islands, many restricted straits and frequent hiding places for pirate craft, the immediate problem for mariners, after Somalia, remains West Africa. It is possible that at some time in the future the South China Sea will reclaim its reputation as the worst pirate hot-spot.

DROUGHT AND FAMINE IN SOMALIA

Drought and famine have been a constant factor of Somali life, and the cycles of deprivation seem to worsen. When drought strikes, due to changes in the El Niño/La Niña cycles, or climate change, it affects a land with a rapidly growing population, creating Malthusian calamities. The Somali population has grown extremely rapidly since independence in 1960. In the 50-year period from 1960 to 2010 the population has grown by 331 per cent, from 2.82 million to 9.36 million (UN estimates).[31]

In the summer of 2011 the UK Disasters Emergency Committee launched an appeal for funds to aid people who were affected by the severe drought in East Africa. The BBC reported that British aid agencies were preparing to expand their activities in Somalia to help some of the 10 million people at risk of starvation in East Africa.[32]

This followed UN reports that in some parts of southern Somalia one in three children were malnourished. In August 2010, the national level of acute malnutrition was 15.2 per cent with 16.6 per cent specifically in southern regions. The Office for the Coordination of Humanitarian Affairs (OCHA) stated that rapid assessments, conducted in April 2011 in the south, confirmed that a sustained crisis existed, 'clearly illustrating the impact of the drought in the south, coupled with insufficient humanitarian assistance'. The OCHA report in June 2011 added:

Somalia is sliding deeper into crisis due to the combination of drought, increasing food prices and conflict. The eastern Horn of Africa, including Somalia, has now experienced two consecutive seasons of significantly below average rainfall, resulting in failed crop production, significant livestock mortality and record food prices.[33]

The UNHCR warned in July 2011 that high levels of malnutrition, combined with ongoing violence in the war-torn Horn of Africa nation, are threatening 'a human tragedy of unimaginable proportions'.[34]

The Dabaab refugee camp across of the border in Kenya was described by journalist Ben Brown in July 2011 as a 'vision of hell'. He said that Dabaab is more like a city than a refugee camp: it sprawls for 30 miles and its population is nearly half a million, and hungry and exhausted people are flocking to it from hundreds of miles around.[35]

Al-Shabaab opened the south of Somalia to aid agencies and in mid-July 2011 UNICEF airlifted five metric tons of emergency nutrition supplies and water-related equipment to Baidoa in southern Somalia, as part of its work to assist drought-affected children in the country. 'It was successful and it was a good step towards airlifting supplies into Somalia. It is the first in two years', said Iman Morooka, the UNICEF spokeswoman for Somalia.[36] In 2009 Al-Shabaab had expelled foreign aid groups, accusing them of being Western spies and Christian crusaders.

By 2011–12 a third of Somalia's population was dependent on aid, and one in six Somali children was acutely malnourished. It is probably true that the fishing grounds off the Somali coast, too long despoiled by foreign fleets, could be better exploited to help support the population, but, except in the irrigated river valleys of the south, agriculture in Somalia will continue to be dependent on the uncertainties of the rains. The over nine million people who currently survive in the Somali territory arguably already exceed the optimum human population that the Somali environment and economy can reasonably sustain in normal conditions, and over-population is itself one of the causes of Somalia's problems, although too long unacknowledged.

It is important to remain aware of the extreme Malthusian pressures in Somalia, and the impact they have. They do much to explain the extraordinary risks that the pirates are prepared to take, their disregard for human life and the lengths they are prepared to go to in order to force ransoms from shipowners.

WESTERN POLICIES IN THE HORN

It is a common, and erroneous, belief held by the average person that the affairs of nations and international bodies are conducted on the basis that policies are determined following a careful analysis of the facts. In practice it could be argued that two irrational tendencies actually play a large part in the affairs of nations. The first is the tendency to develop a 'grand theory' through which all situations are viewed – the 'domino theory' of communist expansion in Southeast Asia, which determined US policy in Vietnam, is one example. The second is the nature of international diplomacy, which follows an established set of instructions or rules – the 'Westphalian' system – which has an internal logic of its own and which is ill-equipped to deal with lawless or ungoverned territories.

International policy towards Somalia was therefore affected by the tendency of the United States, in the early twenty-first century, to see Islamic terrorism as the primary international problem; since 9/11 this was been the grand theory of American policy. Even the rapid rise of Chinese military power has not yet displaced this notion among US policy-makers; although in 2012 there were signs of a realignment of policy, which will doubtless become more obvious after the disengagement from Afghanistan. Because of the dominance of US military power, the UN and other Western states have generally accepted US leadership in the region, though Britain refused in April 2010 to allow the United States to add the names of well-known pirate leaders to the UN sanctions list. Britain also made it known in 2012 that it would not allow British territory, including the RAF base at Akrotiri in Cyprus and the American military facilities located on the British territory of Diego Garcia in the Indian Ocean, to be used for pre-emptive attacks on Iran by the United States.[37]

As the complexities and contradictions of Somalia defy easy solutions, international decision-makers have sought to rely on theory, or unexamined assumptions, as the basis for action. Rory Stewart, writing about Western involvement in Afghanistan, notes how, 'everyone – politicians, generals, diplomats and journalist – feels trapped by our grand theories ... powerful cultural assumptions, historical and economic forces and psychological tendencies'.[38]

Ron Suskind points to a remarkable willingness in the previous US administration to ignore facts. He describes how, in 2003, Senator Biden asked President George W. Bush: 'Mr President, how can you be so sure when you don't know the facts?' George Bush replied: 'My instincts, my instincts.' Suskind said that there was one key feature of the faith-based Bush presidency, 'Open dialogue, based on facts...[was] not seen as something of inherent value.'[39] It is not obvious that such habits of mind have entirely vanished from Washington.

Bronwyn Bruton has written of the dangers of further militarizing the international response to the Somali situation, which she says will probably accomplish little, and 'only aggravate the Somali perception that the country is under attack'.[40] Her opinions appear to be informed and practical, although, as I observed, certain Somalis did not agree with her suggestions; the fact that she is a young woman may have been partly to blame.[41]

As regards the international community's policies in Somalia, the UN and the United States, with the European Union, have long been wedded to what they referred to as the framework of the Djibouti Agreement, between the TFG and the Alliance for Re-liberation of Somalia (ARS) signed on 11 June 2008. This agreement was for long a dead letter and the TFG hung on to a small area of Mogadishu entirely due to the presence of AMISOM's force. However, the TFG was treated by foreign governments as if it actually controlled the territory of Somalia; and it sat as Somalia's representative at the UN. A UN conference in Istanbul, which took place between 21 and 23 May 2010, issued a declaration that said that the conference reflected:

the strong determination of the United Nations, the Government of Turkey and the International Community to work with the Transitional

Federal Institutions and the people of Somalia to defeat the cycle of lawlessness, violence and despair in the country and to build in its place a peaceful and prosperous future for the Somali people.

The conference welcomed the progress made by the TFG, and the TFG reaffirmed:

Its primary responsibility to provide security to the people of Somalia by increasing the number of trained Somali recruits, ensuring integration of all security forces ... and improving the control and command structure of the Somali Forces.[42]

International conferences often have a loose grasp of the facts, but these statements showed a particular failure to deal with reality.

The TFG never was worthy of support and there will be no regrets over its passing, and whatever credibility it may have had rapidly vanished, like morning mist. But because international civil servants could not afford to admit this, they continued with the subterfuge. If the situation were not so tragic it would be laughable. The many tons of American-funded arms supplied to the TFG in 2009 quickly ended up in Mogadishu's arms bazaar, arming all sides in the conflict. In discussions in London with Somalis, the best thing said about Sheikh Sharif was that he was indecisive; other comments were less flattering.

The new Somali government, which replaced the TFG in August 2012 as a result of the Garowe Process,[43] is a development that involves many of the same politicians; to expect the new government to act in a fundamentally different way is unrealistic, because the underlying dynamics of the Somali situation have not altered. The new government is also a transitional one, it was not directly elected and is based on a draft Constitution that still has to be ratified by a public referendum and the members of Parliament were selected by clan chiefs, not elected.[44] Michael Weinstein described the political environment in 2010, and nothing has fundamentally changed:

the political situation in Somalia is so complex, convoluted and fragmented that it is impossible to draw any grounded conclusions about how it will mutate. The myriad interests constituting the country's power configuration include the divided factions within the TFG, the factions of the armed Islamist opposition, Islamists outside the armed opposition with their own militias, clan families, sub-clans, regional power centers, micro-political interests at the local level, legitimate and criminal business interests, [etc.]. On the ground, some of these factions and interests form alliances with each other and then fall out, interests overlap and cross-cut, and uncertainty and distrust proliferate. Both the weak TFG and the coalition of 'stakeholders' are not driving the situation, but are enmeshed in it like all the others.[45]

Ioan Lewis, the great chronicler of modern Somalia, said of international support for the previous incarnation of the TFG: 'European arrogance in these matters is, of course, well-known and seems to flourish in direct proportion to factual ignorance. Having spent so much public money on this highly dubious project, it would also presumably be difficult to admit defeat.'[46] Unfortunately, in 2014, he was still correct.

If there is a better future for Somalia it is likely to be found in the example of Somaliland, imperfect though it is, and in an oil-enriched Puntland, which we hope has cast aside its pirate past. The south and centre of Somalia, with or without Al-Shabaab, is likely to remain a place without law, where clans, warlords, militias, foreign armies and businessmen compete for control of those assets and resources that have value – like the pieces in a perpetual chess game. I hope that I am too pessimistic.

THE GREAT GAME IN THE HORN OF AFRICA

There is now a major, but largely hidden, conflict between regional powers for hegemony over key territories in north-east Africa, including the Horn, in the Arabian Peninsula and the waters between them. The Red Sea is the subject of an undeclared conflict between Saudi Arabia, Egypt and Iran. There is a further potential conflict, for control of the headwaters of the Nile, between Egypt and Ethiopia, which has the potential to spill over into the new state of South Sudan. In addition, there are also subordinate conflicts for the control of southern Arabia and the Horn. On the basis that my enemy's enemy is my friend, the Gaddafi regime in Libya sought to become involved in the region to counteract the influence of Egypt, its main adversary in North Africa. By the same token, Eritrea aligned itself with Ethiopia's enemy Egypt and with Iran. The late Meles Zenawi, when Ethiopian prime minister, announced that he would support Eritrean rebels to overthrow the regime in Asmara. It seems that Ethiopia is still keen to regain a port on the Red Sea, possibly Assab at the southern end of the Red Sea.

Israel has also projected its naval forces south into the Red Sea, used its air force to bomb Sudan, and even sent submarines into the Persian Gulf. Given that Israel publicly regards Iran as its main adversary, then like Iran it will doubtless seek to disguise most of its activities, or even undertake 'false flag' actions designed to discredit Iran. In this area lie and counter-lie serve to confuse what is already an incredibly complex picture.

None of the major regional powers involved appears willing to show any restraint in the aggressive, and secretive, execution of their policies. For example, it appears that Saudi Arabia interferes in the affairs of Ethiopia, Somalia, and Yemen. The United States, although weakened by the heavy financial toll of the Iraqi and Afghan conflict, and with growing doubts about its ability to maintain its previous global political and economic dominance, is seen as still the most effective actor in the region. Arguably the region increasingly resembles Europe in the period before the First World War: there is actual conflict in Somalia and Yemen, active aggression on the borders of Ethiopia and Eritrea, great concern over the division of Sudan and Egypt's interest in Nile water, clandestine support for Sunni Islamic groups by Saudi Arabia, and the promotion of its version of Islam. Even states that are currently peaceful, like Oman, Qatar and the United Arab Emirates, could be unwillingly engulfed in these struggles, and foreign players, including Pakistan and its partner China, together with India and Russia, all have interests in the region (which in geopolitical terms stretches from the White Nile east to the Arabian Sea, and from the Suez Canal south to the Mozambique Channel) and will wish to play their roles.

None of this is good news for weaker states, such as Yemen and Eritrea; that are likely to become the cockpits in which future conflict is played out. Somalia will almost certainly continue to be affected by the complex and deep-rooted intra-state conflicts.

Of the states involved, Israel and Pakistan already have nuclear weapons, and Prince Turki al-Faisal of Saudi Arabia said in June 2011 that if Iran develops nuclear weapons then Saudi Arabia would be compelled to, 'to pursue policies which could lead to untold and possibly dramatic consequences'.[47] Egypt, like Turkey, also has the industrial potential to copy Iran. Turkey is quietly exploring the necessary nuclear technology. Egypt, which stopped its first military nuclear programme in 1973, and has up until now maintained that the whole Middle East should be a nuclear-free area, could change its mind.

Israel, which has around 200 nuclear warheads, has shown no sign of even discussing nuclear disarmament, and in April 2010 refused to participate in a nuclear security summit in Washington DC, organized by President Barack Obama. If there is to be a nuclear-free Iran, as it now appears likely in the light of the Geneva interim agreement, or the Joint Plan of Action, signed on 24 November 2013, it would seem logical that this is in the context of a nuclear-free Middle East that includes Israel. This of course will not happen.

The pressures are now also building up on natural resources. Egypt's fast-growing population is completely dependent on the waters of the Nile, water that Ethiopia and Sudan could undoubtedly use more effectively. Saudi Arabia is afraid that its crude oil production will soon decline; a report by Citicorp has even suggested that Saudi Arabia could cease to export crude oil by 2030.[48] Iran, with its growing population is, with Egypt, one of the largest importers of grain in the world.

The medium-term outlook is poor: the threat does not come from terrorists, who are frequently the secretive infantry of a foreign power, and enable the deniable use of force against a neighbouring state, but from intra-state conflict. Like the tectonic plates that lock the continents together, the once stable states of the region are being forced to move under the influence of immense pressures; these tensions will in turn release great destructive energy, and the landscape of the region will be brutally reworked. The Arab Spring of 2011 marks only the beginning of a period of extraordinary changes.

In such a chaotic environment piracy may continue to operate from places on the margin of the region, but Puntland's interest in oil means that for the first time in the last decade we may be seeing a decline in its influence in Somalia.

WHAT HOPE FOR THE SOMALIAS OF THE WORLD?

This book has looked in some details at the problems of Somalia, the political and social background and the role of Somali elites in taking control of the resources of the state. There have also been questions about the effects of policies based on the paradigm of the 'War on Terror', quoting with approval Hoehne's observation about the 'binary logic' of conflict between the United States and its opponents.

In all honesty it is not clear how the international community can do anything to help Somalia, but it does have the power to make things much worse. The idea that Western governments can walk into a country and make it democratic is a nonsense that has died a death in the deserts of Iraq and the mountains of Afghanistan: George Bush's instincts were wrong. The United States had an earlier experience in Mogadishu in 1993 that convinced it for a time that it should not get involved in countries like Somalia; it relearned the lesson in 2003 in Iraq, and is still relearning it in Afghanistan. The Libyan intervention in 2011 has yet to create stability, and the international powers have no clear ideas on how to deal with the growing sectarian conflicts in Syria and Iraq.

We live in a far more dangerous and difficult world today than the one we inhabited before 9/11. The historians of the future will doubtless look with amazement at the follies of the financial markets, the failure adequately to regulate and control the banks and hedge funds, and at the invasions of Iraq and Afghanistan. They will find it virtually impossible to understand how apparently intelligent people made such a series of basic mistakes, and that, as a result, the United States so rapidly undermined its position in the world, thus opening up the multi-polar world, described by Dilip Hiro, in which no one power has the global authority the United States, until recently, took for granted.[49]

However, human folly, although it is undoubtedly a factor in the affairs of states, is not the only thing that influences the course of history. There is now an intersection of forces – resource depletion, impending food shortages, over-population, and the impact of climate change – that, taken together with the crisis of confidence in the capitalist model of development, means that the shape of the world in the next few years will be very different from the world at the end of the twentieth century. There is not the will to help states in difficulty, and increasingly there will not be the capacity. As the financial crisis led to riots on the streets of Dublin and Athens, and higher food prices threaten hunger in the developing world, while Mexican violence and instability represent a growing threat to the United States, no votes will be gained for sorting out Somalia, the Congo or Guinea. These territories will increasingly be left to sink, or swim, unless they have oil. We have seen how the horrors in the Congo continued without resolution for many years, despite the deaths of millions; while foreign soldiers illegally took Congolese minerals and other natural resources – in the words of the International Court of Justice, 'looting, plundering'.[50] The plundering of the Congo's abundant natural resources created a self-perpetuating system of violence, as the profits of looting pay for conflict, which in turn facilitates plunder. There is no end in sight.

As most navies of the world shrink in size, the world's merchant fleets will need to become more resilient and better able to cope with the ever-growing menace of piracy, one of the few growth industries of the twenty-first century, if not off Somalia, then in other areas.

WE DEPEND ON THE SEA

This book was mainly written in London, one of the great cities of the world – no longer the largest, but a crossroads of cultures and people. London is virtually completely dependent, like the rest of Britain, on the sea. Britain is too densely populated an island to be able to feed itself; it sits at the intersection of great trade routes with goods and materials bought to it from every corner of the Earth. John Maynard Keynes described this situation, when writing about London, just before the First World War, when he said:

> The inhabitant of London could order by telephone, sipping his morning tea in bed, the various products of the whole earth, in such quantity as he might see fit, and reasonably expect their early delivery upon his doorstep; he could at the same moment and by the same means adventure his wealth in the natural resources and new enterprises of any quarter of the world, and share, without exertion or even trouble, in their prospective fruits and advantages ... But, most important of all, he regarded this state of affairs as normal, certain, and permanent, except in the direction of further improvement, and any deviation from it as aberrant, scandalous, and avoidable.[51]

Like the Londoner of July 1914, we regard the state of affairs we have become accustomed to as 'normal, certain, and permanent.'[52] However, nothing in life is certain, as the British found when soon after, on 4 August 1914, the Kaiser marched his troops into Belgium, and Britain declared war on Germany.

Piracy and predatory states, who support piracy by deceit, are a real threat to maritime lines of communication, to the supply of the 'various products of the whole earth'.[53] As any student of the Royal Navy knows, the survival of Britain has at many times been due to the ability of the navy to protect the country's essential lines of communication. In the twenty-first century, this is likely to be proven to be the case once more, and not just for Britain. In times of increasing uncertainty there will be a greater need for maritime security.

PIRACY IS A MANIFESTATION OF CHANGE

As hopefully this book has demonstrated, piracy does not arise just because the geography of an area is suitable; piracy, as seen off Somalia, is a complex organized criminal activity that requires investment and the involvement of political and business elites; it is not driven by the actions of a few fishermen. The Somali model of holding ships and their crews for ransoms requires safe havens and the acquiescence, or active support, of those groups that control the territories where the ships are held. In fact, in Puntland we saw the emergence of the first modern pirate state, a contemporary version of the Barbary Coast, which has now, hopefully, passed into history, as the oil industry develops.

We now stand at a crossroads, from where the global economy may decline, driven by the forces of over-population, resource shortages, climate change and the failure of the international financial system, or from which it will recover, probably on the back of the development of new low carbon technologies and sustainable methods of production of food and manufactures. My own guess is that things will get much worse, at least over the next 20 years, when hopefully a new balance will be created. In this time of chaos we are therefore likely to see further pressures on established states and the spread of predatory forms of control. In these conditions the extension of piracy will be a manifestation of change and a sign of the collapse of established systems of governance: it is the litmus paper of political failure.

A darker period in our history now seems preordained, no matter what we do. Somalia is a warning of what happens when nations fragment and the basest elements take control; we need to learn from this sad experience. Piracy is not about Somalia itself, it is really about human beings trying to exist in a world where they have nothing, where greed is the only guide, and there are no restraints.

It is too early to be optimistic, but two recent developments in Somalia raise the real possibility of an improvement in the country's position. Firstly, as noted above, the prospect of oil discoveries in Puntland have already lead to the development of counter-piracy forces; and, secondly, the decline in Al-Shabaab's position means that the replacement body for the TFG has a greater chance of success than seemed the case in 2011.

Our ships will become more resilient, protected against bullets and grenades, and the rules of engagement given to naval vessels will be much tougher; together with attacks on pirate bases, this will manage, if not remove, the problem. Piracy is now on the increase in the South China Sea and the Gulf of Guinea, and could emerge in South America and the Caribbean. Europe, North America and the more fortunate areas of the world will raise ever higher the barriers to refugees and migrants from famine and conflict. The cargoes of grain and oil will continue to flow past the failed states where hope has died; along the embattled supply lines. The resources of such territories will also continue to flow, managed by predatory elites, their populations excluded from the wealth created.

Most books on piracy end with a few lines recommending a simple 'solution', often based on the re-creation of the Somali state. I apologize for this bleak vision of the future, but for the next generation I believe this is a realistic outlook. We have to face up to the problem. In fact, it seems that Somali piracy has seen its glory days, and is now in decline, but the problem has not gone away. In October 2013 Reuters reported that 'Pirate attacks off Nigeria's coast have jumped by a third this year with ships passing through West Africa's Gulf of Guinea, a major commodities hub, increasingly under threat from gangs wanting to snatch cargoes and crews.'[54] Reuters also reported in November 2013 that 'On November 7, pirates hijacked a tanker carrying marine gasoil in the strait near Pulau Kukup, Malaysia, and stole its cargo before the ship and crew were released. It was the second hijacking in waters around Singapore this year after an attack on a Thai-registered tanker laden with gasoil near Pulau Aur, Malaysia, in the South China Sea on October 10.' We cannot afford to be complacent.[55]

We need to understand that international crime, of which piracy is but a part, threatens the well-being of us all, and that where it is trimphant we face the dangers foreseen by the English philosopher Thomas Hobbes, who had experienced the struggles of the English Civil War:

[W]here every man is enemy to every man, the same consequent to the time wherein men live without other security than what their own strength and their own invention shall furnish them withal. In such condition there is no place for industry, because the fruit thereof is uncertain: and consequently no culture of the earth; no navigation, nor use of the commodities that may be imported by sea; no commodious building; no instruments of moving and removing such things as require much force; no knowledge of the face of the earth; no account of time; no arts; no letters; no society; and which is worst of all, continual fear, and danger of violent death; and the life of man, solitary, poor, nasty, brutish, and short.[56]

He could have been writing about modern Somalia.

NOTES

1 PIRACY: THE BACKGROUND

1 David Anderson, 'Somali piracy: historical context, political contingency', *European Security Forum Working Paper no. 33* (December 2009), CEPS, Brussels, www.ceps.eu (also published in *Readings in European Security*, 6 (2010), p. 4).

2 Marten Scheffer, *Critical Transitions in Nature and Society*, Princeton and Oxford: Princeton University Press, 2009, pp. 11–17.

3 Ibid., p. 23.

4 Ibid., p. 23.

5 Mohamed Ahmed, 'Somali sea gangs lure investors at pirate lair', *Reuters*, 1 December 2009.

6 Ibid.

7 'Travel and tourism in Somalia', *Euromonitor*, Report, April 2009.

8 'Pirate cash suspected cause of Kenya property boom', *The New York Times*, 1 January 2010.

9 David Randall, 'Somali pirates seize British super-freighter', *The Independent*, 3 January 2010.

10 David Anderson, 'Somali piracy: historical context, political contingency', *European Security Forum Working Paper no. 33* (December 2009), CEPS, Brussels, www.ceps.eu (also to be published in *Readings in European Security*, 6 (2010), p. 4).

11 http://janenovak.wordpress.com/2008/08/28/corruption-triggers-media-repression-in-yemen/.

12 http://www.icc-ccs.org/piracy-reporting-centre/piracynewsafigures, 13 January 2013.

13 'Somali pirate king-pin "Afweyne" retires', AFP 10 January 2013, http://www.news24.com/Africa/News/Somali-pirate-king-pin-Afweyne-retires-20130110.

2 THE POLITICAL DEVELOPMENT OF SOMALIA

1 I.M. Lewis, *A Modern History of the Somali*, 4th edn, Oxford: James Currey, 2002, p. 2.

2   Christian Webersik, 'Fighting for the plenty – The banana trade in southern Somalia', Paper presented to the Conference on Multinational Corporations, Development and Conflict, Queen Elizabeth House, Oxford, 6 December 2003, p. 6.

3   I.M. Lewis, *A Modern History of the Somali*, 4th edn, Oxford: James Currey, 2002, p. 3.

4   Ibid., pp. 4–7.

5   Ibid., p. 8.

6   Ibid., p. 11.

7   Ibid., p. 15.

8   Ibid., p. 16.

9   I.M. Lewis, *Understanding Somalia and Somaliland'*, London: Hurst & Company, 2008, p. 22.

10 Bruce Leimsidor, *Conflict in Somalia: International Migration Ramifications*, Università Ca' Foscari, Venezia: DEP, 2009, pp. 3–4.

11 F.L. James, *The Unknown Horn of Africa, An Exploration from Berbera to the Leopard River*, London: George Philip & Son, 1888, pp. 2–3.

12 I.M. Lewis, *A Modern History of the Somali*, 4th edn, Oxford: James Currey, 2002, pp. 41–4.

13 Ibid., p. 43.

14 Ibid., pp. 49–51.

15 I.M. Lewis, *Understanding Somalia and Somaliland*, London: Hurst & Company, 2008, pp. 124–5.

16 Ibid., p. 34.

17 Ibid., p. 35.

18 Basil Davidson, *The Search for Africa: History, Culture, Politics*, London: Times Books, 1994, p. 284.

19 William Shakespeare, *Macbeth*, Act 5, Scene 8, line 68.

20 Ruth Gordon, 'Growing constitutions', *Journal of Constitutional Law*, Vol. 1:3 (1999), p. 574.

21 I.M. Lewis, *A Modern History of the Somali*, 4th edn, Oxford: James Currey, 2002, p. 107.

22 I.M. Lewis, *Understanding Somalia and Somaliland*, London: Hurst & Company, 2008, p. 38.

23 By 1975, 50 per cent of the SRC's members were Darod; in 1976 it was dissolved, being replaced by the Somali Socialist Party. I.M. Lewis, *A Modern History of the Somali*, 4th edn, Oxford: James Currey, 2002, p. 107.

24 Wolfgang Achtner, 'The Italian connection: How Rome helped ruin Somalia', *Washington Post*, 24 January 1993.

25 Ismail I. Ahmed and Reginald Herbold Green, 'The heritage of war and state collapse in Somalia and Somaliland: Low-level effects, external interventions and reconstruction', *Third World Quarterly*, Vol. 20, No. 1 (1999), p. 118.

NOTES

26 I.M. Lewis, *Understanding Somalia and Somaliland*, London: Hurst & Company, 2008, p. 66.

27 *Somalia, A Government at War with its Own People*, New York: The African Watch Committee, 1990, p. 34.

28 Ibid., p. 31.

29 Ibid., p. 43.

30 A segmentary lineage society is characterized by the organization of the society into segments; this is frequently also called a tribal society.

31 I.M. Lewis, *Understanding Somalia and Somaliland*, London: Hurst & Company, 2008, pp. 71–2.

32 Martin Meredith, *The State of Africa: A History of 50 Years of Independence*, London: The Free Press, 2006, ch. 26, 'Black Hawk Down', p. 469.

33 *Somalia: A Government at War with its Own People*, New York: Africa Watch Committee, January 1990.

34 'In 1998, *Famiglia Cristiana*, an Italian weekly magazine, claimed that although most of the waste-dumping took place after the start of the civil war in 1991, the activity actually began as early as 1989 under the Barre government.' Najad Abdullahi, 'Toxic waste behind Somali piracy', *Al Jazeera*, 11 October 2008, http://english.aljazeera.net/news/afri ca/2008/10/2008109174223218644.html.

35 Jean-François Bayart, Stephen Eillis and Béatrice Hibou, *The Criminalization of the State in Africa*, Oxford: James Currey and Indianapolis: Indiana University Press, 1999, p. xv.

36 Ibid.

37 William Reno, 'Sovereign predators and non-state armed group protectors?', presented at Curbing Human Rights Violations of Armed Groups, UBC Centre of International Relations, 13–15 November 2003, p. 12.

38 United Nations Development Programme, *Somalia Human Development Report*, New York: United Nations, 2001, p. 42.

39 George B.N. Ayittey, 'The Somali crisis, time for an African solution', CATO Policy Analysis No. 205, 28 March 1994, www.cato.org/pubs/pas/pa-205.html.

40 Christian Webersik, 'Fighting for the plenty – The banana trade in southern Somalia', Paper presented to the Conference on Multinational Corporations, Development and Conflict, Queen Elizabeth House, Oxford, 6 December 2003, p. 4.

41 Dustin Dehérez, 'The scarcity of land in Somalia, natural resources and their role in the Somali conflict', Bonn International Center for Conversion, April 2009, Bonn, Germany.

42 Meeting at Chatham House, London, 28 October 2009: www.chathamhouse.org.uk/files/ 15071_281009sharmarke.pdf. I questioned the prime minister during this meeting and he confirmed that the TFG regarded the pre-1991 borders of Somalia as still valid.

43 Catherine Besteman, 'Genocide in Somalia's Jubba Valley and Somali Bantu refugees in the US', *SSRC*, 9 April 2007, http://hornofafrica.ssrc.org/Besteman/.

44 *Report of the Monitoring Group on Somalia and Eritrea*, S/2011/433, New York: The United Nations, July 2011, p. 16.

45 Bronwen Maddox, 'America counts the cost of going to war', *The Times*, 29 March 2010.

46 I.M. Lewis, *Understanding Somalia and Somaliland*, London: Hurst & Company, 2008, p. 76.

47 Mark Bowden, *Black Hawk Down: A Story of Modern War*, New York: Atlantic Monthly Press, 1999.

48 Ibid., p. 80.

49 Abdi Ismail Samatar and Ahmed I. Samatar, *Bildhaan*, vol. 5.

50 Bronwyn E. Bruton, 'Somalia, a new approach', Council for Foreign Relations, Special Report No. 52, March 2010, Washington DC, p. 7.

51 I.M. Lewis, *Understanding Somalia and Somaliland*, London: Hurst & Company, 2008, p. 91.

52 'Somalia: An opportunity that should not be missed', International Crisis Group, Africa Briefing No. 87, Nairobi and Brussels, 22 February 2012, p. 3.

53 Napoleon A. Bamfo, 'Ethiopia's invasion of Somalia in 2006: Motives and lessons learned', *African Journal of Political Science and International Relations*, Vol. 4(2) (February 2010), p. 60.

54 The USAF also uses a later model A-130 gunship the A-130U Spooky, but the indications are that the AC-130H was based in Djibouti in 2006–7.

55 Karen DeYoung, 'US strike in Somalia targets Al-Qaeda figure', *Washington Post*, 9 January 2007, www.washingtonpost.com/wp-dyn/content/article/2007/01/08/AR200701 0801635.html.

56 Daveed Gartenstein-Ross, 'America's boots on the ground in Somalia', 9 January 2007, http://counterterrorismblog.org/mt/pings.cgi/3529.

57 Stephanie McCrummen, 'US troops went into Somalia after raid', *Washington Post*, 12 January 2007, www.washingtonpost.com/wp-dyn/content/article/2007/01/11/ AR2007011102329.html.

58 'Aden Hashi Ayro', *The Times*, 21 May 2008.

59 Ibid.

60 Ann Talbot, 'Washington admits role in illegal war: US troops took part 1', *Garre Forum*, 17 January 2007, http://garreonline.com.

61 'Sheikh Shariif sets conditions to release 11 US soldiers seized in Somalia', *kavkazcenter.com*, 1 February 2007, www.kavkazcenter.com.

62 Jeffrey Gettleman, 'US strikes inside Somalia, bombing suspected militant hide-out', *The New York Times*, 3 June 2007, www.nytimes.com/2007/06/03/world/africa/03somalia.html.

63 '"Why am i still here?" The 2007 Horn of Africa renditions and the fate of those still missing', *Human Rights Watch* (October 2008), p. 13.

64 Ibid., p. 11.

65 *Routinely Targeted, Attacks on Civilians in Somalia*, London: Amnesty International, 2008, AFR 52/009/2008, pp. 9–10.

66 Mohammed Ibrahim and Jeffrey Gettleman, 'Strategic Somali Town Is Seized by Ethiopians', *The New York Times*, 31 December 2011.

67 'Somalia al-Shabab militant base of Baidoa captured', BBC, 22 February 2012 http://www.bbc.co.uk/news/world-africa-17127353.

68 'African Union, Somali troops capture Shebab stronghold', 10 December 2012, *The Nation*, Lahore, Pakistan, http://www.nation.com.pk/pakistan-news-newspaper-daily-english-online/international/10-Dec-2012/african-union-somali-troops-capture-shebab-stronghold.

69 Jeffrey Gettleman, 'US aiding Somalia in its plan to retake its capital', *The New York Times*, 5 March 2010.

70 Testimony by Ted Dagne, Congressional Research Service, 'The Horn of Africa: Current conditions and US policy', before the Subcommittee on Africa and Global Health, House Foreign Affairs Committee, 17 June 2010, Washington DC, p. 3.

71 Markus Virgil Hoehne, *Counter-Terrorism in Somalia: How External Interference Helped to Produce Militant Islamism*, Halle/Saale, Germany: Max Planck Institute for Social Anthropology, 2009, pp. 2–3.

72 Ibid., p. 26.

73 Ibid.

74 'UN envoy urges Somalis to finalize list of new parliamentarians', UN News Centre, 25 August 2012, www.un.org/apps/news/story.asp?NewsID=42,740&Cr=somalia&Cr1.

75 Jason Mosley, 'End of the Roadmap: Somalia after the London and Istanbul Conferences', Africa Programme Paper AFP PP2012/04, Chatham House, London, June 2012, p. 2.

76 *UN Monitoring Group on Somalia and Eritrea*, S/2012/544, preliminary draft (advanced copy) dated 27 June 2012, p. 5.

77 'World Report 2011: Somalia', *Human Rights Watch*, 2011, www.hrw.org/en/world-report-2011/somalia.

78 Rashid Abdi and Ernest Jan Hogendoorn, 'It's not too late to rescue Somali Islamists from the jihadis who have hijacked them', *The East African*, 2 May 2010, www.hiiraan.com/print2_op/2010/may/it_s_not_too_late_to_rescue_somali_islamists_from_the_jihadis_who_have_hijacked_them.aspx.

79 *Report of the Monitoring Group pursuant to Security Council Resolution 1853 (2008)*, S/2010/91, 26 February 2010, Matt Bryden, coordinator, p. 6.

80 'Somalia: Fistfight in Somali parliament over speaker election', *AllAfrica.com*, 5 January 2012, http://allafrica.com/stories/201201051340.html.

81 Security Council, 6729th Meeting, SC/10566, UN Department of Public Information, News and Media Division, New York, USA, 5 March 2012.

82 The International Crisis Group, 'Somalia: the Transitional Government on life support', Africa Report No. 170, Brussels, Belgium, 21 February 2011, p. 3.

83 Ibid., p. 3.

84 Security Council, 6729th Meeting, SC/10566, UN Department of Public Information, News and Media Division, New York, USA, 5 March 2012.

85 Jeffrey Gettleman, 'A taste of hope in Somalia's battered capital', *The New York Times*, 3 April 2012.

86 UN Monitoring Group 2012, ibid., p. 14.

87 Ibid.

88 UN Monitoring Group, 10 March 2010, p. 7.

89 Ibid., p. 49.

90 'US gives Somalia about 40 tons of arms, ammunition', *Reuters*, 27 June 2009.

91 *Report of the Monitoring Group pursuant to Security Council Resolution 1853 (2008)*, S/2010/91, 26 February 2010, Matt Bryden, coordinator, p. 54.

92 Andre Le Sage, 'Somalia: Sovereign disguise for a Mogadishu Mafia', *Review of African Political Economy*, vol. 29, no. 91 (March 2002), p. 134.

93 Ibid., p. 136.

94 Ibid., p. 136.

95 Bank of England, Bank of Scotland, Royal Bank of Scotland, Clydesdale Bank, Bank of Ireland, First Trust Bank, Northern Bank and Ulster Bank.

96 Ibid., pp. 137–8.

97 Barney Jopson, 'China wins permit to look for oil in Somalia', *Financial Times*, 14 July 2007.

98 Mark Fineman, 'The oil factor in Somalia', *Los Angeles Times*, 18 January 1993.

99 Katrina Manson, Somalia deal raises concerns about oil risks, *Financial Times*, 12 August 2013, http://www.ft.com/intl/cms/s/0/b9fd1418-034d-11e3-b871-00144feab7 de.html#axzz2i936k4TB.

100 'Kilimanjaro to Assume Pivotal Role in Somalia Oil Project', *Wall Street Journal*, 30 September 2013, http://online.wsj.com/article/PR-CO-20130930-904849.html?mod= googlenews_wsj.

101 'Troubled Somalia hustles Big Oil to resume exploration', *UPI*, 16 October 2013 http://www.upi.com/Business_News/Energy-Resources/2013/10/16/Troubled-Somalia-hustles-Big-Oil-to-resume-exploration/UPI-31691381942688/#ixzz2i91wiKNK.

102 *UN Security Counctil Report pursuant to resolutions 751 (1992) and 1907 (2009) concerning Somalia and Eritrea* 12 July 2013, S/2013/413, New York, p. 25.

103 'Somalia–Chinese engagement', US Embassy Nairobi, 12 February 2010, published by WikiLeaks.

104 Ibid.

105 *Report of the Monitoring Group pursuant to Security Council Resolution 1853 (2008)*, S/2010/91, 26 February 2010, Matt Bryden, coordinator, p. 7.

106 Jaco Maritz, 'Running a thriving money transfer business from Somalia', *howwemadeitinafrica.com*, 5 October 2010, www.howwemadeitinafrica.com/running-a-thriving-money-transfer-business-from-somalia/4118/.

107 'Somalia calling: An unlikely success story', *Economist*, 20 December 2005.

108 *Report of the Monitoring Group pursuant to Security Council Resolution 1853 (2008)*, S/2010/91, 26 February 2010, Matt Bryden, coordinator, p. 33.

109 Ibid., p. 34.

110 Ibid., p. 35.

111 *Weekly Humanitarian Bulletin*, Issue 47 (26 November–3 December 2010), UNOCHA Somalia.

112 *Hard News, Journalists' Lives in Danger in Somalia,* London: Amnesty International, 2010, p. 8.

113 Will Ross, 'EU hopes new recruits can shore up Somalia's defences', *BBC News,* 5 October 2010, www.bbc.co.uk/news/world-africa-11475551.

114 Katharine Houreld, 'Unpaid Somali soldiers desert to insurgency', *Associated Press,* 27 April 2010.

115 The International Crisis Group, 'Somalia: The Transitional Government on life support', Africa Report No. 170, Brussels, Belgium, 21 February 2011, p. 3.

116 Rt. Hon. William Hague, MP, foreign secretary UK, 'A new effort to help Somalia', Chatham House, 8 February 2012, p. 4.

117 Mohammed Ibrahim, 'Somalia selects an activist as leader', *The New York Times,* 10 September 2012.

118 'Outsider Hassna Mohamud wins Somali presidential race', *Agence France Presse English Wire,* 10 September 2012.

119 'Somalia: UN officials condemn attack on hotel during new president's press conference', UN News Centre, 12 September 2012, www.un.org/apps/news/story.asp?News ID=42870&Cr=somalia&Cr1=#.UFF9MlFciSo.

120 Tristan McConnell, 'Al-Shabaab branches out beyond Somalia', *Global Post,* 10 September 2012, www.globalpost.com/dispatch/news/regions/africa/120907/al-qaeda-al-shabaab-somalia?page=0,1.

121 *Report of the Secretary-General on Somalia,* S/2012/643, 22 August 2012, New York, p. 15.

122 Helen Epstein, 'Cruel Ethiopia', *New York Review of Books,* 13 May 2010.

123 *So Much to Fear, War Crimes and the Devastation of Somalia,* Washington DC, Human Rights Watch, 2008, p. 58.

124 Ibid, p. 62.

125 'Ethiopia: Insecurity threatens oil', *Africa Research Bulletin: Economic, Financial and Technical Series,* vol. 44, Issue 10 (December 2007), pp. 17587B–C.

126 'Ethiopia: Ethnic federalism and its discontents', The International Crisis Group, Brussels, Africa Report No. 153, 4 September 2009, p. 32.

127 Gregory R. Copley, 'Energy and security issues in the Red Sea transforming as "the Age of Gas" begins in earnest', *OilPrice.com,* 19 August 2010 (email).

128 Ibid.

129 Colonel Yusuf died in Dubai in March 2012.

130 Kareen Fahim, 'Yemen: Defiant commander gives up', *The New York Times,* 25 April 2012.

131 Wikileaks, US Embassy Sanaa, REF: SANAA 01549, cable 15 September 2009, 'SUBJECT: BRENNAN-SALEH MEETING SEP 6, 2009'.

132 Dominic Rushe, Chris McGreal, Jason Burke and Luke Harding, 'Anwar al-Awlaki death: US keeps role under wraps to manage Yemen fallout', 30 September 2011, *Guardian,* www.guardian.co.uk/world/2011/sep/30/anwar-al-awlaki-yemen.

133 'Yemen', *The New York Times,* 21 May 2012, http://topics.nytimes.com/top/news/internati onal/countriesandterritories/yemen/index.html.

134 Adam Baron and Richard Spencer, 'Al-Qaeda kills nearly 100 soldiers in Yemen attack', *The Daily Telegraph*, 21 May 2012.

135 Ronald K. McMullen, 'Bio notes on Eritrean President Isaias Afwerki – Is Isaias unhinged?', US Embassy Asmara, 12 November 2008, published by WikiLeaks.

136 Ronald K. McMullen, 'Eritrea's squabbling colonels, fleeing footballers, frightened librarians', US Embassy Asmara, 15 December 2009, published by WikiLeaks.

137 'Security Council imposes sanctions on Eritrea over its role in Somalia', UN Security Council, New York, SC/9833, 23 December 2009, www.un.org/News/Press/docs/2009/sc9833.doc.htm.

138 *Report of the Monitoring Group on Somalia pursuant to Security Council Resolution 1853 (2008)*, S/2010/91, New York: United Nations, 10 March 2010, p. 21.

139 Ibid., p. 23.

140 Mark Tran, 'Somalia conference is a turning point, says Cameron', *Guardian*, 23 February 2012.

141 Ibid.

142 Christopher Clapham, 'Rethinking African states', *African Security Review* 10 (3) (2001), p. 13.

143 Ibid., p. 14.

144 Ibid., p. 15.

145 Julian Borger and Mark Tran, 'UN votes to increase Somalia peacekeeping force', *Guardian*, 22 February 2012.

146 Ibid.

147 William Reno, *Corruption and State Politics in Sierra Leone*, Cambridge: Cambridge University Press, 1995, p. 188.

148 Tacitus, *The Annals of Imperial Rome* (trs. Michael Grant), London: Penguin Books, 1996, p. 353.

149 *Al-Qa'ida's (Mis)Adventures in the Horn of Africa*, Combating Terrorism Center: West Point, 2007, p. iii.

150 Ibid., pp. iii and iv.

151 Patrick Chabal and Jean-Pascal Daloz, *Africa Works: Disorder as Political Instrument*, Oxford: The International African Institute in association with James Currey, 1999, p. 16.

152 Ibid., p. 85.

3 STATELESS TERRITORIES AND CLANDESTINE NETWORKS

1 Lorenzo I. Bordonaro, 'Introduction: Guinea-Bissau today – The irrelevance of the state and the permanence of change', *African Studies Review*, vol. 52, no. 2 (September 2009), p. 37.

2 Patrick Chabal and Jean-Pascal Daloz, *African Works: Disorder as Political Instrument*, Oxford: International African Institute in association with James Currey, 1999, p. 16.

3   Lorenzo I. Bordonaro, 'Introduction: Guinea-Bissau today – The irrelevance of the state and the permanence of change', *African Studies Review*, vol. 52, no. 2 (September 2009), p. 36.

4   Ibid., p. 37.

5   Ian Taylor, 'Conflict in central Africa: Clandestine networks and regional/global configurations', *Review of African Political Economy*, no. 95 (2003), p. 46.

6   Christopher Clapham, 'The global–local politics of state decay', in Robert I. Rotberg (ed.), *When States Fail, Causes and Consequences*, Princeton: Princeton University Press, 2004, pp. 77–9.

7   Peter Eichstaedt, *Pirate State*, Chicago: Lawrence Hill Books, 2009, p. 109.

8   Andre Le Sage, 'Stateless justice in Somalia, formal and informal rule of law initiatives', July 2005 Report, Centre for Humanitarian Dialogue, Geneva, Switzerland, 2005, pp. 32–3.

9   Ibid., p. 33.

10   I.M. Lewis, *A Modern History of the Somali*, 4th edn, Oxford: James Currey, 2002, p. 11.

11   Ibid., p. 11.

12   'Somalia pirates release Panama-flagged bitumen cargo ship', *Reuters*, 15 April 2011, http://af.reuters.com/article/somaliaNews/idAFLDE73E1LA20110415.

13   J Gundel, 'The predicament of the Oday: The role of traditional structures in security, rights, law and development in Somalia', Danish Refugee Council & Novib/Oxfam, Nairobi, Kenya, November 2006, p. iii.

14   Carolyn Nordstrom, 'Out of the shadows', in Thomas Callaghy, Ronald Kassimir and Robert Latham (eds), *Intervention and Transnationalism in Africa, Global-Local Networks of Power*, Cambridge: Cambridge University Press, 2001, p. 225.

15   Carolyn Nordstrom, *Global Outlaws, Crime, Money, and Power in the Contemporary World*, Berkeley: University of California Press, 2007.

16   Ibid., p. 162.

17   Ibid., p. 207.

18   Ibid., p. 206.

19   Ibid., p. 205.

20   Carolyn Nordstrom, 'Out of the shadows', in Thomas Callaghy, Ronald Kassimir and Robert Latham (eds), *Intervention and Transnationalism in Africa, Global-Local Networks of Power*, Cambridge: Cambridge University Press, 2001, p. 225.

21   Ibid., pp. 238–9.

22   Gregory David Roberts, *Shantaram*, London: Abacus, 2005.

23   United Nations Office on Drugs and Crime, *Global Report on Trafficking in Persons*, Vienna: UNODC, 2009.

24   Boris Groendahl, 'UN crime chief says drug money flowed into banks', *Reuters*, 25 January 2009, quoting an interview in the Austrian magazine *Profil*, www.reuters.com/article/2009/01/25/financial-un-drugs-idUSLP65079620090125.

25   There is also pressure on Indian seamen, from their shipping companies, not to talk about their experiences when they return from Somalia.

26 Frank G. Madsen, *Transnational Organized Crime*, London and New York: Routledge, 2009, p. 81.

27 James R. Richards, *Transnational Criminal Organizations, Cybercrime and Money Laundering*, Boca Raton, Florida: CRC Press, 1999, p. 3.

28 Frank G. Madsen, *Transnational Organized Crime*, London and New York: Routledge, 2009, p. 53.

29 Tamara Makarenko, 'The crime–terror continuum: Tracing the interplay between transnational organised crime and terrorism', *Global Crime*, Vol. 6, No. 1 (February 2004), p. 132.

30 'Northern Ireland: IRA dissidents find new cause in drug war', *Irish Independent*, 20 September, 2010.

31 Juan Carlos Garzón, *Mafia & Co.: The Criminal Networks in Mexico, Brazil, and Columbia*, (trans. Kathy Ogle), Washington DC: Woodrow Wilson International Center for Scholars, 2010.

32 John Rollins, Liana Sun Wyler and Seth Rosen, 'International terrorism and transnational crime: Security threats, US policy, and considerations for Congress', US Congressional Research Service, Washington DC,7-5700, www.crs.gov, R41004, 5 January 2010, p. 15.

33 Ibid., p. 16.

34 Ed Vulliamy, 'How a big US bank laundered billions from Mexico's murderous drug gangs', *Observer*, 3 April 2011.

35 Misha Glenny, *McMafia, Crime Without Frontiers*, London: The Bodley Head, 2008, p. 393.

36 Jeffrey Robinson, *The Sink*, London: Constable, 2003, p. 339.

37 UNODC, Afghan Opium Trade_2009, www.unodc.org/documents/data-and-analysis/Afghanistan/Afghan_Opium_Trade_2009_web.pdf.

38 www.reuters.com/article/idUSLR485931.

39 'Somali pirates receive record ransom for ships' release', *BBC News*, 6 November 2010, www.bbc.co.uk/news/world-africa-11704306.

40 'Somali pirates free Irene SL tanker -Greek coastguard', *Reuters AlertNet*, 8 April 2011, www.trust.org/alertnet/news/somali-pirates-free-irene-sl-tanker–greek-coastguard/.

41 Martin Abbugao, 'Somali pirates controlled by syndicates: Interpol', *AFP*, 14 October 2009, www.google.com/hostednews/afp/article/ALeqM5hPsfTb5MwUq0regWvnBc74PNdj3g.

42 Mary Harper, 'Chasing the Somali piracy money trail', *BBC News*, 24 May 2009, http://news.bbc.co.uk/go/pr/fr/-/1/hi/world/africa/8061535.stm.

43 Anna Lindley, 'Between "dirty money" and development capital: Somali money transfer infrastructure under global scrutiny', *African Affairs*, 108/433, August 2009, p. 522.

44 President George W. Bush, 'Terrorist financial network fact sheet', The White House, Washington DC, Office of the Press Secretary, 7 November 2001, http://georgewbush-whitehouse.archives.gov/news/releases/2001/11/20011107-6.html.

45 Anna Lindley, 'Between "dirty money" and development capital: Somali money transfer infrastructure under global scrutiny', *African Affairs*, 108/433, August 2009, p. 529.

46   Ibrahim Warde, *The Price of Fear, Al-Qaeda and the Truth Behind the Financial War on Terror*, London: I.B.Tauris, 2007, pp. 96–7.

47   Khalid M. Medani, 'Financing terrorism or survival? Informal finance and state collapse in Somalia, and the US war on terrorism', *Middle East Report* 223 (Summer 2002), p. 4.

48   Anna Lindley, 'Between "dirty money" and development capital: Somali money transfer infrastructure under global scrutiny', *African Affairs*, 108/433, August 2009, p. 524.

49   Ibid., p. 527.

50   William Reno, 'Illicit commerce in peripheral states', in H. Richard Frimen (ed.), *Crime and the Global Political Economy*, Boulder and London: Lynne Rienner, 2010, p. 68.

51   'L'afro-pessimisme par le bas', *Politique africaine* 40, December 1990, p. 106, quoted in Jean-François Bayart, Stephen Eillis and Béatrice Hibou, *The Criminalization of the State in Africa*, Oxford: James Currey and Indianapolis: Indiana University Press, 1999, p. xiv.

52   William Reno, 'Illicit Commerce in Peripheral States', in H. Richard Frimen (ed.), *Crime and the Global Political Economy*, Boulder and London: Lynne Rienner, 2010, p. 78.

53   'Piracy off coast of Somalia Outpacing international efforts to defeat it', UN Doc S/2010/556, Security Council, 6417th Meeting (AM), 9 November 2010, www.un.org/News/Press/docs/2010/sc10079.doc.htm.

54   Peter Lewis, 'From prebendalism to predation: The political economy of decline in Nigeria', *Journal of Modern African Studies*, 34 (1) (1996), p. 101.

55   Jeffrey Gettleman, 'US aiding Somalia in its plan to retake its capital', *The New York Times*, 5 March 2010.

56   Robert Jackson, *Quasi-States: Sovereignty, International Relations and the Third World*, New York: Cambridge University Press, 1990, p. 21.

4   THE PIRATE COAST

1   William Reno, 'Somalia and survival in the shadow of the global economy', QEH Working Paper No. 100, ODID, Queen Elizabeth House, Oxford, February 2003, p. 16.

2   Mohammed Ibrahim, 'Abdullahi Yusef Ahmed, former Somali strongman, dies at 77', *The New York Times*, 23 March 2012.

3   'Somalia: Col. Abdullahi Yusuf laid to rest', *AllAfrica*, 25 March 2012, http://allafrica.com/stories/201203260082.html.

4   William Reno, 'Somalia and survival in the shadow of the global economy', QEH Working Paper No. 100, ODID, Queen Elizabeth House, Oxford, February 2003, p. 37.

5   Ibid., p. 35.

6   H.E. Abdirahman Mohamud Farole, 'Puntland and Somalia: The year ahead', Transcript of his address at Chatman House, London, 10 October 2011, p. 5.

7   'Piracy hits Puntland economy, brings vices-leader', *Reuters*, 9 April 2010.

8   'Somalia's Puntland police arrest 11 pirates', *Reuters*, 28 May 2012.

9   It has been alleged that the death of Lodewyk Pietersen in April 2012 during an operation against pirates near Hul-Anod, was due to panicking members of the force firing wildly in

an attempt to warn the pirates; while urging the men forward Pietersen was shot and killed: Robert Young Pelton, 'Expat mentor killed on anti-piracy operation', *SomaliaReport.com*, 27 April 2012, www.somaliareport.com/index.php/post/3280.

10 Peter Eichstaedt, 'Pirate state: Inside Somalia's terrorism at sea', *Chicago Review Press*, 2010, p. 63.

11 Ibid. pp. 62–3.

12 Stig Jarle Hansen, 'Piracy in the greater Gulf of Aden: Myths, misconceptions and remedies', Norwegian Institute for Urban and Regional Research, Oslo, Norway, October 2009, p. 5.

13 *Report of the UN Monitoring Group on Somalia and Eritrea*, S/2011/433, 18 July 2011, pp. 36–7.

14 Ibid., p. 38.

15 Ibid., p. 38.

16 Ibid., p. 38.

17 Ibid., pp. 38–39.

18 Ibid., p. 39.

19 *Report of the Monitoring Group pursuant to Security Council Resolution 1853 (2008)*, S/2010/91, 26 February 2010, Matt Bryden, coordinator, p. 7.

20 Ibid.

21 Geoffrey Gettleman, 'Somalia's President Assails U.N. Report on Corruption', *New York Times*, 16 March 2010.

22 Robert Young Pelton, 'Does the US, UN and ANISOM supply Al-Shabaab?', *Somalia Report*, 30 July 2011, http://somaliareport.com/index.php/post/1253/US_Supplying_Ammunition_To_Al_Shabaab.

23 Robert Young Pelton, 'Puntland marine police force enter Eyl', *Somalia Report*, 2 March 2011, www.somaliareport.com/index.php/post/2978.

24 *Report of the UN Monitoring Group on Somalia and Eritrea*, S/2011/433, 18 July 2011, p. 39.

25 Ibid., p. 39.

26 Ibid., p. 39.

27 Said Shiiq, 'Puntland: The epicenter of Somalia's piracy and human trafficking', *Hiiraan Online*, 27 December 2007, www.hiiraan.com.

28 Stig Jarle Hansen, 'Piracy in the greater Gulf of Aden: Myths, misconceptions and remedies', Norwegian Institute for Urban and Regional Research, Oslo, Norway, October 2009, pp. 30–1.

29 Jay Bahadur, 'Of coast guards and pirates', 9 August 2011, http://jaybahadur.blogspot.com/2011/08/of-coast-guards-and-pirates.html.

30 Jay Bahadur, *Deadly Waters: Inside the Hidden World of Somalia's Pirates*, London: Profile Books, 2011, p. 69.

31 Roger Middleton, 'Piracy in Somalia, threatening global trade, feeding local wars', Chatham House Briefing Paper, London, October 2008, p. 5.

32 Jonathan Clayton, 'Millions are starving in Somalia, but in Eyl Piracy is big business', *Times*, 19 November 2008.

33 Aidan Hartley, 'The terror of Tesco's finest...', *Daily Mail*, 23 May 2008.

34 Ibid.

35 Gregory R. Copley, 'Yemen hysteria hides deeper strategic matrix of long-term importance', *Oilprice.com*, 19 January 2010, www.resourceinvestor.com/2010/01/19/yem en-hysteria-hides-deeper-strategic-matrix-of-lo (accessed 20 January 2010).

36 Abdulaziz Al-Mutairi, 'Puntland's lucrative piracy business', *Arab News*, 2 November 2008, www.ArabNews.com.

37 Ibid.

38 *Report of the Monitoring Group pursuant to Security Council Resolution 1853 (2008)*, S/2010/91, 26 February 2010, Matt Bryden, coordinator, p. 25.

39 Ibid., p. 33.

40 Ibid., p. 39.

41 Ibid., p. 37.

42 Ibid., p. 38.

43 William Reno, 'Somalia and survival in the shadow of the global economy', QEH Working Paper No. 100, ODID, Queen Elizabeth House, Oxford, February 2003, p. 38.

44 Ibid., p. 42.

45 '20 slain in Puntland inter-clan fighting', *Press TV*, 21 November 2010, www.hiiraan.com/ news2/2010/nov/20_slain_in_puntland_inter_clan_fighting.aspx (accessed 16 January 2011).

46 'Puntland pleas to UN over piracy', *Somalia Report*, 23 July 2011, www.somaliareport. com/index.php/post/1206.

47 'Somalia: Benefits – and risks – of Puntland oil', IRIN (UN Office for the Coordination of Humanitarian Affairs, Nairobi, 8 March 2012.

48 www.africaoilcorp.com/s/Puntland.asp?ReportID=505141 (accessed 28 May 2012).

49 Ibid.

50 'Update 2 – Horn Petroleum suspends drilling well', *Reuters*, 17 May 2012 www.reuters. com/article/2012/05/18/ozabs-hornpetroleum-idAFJOE84H00H20120518.

51 2012 Third Quarter Report, http://www.africaoilcorp.com/s/Operations_Update.asp.

52 Sandeep Dikshit, 'And now, an offer of oil from Puntland', *The Hindu*, 16 May 2012.

53 'Somalia: Benefits – and risks – of Puntland oil', IRIN (UN Office for the Coordination of Humanitarian Affairs), Nairobi, 8 March 2012.

54 Alisha Ryu, 'Clan rivalry complicates terrorism fight in Puntland', VOANews.com, 29 September 2010, www.voanews.com/english/news/africa/Clan-Rivalry-Complicates-Terrorism-Fight-in-Puntland-104017374.html.

55 Africa Oil Corporation website, www.africaoilcorp.com/s/Nogal.asp (accessed 15 January 2011).

56 Alisha Ryu, 'Clan rivalry complicates terrorism fight in Puntland', VOANews.com, 29 September 2010, www.voanews.com/english/news/africa/Clan-Rivalry-Complicates-Terrorism-Fight-in-Puntland-104017374.html.

57 Dahir Kahin, 'Puntland's anti-piracy forces – Smokescreen for hunting oil & minerals unlawfully', *Somaliland Press*, [4] January 2011.

58 Ibid.

59 Alisha Ryu, 'Clan rivalry complicates terrorism fight in Puntland', VOANews.com, 29 September 2010, www.voanews.com/english/news/africa/Clan-Rivalry-Complicates -Terrorism-Fight-in-Puntland-104017374.html.

60 Jaale Cali Justice, 'Brilliant politician speak about uprooted community', Galgala News Agency, 15 August 2010, Wehelkaaga Ka Dhigo Galgala News (GNA), http:// galgalanews.com/?p=3760.

61 Abdulazez Al-Motairi, 'Puntland's tin mineral war; South African mercenaries; Ugandan gang trainers', *American Chronicle*, 17 December 2010, www.americanchronicle.com.

62 Jaale Cali Justice, 'Brilliant politician speak about uprooted community', 15 August 2010, Galgala News Agency, Wehelkaaga Ka Dhigo Galgala News (GNA), http://galgalanews. com/?p=3760 (no longer active).

63 Abdi Sheikh, 'Islamist rebels vow Jihad on Somalia's Puntland', *Reuters*, 28 July 2010.

64 *Report of the Monitoring Group on Somalia and Eritrea*, S/2011/433, New York: United Nations, 18 July 2011, p. 19.

65 Ibid., pp. 20–1.

66 'Puntland claims Somaliland harbors al-Shabaab Group', Muqdisho News, 2 January 2011, www.muqdishonews.com/2011/01/02/puntland-claims-somaliland-harbors-al-shabaab-groub/ (not active).

67 Hussein Ali Noor, 'Somaliland says Shabaab ties claim a smokescreen', *Reuters*, 3 January 2011.

68 Ibid.

69 'Puntland signed an agreement with Saracen company to train its marine forces', *Garoweonline.com*, 18 November 2010.

70 H.E. Abdirahman Mohamud Farole, 'Puntland and Somalia: The year ahead', Transcript of his address at Chatman House, London, 10 October 2011, p. 5.

71 *UN Monitoring Group on Somalia and Eritrea Report*, S/2011/433, New York: United Nations, 18 July 2011, p. 273, referring to Security Council Resolutions 751 (1992), and 1907 (2009), p. 53.

72 Ibid., p. 53.

73 Ibid., p. 273.

74 Katharine Houreld, 'Blackwater founder trains Somalis', *ABC News/Associated Press*, 20 January 2011, http://abcnews.go.com/International/wireStory?id=12723737.

75 Ibid.

76 *UN Monitoring Group on Somalia and Eritrea Report*, S/2011/433, New York: United Nations, 18 July 2011, p. 276.

77 Galmudug (Galmudug State) was formed from Galguduud province and part of Mudug province on 14 August 2006.

78 Ibid., p. 282.

79 Ibid., p. 283.

80 Richard Meade, 'Puntland counter-piracy forced poised for launch', *Lloyds List*, London, 23 February 2012.

81 http://pmpf.net.

82 'Arrival of Puntland maritime police force drives pirates from town of Iskushuban', Puntland Maritime Police Force press release, 26 April 2012, http://pmpf.net/arri val-of-puntland-maritime-police-force-drives-pirates-from-town-of-iskushuban/.

83 Robert Young Palton, 'Puntland captures seven suspects in Hafun', *Somalia Report*, 27 May 2012, www.somaliareport.com/index.php/topic/29.

84 Robert Young Palton, 'Puntland marine police force enter Eyl', *Somalia Report*, 2 March 2012, www.somaliareport.com/index.php/post/2978.

85 Andrew Hudson, "South African-led operation frees hostages from Somali pirates", Defence Web, 29 January 2013, http://www.defenceweb.co.za/index.php?option=com_ content&task=view&id=29219&Itemid=233 (accessed 15 December 2013)

86 Bryden, Matt, Deisser, Emmanuel et al.,'Report focusing on Somalia of the Monitoring Group on Somalia and Eritrea', S/2012/544, United Nations, New York, 13 July 2012, para. 66, p. 23.

87 Ibid., para. 66.

88 Robert Young Palton, 'Puntland marine police force enter Eyl', *Somalia Report*, 2 March 2012, www.somaliareport.com/index.php/post/2978.

89 UN Monitoring Group report on Somalia S/2012/544, 13 July 2012, para. 63, p. 22.

90 Ibid., para. 64.

91 UNODC Counter-Piracy Programme, *Support to the Trial and Related, Treatment of Piracy Suspects*, Issue Eight (February 2012), Nairobi, Kenya: UNODC, pp. 4–15.

92 *Report of the Monitoring Group on Somalia pursuant to Security Council Resolution 1811 (2008)*, S/2008/769, Matt Bryden, coordinator, p. 6.

93 Ibid., p. 30.

94 Ibid., p. 30.

95 *UN Monitoring Group Report 2012*, p. 19.

96 *Report of the Monitoring Group on Somalia pursuant to Security Council Resolution 1630 (2005)*, S/2006/2293, Bruno Schiemsky, chairman, p. 27.

97 Ibid.

98 Ibid.

99 Ibid., pp. 39–40.

100 *Report of the Monitoring Group pursuant to Security Council Resolution 1853 (2008)*, S/2010/91, 26 February 2010, Matt Bryden, coordinator, pp. 37–8.

101 Ibid., p. 38.

102 William Reno, 'Somalia and survival in the shadow of the global economy', QEH Working Paper No. 100, ODID, Queen Elizabeth House, Oxford, February 2003, p. 40.

103 House of Lords, European Union Committee, 12th Report of Session 2009–10, 'Combating Somali piracy: the EU's naval operation Atalanta', Report with Evidence, HL Paper 103, London: The Stationery Office Ltd, 14 April 2010, p. 10.

104 Stig Jarle Hansen, 'Piracy in the greater Gulf of Aden: Myths, misconceptions and remedies', Norwegian Institute for Urban and Regional Research, Oslo, Norway, October 2009, p. 23.

105 Ibid., p. 24.

106 Ibid., p. 25.

107 *Report of the Monitoring Group pursuant to Security Council Resolution 1853 (2008)*, S/2010/91, 26 February 2010, Matt Bryden, coordinator, pp. 37–8.

108 Ibid., p. 38.

109 Daniel Howden, 'Gaddafi's forty years in power celebrated with a gallery of grotesques', The *Independent*, 2 September 2009.

110 *Report of the Monitoring Group pursuant to Security Council Resolution 1853 (2008)*, S/2010/91, 26 February 2010, Matt Bryden, coordinator, p. 39.

111 *Report of the UN Monitoring Group on Somalia and Eritrea*, S/2011/433, 18 July 2011, p. 41.

112 Charlotte McDonald-Gibson, 'The Pirate who fell into a movie trap', *The Independent*, London, 15 October 2013.

113 Jay Bahadur, 'The pirate king of Somalia', *Globe and Mail*, 26 April 2009.

114 www.alarabiya.net/articles/2009/04/13/70528.html and http://mobile.france24.com/.

115 'Pirates stage rocket attack on US freighter', *Agence France Presse*, 13 April 2009, http://rawstory.com/news/2008/Pirates_stage_rocket_attack_on_US_0415.html.

116 *Report of the Monitoring Group pursuant to Security Council Resolution 1853 (2008)*, S/2010/91, dated 10 March 2010, Matt Bryden, coordinator, pp. 42–3.

117 Stig Jarle Hansen, 'Piracy in the greater Gulf of Aden: Myths, misconceptions and remedies', Norwegian Institute for Urban and Regional Research, Oslo, Norway, October 2009, p. 26.

118 Ibid., p. 57.

119 'Garaad Mohammed, Pirate, Somalia Inc.', *Lloyd's List*, 14 December 2010.

120 *Report of the Monitoring Group pursuant to Security Council Resolution 1853 (2008)*, S/2010/91, 10 March 2010, Matt Bryden, coordinator, pp. 42–3.

121 Ibid., p 41.

122 Jay Bahadur, 'I'm not a pirate, I'm the saviour of the sea', *The Times*, 16 April 2009.

123 Jeffrey Gettleman, 'For Somali pirates, worst enemy may be on shore', *The New York Times*, 9 May 2009.

124 *Report of the Monitoring Group pursuant to Security Council Resolution 1853 (2008)*, S/2010/91, 26 February 2010, Matt Bryden, coordinator, p. 42.

125 Stig Jarle Hansen, 'Piracy in the greater Gulf of Aden: Myths, misconceptions and remedies', Norwegian Institute for Urban and Regional Research, Oslo, Norway, October 2009, p. 39.

126 *Report of the Monitoring Group pursuant to Security Council Resolution 1853 (2008)*, S/2010/91, 26 February 2010, Matt Bryden, coordinator, p. 40.

127 Ibid., pp. 40–1.

128 Ibid., p. 45.

129   Ibid., p. 45.

130   Stig Jarle Hansen, 'Piracy in the greater Gulf of Aden: Myths, misconceptions and remedies', Norwegian Institute for Urban and Regional Research, Oslo, Norway, October 2009, p. 19.

131   Ibid., pp. 32–3.

132   Ibid., p. 27.

133   'Islamists take pirate town', *Times*, 3 May 2010 (AP report).

134   Stig Jarle Hansen, 'Piracy in the greater Gulf of Aden: Myths, misconceptions and remedies', Norwegian Institute for Urban and Regional Research, Oslo, Norway, October 2009, p. 8.

135   Ken Menkhaus, 'Dangerous waters', *Survival* 51:2 (2009), p. 22.

136   Stig Jarle Hansen, 'Piracy in the greater Gulf of Aden: Myths, misconceptions and remedies', Norwegian Institute for Urban and Regional Research, Oslo, Norway, October 2009, p. 10.

137   Ibid., p. 34.

138   *AFP,* 14 October 2009.

139   *Report of the UN Monitoring Group on Somalia and Eritrea*, S/2011/433, New York: United Nations, 18 July 2011, pp. 225–6.

140   Johann Hari, *The Independent*, 5 January 2009.

141   Ibid.

142   *Report of the UN Monitoring Group on Somalia and Eritrea*, S/2011/433, 18 July 2011, p. 40.

143   Ibid.

144   Kerin Backhaus, 'Piracy in the Puntland region of Somalia', *Oilprice.com* (accessed 15 May 2010).

145   Gregory R. Copley, 'Yemen hysteria hides deeper strategic matrix of long-term importance', *OilPrice.com*, 19 January 2010, www.oilprice.com (accessed 20 January 2010).

146   www.globalsecurity.org/military/world/yemen/corruption.htm.

147   Ibid.

148   *UN Monitoring Group on Somalia Report 2008*, p. 26.

149   Ibid., p. 27.

150   Ibid., pp. 29–30.

151   Ibid., p. 32.

5   THE GEOGRAPHY OF PIRACY

1   'Factbox – The Strait of Hormuz, key oil shipping route', Reuters.com, 28 July 2010 www.reuters.com/article/2010/07/28/japan-explosion-hormuz-idUSLDE66R1142010 0728.

2   'Factbox: Pirates stalk shipping lanes', Reuters, 9 February 2011, http://www.reuters.com/article/2011/02/09/us-oman-tanker-lanes-factbox-idUSTRE7184SD20110209.

3 *UN Monitoring Group on Somalia Report 2008*, p. 29.

4 Ibid., pp. 45–6.

5 Gulf Daily News, Manama, Bahrain, 14 August 2009.

6 Confidential information from a maritime training company.

7 Private briefings.

8 www.mschoa.eu.

9 Ships can telephone UKMTO on +971 50 552 3215.

10 At 12°58N 048°34E.

11 www.armybase.us/2009/08/somali-piracy-reduced-but-still-a-threat-adm-gary-roug-head/ (accessed 24 August 2009).

12 Ramola Talwar Badam and Preeti Kannan, 'Hostages on Dubai's MV Iceberg 1 freed in rescue operation', The National, Abu Dhabi, 24 December 2012, http://www.thenational.ae/news/uae-news/hostages-on-dubais-mv-iceberg-1-freed-in-rescue-operation.

13 At 24°23N 060°02E.

14 At 22°00N 064°00E.

15 'Advisory HoA 09/2011 Hijack MV *Sinin*', Dryad Maritime Ltd.

16 International Transport Workers' Federation, Press Statement, 2 February 2011, www.itfglobal.org/press-area/index.cfm/pressdetail/5598.

17 At 09°40S 045°05E.

18 At 01.53°N 060.05°E.

19 At 0.35°S 062°.40E, and 2° beyond the 60° east line of longitude.

20 At 1°10S and 61°32E.

21 Automatic position transmitter.

22 Information given to the author.

23 Jama Deperani and Iddi Shabeel, 'The "pirate-satellite" is a magic man', *The Somali Marine and Coastal Monitor & Ecoterra*, 11 June 2011.

24 At 17°11N and 66°05E.

25 Adam J. Young, *Contemporary Maritime Piracy in Southeast Asia, History, Causes and Remedies*, Leiden, The Netherlands, and Institute of Southeast Asian Studies, Singapore: International Institute for Asian Studies, 2007, p. 3.

26 Robert Antony, *Like Froth Floating on the Sea: The World of Pirates and Seafarers in Late Imperial South China*, China Research Monographs, No. 56, Berkeley: University of California Press: Institute for East Asian Studies, 2003.

27 Adam J. Young, *Contemporary Maritime Piracy in Southeast Asia, History, Causes and Remedies*, Leiden, The Netherlands, and Institute of Southeast Asian Studies, Singapore: International Institute for Asian Studies, 2007, p. 31.

28 John S. Burnett, *Dangerous Waters, Modern Piracy and Terror on the High Seas*, New York: Plume, 2002, p. 39.

29 Catherine Zara Raymond, 'Piracy in southeast Asia: New trends, issues and responses', *Harvard Asia Quarterly*, Vol. IX, No. 4 (Fall 2005).

30 John S. Burnett, *Dangerous Waters, Modern Piracy and Terror on the High Seas*, New York: Plume, 2002, pp. 218–19.

31 Ibid., pp. 227–9.

32 ICC Commercial Services, 'Piracy doubles in first six months of 2009', 15 July 2009, http://www.icc-ccs.org/news/332-piracy-doubles-in-first-six-months-of-2009, accessed 16 October 2013.

33 Henry Keppel and James Brooke, *The Expedition to Borneo of H.M.S. Dido for the Suppression of Piracy; With Extracts from the Journal of J. Brooke Esq., of Sarawak*, London, 1846.

34 Carolin Liss, 'The roots of piracy in Southeast Asia', APSNet Policy Forum, 22 October, 2007, Nautilus Institute, Berkeley, California, USA, http://nautilus.org/apsnet/the-roots-of-piracy-in-southeast-asia/.

35 Moro Islamic Liberation Front.

36 Bin Dong and Benno Torgler, 'The causes of corruption: Evidences from China', CREMA, Working Paper No. 2010–07, Basel, Switzerland, 2010.

37 Frederic Dannen, 'Partners in crime', *The New Republic*, 14 and 21 July 1997.

38 Carlyle A. Thayer, 'Vietnam and the challenge of political civil society', *Contemporary Southeast Asia*, Vol. 31, No. 1 (2009), p. 2.

39 Jack A. Gottschalk and Brian P. Flanagan, *Jolly Roger with an UZI, The Rise and Threat of Modern Piracy*, Annapolis, Maryland: Naval Institute Press, 2000, p. 79.

40 Stefan Eklöf, *Pirates in Paradise, A Modern History of Southeast Asia's Maritime Marauders*, Copenhagen, Denmark: Nias Press, 2006, p. 81.

41 ICC International Maritime Bureau, *Piracy and armed robbery, against ships, Annual report, 1 January – 31 December 2009*, London, 2010, p. 37

42 IMB Piracy Incident Report.

43 Ibid., 6 February 2010.

44 Ibid., 19 April 2010.

45 'Office of Naval Intelligence – world wide piracy report', 19 May 2010 http://msi.nga.mil/MSISiteContent/StaticFiles/MISC/wwtts/wwtts_20100519100000.txt.

46 IMB Piracy Incident Report, 7 April 2010.

47 Susan Njanji, 'Nigeria "Rapidly Becoming Like Somalia"', *Daily Telegraph* (AFP), 8 January 2010.

48 'Benin, Nigeria: A Hijacked oil tanker', *Stratfor Global Intelligence*, 24 November 2009.

49 Nigeria's fiscal deficit is forecast to increase to 5.43 per cent of GDP as the government collects less revenue: Camillus Eboh, 'Nigeria leader proposes budget revisions, supplement', *International Business Times*, 2 June 2010, http://uk.ibtimes.com/articles/26391/20100602/nigeria-leader-proposes-budget-revisions-supplement.htm.

50 Report in Vanguard quoted by *Africanloft.com*, www.africanloft.com/retired-military-generals-engage-nigeria-in-oil-bunkering-war/ (accessed 30 June 2010).

51 Peter Lewis, 'From prebendalism to predation: The political economy of decline in Nigeria', *Journal of Modern African Studies*, 34 (1) (1996), p. 101.

52 Ben Agande, 'Chief of naval staff knows about missing ship', *Online Nigeria*, 25 November 2004, http://nm.onlinenigeria.com/templates/?a=286&z=17 (accessed 30 June 2010).

53 'Nigeria: Conviction of admirals confirms navy role in oil theft', *IRIN*, 6 January 2005, www.irinnews.org/report.aspx?reportid=52598 (accessed 30 June 2010).

54 Peter Lewis, 'From prebendalism to predation: The political economy of decline in Nigeria', *Journal of Modern African Studies*, 34 (1) (1996), p. 103.

55 'Ghana returns Nigeria oil tanker after pirate attack', BBC News, 1 December 2009, http://news.bbc.co.uk/1/hi/8389284.stm.

56 'Piracy incidents rise for third consecutive year', IMB, 15 January 2010.

57 *International Maritime Bureau Report 2009/187.*

58 Jack A. Gottschalk and Brian P. Flanagan, *Jolly Roger with an UZI, The Rise and Threat of Modern Piracy*, Annapolis, Maryland: Naval Institute Press, 2000, pp. 58 and 62.

59 'The failed states index 2010', *Foreign Policy and The Fund for Peace*, www.foreignpolicy.com/articles/2010/06/21/2010_failed_states_index_interactive_map_and_rankings.

60 Stephan Faris, Forecast: *The Consequences of Climate Change, From the Amazon to the Arctic, from Darfur to Napa Valley*, New York: Henry Holt, 2009.

6 PIRATE OPERATIONS

1 Ben Macintyre, 'The battle against piracy begins in Mogadishu', *The Times*, 16 April 2009.

2 Jay Bahadur, 'Pirates Inc.', *Financial Times*, 25 June 2010.

3 *Report of the Secretary-General on Children and Armed Conflict in Somalia*, S/2010/557, 9 November 2010, New York: United Nations, p. 15.

4 Mohamed Ahmed – 'Somalia pirates undaunted by navy patrols', Reuters 16 April 2010, www.reuters.com/article/2010/04/16/idUSLDE63D0HO.

5 Stewart Bell, 'Somali militants training pirates', *National Post*, Don Mills, Ontario, Canada, 3 December 2009,

6 'Somali pirates may have been forced', *United Press International*, 18 November 2010, www.upi.com/Top_News/US/2010/11/18/Somali-pirates-may-have-been-forced/UPI-64,96129,0116847/.

7 *Report of the Monitoring Group on Somalia pursuant to Security Council Resolution 1853 (2008)*, 26 February 2010, Matt Bryden, coordinator, p. 86.

8 Randeep Ramesh, 'Pirate ship sunk by Indian navy was hijacked Thai trawler', *Guardian*, 26 November 2008, www.guardian.co.uk/world/2008/nov/26/piracy and 'Somali pirate "mother ship" sunk by Indian navy turns out to be Thai trawler', *Daily Mail*, 26 November 2008.

9 Jean-Marc Mojon, 'Pirates free Taiwan ship, 3 crew dead: watchdog', *AFP*, 11 February 2010, www.google.com/hostednews/afp/article/ALeqM5gp8E5qx56e0U_cQnUdq8AXQ5deMg.

10 Details of Hijacked Ship's Fate, Somalia report, 29th May 2011, http://www.somaliareport.com/index.php/post/859 (accessed 16 December 2013).

11 Press Statement, Allied Maritime Command Headquarters, Northwood, 18 May 2011, http://www.manw.nato.int/pdf/Press%20Releases%202011/Press%20releases% 20Jan-June%202011/SNMG2/180511%20GB%20PAO%20%20BAIN%20SWG%20 ESSN%20%20round%20up.pdf (accessed 16 December 2013).

12 *Turkish Maritime*, 19 March 2008, www.turkishmaritime.com.tr/news_detail.php? id=1240.

13 'Status of Seized Vessels and Crews in Somalia and the Indian Ocean', *Ecoterra*, 5 July 2010.

14 Unfortunately some yachtsmen have disregarded the clear advice not to sail in the Indian Ocean, to their cost.

15 *Ecoterra*, 13 November 2009, Issue 287 (note this Somali source while not always reliable does also have excellent sources within Somalia) and *Reuters*, 3 December 2009, 'Factbox – Ships held by Somali pirates', www.reuters.com/article/idUSGEE5B22CA.

16 Tristan McConnell, 'Security guards shoot dead Somali pirate in attack on MV Almezaan cargo ship', *The Times*, 25 March 2010.

17 Roba Sharamo and Berouk Mesfin, 'Regional Security in the post-Cold War Horn of Africa', Monograph 178, April 2011, Institute for Security Studies, Pretoria, South Africa, p. 17.

18 'Somali cook gives guns to hostage crew who kill pirate captors', *Neptune Maritime Security*, 19 June 2010, http://neptunemaritimesecurity.posterous.com/somali-cook-gives -guns-to-hostage-crew-who-ki.

19 'Crew of the hijacked MV *Rim* retake control from Pirates, EU NAVFOR warship *SPS Victoria* gives medical support', EU NAVFOR press statement, 2 June 2010, www.eunavfor.eu/2010/06/crew-of-the-hijacked-mv-rim-retake-control-from-pirates- eu-navfor-warship-sps-victoria-gives-medical-support/.

20 'The Kosovo Liberation Army (KLA) and "Organ Harvesting"', *Global Research*, 22 January 2010, www.globalresearch.ca/index.php?context=va&aid=17,125.

21 'Routinely Targeted, Attacks on Civilians in Somalia', Amnesty International, London, 6 May 2008, p. 25.

22 Report of the Monitoring Group on Somalia, 24 April 2008, S/2008/274, p. 6.

23 S/2008/769.

24 Ibid.

25 *Report of the Monitoring Group pursuant to Security Council Resolution 1853 (2008)*, S/2010/91, 26 February 2010, Matt Bryden, coordinator.

26 *Report of the Monitoring Group pursuant to Security Council Resolution 751 (1992)* concerning Somalia, and in accordance with para. 3 (i) of Security Council resolution 1811 (2008), S/2008/769, 10 December 2008, United Nations, New York, p. 6.

27 Ibid., p. 49.

28 Ibid., p. 69.

29 *Report of the Monitoring Group on Somalia and Eritrea*, S/2011/433, 18 July 2011, New York: United Nations, p. 43.

30 Ibid., p. 44.

31 'Somalia: Airplanes carrying weapons land at Dhusamareb Airport', *RBC Radio*, 3 July 2010,

32 *Report of the Monitoring Group on Somalia and Eritrea*, S/2011/433, 18 July 2011, New York: United Nations, p. 42.

33 The UN arms embargo was partially lifted in March 2013 to allow the new Somali government to buy arms; see, Michell Nichols, 'U.N. partially lifts arms embargo on Somalia for a year', *Reuters*, 6 March 2013, http://www.reuters.com/article/2013/03/06/us-somalia-arms-un-idUSBRE92514A20130306.

34 Larry Kahaner, 'Weapon of mass destruction', *Washington Post*, 26 November 2006.

35 *Report of the Monitoring Group pursuant to Security Council Resolution 1853 (2008)*, S/2010/91, 26 February 2010, Matt Bryden, coordinator, p. 75.

36 Ibid., p. 86.

37 *Report of the Monitoring Group pursuant to Security Council Resolution 751 (1992) concerning Somalia, and in accordance with paragraph 3 (i) of Security Council resolution 1811 (2008)*, S/2008/769, 10 December 2008, United Nations, New York, p. 25.

38 Ibid., p. 25.

39 Ibid., p. 25.

40 Lt Col. Vladimir Karpov, 20 October 1999, http://fofanov.armor.kiev.ua/Tanks/TRIALS/19991020.html.

41 'Mystery widens on Greek tanker fire and pirates off Somalia', *Maritime Security Asia*, 13 July 2011, http://maritimesecurity.asia/free-2/piracy-update/mystery-widens-on-greek-tanker-fire-and-pirates-off-somalia/.

42 Wendell Roelf, 'Analyst says Somali pirates have new weapons from Libya', *Reuters*, 12 April 2012, www.reuters.com/article/2012/04/12/us-africa-pirates-idUSBRE83B0HO20120412.

43 Larry Shaughnessy, 'Libyan weapons falling into Somali al Qaeda's hands, U.S. official warns', *CNN*, 18 June 2012, http://security.blogs.cnn.com/2012/06/18/libyan-weapons-falling-into-somali-al-qaedas-hands-u-s-official-warns/.

44 Auslan Crumb, 'Sailor tells of the moment pirates captured the Sirius Star', *Daily Telegraph*, 29 January 2009, www.telegraph.co.uk/news/worldnews/africaandindianocean/somalia/4389151/Sailor-tells-of-the-moment-pirates-captured-the-Sirius-Star.html.

45 Michelle Wiese Bockmann, 'Armed Guards Can Help Cut Insurance Shipping Costs', *Bloomberg*, 23 May 2012, http://www.bloomberg.com/news/2012-05-11/armed-guards-can-help-cut-insurance-costs-for-shipping-companies.html.

46 'Somali pirates use new boarding methods' Somali pirates use new boarding methods' www.gaops.com/index.php?option=com_content&view=article&id=335:02-july-2010-somali-pirates-use-new-boarding-techniques&catid=3:news&Itemid=13, Marinelog, 2 July 2012, www.marinelog.com/DOCS/NEWSMMIX/2010jul00020.html.

47 'Pirates capture Saudi oil tanker', *BBC News*, 18 November 2009, http://news.bbc.co.uk/1/hi/7733482.stm, accessed 1 July 2010.

48 INTERPOL maritime piracy working group aims to enhance international police collaboration – 17 September 2009, INTERPOL Press Release, http://www.interpol.int/News-and-media/News-media-releases/2009/PR081.

49 Alex Kennedy, 'Somali police chief laments lack of progress on curbing piracy', *The Associated Press*, 14 October 2009.

50 www.aislive.com/services.html.

51 http://www.fleetmon.com/live_tracking/fleetmon_explorer, accessed 31 May 2014.

52 Division for Investigation of Maritime Accidents, Danish Maritime Authority, Case: 200711082, 16 November 2007, p. 11.

53 Giles Tremlett, 'This is London – the capital of Somali pirates' secret intelligence operation', *Guardian*, 11 May 2009.

54 Ibid.

55 Ibid.

56 Ibid.

57 *UN Monitoring Group Report*, February 2010, p. 99.

58 Bahadur, Jay. 'Pirates Inc'., *Financial Times*, June 2010

59 *UN Monitoring Group Report*, February 2010, p. 99.

60 Gerard W. Gawalt, 'America and the Barbary pirates: An international battle against an unconventional foe', US Library of Congress, http://memory.loc.gov/ammem/collections/jefferson_papers/mtjprece.html.

61 House of Lords, European Union Committee, 12th Report of Session 2009–10, 'Combating Somali piracy: the EU's naval operation Atalanta', Report with Evidence, HL Paper 103, London: The Stationery Office Ltd. 14 April 2010.

62 Jon Gambrell, 'Company: Nigerian navy retakes hijacked oil tanker Indian sailors unhurt', *Associated Press*, 5 September 2012.

63 'Pirates release Greek tanker and crew after stealing ship's fuel', *maritime-executive.com*, 30 August 2012, www.maritime-executive.com/article/pirates-release-greek-tanker-and-crew-after-stealing-ship-s-fuel.

64 Martin N. Murphy, *Small Boats, Weak States, Dirty Money: The Challenge of Piracy*, New York: Columbia University Press, 2009, p. 111.

65 Ibid.

66 'Felix Batista, anti kidnapping expert is himself kidnapped while his wife pleas for his life', *Legal Pub*, 8 January 2009, http://legalpublication.blogspot.com/2009/01/felix-batista-anti-kidnapping-expert-is.html.

67 'Somali pirates free Bermuda-flagged ship, ransom paid', *Reuters*, 11 May 2010, www.alertnet.org/thenews/newsdesk/LDE64A149.htm.

68 Mohamed Ahmed, 'Somali pirates release cargo ship, ransom paid', *Reuters*, 1 February 2010, www.reuters.com/article/idUSTRE61,06152,0100201.

69 *Report of the UN Monitoring Group on Somalia and Eritrea*, 18 July 2011, S/2011/433, p. 212.

70 'Somali pirates receive record ransom for ships' release', *BBC News*, 6 November 2010, www.bbc.co.uk/news/world-africa-11704306.

71 John Frum (or Jon Frum, or John From) is a figure associated with cargo cults on the island of Tanna in Vanuatu, where supplies from US forces, dropped during World War Two, were thought to be from local gods.

72 Abdi Guled and Abdi Sheikh, 'Somali pirates free oil tanker after record ransom', *Reuters*, 18 January 2010, http://mobile.reuters.com/article/worldNews/idUSTRE60H1XX 20100118?src=RSS-WOR.

73 *Report of the UN Monitoring Group on Somalia and Eritrea*, S/2011/433, 18 July 2011, p. 221.

74 Ibid., pp. 221–2.

75 Ibid., p. 223.

76 Katrin Bennhold, 'Piracy, kidnapping and rescue', *The New York Times*, 15 April 2008, www.nytimes.com/2008/04/15/world/europe/15iht-france.4.12016721.html.

77 'Somali pirates using hostages as human shields', *Daily Telegraph*, 3 February 2011.

78 Kaija Hurlburt, and D. Conor Seyle, *The Human Cost of Maritime Piracy 2012*, Oceans Beyond Piracy and the One Earth Future Foundation: Broomfield, Colorado, 2012, p. 7.

79 Vijay Mohan, 'For 11 months, they stared death in the face', *Tribune News Service*, 23 April 2011.

80 Frank Gardner, 'The long road to the Chandlers' release', *BBC News*, 14 November 2010, www.bbc.co.uk/news/uk-11,753927.

81 Wang Qian, 'Held by pirates for 202 days', *China Daily/Asia News Network*, 5 January 2009.

82 'Somalia pirates release German ship', *Reuters*, 13 April 2011, http://af.reuters.com/article/ somaliaNews/idAFLDE73C17H20110413?pageNumber=&virtualBrandChannel=0.

83 *Ecoterra*, 11 February 2010.

84 http://wap.odessacrewing.borda.ru/?1-20-0-00000112-000-480-0, accessed 17 October 2013.

85 Venatrix Fulmen, 'Pirate update: Ariana crew abandoned again', Salem-News.com, 25 December 2009, www.salem-news.com/articles/december252009/ariana.php.

86 Ibid.

87 Ibid.

88 Ibid.

89 Ibid.

90 Martin Barillas, 'Spanish crewmembers recount horror of captivity and rape by Somali pirates', *The Cutting Edge*, 30 November 2009, www.thecuttingedgenews.com/index. php?article=11810&pageid=17&pagename=News.

91 Siddharth Srivastava, 'We'd like to go home, Pirates demand release of their mates by Indian authorities', *Asian Sentinel*, 29 April 2011, www.asiasentinel.com/index.php?opti on=com_content&task=view&id=3160&Itemid=225.

92 Mohamed Ahmed, 'Somali pirates say to hold any Indian crews hostage', *Reuters*, 16 April 2011, www.reuters.com/article/2011/04/16/somalia-piracy-idUSL-DE73F05D20110416.

93 'Murder of sailor by pirates shocks seafarers', *New Indian Express*, 10 February 2011, http://newindianexpress.com/cities/kochi/article39,5309.ece.

94 Hyung-Jin Kim, 'Freed sailor: "Pirates trampled and beat me"', *msnbc.com* (Associated Press), 2 February 2011, www.msnbc.msn.com/id/41,384058/.

95 Surabhi Vaya, '"Speech impaired" pirate finally speaks', *Hindustan Times*, 4 May 2011.

96 Robert Young Pelton, 'Weekly piracy report', *Somalia Report*, 14 August 2012, www.somaliareport.com/index.php/post/3584/Weekly_Piracy_Report.

97 'Somali Pirates who hijacked MV Orna kill a hostage and wound another', *The National*, 2 September 2012.

98 UPDATE – MV Albedo Lifeboats Sighted On Somali Beach, EU NAVFOR press release, 10 July 2013, http://eunavfor.eu/update-mv-albedo-lifeboats-sighted-on-somali-beach/ (accessed 22 December 2013).

99 Thaindian News, 9 August 2012, http://www.thaindian.com/newsportal/health/captive-sailors-family-pleads-with-government_100637081.html and also Anand Bodh, 'Parents of Himachal youth caught by Somali pirates seek govt help', *The Times of India*, 9 August 2012.

100 'Pirates, Investors Fight Over MV Albedo Ransom' Somali Report, 6 August 2012, http://www.somaliareport.com/index.php/post/3573/Pirates_Investors_Fight_Over_MV_Albedo_Ransom (accessed 22 December 2013).

101 Muaz Shabandri –'They treated us like animals: Piracy victim', Khaleej Times, Dubai, UAE, 11 September 2013 http://www.khaleejtimes.com/kt-article-display-1.asp?xfile=data/crime/2013/September/crime_September49.xml&section=crime (accessed 23 December 2013).

7 THE IMPACT ON THE SHIPPING INDUSTRY

1 Unless otherwise stated the figures in this Chapter 7 are from the 'Review of Maritime Transport 2013', United Nations Conference on Trade and Development, UNCTAD/RMT/2013, Geneva, Switzerland, 2013, this covers data and events from January 2012 until June 2013. Figures have also been used from earlier UNCTAD reports, including the 'Review of Maritime Transport 2010'.

2 UNCTAD Secretariat, 2009, p. 65.

3 http://www.worldslargestship.com.

4 Eoghan Macguire "Dawn of the super-ports? Mammoth ships force ports to adapt", CNN, 4 October 2013, http://edition.cnn.com/2013/10/04/business/dawn-super-port-mammoth-ships/ (accessed 21 December 2013).

5 Review of Maritime Transport 2013', United Nations Conference on Trade and Development, UNCTAD/RMT/2013, Geneva, Switzerland, 2013, p. 37.

6 Robert Wright, 'Collapse in dry bulk shipping rates unprecedented in its severity', *Financial Times*, 1 December 2008.

7 Data from Bloomberg.

8   Robert Wright, Leslie Hook and Joe Leahy - "China allows huge Valemax ship to dock", *Financial Times*, 29 December 2011, http://www.ft.com/cms/s/0/77a8da68-3219-11e1-b4ba-00144feabdc0.html#axzz2neO5P98e (accessed 16 December 2013).

9   Oman Shipping Company Website http://www.omanship.co.om/Default.aspx (accessed 16 December 2013).

10 'Trade flows collapse continues in first quarter 2009', OCED news release, OECD International Trade Statistics, Paris, 15 July 2009.

11 Ibid.

12 'Trade flows continue to grow in the first quarter of 2010 but at a slower pace', OECD News release, OECD International Trade Statistics, Paris, 21 July 2010.

13 9 September 2013 Press Release – 'WTO sees gradual recovery in coming months despite cut in trade forecasts', World Trade Organization.

14 UNCTAD Secretariat, 2009, p. 62.

15 Ibid., p. 70.

16 UNCTAD, 2013, p. 59.

17 Ibid., p. 36.

18 Simon Parry, 'Revealed: The ghost fleet of the recession anchored just east of Singapore', *Daily Mail*, 28 September 2009.

19 UNCTAD Secretariat, 2009, p. 72.

20 Barry Rogliano Salles, Shipping and Shipbuilding Markets, Annual Review 2011, Paris, 2011, p. 3.

21 J. Frank and D. Osler, 'Piracy could add $400 m to owners' insurance costs', *Lloyd's List*, 20 November 2008.

22 Rawle O. King, 'Ocean piracy and its impact on insurance', *Congressional Research Service*, 6 February 2009, http://fpc.state.gov/documents/organization/162745.pdf.

23 Carolyn Bandel and Kevin Crowley, 'Somali pirate attacks sink premiums as insurers leap aboard', *Bloomberg.com*, 3 August 2010, www.bloomberg.com/news/2010-08-02/somali-piracy-attacks-surge-premiums-sink-as-more-insurers-leap-aboard.html.

24 'Sue and labour' is a standard clause in a maritime insurance policy that allows the insured to recover from the insurer any reasonable expenses incurred by the insured in order to minimize or avert a loss to the insured property, for which loss the insurer would have been liable under the policy.

25 Carolyn Bandel and Kevin Crowley, 'Somali pirate attacks sink premiums as insurers leap aboard', *Bloomberg.com*, 3 August 2010, www.bloomberg.com/news/2010-08-02/somali-piracy-attacks-surge-premiums-sink-as-more-insurers-leap-aboard.html.

26 D. Olser, 'The long way round', *Lloyd's List*, 26 November 2008.

27 PowerPoint presentation of G. De Monie, senior director, Policy Research Corporation, European Commission, in the Seminar, 'Piracy and armed robbery against shipping', 21 January 2009, cited by UNCTAD Secretariat, 2009, p. 10.

28 'Maersk to route Asia–Europe service around Africa', *Fresh Plaza*, 21 January 2009, www.freshplaza.com/news_detail.asp?id=37361.

29 www.bunkerworld.com/markets/surcharges/tsa.

30 http://www.bunkerworld.com/prices/ (accessed 16 December 2013).

31 Owen Bowcott, 'Round-the-world cruise liner flees suspected Somali pirates', *Guardian*, 5 March 2009.

32 Arjun Ramachandran, 'Aussie tells of terror of pirate attack', *Sydney Morning Herald*, 29 April 2009, www.smh.com.au/travel/travel-news/aussie-tells-of-terror-of-pirate-attack-20090429-amlw.html.

33 Matthias Gebauer and Dietmar Hipp, 'Passengers Fought Pirates with Tables and Deck Chairs', *Spiegel Online*, 28 April 2009, http://www.spiegel.de/international/world/0,1518,621708-2,00.html.

34 Matthias Gebauer and Dietmar Hipp, 'Passengers fought pirates with tables and deck chairs', *Spiegel Online*, 28 April 2009, www.spiegel.de/international/world/0,1518,621708-2,00.html.

35 Martin Cox, 'No peace for *Peace Boat*', *Maritime Matters*, 10 May 2010, http://maritimematters.com/2010/05/no-peace-for-peace-boat/.

36 George Thande, 'Seychelles deploys troops after pirate attacks', *Reuters*, 2 April 2009.

37 Victoria Mahé, 'Seychelles/TOPAZ repels pirate attack', *African Press Organization*, 30 March 2010.

38 'EU NAVFOR destroys 2 more pirate action groups (PAG)', *EU NAVFOR*, 16 March 2010, www.eunavfor.eu/2010/03/eu-navfor-destroy-2-more-pirate-action-groups-pag/.

39 'Pirate action group disrupted due to excellent cooperation between EU NAVFOR and the Seychelles Coast Guard', *EU NAVFOR*, 30 May 2010, www.eunavfor.eu/2010/05/pirate-action-group-disrupted-due-to-excellent-cooperation-between-eu-navfor-and-the-seychelles-coast-guard/.

40 MSC Cruises http://www.cruiseshipcenters.com/en-CA/winnipeg/cruise-line-details/MSC-Cruises.

8 LEGAL AND INSURANCE ISSUES

1 Nicolette Jones, *The Plimsoll Sensation, The Great Campaign to Save Lives at Sea*, London: Abacus, 2007, pp. 266–7.

2 www.lloyds.com/Common/Help/Glossary.

3 The UK Marine Insurance Act 1906, 6 Edw. 7 c.41, His Majesty's Stationery Office, London, it can be accessed at http://www.legislation.gov.uk/ukpga/Edw7/6/41.

4 Ibid.

5 Ibid.

6 The UK Marine Insurance Act 1906, 6 Edw. 7 c.41, His Majesty's Stationery Office, London.

7 John Knott and Toby Stephen, *Piracy and Terrorism at Sea*, London: HFW, 2008.

8 Jonathan Steer, 'Piracy and general average – A look at some of the pitfalls', *Maritime Risk International*, 1 October 2009.

9 Ibid.

10 *North Star Shipping Ltd v. Sphere Drake Plc* [2004] EWHC 2457 (Comm).

11 'Charterparty piracy technical paper', 'Charterparty Piracy Clauses and Marine Insurances', *Marsh's Global Marine Practice*, London: Marsh Ltd., 2009.

12 *Royal Boskalis Westminster NV* v. *Mountain* [1999] QB 674.

13 Jonathan Bruce, 'Piracy: Whose risk is it anyway?', *Lloyd's List*, 31 December 2008.

14 Ibid.

15 Ibid.

16 'Charterparty Piracy Clauses and Maritime Insurances', *Marsh's Global Marine Practice*, London: Marsh Ltd., 2009.

17 The common law doctrine of contractual frustration applies when after the formation of a contract, an event occurs that is due to no fault of either party and that renders performance of the contract by one or both parties physically and commercially impossible. The parties are then released from any further obligation and the contract is prima facie dissolved. A leading case, which is cited in legal textbooks, is *Taylor* v. *Caldwell* (1863) 3 B & S 826, where a contract was entered into to use a music hall. However, the music hall was destroyed by an accidental fire. The claimant sought to bring an action for breach of contract for failing to provide the hall and claiming damages for the expenses incurred. The claimant's action for breach of contract failed and the court held that the contract had been frustrated because the contract was impossible to perform.

18 *Masefield AG* v. *Amlin Corporate Member Ltd* [2010] EWHC 280 (Comm).

19 Ibid.

20 Ibid.

21 It was understood that the bunker barge *Al-Nisr-Al-Saudi* was empty, so this is a hypothetical example.

22 Rear Admiral Hudson, evidence to the House of Lords, European Union Committee, 12th Report of Session 2009–10, 'Combating Somali piracy: the EU's naval operation Atalanta', Report with Evidence, HL Paper 103, London: The Stationery Office Ltd, 14 April 2010.

23 Note, I am a director of Idarat Ltd. We provide advice to shipowners and the insurance industry.

24 SOLAS: the International Convention for the Safety of Life at Sea, 1974, The International Maritime Organization, October 1998, www.imo.org/about/conventions/statusofconventions/documents/status%20-%202012.pdf.

25 House of Lords' EU Committee, 'Money laundering and the financing of terrorism', HL Paper 132-I, published 22 July 2009, para. 222, www.publications.parliament.uk/pa/ld200809/ldselect/ldeucom/132/13209.htm#a76.

26 Ibid., para. 226.

27 Ibid., para. 171.

28 Ibid., para. 170.

29 Ibid., para. 166.

30 Ibid., para. 167.

31 Ibid., para. 168

32　Ibid., paras 168–9.

33　House of Lords, *Hansard*, 7 December 2009, cols 977–8.

34　United Nations, Security Council, 'List of Individuals Identified Pursuant to Paragraph 8 of Resolution 1844' (2008), SC/9904, Department of Public Information, News and Media Division, 12 April 2010, New York.

35　'Obama piracy order "unhelpful," ship owner groups say', *Bloomberg*, 31 May 2010.

36　Executive Order, 'Blocking property of certain persons contributing to the conflict in Somalia', White House, Washington DC, 13 April 2010, www.whitehouse.gov/the-press-office/executive-order-concerning-somalia.

37　Ibid.

38　'Somalia pirates free MV Panama after $7 million ransom paid', *Reuters*, 6 September 2011, http://www.reuters.com/article/2011/09/06/us-somalia-piracy-idUSTRE7852U H20110906.

39　Michael Peel, 'UK blocks UN move to end pirate funding', *Financial Times*, 8 August 2010.

40　Council Regulation (EU) No. 356/2010, 26 April 2010, *Official Journal of the European Union* L 105/1, 27 April 2010.

41　Ibid.

42　Ibid.

43　US Presidential Executive Order Concerning Somalia, 'Blocking property of certain persons contributing to the conflict in Somalia', 13 April 2010, The White House, Washington DC.

44　Council Regulation (EU) No. 356/2010, 26 April 2010, Official Journal of the European Union L 105/1, 27 April 2010, art. 2.

45　HM Treasury Financial Sanctions Notice, Somalia, Council Regulation (EU) No 356/2010, 28 April 2010.

46　Jay Bahadur, 'The pirate king of Somalia', *Globe and Mail*, 26 April 2009.

47　*Report of the Monitoring Group on Somalia pursuant to Security Council Resolution 1853 (2008)*, S/2010/91, United Nations, New York, 10 March 2010, p. 42.

48　Ibid., New York, p. 41.

49　Jane Novak, 'US Treasury freezes Fares Manna's assets', *Armies of Liberation*, 14 April 2010, http://armiesofliberation.com/archives/2010/04/14/us-treasury-freezes-fares-mannas-assets/.

50　'Security Council Committee on Somalia and Eritrea Issues List of Individuals, Identified Pursuant to Paragraph 8 of Resolution 1844 (2008)' UN Security Council, Department of Public Information, News and Media Division, New York, 12 April 2010, SC/9904.

51　Phillip Carter of the Bureau of African Affairs of the United States State Department, 'The US Government's Approach to Somalia', transcript of address, 22 July 2009, Chatham House, London.

52　Ibid.

53　Murithi Mutiga, 'Al Qaeda veterans now run Al-Shabaab Militia', *East African*, 26 July 2010, http://allafrica.com/stories/printable/201007261357.html.

54 Stephen Askins, *Paying Ransoms – Could the US make this more difficult?*, London: Ince & Co., 2010.

55 [2010] EWHC 280 (Comm).

56 Ibid.

57 'EU NAVFOR warship SPS Victoria apprehends pirate attack skiff', *EU NAVFOR* 3 August 2010, www.eunavfor.eu/2010/08/eu-navfor-warship-sps-victoria-apprehends-pirate-attack-skiff/.

58 'Detained suspects sent back to Somalia', *EU NAVFOR*, 5 August 2010, www.eunavfor.eu/2010/08/detained-suspects-sent-back-to-somalia/.

59 Recommendation 1913 (2010) Parliamentary Assembly of the Council of Europe, http://assembly.coe.int/Main.asp?link=/Documents/AdoptedText/ta10/EREC1913.htm.

60 Ibid., 3.2.

61 Ibid., 3.4.

62 Craig Whitlock, 'Lack of prosecution poses challenge for foreign navies that catch Somali pirates', *Washington Post*, 24 May 2010, www.washingtonpost.com/wp-dyn/content/article/2010/05/23/AR2010052303893.html.

63 Press Association report, 8 July 2010, citing Commodore Tim Lowe, RN, former commander of Royal Navy forces in the Middle East, cited in John Knott, 'New strategies and ideas for countering piracy off Somalia; Piracy prosecutions; human rights issues', 22 July 2010, www.idaratmaritime.com/wordpress/?p=261, to which article I am greatly indebted.

64 Address by the executive director of UNODC to the United Nations sixty-fourth General Assembly, Informal Meeting of the Plenary on Piracy, 14 May 2010, GA/10940.

65 UK Foreign & Commonwealth Office statement, 12 March 2010.

66 BBC News, 1 November 2006.

67 *Daily Nation* online, 21 May 2010.

68 UNODC 25 June 2010.

69 www.idaratmaritime.com/wordpress/?p=261.

70 *Agence France Presse*, 15 July 2010.

71 Mike Pflanz, 'At last, a court to try Somali pirates', *Christian Science Monitor*, 8 July 2010, www.csmonitor.com/World/Africa/2010/0708/At-last-a-court-to-try-Somali-pirates.

72 Somali pirate sentenced to 33 years in US prison, *BBC News*, 16 February 2011, www.bbc.co.uk/news/world-us-canada-12486129, accessed 4 December 2012.

73 'Somali admits in US court to ship hijacking', *Reuters*, 18 May 2010, www.alertnet.org/thenews/newsdesk/N18159113.htm.

74 Colin Freeman, 'Somali pirates on trial in Holland', *The Sunday Telegraph*, 13 June 2010.

75 'Yemen court sentences six Somali pirates to death', *Reuters*, 18 May 2010, www.reuters.com/article/idUSTRE64H3EL20100518.

76 Nick Hopkins, 'Outgunned Somali pirates can hardly believe their luck', *Guardian*, 8 May 2012.

77 House of Commons, *Hansard*, 12 January 2009, col. 108 W.

78 John S. Burnett, 'Captain Kidd, human-rights victim', *The New York Times*, 20 April 2008.

79 The West of England (insurer) 1 April 2011, www.westpandi.com/Publications/News/Archive/South-Africa/.

80 Ramola Talwar Badam, 'UAE Coastguard detains floating weapons arsenal off Fujairah', *The National*, Abu Dhabi, 17 October 2012, www.thenational.ae/news/uae-news/uae-coastguard-detains-floating-weapons-arsenal-off-fujairah, accessed 7 December 2012.

81 Aislinn Laing, 'Brits detained in Eritrea for "espionage" released', *The Daily Telegraph*, London, 12 June 2012, http://www.telegraph.co.uk/news/worldnews/africaandindian ocean/eritrea/8571226/Brits-detained-in-Eritrea-for-espionage-released.html, accessed 7 December 2012.

82 Ibid.

83 Bryden, Matt, Deisser, Emmanuel et al., 'A report focusing on Somalia of the Monitoring Group on Somalia and Eritrea', 13 July 2012, S/2012/544, United Nations, New York, p. 280.

84 'IMO plans to launch global standards for armed guards', *Lloyd's List*, 18 May 2012.

85 Annie Banerji, 'Italy challenges India in Supreme Court over fishermen's deaths', *Reuters*, 29 August 2012, http://in.reuters.com/article/2012/08/29/india-italy-marines-idIN DEE87S0CQ20120829, accessed 6 December 2012.

86 Rahul Das, 'Mistaken for pirate, Indian fisherman shot off Oman coast', *The Indian Express*, 22 April 2010, www.indianexpress.com/news/mistaken-for-pirate-indian-fis herman-shot-off-oman-coast/609609/, accessed 5 September 2012.

87 International Tribunal for the Law of the Sea, 1 July 1999, the *M/V 'Saiga' (No. 2)* case (*Saint Vincent and The Grenadines* v. *Guinea*).

88 *Best Management Practices Version 4*, Edinburgh: Witherby Publishing Group Ltd., 2011, p. 23.

89 Ibid., p. 40.

90 MSC 78/26/Add 1. Annex, Resolution MSC. 153 (78) (adopted on 20 May 2004, Adoption of Amendments to the International Convention for the Safety of Life at Sea, 1974, as amended, International Maritime Organization, London, 2004 http://www.imo. org/OurWork/Facilitation/IllegalMigrants/Documents/Resolution%20MSC.153(78)-MSC%2078.pdf.

91 'Revised interim guidance to shipowners, ship operators and shipmasters on the use of privately contracted armed security personnel on board ships in the high risk area', MSC. 1/Circ. 1405/Rev 2, International Maritime Organization, London, 25 May 2012, Annex p. 1.

92 Ibid., Annex p. 1.

93 Ibid., Annex p. 3.

94 BMP 4 Best Management Practices for Protection against Somalia Based Piracy, SIGTTO, INTERTANKO et al., Version 4 – August 2011, Witherby Publishing Group Ltd., Edinburgh, para. 8.15, p. 40.

9 VESSEL DEFENCE

1 'American Peace Commissioners to John Jay', 28 March 1786, 'Thomas Jefferson Papers', Series 1. General Correspondence. 1651–1827, Library of Congress. LoC: 28 March 1786 and *The Atlantic Monthly* vol. 30, Issue 180, October 1872. 'Jefferson, American Minister in France', http://cdl.library.cornell.edu/cgi-bin/moa/pageviewer? ammem/coll=moa&root=/moa/atla/atla0030/&tif=00419.TIF&view=50&frames=1.

2 'Tough self protection measures by MV BW Lion evade pirates', 10 November 2009, EUNAVFOR, http://eunavfor.eu/tough-self-protection-measures-by-mv-bw-lion-evade-pirates/.

3 Ibid.

4 'Dutch captain tells of escape from pirates', *Radio Netherlands Worldwide*, 5 January 2010, http://www.rnw.nl/international-justice/article/dutch-captain-tells-escape-pirates.

5 Ibid.

6 Ibid.

7 Ibid.

8 Ibid.

9 Ibid.

10 Fergal Keane, 'British captain's Somali pirate nightmare', BBC News, 19 January 2010, http://news.bbc.co.uk/1/hi/world/africa/8465770.stm.

11 Ibid.

12 Ibid.

13 gCaptain.com, 15 April 2009, http://gcaptain.com/forum/professional-mariner-forum/1514-letter-maersk-alabama.html.

14 'Crewman's e-mail gives harrowing details of hijacking', *CNN*, 20 April 2009, http://edition.cnn.com/2009/WORLD/africa/04/16/somalia.hijacked.ship.email/index.html.

15 gCaptain.com, 15 April 2009, http://gcaptain.com/forum/professional-mariner-forum/1514-letter-maersk-alabama.html.

16 Ibid.

17 Ibid.

18 Ibid.

19 The fantail is an overhang at the extreme rear of the ship, to the rear of the poop deck.

20 A padeye is a type of fitting on a boat that incorporates a loop or ring that can be used as an attachment point.

21 A fairlead is a block, padeye, ring or any other device that controls the path of a line on a boat.

22 Ibid.

23 Ibid.

24 Ibid.

25 Ibid.

26 gCaptain.com, 15 April 2009, http://gcaptain.com/forum/professional-mariner-forum/ 1514-letter-maersk-alabama.html.

27 'US captain rescued from pirates', *BBC News*, 13 April 2009, http://news.bbc.co.uk/1/hi/ world/africa/79,96087.stm.

28 Mike Perry (chief engineer); Ken Quinn (second mate); Matt Fisher (first engineer); Dick Mathews (second engineer); John Cronan (third engineer); William Rios (BOSN); Richard Hicks (steward); John White (electrician); Jimmy Sabga (qualified member of engine department (QMED)); Miguel Ruiz (wiper); ATM Reza (able-bodied seaman); Andrew Brzezinski (able-bodied seaman); Mohammad Abdlawahab (able-bodied seaman); Hector Sanchez (able-bodied seaman); Husain Salah (steward assistant); Mario Clotter (cook).

29 Drew Griffin and David Fitzpatrick, 'Hero skipper ignored pirate warnings, crew says', CNN Special Investigations Unit, 25 May 2010, http://edition.cnn.com/2010/US/05/21/ siu.phillips.pirates/ (accessed 16 December 2013).

30 'Capt. Richard Phillips Risked Crew's Lives Before Hijacking, Suit Alleges', ABC News, 2 October 2013, http://abcnews.go.com/blogs/entertainment/2013/10/capt-richard-phillips-risked-crews-lives-before-hijacking-suit-alleges/ (accessed 16 December 2013).

31 Andrew Dansby, "Colin Wright, the third mate on the Alabama, has his own story to tell", *The Houston Chronicle*, 13 October 2013, http://www.houstonchronicle.com/ entertain-ment/article/Colin-Wright-the-third-mate-on-the-Alabama-has-4888687.php (accessed 16 December 2013).

32 www.pravenue.com/newsletter.asp?article=4234.

33 Richard Phillips, *A Captain's Duty: Somali Pirates, Navy SEALs, and Dangerous Days at Sea*, London: Hyperion Books, 2010.

34 Ben Child, 'Captain Phillips "no hero" in real life, say ship's crew', *Guardian*, 14 October 2013.

35 Rob Walker, 'Inside story of Somali pirate attack', *BBC News*, 4 June 2009.

36 'Hijacked oil tanker Moscow University freed in dramatic rescue – pirates captured', *EU NAVFOR*, 6 May 2010, www.eunavfor.eu/2010/05/hijacked-oil-tanker-moscow-university-freed-in-dramatic-rescue-%E2%80%93-pirates-captured/.

37 'Pirate killed in Russian rescue of sailors', *AP*, *Guardian*, 6 May 2010, www.guardian.co. uk/world/2010/may/06/sailors-russian-tanker-hijacked-somali-pirates.

38 'US Navy thwarts pirate attack off Oman, officials say', *CNN World*, 25 March 2011, http://articles.cnn.com/2011-03-25/world/oman.navy.pirates_1_pirate-attack-european-union-naval-force-vessel?_s=PM:WORLD.

39 'Moscow University: All pirates killed – Voitenko', *Flags of Convenience*, 11 May 2010, http://convenientflags.blogspot.com/2010/05/moscow-university-pirates-all-killed.html.

40 'Somalia calls Russia to account over pirate deaths', *Radio Netherlands Worldwide*, 14 May 2010, www.rnw.nl/international-justice/article/somalia-calls-russia-account-over-pirate--deaths.

41 'Piracy – the East African/Somalia situation', *OCIMF*, 2009, www.ocimf.com/Library/ Information-Papers.

42 Captain Peter Corbett, *A Modern Plague of Pirates*, East Mersea, Essex: Off Shore Marine, 2009.

43 Here I declare an interest, as a director of Idarat Ltd, because we provide advice to shipowners and the insurance industry.

44 David Osler, 'Sonic solution may not be a sound investment', *Lloyd's List*, 2 December 2008.

45 Ed Cumming, 'The Active Denial System: the weapon that's a hot topic', *The Daily Telegraph*, 20 July 2010.

46 UK Department of Transport, 'Interim Guidance to UK Flagged Shipping on the Use of Armed Guards to Defend Against the Threat of Piracy in Exceptional Circumstances', London, 2012, version 1.1 (updated June 2012).

47 Commander Dow, 14 January 2010, evidence to the House of Lords, European Union Committee, 12th Report of Session 2009–10, 'Combating Somali piracy: The EU's naval operation Atalanta', Report with Evidence, HL Paper 103, The Stationery Office Ltd, London, published 14 April 2010.

48 Rear Admiral Hudson, 14 January 2010, evidence to the House of Lords, European Union Committee, 12th Report of Session 2009–10, 'Combating Somali piracy: The EU's naval operation Atalanta', Report with Evidence, HL Paper 103, The Stationery Office Ltd, London, published 14 April 2010, p. 10.

49 'Pirate attacks cut dramatically by navies, US admiral says', *Bloomberg.com*, 27 January 2009, www.bloomberg.com/apps/news?pid=newsarchive&sid=aXR8.j52hcpo&refer=uk.

50 'Somali piracy reduced but still a threat: Adm. Gary Roughead', *World Military Forum*, 24 August 2009, www.armybase.us/2009/08/somali-piracy-reduced-but-still-a-threat-adm-gary-roughead/.

10 ARE THERE ANSWERS?

1 Markus Virgil Hoehne, *Counter-Terrorism in Somalia: How External Interference Helped to Produce Militant Islamism*, Halle/Saale: Max Planck Institute for Social Anthropology, 2009, p. 26.

2 *Report of the Monitoring Group on Somalia and Eritrea*, S/2011/433, 18 July 2011, New York: United Nations, p. 17.

3 'Indian navy foils another piracy attempt', *NewKerala.com*, 12 November 2010, www.newkerala.com/news/world/fullnews-82760.html.

4 At a seminar in March 2011, subject to Chatham House Rules.

5 'Crew uses safe room to foil Somali pirate attack', *Associated Press*, *Bloomberg.com*, 4 January 2011.

6 Meeting on board *HMS Cornwall*, February 2011, moored at Dubai, with Commander David Wilkinson, RN, and other officers.

7 International Safety Management Code (ISM Code) and Guidelines on Implementation the ISM Code (2010 Edition) International Maritime Organization, London.

8   Oil Companies International Marine Forum, London, 2009.

9   House of Lords, European Union Committee, 12th Report of Session 2009–10, 'Combating Somali piracy: The EU's naval operation Atalanta', Report with Evidence, HL Paper 103, The Stationery Office Ltd, London, published 14 April 2010.

10 'Better management practice rather than force the key to beating piracy', *Ship Management International*, 1 October 2010.

11 DNK Oslo Maritime Security Seminar, 5 November 2010, my own notes. In addition to Major General Buster Howes (commander EU NAVFOR), Vice Admiral Xavier Magne (French Navy) and Rear Admiral Robert O. Wray (USN) spoke.

12 Frank Gardner, 'Somali piracy: A broken business model?', BBC News, 29 November 2012, www.bbc.co.uk/news/world-africa-20549056, accessed 29 November 2012.

13 'Somali piracy: EU forces in first mainland raid', BBC News, 15 May 2012, www.bbc.co.uk/news/world-africa-18069685, accessed 10 December 2012.

14 Jean Marc Mojon, 'The wretched of the sea: piracy's 600 anonymous hostages', *Agence France Presse*, 17 December 2010.

15 Ibid.

16 'Somali pirates fire at Spanish warship: EU', *Safe Seas* (AFP), 8 November 2010, http://safewaters.wordpress.com/2010/11/08/piracy-somali-pirates-fire-at-spanish-warship-eu/.

17 Jeffrey Gettleman and Mohamed Ibrahim, 'Insurgents' seizure of a pirate base in Somalia raises questions about its future', *The New York Times*, 2 May 2010, www.nytimes.com/2010/05/03/world/africa/03somalia.html.

18 Jonathan Saul, 'Somali pirates use Yemen island as fuel base', *Reuters Africa*, 5 July 2011.

19 Position: 00°38N 063°59E, course 145°, speed 2.2 knots.

20 Position: 12°38N 059°00E, course 310°, speed 12 knots.

21 Position: 13°27S 053°03E, course 102°, speed 9.1 knots.

22 Position: 00°50N 050°09E, course 342°, speed 13.4 knots.

23 Gill Charlton, 'Kenyan tourism hurt by new kidnapping', *Daily Telegraph*, 8 October 2011.

24 *Cargoes* by John Mansfield, published in *Ballads*, 1903, Elkin Mathews, London.

25 Giffen goods: inferior quality goods, whose demand is driven by poverty, a quotation from Veeresh Malik's, 'An Indian view of piracy', *Idarat* blog, 7 March 2011, www.idaratmaritime.com/wordpress/?p=317.

26 Jared Diamond, *Collapse, How Societies Choose to Fail or Succeed*, New York: Viking, 2005, p. 276.

27 W.B. Yeats, 'The Second Coming' (1920).

28 'Corruption and its consequences in Equatorial Guinea', Briefing Paper, March 2010, Open Society Justice Initiative, Washington DC, p. 3.

29 'GUINEA: Reputation for corruption worsens', *IRIN*, 24 September 2008, www.irinnews.org/report.aspx?ReportId=80575.

30 Sara Schonhardt, 'Spike in pirate attacks in Indonesian waters raises warnings', *Voice of America*, 6 September 2010, www.voanews.com/english/news/Spike-in-Pirate-Attacks-in-Indonesian-Waters-Raises-Warnings-102283754.html.

31   UNICEF, www.unicef.org/infobycountry/somalia_865.html, accessed 22 August 2010.

32   'Horn of Africa drought: UK charities boost Somalia aid', *BBC News*, 13 July 2011, www.bbc.co.uk/news/uk-14132721.

33   Weekly Humanitarian Report OCHA, Issue #25, 17–24 June 2011, UNOCHA Somalia, Nairobi.

34   Zoe Flood, 'UN refugee agency warns of crisis "of unimaginable proportions" in Somalia drought', *Daily Telegraph*, 6 July 2011, www.telegraph.co.uk/news/worldnews/africaandi ndianocean/somalia/8621079/UN-refugee-agency-warns-of-crisis-of-unimaginable-proportions-in-Somalia-drought.html.

35   Ben Brown, 'Horn of Africa drought: A vision of hell at the Dabeeb refugee camp', *Daily Telegraph*, 9 July 2011.

36   'UN makes first aid airlift to rebel-held Somali region', *Independent Online, South Africa*, 18 July 2011, www.iol.co.za/news/africa/un-delivers-aid-to-somalia-1.1100523#. UMCAu4PqnE0, accessed 6 December 2012.

37   'Britain views pre-emptive strike on Iran nuclear facilities as illegal', *The Daily Telegraph*, London, 26 October 2012, www.telegraph.co.uk/news/worldnews/middleeast/iran/ 9636134/Britain-views-pre-emptive-strike-on-Iran-nuclear-facilities-as-illegal.html, accessed 10 December 2012.

38   Rory Stewart, 'The real reason we are in Afghanistan', *Spiegel Online*, 7 January 2010, www.spiegel.de/international/world/0,1518,703408,00.html.

39   Ron Suskind, 'Faith, certainty and the presidency of George W. Bush', *The New York Times*, 17 October 2004.

40   Bronwyn E. Bruton, 'Somalia, a new approach', Council on Foreign Affairs Special Report No. 52. March 2010, Washington DC, p. 32.

41   'Somalia: A new approach', an event at Chatham House, London, on 21 July 2010 with Bronwyn Bruton.

42   Istanbul Declaration, Istanbul, Turkey, 22 May 2010, United Nations.

43   See International Contact Group on Somalia, 5–6 February 2012, Djibouti, Final Communiqué, http://unpos.unmissions.org/LinkClick.aspx?fileticket=pnYyg_OMs K8%3D&tabid=9748&language=en-US, accessed 10 December 2012.

44   'Somalia', *The New York Times*, 5 October 2012, http://topics.nytimes.com/top/news/i nternational/countriesandterritories/somalia/index.html, accessed 10 December 2012.

45   Michael Weinstein, 'No simple narrative in Somalia drama', Center for Strategic and International Studies, Washington DC, 2010, http://csis.org/print/13921, accessed 10 December 2012.

46   Ioan M. Lewis, *Making and Breaking States in Africa, The Somali Experience*, Trenton, New Jersey and Asmara, Eritrea: The Red Sea Press, 2010, p. xix.

47   Jason Burke, 'Riyadh will build nuclear weapons if Iran gets them, Saudi prince warns', *Guardian*, 29 June 2011, www.guardian.co.uk/world/2011/jun/29/saudi-build-nuclear-weapons-iran.

48   Heidy Rehman, Citigroup, September 2012, cited by Christopher Helman in Forbes 4 September 2012, www.forbes.com/sites/christopherhelman/2012/09/04/saudi-arabia-

to-become-an-oil-importer-heres-how-they-can-avoid-it/?utm_source=dlvr.it&utm_medium=twitter, accessed 6 September 2012.

49 Dilip Hiro, *After Empire, The Birth of a Multipolar World*, New York: Nation Books, 2010.

50 International Court of Justice, *Armed Activities on the Territory of the Congo (DRC* v. *Uganda)*, 19 December 2005.

51 John Maynard Keynes, *The Economic Consequences of the Peace*, London: Macmillan and Co. Ltd, 1919, pp. 9–10.

52 Ibid.

53 Ibid.

54 Jonathan Saul, 'Pirate attacks by heavily armed gangs surge off Nigerian coast', Reuters, London, 17 October 2013, http://www.reuters.com/article/2013/10/17/us-shipping-piracy-idUSBRE99G16320131017 (accessed 23 December 2013).

55 Keith Wallis, 'Tanker hijackings raise piracy concerns in seas around Singapore', Reuters, Singapore, 12 November 2013, http://www.reuters.com/article/2013/11/12/us-shipping-singapore-piracy-idUSBRE9AB06420131112 (accessed 23 December 2013).

56 Thomas Hobbes, *Leviathan or The Matter, Forme and Power of a Common Wealth Ecclesiasticall and Civil*, London: Andrew Crooke, 1651, ch. 13.

BIBLIOGRAPHY

Abbugao, Martin. 'Somali pirates controlled by syndicates: Interpol'. *Yahoo! News*, 14 October 2009.

Abdi, Sahra. 'Sufi group vows to rid Somalia of radical Islamists'. *Reuters.com*, 28 March 2010. www.reuters.com (accessed 2 April 2010).

Adbullahi, Zam Zam. 'Struggling for women's rights in Somalia'. *Amnesty International*, 20 January 2009. www.amnesty.org/en/news-and-updates/feature-stories/struggling-womens-rights-somalia-20090120.

African Watch Committee. *Somalia, A Government at War with its Own People*. New York: The African Watch Committee, 1990.

Ahmed, Ismail I. and Reginald Herbold Green. 'The heritage of war and state collapse in Somalia and Somaliland: Low-level effects, external interventions and reconstruction'. *Third World Quarterly* 20, no. 1 (1999): 113–27.

Ali, M.Y. 'Hydrocarbon potential of Somaliland'. *First Break* 24 (August 2006).

Al-Nasser, Nassir Abdulaziz. *Report of the Monitoring Group on Somalia pursant to Security Council Resolution 1630 (2005)*. New York: United Nations, May 2006.

—— *Report of the Monitoring Group on Somalia pursant to Security Council Resolution 1676 (2006)*. New York: United Nations, November 2006.

Alston, Philip, special rapporteur on extrajudical, summary or arbituary executions. *Report to the 64th Session of the United Nations General Assembly, Third Committee, 27 October 2009, New York*. New York: The United Nations, 2009.

Amnesty International. *Blood at the Crossroads, Making the Case for a Global Arms Trade Treaty*. London: Amnesty International, 2008.

Amr, Hady. 'Saving a failed state'. 12 February 2010. www.brookings.edu (accessed 27 March 2010).

Antony, Robert. *Like Froth Floating on the Sea: The World of Pirates and Seafarers in Late Imperial South China*. Vols. Institute for East Asian Studies, China Research Monographs. Berkeley, California: University of California Press, 2003.

Armed Activities on the Territory of the Congo (DRC v. Uganda). International Court of Justice, The Hague, 19 December 2005.

Arshad, Mohammed. 'US gives Somalia about 40 tons of arms, ammunition'. *Reuters Alert Net*. 27 June 2009. www.alertnet.org, accessed 27 October 2009.

Badr, Ashraf. 'Egypt to grant South Sudan $300 m for projects'. *Reuters.com*. 11 July 2010. www.reuters.com/article/idUSLDE66A04120100711 (accessed 18 August 2010).

Bahadur, Jay. 'Pirates Inc'. *Financial Times*, June 2010.

—— *Deadly Waters, Inside The Hidden World of Somalia's Pirates*. London: Profile Books, 2011.

Baja, Lauro L. Jr. *Report of the Monitoring Group on Somalia Pursuant to Security Council Resolution 1519 (2003)*. New York: United Nations, August 2004.

—— *Report of the Monitoring Group on Somalia Pursuant to Security Council Resolution 1587 (2005)*. New York: United Nations, October 2005.

Bakonyi, Jutta. 'Between protest, revenge and material interests: A phenomenological analysis of looting in the Somali war'. *Disasters* (Blackwell Publishing/Overseas Development Institute) 34, no. S2 (2010): S238–S255.

Bamfo, Napoleon A. 'Ethiopia's invasion of Somalia in 2006: Motives and lessons learned'. *African Journal of Political Science and International Relations* 4, no. 2 (February 2010): 55–66.

Bates, Robert H. 'Political conflict and state failure'. Chap. 7. In Benno Ndulu, Stephen A. O'Connell, Robert H. Bates, Paul Collier, Chukwuma C. Soludo, Jean-Paul Azam, Augustin K. Fosu, Jan Willem Gunning (eds), Dominique Njinkeu (auth.). *The Political Economy of Economic Growth in Africa, 1960–2000*. Vol. 1. Cambridge: Cambridge University Press, 2008.

Bayart, Jean-François, Stephen Eillis and Béatrice Hibou. *The Criminalization of the State in Africa*. Oxford: James Currey, 1999.

BBC. 'US to resume engagement with ICC'. *BBC*. 16 November 2009. http://news.bbc.co.uk/1/hi/8363282.stm (accessed 1 March 2010).

Beaumont, Peter. 'Violence, fear and confusion: Welcome to the Horn of Africa'. *The Observer*. 10 January 2010.

Bell, Stewart. 'Somali militants training pirates'. *NationalPost.com*, 3 December 2009. www.nationalpost.com (accessed 7 January 2010).

Berube, Claude. 'Marine corps, private security companies and piracy'. *Janes Intelligence Review*, March 2009: 34–7.

Birdsall, Nancy. *Do No Harm: Aid, Weak Institutions, and the Missing Middle in Africa*. Center for Global Development, Center for Global Development, March 2007: 1–32.

Bohn, Michael K. *The Achille Lauro Hijacking, Lesson in the Politics and Prejudice of Terrorism*. Washington DC: Potomac Books Inc., 2004.

Bordonaro, Lorenzo I. 'Introduction: Guinea-Bissau today – the irrelevance of the state and the permanence of change'. *African Studies Review* 52, no. 2 (September 2009): 35–45.

Bowden, Mark. *Black Hawk Down: A Story of Modern War*. New York: Atlantic Monthly Press, 1999.

Branfman, Fred. 'Mass assassinations lie at the heart of America's military strategy in the Muslim world'. *AlterNet*. 24 August 2010. www.alternet.org/.

Bryden, Matt, Deisser, Emmanuel et al., 'A report focusing on Eritrea of the Monitoring Group on Somalia and Eritrea', 13 July 2012, S/2012/545, United Nations, New York.

—— 'A report focusing on Somalia of the Monitoring Group on Somalia and Eritrea', 13 July 2012, S/2012/544, United Nations, New York.

Bruton, Bronwyn E. *Somalia: A New Approach*. New York: Council on Foreign Relations, March 2010.

Burgess, Stephen F. 'Stabilization, peacebuilding, and sustainability in the Horn of Africa'. *Strategic Studies Quarterly*, Spring 2009: 81–118.

Burnett, John S. *Dangerous Waters, Modern Piracy and Terror on The High Seas*. London: PLUME, 2003.

BIBLIOGRAPHY

Burton, Fred and Scott Stewart. 'Al-Qaeda in the Arabian peninsula: Desperation or new life?' *www.stratfor.com*, 28 January 2009. www.stratfor.com/weekly/20090128_al_qaeda_ara-bian_peninsula_desperation_or_new_life (accessed 22 July 2012).

Byman, Daniel L. 'Our two-faced friends in Sanaa'. *Brookings Institute*, 27 March 2010. www.brookings.edu (accessed 30 March 2010).

Cable, James. *Navies in Violent Peace*. Basingstoke, Hampshire: Macmillan, 1989.

Carr, Matthew. *The Infernal Machine*. New York: The New Press, 2006.

Cassanelli, Lee V. 'Somali land resource issues in historical perspective'. In Jeffrey Herbst and Walter S. Clarke (eds). *Learning from Somalia: Lessons of Armed Humanitarian Intervention*. Boulder, Colorado: Westview Press, 1997.

Cawthorne, Nigel. *Pirates of the 21st Century, How Modern-Day Buccaneers are Terrorising The World's Oceans*. London: John Blake, 2009.

Charbonneau, Loius. 'Somali tied to Islamists worked with two UN agencies'. *Reuters*, 11 March 2010.

Chomsky, Noam. *Pirates and Emperors, Old and New, International Terrorism in the Real World*. London: Pluto Press, 2002.

—— *What We Say Goes Conversations on US Power in a Changing World (interviews with David Barsamian)*. New York: Metropolitan Books, 2007.

Clarke, Walter and Jeffrey Herbst (eds). *Learning from Somalia Walter, The Lessons of Humanitarian Intervention*. Boulder, Colorado: Westview Press, 1997.

Colangelo, Anthony J. 'Constitutional limits on extraterritorial jurisdiction: Terrorism and the intersection of national and international law'. *Harvard International Law Journal* 48, no. 1 (Winter 2007).

Collier, Paul, Gordon Conway and Tony Venables. 'Climate change and Africa'. *Oxford Review of Economic Policy*, 2008: 337–53.

Combating Terrorism Center. 'Al-Qaida's (mis)adventures in the Horn of Africa'. *Harmony Project*, 2007.

Copley, Gregory R. 'Yemen hysteria hides deeper strategic matrix of long-term importance'. *OilPrice.com*, 19 January 2010. www.oilprice.com (accessed 20 January 2010).

Daily Mail. 'Terror for 1,200 Britons as Somali pirates with rocket launchers attack cruise ship', 5 March 2009.

Daloz, Jean-Pascal and Patrick Chabal. *African Works: Disorder as Political Instrument*. Oxford: International African Institute in association with James Currey, 1999.

Danish Maritime Authority. *Danica White Pirate Attack and Hijacking on 1 June 2007*. Cophenagen, Denmark: Danish Maritime Authority, 2007.

Davies, Charles E. *The Blood-Red Arab Flag, An Investigation into Qasimi Piracy 1797–1820*. Exeter, Devon: University of Exeter Press, 1997.

Defoe, Daniel (attr.). *A General History of the Pyrates*. New York: Dover Publications, 1999 (1724).

Dickens, Charles. *A Christmas Carol*. London: Elliot Stock, 1843.

Doornbos, Martin and Mohamud H. Khalif. 'The Somali region in Ethiopia: A Neglected human rights tragedy'. *Review of African Political Economy* 91 (2002): 73–94.

Drakard, Martyn. 'The edge of piracy: Somalia's challenge to the world'. *The Cutting Edge*. 8 February 2010. www.thecuttingedgenews.com/index.php?article=11955 (accessed 22 February 2010).

Drake, John. 'New Somali clans to join pirate trade'. *Lloyd's List*, 6 November 2009.

Eichstaedt, Peter. *Pirate State, Inside Somalia's Terrorism at Sea*. Chicago, Illinois: Lawrence Hill Books, 2010.

Eizenstat, Stuart E., John Edward Porter, Jeremy M. Weinstein. 'Rebuilding weak states'. *Foreign Affairs* 84, no. 1 (January/February 2005): 134–46.

EU NAVFOR. 'Detained suspects sent back to Somalia'. *www.eunavfor.eu. 5 August 2010. www.eunavfor.eu/2010/08/detained-suspects-sent-back-to-somalia* (accessed 5 August 2010).

Falola, Toyin. *Violence in Nigeria, The Crisis of Religious Politics and Secular Ideologies*. Rochester, New York: University of Rochester Press, 1998.

Fineman, Mark. 'The oil factor in Somalia'. *The Los Angeles Times*, 18 January 1993.

Fletcher, Martin. 'Danish special forces storm cargo ship to Thwart Somali pirate attack'. *The Times*, 6 February 2010.

Foreign Policy and the Fund for Peace. 'Failed states index 2009'. *Foreign Policy*. 22 June 2009. www.foreignpolicy.com/articles/2009/06/22/2009_failed_states_index_interactive_map_and_rankings (accessed 2 April 2010).

Frankel, Matthew. 'What can Pakistan teach us about Yemen?' *Brookings Institute*. 26 February 2010. www.brookings.edu (accessed 27 March 2010).

Friedman, Thomas L. *Hot, Flat and Crowded*. London: Allen Lane, 2008.

Gettleman, Jeffrey. 'Somalia's president assails UN report on corruption'. *The New York Times*, March 2010.

―――― 'US Aiding Somalia in Its Plan to Retake Its Capital'. *The New York Times*, 5 March 2010.

Glocer, Karen A. and Angela Telerski, Paul Viotti. 'Viewing predator behavior through the lens of microeconomics'. March 2002, University of California, Santa Cruz.

Gordon, Ruth. 'Growing constitutions'. *Journal of Constitutional Law* 1, no. 3 (1999): 528–83.

Greenberg, Michael D., Peter Chalk, Henry H. Willis, Ivan Khilko, David S. Ortiz. *Maritime Terrorism, Risk and Liability*. Santa Monica, California: RAND Corporation, 2006, pp. 1–199.

Guled, Abdi. 'Somali Al-Shabaab Rebel Commander Shot Dead'. 20 March 2010. www.reuters.com (accessed 2 April 2010).

―――― 'Somali rebels planning attack on Mogadishu port-sources'. *Reuters.com*. 2 April 2010. www.reuters.com/article/latestCrisis/idUSLDE63103J (accessed 2 April 2010).

Hagmann, Tobias and Markus V. Hoehne. 'Failures of the state failure debate: Evidence form the Somali territories'. *Journal of International Development* 21 (2009): 42–57.

Hague, Rt Hon. William (MP) foreign secretary, UK, 'A new effort to help Somalia'. Chatham House, London. 8 February 2012. Transcript of speech delivered at the conference, British Government Consultation on Somalia, organized by the Chatham House Africa Programme.

Haldi, Stacy Bergstrom. *Why Wars Widen, A Theory of Predation and Balancing*. Portland, Oregon: Frank Cass, 2003.

Hanlon, Joseph. 'Bank corruption becomes site of struggle in Mozambique'. *Review of African Political Economy* 29, no. 91 (2002): 53–72.

Hansen, Stig Jarle. *Piracy in the Greater Gulf of Aden, Myths, Misconceptions and Remedies*. Oslo: Norwegian Institute for Urban and Regional Research, 2009: 1–74.

Harris, David. 'From "warlord" to "democratic" president: How Charles Taylor won the 1997 Liberian elections'. *Journal of Modern African Studies* 37, no. 3 (1999): 431–55.

Hartmann, Ingrid and Sugulle, Ahmed J. 'Report: The impact of cimate change on pastoral societies in Somaliland'. Djibouti: Candlelight for Health, Education & Environment, November 2009.

Healy, Sally. 'Hostage to conflict prospects for building regional economic cooperation in the Horn of Africa'. London: Chatham House, November 2011

Heilprin, John. 'Most hijacked ships ignored safety precautions'. *Associated Press*. 28 January 2010. www.ap.org (accessed 30 January 2010).

Heller, Claude. 'Report of the Monitoring Group on Somalia Pursuant to Security Council Resolution 1858 (2008)'. United Nations, New York, 10 March 2010, 1–110.

Heller-Roazen, Daniel. *The Enemy of All, Piracy and the Law of Nations*. New York: Zone Books, 2009.

Herbst, Jeffrey. *States and Power in Africa*. Princeton, New Jersey: Princeton University Press, 2000.

Hill, Charles S. *Episodes of Piracy in the Eastern Seas 1519 to 1852*. Bombay, India: Mazaon, 1920.

Hill, Ginny. *Yemen: Fear of Failure*. Briefing Paper, London: Chatham House, January 2010.

Hiro, Dilip. *After Empire, The Birth of a Multipolar World*. New York: Nation Books, 2010.

Hobbes, Thomas. *Leviathan or The Matter, Forme and Power of a Common Wealth Ecclesiasticall and Civil*. London: Andrew Crooke, 1651.

Hodges, Michael. *AK 47: The Story of a Gun*. n.d.

Hoehne, Markus Virgil. *Counter-Terrorism in Somalia: How External Interference Helped to Produce Militant Islamism*. Halle/Saale: Max Planck Institute for Social Anthropology, 2009.

Hoehne, Tobias and Markus V. Hagmann. 'Failures of the state failure debate: Evidence from the Somali territories'. *Journal of International Development* 21 (2009): 42–57.

Hopkins, Donna. 'The changing threat from Somali pirates and their major centers of activity in 2012'. Article commissioned by Institute for Near East and Gulf Military Analysis (INEGMA) on behalf of second United Arab Emirates Counter Piracy Conference, 'A regional response to maritime piracy: Enhancing public–private partnerships and strengthening global engagement', organized by the UAE Ministry of Foreign Affairs in partnership with DP World, held in Dubai in June 2012.

Hornby, Lucy. 'Hijacked China ship shows Somali pirates extending reach. *Reuters*. 20 October 2009.

House of Commons Transport Committee. *Piracy: Government Response to the Committee's Eighth Report of the Session 2005–06*. London: The Stationery Office, 2 November 2006.

House of Lords, European Union Committee. *12th Report of Session 2009–10: 'Combating Somali Piracy: the EU's Naval Operation Atalanta'*, Report with Evidence. London: The Stationery Office Ltd, 14 April 2010.

Howden, Daniel. 'Gaddafi's forty years in power celebrated with a gallery of grotesques'. *The Independent*, 2 September 2009.

Human Rights Watch. '"Why am i still here?", The 2007 Horn of African renditions and the fate of those still missing'. *Human Rights Watch*, October 2008.

———— 'Ethiopia: Country summary', January 2010.

Human Rights Watch, Amnesty and others. 'Off the record, US responsibility for enforced disappearances in the "War on Terror"'. *Human Rights Watch*, June 2007.

Huxley, Tim. *Disintegrating Indonesia? Implications for Regional Security*. London: Oxford University Press/The International Institute for Strategic Studies, 2002.

Hynes, Paul, Richard Furlong, Nathaniel Rudolf. *International Money Laundering and Terrorist Financing: a UK Perspective*. London: Sweet & Maxwell, 2009.

Ibrahim, Mohamed and Duncan Miriri. *Somali Pirate Killed in Cargo Ship Hijack Shooting*. 24 March 2010. www.reuters.com (accessed 2 April 2010).

Ignatius, David. 'What the partisan squabbles miss on Obama's terror response'. *The Washington Post*. 17 February 2010. www.washingtonpost.com/wp-dyn/content/article/2010/02/16/AR2010021605043.html?hpid=opinionsbox1 (accessed 5 March 2010).

International Crisis Group. 'Counter-terrorism in Somalia: Losing hearts and minds?' Brussels, 11 July 2005, 1–28.

—— 'Somalia's Islamists'. Brussels, 12 December 2005.

—— 'Somalia: To move beyond the failed state'. Nairobi/Brussels, 23 December 2008: 1–45.

—— 'Somalia: The tough part is ahead'. 26 January 2007. www.crisisgroup.org/library/documents/africa/horn_of_africa/b45_somalia___the_tough_part_is_ahead.pdf (accessed 1 April 2010).

International Maritime Organization. 'The Djibouto meeting'. *Adoption of the Code of Conduct Concerning the Repression of Piracy and Armed Robbery Against Ships in the Western Indian Ocean and the Gulf of Aden*. London: International Maritime Organization, 2010.

Jackson, Robert. *Quasi-States: Sovereignty, International Relations and the Third World*. New York: Cambridge University Press, 1990.

Jamestown Foundation. 'Somalia's Hizb Al-Islam pledges to retake territory lost to Al-Shabaab rivals'. *Terrorism Monitor* 8, no. 10 (March 2010).

Jervis, Robert. *Perception and Misperception in International Politics*. Princeton, New Jersey: Princeton University Press, 1976.

Johnston, Cynthia. *US Warns Ships off Yemen of Possible Al-Qaeda Attack*. 22 March 2010. www.reuters.com (accessed 2 April 2010).

Kaplan, Seth. 'Rethinking state-building in a failed state'. *The Washington Quarterly* (Center for Strategic and International Studies) 33, no. 1 (January 2010): 81–97.

Keaten, James. 'AP interview: Interpol hunting pirate money'. 20 January 2010. INO.com (accessed 21 January 2010).

Keynes, John Maynard. *The Economic Consequences of the Peace*. London: Macmillan and Co. Ltd, 1919.

Kilcullen, David. 'Death from above, outrage down below'. *The New York Times*, 16 May 2009.

Kimenyi, Mwangi S. 'Fractionalized, armed and lethal: Why Somalia matters'. *The Brookings Institute*. 3 February 2010. www.brookings.edu (accessed 27 March 2010).

Knott, John. 'Somali piracy: The effect of ship hijacking on marine insurance policies'. *Mondaq.com*. 23 February 2010. www.mondaq.com (accessed 25 February 2010).

Kumalo, Dumisani Shadrack. *Report of the Panel of Experts on Somalia Pursuant to Security Council resolution 1474 (2008)*. New York: United Nations, 2008.

Langewiesche, William. 'The pirate latitudes'. *Vanity Fair*, April 2009.

Leeson, Peter T. 'Better off stateless: Somalia before and after government collapse'. *Journal of Comparative Economics* 35, no. 4 (2007): 689–710.

——— 'The invisible hook: The law and economics of pirate tolerance'. *New York University Journal of Law and Liberty* 4, no. 2 (2009): 139–71.

Leimsidor, Bruce. *Conflict in Somalia: International Migration Ramifications.* Università Ca' Foscari. Venezia: DEP, 26 October 2009.

Leonard, David K. 'Recreating political order: The Somali systems today'. Instiute of Development Studies, no. 316 (January 2009): 1–23.

Lewis, I.M. *A Pastoral Democracy: A Study of Pastoralism and Politics among the Northern Somali of the Horn of Africa.* London, 1961.

——— *A Modern History of the Somali, Nation and State in the Horn of Africa.* 4th edn. Oxford: James Currey, 2002.

——— *Understanding Somalia and Somaliland, Culture, History, Society.* London: Hurst & Company, 2008.

——— *Making and Breaking States in Africa, The Somali Experience.* Trenton, New Jersey and Asmara, Eritrea: The Red Sea Press, 2010.

Lewis, Peter M. 'From pre-bendalism to predation: The political economy of decline in Nigeria'. *Journal of Modern African Studies* 34, no. 1 (1996): 79–103.

Liss, Carolin. 'The roots of piracy in southeast Asia'. *Austral Policy Forum 07-18A.* 2007. 1–8.

Long, Larry and Colleen Neumeister. 'Abdiwali Abdiqadir muse: Prosecutors say teenage Somali pirate was brazen ringleader of crew'. *Associated Press,* 22 April 2009.

Love, Roy. 'Economic drivers of conflict and cooperation in the Horn of Africa, a regional perspective and overview'. Chatham House, Briefing Paper, December 2009: 1–16.

Mahbubani, Kishore. *Report of the Panel of Experts pursuant to Security Council Resolution 1343 (2001) paragraph 19, concerning Liberia.* New York: United Nations, 2001.

Marchal, Roland. 'Warlordism and terrorism: how to obscure an already confusing crisis? The case of Somalia'. *International Affairs* 83, no. 6 (2007): 1091–106.

Mayer, Jane. 'The predator war, what are the risks of the CIA's covert drone program?' *The New Yorker.* 26 October 2009. www.newyorker.com/reporting/2009–10/26/091026fa_fact_-mayer (accessed 5 March 2010).

McGregor, Andrew. 'The leading factions behind the Somali insurgency'. *Terrorism Monitor* 5, no. 8 (April 2007).

Menkhaus, Ken. 'Vicious circles and the security development nexus in Somalia'. *Conlfict, Security & Development* 4, no. 2 (August 2004): 149–65.

——— 'Governance without government in Somalia: Spoilers, state building, and the politics of coping'. *International Security* 31, no. 3 (Winter 2006/07): 74–106.

——— 'The crisis in Somalia: Tradegy in five acts'. *African Affairs* 106, no. 204 (2007): 357–90.

Meredith, Martin. The State of Africa: A History of 50 Years of Independence. London: The Free Press, 2006.

Middleton, Roger. *Piracy in Somalia, Threatening Global Trade, Feeding Local Wars.* London: Chatham House, October 2008, 1–12.

——— 'Pirates and how to deal with them'. Chatham House, Briefing Note, April 2009: 1–8.

Mohamoud, Abdullah A. *State Collapse and Post Conflict Development in Africa, The Case of Somalia 1960 2001.* West Lafayette, Indiana: Purdue University Press, 2006.

Moller, Bjorn. *Somalia: From Stateless Order to Talibanisation?* Madrid: Real Instituto Elcano, 13 March 2009, 1–5.

Murphy, Martin N. 'Small boats, weak states, dirty money: The challenge of piracy'. New York: Columbia University Press, 2009.

—— *Somalia The New Barbary?* 1st edn. London: C Hurst & Co Publishers Ltd, 2010.

Nordstrom, Carolyn. 'Out of the shadows'. chap. 10. In Thomas M. Callaghy, Ronald Kassimir and Robert Latham (eds). *Intervention and Transnationalism in Africa.* Cambridge: Cambridge University Press, 2001: 216–39.

Orogun, Paul S. 'Plunder, predation and profiterring: The political economy of armed conflicts and economic violence in modern Africa'. *Perspective on Global Development and Technology* 2, no. 2 (2003): 283–313.

Osman, Abdulahi A. and Issaka K. Souaré (eds). *Somalia at the Crossroads, Challenges and Perspectives on Reconstituting a Failed State.* London: Adonis & Abbey, 2007.

Page, Jeremy. 'A monster out of control: Pakistan secret agents tell of militant links'. *The Times,* December 2008.

Patman, Robert G. *Strategic Shortfall, The Somalia Syndrome and the March to 9/11.* Santa Barbara, California: Praeger, 2010.

Patrick, Stewart. 'Weak states and global threats: Fact or fiction?' *The Washington Quarterly* (The Center for Strategic and International Studies and the Massachusetts Institute of Technology), Spring 2006: 27–53.

Peel, Michael. *A Swamp Full of Dollars, Pipelines and Paramilitaries at Nigeria's Oil Frontier.* London: I.B.Tauris, 2009.

Piazza, James A. 'Incubators of terror: Do failed and failing states promote transnational terrorism?' *International Studies Quarterly* 52 (2008): 469–88.

'Pirate payoffs feed big-money lifestyle in Somalia'. 7 December 2009. http://insidesomalia.org/20,09120,72707/News/Business/Pirate-Payoffs-Feed-Big-Money-Lifestyle-in-Somalia.html (accessed 22 August 2010).

RAND Corporation. 'Piracy reconsidered: Perspectives for the 21st century'. Arlington, Virginia: RAND Corporation, 11–12 March 2009.

Reeve, James. *International Law and the Use of Force in Self-Defence: The Legality and Significance of Ethiopian and United States Military Action in Somalia, 2006–7.* International Studies and Diplomacy, SOAS University of London, 2007.

Reno, William. 'Foreign firms and the financing of Charles Taylor's NPFL'. *Liberian Studies Journal* 18, no. 2 (1993): 175–88.

—— 'Sovereign predators and non-state armed group protectors?' *Curbing Human Rights Violations of Armed Groups, UBC Centre of International Relations,* 13–15 November 2003.

—— 'Explaining patterns of violence in collapsed states'. *Contemporary Security Policy* 30, no. 2 (August 2009): 356–74.

'Review of Maritime Transport 2013', United Nations Conference on Trade and Development, UNCTAD/RMT/2013, Geneva, Switzerland, 2013.

Riede, Bruce. *The Search for Al-Qaeda, Its Leadership, Ideology, and Future.* Washington DC: Brookings Institution Press, 2008.

Rotberg, Robert I. (ed.). *When States Fail, Causes and Consequences.* Princeton, New Jersey: Princeton University Press, 2004.

—— 'Weak and failing states: Critical new security issues'. *Turkish Policy Quarterly* 3, issue 2 (Summer 2004): 57–69.

Le Sage, Andre. 'Somalia: Sovereign disguise for a Mogadishu Mafia'. *Review of African Political Economy* 29, no. 91 (March 2002): 132–8.

Salem-News.com. 'Somali pirates are guided by a London-based intelligence team'. *Salem News*. 13 May 2009. www.salem-news.com (accessed 28 November 2009).

Sandal, Constanse M. 'The Somali integration conundrum'. *Migration*, Autumn 2009: 34–5.

Saul, Jonathan. *Somali Pirates Widening Attack Area – US Admiral*, 25 March 2010. www.reuters.com (accessed 2 April 2010).

Savage, Kevin, Mulbah S. Jackollie, D. Maxim Kumeh and Edwin Dorbor. *Corruption Perceptions and Risks in Humanitarian Assistance: A Liberia Case Study*. London: Humanitarian Policy Group, Overseas Development Institute, April 2007.

Schonhardt, Sara. 'Spike in pirate attacks in Indonesian waters raises warnings'. *Voice of America*. 6 September 2010. www.voanews.com/english/news/Spike-in-Pirate-Attacks-in-Indonesian-Waters-Raises-Warnings-10,2283754.html (accessed 22 July 2012).

Shakil, Sakina. 'AU base in Mogadishu struck by Al-Shabaab suicide bombers'. *The International*, 28 September 2009. www.theinternationalonline.com/articles/88-au-base-in-mogadishu-struck-by-al-shabaab (accessed 2 April 2010).

Shinn, David H. 'Al-Qaeda in East Africa and the Horn'. *The Journal of Conflict Studies* 27, no. 1 (2007): 47–75.

—— 'Terrorism in East Africa and the Horn: An overview'. *The Journal of Conflict Studies* 23, no. 2 (Fall 2003): 79–91.

Smillie, Ian, Lansara Gberie, Ralph Hazleton. *The Heart of the Matter: Sierra Leone, Diamonds & Human Security*. Ottawa, Ontario: Partnership Africa Canada, January 2000.

Smith, Oliver. 'Pirates attack cruise ship off Somali coast'. *The Daily Telegraph*, 1 December 2008.

Somaliland Ministry of Water & Mineral Resources. 'Somaliland country background and hydrocarbon potential'. Government of Somaliland, 2008.

Spatafora, Marcello. *Report of the Panel of Experts on Somalia Pursuant to Security Council Resolution 1474 (2007)*. New York: United Nations, 2007.

Spencer, Richard, Adrian Blomfield, Mike Pflanz, Ben Farmer, Colin Freeman, Sean Rayment. 'Recruits seek out al-Qaeda's deadly embrace across a growing arc of jihadist terror'. *The Daily Telegraph*, 31 January 2010.

Steer, Jonathan. 'Piracy and general average – A Look at some of the pitfalls'. *Maritime Risk International*, October 2009.

Sterns, Scott. 'Kidnappers make ransom demand for Chinese fishermen'. *VOANews.com*, 15 March 2010. www1.voanews.com/english/news/africa/Kidnappers-Make-Ransom-Demand-for-Kidnapped-Chinese-Fishermen-87653512.html (accessed 15 March 2010).

Stewart, Rory. 'The real reason we are in Afghanistan'. *Spiegel Online*, 7 January 2010. www.spiegel.de/international/world/0,1518,70,3408,00.html (accessed 21 September 2010).

Sunderland, Ruth. 'Rising wave of piracy sends shipowners' cost soaring'. *The Observer*, August 2009.

Suskind, Ron. 'Faith, certainty and the presidency of George W. Bush'. *The New York Times*, 17 October 2004.

Sutton, Jane. 'US to require ships sailing off Somalia to post guards'. *Insurance Journal*, 12 May 2009.

Swart, Gerrie. 'Pirates of Africa's Somali coast: On terrorism's brink?' *Scientia Militaria: South African Journal of Military Studies* 37, no. 2 (2009): 43–62.

—— 'The Role of Africom: Observer, enforcer or facilitator of peace?' *Conflict Trends*, no. 4 (2007): 9–14.

Tafrov, Stefan. *Report of the Panel of Experts on Somalia Pursuant to Security Council Resolution 1425 (2002)*. New York: United Nations, March 2003.

—— *Report of the Panel of Experts on Somalia Pursuant to Security Council Resolution 1474 (2003)*. New York: United Nations, 2003.

—— *Report of the Team of Experts Appointed Pursuant to Security Council Resolution 1407 (2002), paragraph 1, concerning Somalia*. New York: United Nations, July 2002.

Tainter, Joseph A. *The Collapse of Complex Societies*. Cambridge: Cambridge University Press, 1988.

Tenenti, Alberto. *Piracy and the Decline of Venice 1580–1615*. London: Longmans, 1967.

Thiers, Cameron G. 'Conflict, geography, and natural resources: The political economy of state predatory in Africa'. *Polity* 41, no. 4 (October 2009).

Tremlett, Giles. 'This is London – the capital of Somali pirates' secret intelligence operation'. *Guardian*, 11 May 2009.

Trinkunas, Anne L. and Harold A. Clunan (eds). *Ungoverned Spaces, Alternative to State Authority in an Era of Softened Soverignty*. Stanford, California: Stanford University Press, 2010.

United Nations Office on Drugs and Crime. 'Counter-piracy programme support to the trial and related treatment of piracy suspects. Issue 8 (February 2012), Nairobi, Kenya

UNCTAD Secretariat. *Review of Maritime Transport 2009*. Geneva: United Nations, 2009.

United Nations. *Interim Report of the Panel of Experts Established Pursuant to Resolution 1591 (2005) Concerning Sudan, Submitted Pursuant to Resolution 1713 (2006)*. New York: United Nations, 2006.

—— 'Istanbul Declaration'. Istanbul, Turkey: United Nations, 22 May 2010.

United Nations Development Programme. *Somalia Human Development Report*. New York: United Nations, 2001.

United Nations Monitoring Group on Somalia and Eritrea. *Report of the Monitoring Group on Somalia and Eritrea*. New York: United Nations, 2011.

—— *Report of the Monitoring Group on Somalia and Eritrea (advance copy)*. New York: United Nations, 27 June 2012.

United Nations Office on Drugs and Crime. *Counter Piracy Programme*. Nairobi, Kenya: United Nations, November 2009.

United Nations, Security Council, *Report of the Team of Experts Appointed Pursuant to Security Council Resolution 1407 paragraph 1, (2002) concerning Somalia, S/2002/722*. New York: United Nations, 3 July 2002.

—— *Report of the Panel of Experts on Somalia, Pursuant to Security Council Resolution 1425 (2002), S/2003/223*. New York: United Nations, 25 March 2003.

—— *Report of the Monitoring Group on Somalia Pursuant to Security Council Resolution 1519 (2003), S/2004/604*. New York: United Nations, 11 August 2004.

—— *Report of the Monitoring Group on Somalia Pursuant to Security Council Resolution 1558 (2004), S/2005/153*. New York: United Nations, 9 March 2005.

——— *Report of the Monitoring Group on Somalia Pursuant to Security Council Resolution 1587 (2005)*, S/2005/625. New York: United Nations, 4 October 2005.

——— *Report of the Monitoring Group on Somalia Pursuant to Security Council Resolution 1630 (2005)*, S/2006/229. New York: United Nations, 4 May 2006.

——— *Report of the Monitoring Group on Somalia Pursuant to Security Council Resolution 1676 (2006)*, S/2006/913. New York: United Nations, 22 November 2006.

——— *Report of the Secretary-General on Somalia*, 24 April 2008, S/2008/274, New York.

——— *Annual Report of the Security Council Committee Established Pursuant to Resolution 751 (1992) concerning Somalia*, S/2008/806. New York: United Nations, 23 December 2008.

——— *Report of the Monitoring Group on Somalia Pursuant to Security Council Resolution 1811 (2008)*, S/2008/769. New York: United Nations, 23 December 2008.

——— *Report of the Secretary-General on Somalia*, 8 January 2010, S/2009/684, New York.

——— *Report of the Secretary-General on Somalia*, 10 March 2010, S/2010/91, New York.

——— *Report of the Secretary-General pursuant to Security Council resolution 1897 (2009)*, 27 October 2010, S/2010/556, New York.

——— *Report of the Secretary-General on Somalia*, 30 December 2010, S/2010/675, New York.

——— *Report of the Secretary-General concerning Somalia*, 13 July 2011, S/2012/544, New York–Somalia Report.

——— *Report of the Secretary-General concerning Somalia and Eritrea*, 13 July 2011, S/2012/545, New York–Eritrea Report.

——— *Report of the Secretary-General concerning Somalia and Eritrea*, 18 July 2011, S/2011/433, New York.

——— *Report of the Secretary-General on Specialized Anti-Piracy Courts in Somalia and Other States in the Region*, S/2012/50. New York: United Nations, 20 January 2012.

——— *Report of the Secretary-General on Somalia*, S/2012/283. New York: United Nations, 1 May 2012.

——— *Report of the Secretary-General on Somalia*, S/2012/643. New York: United Nations, 22 August 2012.

——— *Report of the Secretary-General pursuant to Security Council resolution 2020 (2011) on the implementation of the resolution and on the situation with respect to piracy and armed robbery at sea off the coast of Somalia*, 22 October 2012, S/2012/783, New York.

——— *Report of the Secretary-General on Somalia*, 31 January 2013, S/2013/69, New York.

——— *Report of the Secretary-General on Somalia*, 31 May 2013, S/2013/326, New York.

——— *Report of the Secretary-General pursuant to resolutions 751 (1992) and 1907 (2009) concerning Somalia and Eritrea*, 12 July 2013, S/2013/413, New York.

United States Department of State. *2012 Trafficking in Persons Report – Somalia*, 19 June 2012.

US Government Accountability Office. *Somalia: Challenges and Development Efforts*. New York: Novinka Books, 2008.

Vaccani, Matteo. *Alternative Remittance Systems and Terrorism Financing, Issues in Risk Management*. Washington DC: The World Bank, 2010.

Warde, Ibrahim. *The Price of Fear, Al-Qaeda and the Truth Behind the Financial War on Terror*. London: IB Tauris, 2007.

Webersik, Christian. 'Fighting for the plenty – The banana trade in southern Somalia'. *Conference on Multinational Corporations, Development and Conflict*. Oxford, 6 December 2003.

Whipple, A.B.C. *To the Shores of Tripoli, The Birth of the US Navy and Marines.* New York: William Morrow and Company, Inc., 1991.

Woods, Emira. 'Somalia'. *Foreign Policy in Focus*, 1 January 1997. www.fpif.org/reports/somalia.

World Bank. *Conflict in Somalia: Drivers and Dynamics.* Washington DC, January 2005.

—— *Somalia, From Resilience Towards Recovery and Development, A Country Economic Memorandum for Somalia*, Report No. 34356-SO, Washington DC, 11 January 2006.

Wrong, Michela. *It's Our Turn to Eat, The Story of a Kenyan Whistleblower.* London: Fourth Estate, 2009.

Young, Adam J. *Contemporary Maritime Piracy in Southeast Asia, History, Causes and Remedies.* Leiden, The Netherlands: International Institute for Asian Studies, 2007.

INDEX